Praise for Tom Patterson's *Mapping Security*

"Tom Patterson captures a compelling and practical view of security in a multinational environment. Your CSO needs to read this book!"
—Dr. Vint Cerf, senior vice president of Technology Strategy at MCI and founder of Internet Protocol (IP)

"The power of the Internet is that it's a global network, seamlessly crossing borders. But it also brings security risks that can cross borders just as easily. Patterson has more than a decade of first-hand experience in defending against such risks and it shows. He uses real-world examples and stories, many from his own career, and offers clear, action-oriented descriptions of the different threats and how to deal with them. This book avoids security jargon and speaks directly to businesspeople around the globe."
—Chris Anderson, Editor in Chief, Wired Magazine

Whether consumers or global giants, we all need to be spending a greater share of our budgets on security. The threats are greater than ever and increasing daily, and yet there is a challenge as to how to justify the expenditure. Mapping Security offers business-oriented and in-depth thinking on how and why to build security into the fabric of the organization. After reading Tom Patterson's book, you will want to make changes with a sense of urgency.
—John R Patrick, president of Attitude LLC and former vice president of Internet Technology at IBM Corporation

As companies of all sizes go global in their search for profit and growth, they will need to understand how to use security as a tool for success in different markets, and Mapping Security shows them how.
—Dr. Craig Fields, former director of Advanced Research Projects Agency (ARPA) for the U.S. Government

MAPPING SECURITY

THE CORPORATE SECURITY SOURCEBOOK FOR TODAY'S GLOBAL ECONOMY

MAPPING SECURITY

THE CORPORATE SECURITY SOURCEBOOK FOR TODAY'S GLOBAL ECONOMY

TOM PATTERSON

WITH SCOTT GLEESON BLUE

✦Addison-Wesley

Upper Saddle River, NJ • Boston • Indianapolis • San Francisco

New York • Toronto • Montreal • London • Munich • Paris • Madrid

Capetown • Sydney • Tokyo • Singapore • Mexico City

Symantec Press Publisher: Linda McCarthy
Editor in Chief: Karen Gettman
Acquisitions Editor: Jessica Goldstein
Cover Designer: Alan Clements
Managing Editor: Gina Kanouse
Project Editor: Christy Hackerd
Copy Editor: Keith Cline
Indexer: Angie Bess
Compositor: Tolman Creek Design
Manufacturing Buyer: Dan Uhrig

The publisher offers excellent discounts on this book when ordered in quantity for bulk purchases or special sales, which may include electronic versions and/or custom covers and content particular to your business, training goals, marketing focus, and branding interests. For more information, please contact:

U. S. Corporate and Government Sales
(800) 382-3419
corpsales@pearsontechgroup.com

For sales outside the U. S., please contact:

International Sales
international@pearsoned.com

Visit us on the Web: www.phptr.com

Library of Congress Catalog Number:

2004113324

ISBN 0-321-30452-7

Text printed in the United States on recycled paper at Phoenix BookTech in Hagerstown, Maryland.
First printing, *December 2004*

This book is dedicated to the memory of Jon Postel, who saw all of this coming years before any of us, and the security folks around the world focused on making security work. "Lo."

Table of Contents

Table of Contents

Acknowledgments

The authors would like to thank the many people that made this book possible. First and foremost, we thank the dozens of experts who lent their time, energy, wit, and wisdom in sitting through the extensive interview process. Each of you, those listed by name in the book and those who chose to provide input anonymously, are the reason that this book can provide the type of local insight that it does.

We also want to thank the *Mapping Security* volunteers, who helped with the research, organization, and Web site of the book. This group includes Jordan Fishler, John Kienast, Larissa Artagaveytia, Jen Handshew, and Adam Rosenblum, plus experts Peter Czerniawsky, NP, MF, and more.

Tom Patterson would specifically like to thank Mr. Griffin, his seventh grade math teacher, who taught him how to think outside the box; Dr. Ed Azar, who in college taught him how people think around the world; and Dr. Craig Fields, who aside from being a long-time business mentor, taught him how to put all this thinking to best use. He also thanks the great teams he has had the opportunity to work with at Centel, MCC, IBM, KPMG, and Deloitte throughout his career; his agent, Gary Reznik of the Greater Talent Network; Brian Foremny for his consistently good legal advice; and his PR firm of choice, Allison & Partners. Finally, thanks to his wonderful family, Deirdre and Will, who have traveled the world with him and made everything an adventure.

Scott Gleeson Blue wishes to express abiding gratitude foremost to Jennifer, his one true love and wife, for her encouragement, patience, and friendship throughout this project. He would like to recognize Dr. Monica Ganas, Dr. Paul Ashdown, and Susan Donaldson—his writing and life mentors. Thanks also to

Scott Allison, Andy Hardie-Brown, and Scott Pansky of Allison & Partners for bringing him in to work with Tom on that first emergency project. He also sends affection and thanks to the Niños.

Finally, the authors would like to thank the publishing team, co-led by the fantastic Jessica Goldstein and the team at Addison-Wesley, and incredible Linda McCarthy and her team at Symantec Press. They both understood that this book was different, and used all of their considerable talents to help make a book out of our discussions. The publishing team also includes our reviewers, including early reviewers Craig Fields, Vint Cerf, and Mark Bentley, plus several others who looked at country-specific sections for us. Also thanks to the reviewers at the end of the process, including Marcia Robinson, who provided some real insight based on her strong business experience.

There are lots of thoughts and opinions contained in this book, some gained by specific interviews and others gained throughout the authors' lives. Any mistakes are clearly ours and not the experts quoted.

About the Author

Tom Patterson is a business advisor in the areas of security, commerce, and governance.

Patterson has been a successful international security and eCommerce partner at both KPMG and Deloitte, a strategy executive with IBM's Internet Division, and a director of security at MCC, Americas leading R&D consortium. Tom has been a board member of several public companies, has advised all three branches of the U.S. government on Internet and security policy, and is a trusted advisor to company executives around the world.

Patterson regularly comments on the security issues of the day for CNBC and other major media outlets. His track record of success in large scale eCommerce, with three separate projects that have each generated over 500 million dollars online, has him in demand as an author, public speaker, board member, and business advisor.

He currently resides in Pacific Palisades, California, with his wife and son. More information about the author is available at www.TPatterson.NET.

Foreword

Security obviously means different things to different people. In the post 9-11 world in which we live, most people think of security as protection from physical harm. Certainly, physical security is, and always will be, a top priority—but it's not the only kind of security to which we as individuals, businesses, and nations need to pay attention. As U.S. companies grow increasingly dependent upon computer networks, information security becomes a prominent national issue. And as these companies increasingly have global presences, global information security becomes part of this concern, too.

Security folks say, "Security is not a destination, it's a journey." My journey began over 37 years ago, and it still surprises me to see how many businesspeople think they can outsource their security issues to others and how little they actually know about a subject that is so critical to their success. Especially now, given the global nature of our business, it is more important than ever for everyone to understand what role security should play in their daily lives.

I began my career in security when I joined the military at age 18. There, everything was about Operational Security ("Op-Sec"), Communications Security ("Com-Sec"), and physical security. When I became a law enforcement officer with the Chandler police department in the early 1980s, security discussions became ingrained in my day-to-day life. My job was to keep people safe in their homes, businesses, and cars, and I was constantly surprised that my fellow officers did not consider computer-related crimes to be very important. That's when I started campaigning to raise the profile of computer-related crime and that campaign has now turned into a life-long calling.

Since my military and police officer days, my work experiences have done nothing but underscore how often information security is a matter of national security and how tremendously dependent society is on information technology and information technology systems. In the public sector, I have taught computer crimes with the FBI, helped assemble the Computer Exploitation Team at the National Drug Intelligence Center, and served as Director of the Computer Crime and Information Warfare directorate for the Air Force Office of Special Investigations.

In the private sector, first as Chief Security Officer for Microsoft and now for eBay, it became obvious to me that security is not a roadblock to business—it is a business enabler. It can be challenging to convince management to exercise caution and perform extensive testing in a business climate that pressures companies to be first to market, but security is just as important to business as it is to the Department of Defense. This cause is worth fighting for in your business, today.

Most recently, I have served as a Special Advisor to the Executive Office of the President and Vice Chair and Chair of the President's Critical Infrastructure Protection Board. In this role, I argued that securing our nation's critical infrastructure is not simply a project that will be completed within a certain budget and timeline. This entire journey underscores the importance of security in all aspects of business today.

Having established the importance of security, we must ask who bears the primary responsibility for it. Is it the security professional, the risk manager, the government employee, or individual citizens? My answer is, and has always been, "All of us." It is everyone's responsibility and everyone's task to be secure. Now, this does not mean that everyone has to go to "security school" and become an expert, but it does mean that we all have to understand the basics and how we all fit into the security picture, and that's where books like this one come in. One mistake of the past is that there was not enough appreciation for the different facets of security, and how best to apply them to the business world. Tom's book helps address that problem by writing in a clear business style, including entertaining anecdotes that teach important lessons and avoiding the jargon that often bogs down a business security discussion.

Those that create the software and hardware that run our critical infrastructure have taken unprecedented actions to make their products more secure, often at tremendous cost and effort. What was once viewed as just one of many priorities for companies creating the great products we now use has now become the number one priority. However, no matter the improvements we make to software and hardware security, humans still create and use these technologies and human involvement always entails a certain degree of human error.

What's more, many people and organizations do not understand how interconnected the world is today and how the actions of some people can affect the security of others. Most of us live in a fairly closed world, but the online world is changing us in fundamental ways. All it takes is 10 to 20,000 users to overlook performing basic security measures and we could have a very negative effect on businesses and government systems. That's a byproduct of our interconnected world and that's another reason why everyone must understand his or her role.

Today, there are an estimated 840 million users online and they have to do their part to secure cyberspace alongside the professionals. It sounds like an impossible task to deal with all of the challenges that we face, but there are more resources to educate and inform than ever before. It takes more than technology to solve the problems of personal, business, and national security. That's why I agreed to write the foreword for Tom's book.

As I look at businesses today, I see an ever-growing number expanding their international reach. Supply chains relocate. Customers come from all over the world. Businesses outsource parts of their operation. All of these activities affect a business's bottom line and all of these activities carry security risks. If you work for a business that has gone global—or has plans to do so—I urge you to read this book. Tom Patterson has also been on a long security journey, very much focused on helping businesses around the world leverage the benefits of security, and he has important and insightful things to say about the security implications of working on a global scale. Tom's book will increase your international security savvy and help you protect yourself, your business, and the bottom line.

—Howard A. Schmidt
November 2004

The Five Ws of Mapping Security

Why Mapping Security

I have written *Mapping Security* in response to questions I have fielded from corporate executives, businesspeople, corporate security officers, and people seated next to me on airplanes. The queries usually fall along the same lines, as follows:

- How much should my company be spending on security?
- What do these new security and privacy rules really mean to my organization?
- What are my peers doing about security?
- Now that I have gone global, what else do I have to do? (perhaps the most frequently asked question).

Importantly, I wrote this book because I have found that many of the answers to questions about security are the same around the world, and—critically—many of the answers are different, depending on where in the world you are working. This reality—linked closely to country-by-country nuances—is reinforced as you read on.

Even though I have now already used the word *security* six times the first two paragraphs alone, guess what: *Mapping Security* is not a run-of-the-mill, technically written volume like the vast majority of its predecessors. This book does not show you how to write a security plan or write an encryption algorithm. It is really a business book that is enabled by a business understanding of what is important in managing your corporate risk. It is written for business people around the world, and it is written with today's global economy in mind.

If Not Now, When?

Okay, so that's the reason *why* I wrote this book. *When* is a function of today's global economy and the risks from our increased reliance on technology. Because of supply chains, customer bases, outsourcing, and just traditional growth, more organizations than ever before are crossing borders. Therefore they are now doing business in different countries and having to change the way they look at security for the first time. Combine this global nature of business today with our great reliance on computers and communications, and we have the highest levels of threats to integral business infrastructure in history.

It is time security moves to the front and center of the corporate psyche. To do that, we need a security map that spells out the realities of security, embraces all aspects of a global business, demystifies it with straight talk, and makes it accessible to entire organizations. Everyone today needs to be well armed with an understanding of the facts.

Security has traditionally hidden behind esoteric discussions of cryptographic key lengths, seemingly unfathomable rules and regulations, a hacker mystique, and, often, deliberate doublespeak. Now, with technology poised to deliver the cost savings and growth needed to survive and thrive in today's global economy, it is the right time to cultivate corporate-wide understanding that leads to embracing security as the business enabler that it can be. Because companies are now working across foreign borders—and must understand foreign security rules, regulations, best practices, and the local security cultures—I have pulled together dozens of experts from different locales around the world, all of whom help to explain "their side" of the security equations you must deploy. Today is *when* we need solutions that both protect us and enable our growth.

What Makes This Book Different?

The *what* of *Mapping Security* is straightforward and comprises three simple parts. Part 1, "Charting a Course," will help people in any organization, anywhere in the world, reduce their risks and maximize their rewards. It outlines and illustrates six business "insider" tips for dealing with the realities of a global security plan—

realities such as shrinking budgets/staff; old-security thinking that holds back the use of new technologies; and the growing maze of rules, regulations, and standards that apply. It shows you how to correlate your security to appropriate rules, stretch your security budget, increase buy-in from all business units of your organization, keep an eye on what is happening in terms that make sense, and finally, incorporate constant vigilance over the evolving threats, countermeasures, technology and regulations. The chapters of Part 1 address these business tips as follows:

1. Establishing Your Coordinates
2. Building The Base
3. Enabling The Businesses and Enhancing the Processes
4. Developing Radar
5. Constant Vigilance

Part 2, "Reality, Illusion, and the Souk," takes a tour of more than 30 countries/regions around the world, taking an honest (sometimes painfully so) look at how security is practiced in each country. Although every organization in the world can benefit from the lessons learned from Part 1, Part 2 offers a discussion of the important local security rules, information from local security and business experts and stories that help illustrate the sometimes difficult cultural issues that are of most significant concern for a global security rollout. Filled with quotes and anecdotes from the frontlines of local environments, and it will give you a good global understanding of the differences between various countries. Of course, its description of the local laws and regulations is designed to be heavily dog eared as a reference section to help you navigate the future, but there's another reason to turn back to it again and again—the *Mapping Security Index* (MSI).

The MSI will help you speed decision making, improve cross-border understanding, and aid in quantifying a highly qualitative process. It is my exclusive formula for making accessible the risks and benefits of moving security into a new country. I created it by combining four scores that make up some of the aspects of understanding good security:

- Information risks
- Communications connectivity
- Political risks
- Cultural diversity

Based on actual historical numbers, expert rankings, and a subjective *Cross-Border Index* (CBI), the MSI score has been tabulated for each country. Incidentally, whereas most people who have reviewed my work believe that "their" country score is too low, they tend to think all the others are just about right. Nonetheless, and at the risk of causing passionate debates in blogs and forums around the world, I have included an MSI score for each of the countries that I covered, to help give you an instant snapshot of the local security scene.

Part 3, "Whose Law Do I Break?" ties the book together by showcasing some old (sorry guys) sages from the worlds of business and security to help solve some of the conflicts that will arise when you put what you have learned from Parts 1 and 2 into global practice. Understanding what to do when laws collide, leveraging technology even on a low budget, and solving important cultural issues are explored. Part 3 helps tie it all together, with plain talk from very experienced folks who have been doing cross-border security for a long time.

Following the book's three-part design is a thorough appendix, organized by country, with descriptions and pointers to the best local information that I have been able to find both in my career, and, specifically, in researching this book. I have always wanted a list like this, and now I (and you) have got one.

Who Would Write a Book Like This?

As for *who*, I have been a consumer of security services while living in the Middle East, a maker of security products, and a consultant of security services to governments and companies around the world, and I have used my understanding of security to enable three separate businesses that each transacted more than $500 million online. I have been in the trenches, run large businesses, and sat on boards of directors. I have spent the past two decades explaining security to business leaders around the word, and I recently completed a two-year tour, living and working overseas, focused exclusively on cross-border security. Living much of my adult life both working in the security world and working *outside* the United States, I have developed a good appreciation for what this world has to offer and have honed strategies for overcoming its associative risks.

The *who* also includes Scott Gleeson Blue, a talented writer and interviewer, whose tireless efforts to get the stories straight and help write them clearly are a big reason the book has turned out as it has. Scott is a Philadelphia-based author/journalist and an instructor at Neumann College (Aston, Pennsylvania). In addition to collaborating with me on security publications in the past, Scott has covered technology, consumer and popular culture, marketing, sports, and the performing arts for various publications in Europe and America. This breadth of background has lent important insight into the expert stories that we used to explain cultural differences around the world.

Finally, the *who* would not be complete without recognizing the dozens of security and business experts who agreed to be interviewed for this book, Howard Schmidt for lending his considerable insight for the Foreword, and the *Mapping Security* volunteer army of researchers. As always, their wisdom and wit are greatly appreciated, and any errors are most certainly my translations, and not their thoughts.

Where in the World Are We?

Oh, and that leaves *where*. Notice that in this book's title, *map* is used as a verb. This book is active and organic, and it was written for businesses that work somewhere on this planet. It was written from 30 different countries, with local voices and local opinions. The Foreword was written by Howard on several airplane trips between Shanghai and Beijing, the opening letter in Part 2 was written among the ancients in Luxor, and the quotes and interviews came from each of the individual countries listed. One quote came from an expert just back from a country where he lamented that the local security folks all have their own body armor, and he had to rent! So you see, this book was written in the same *where* that you are now doing business: every*where*.

So that's the who, what, where, when, and why of the book. Straightforward, demystifying (and at the same time a new and unique sourcebook for whatever and wherever you are looking for security). I hope it helps.

Chapter 1

The Historian and the Security Guy

The need for a common knowledge of the general facts of human history throughout the world has become very evident during the tragic happenings of the last few years. Swifter means of communications have brought all men closer to one another for good or for evil.

—H. G. Wells, *The Outline of History* (1920)

Through *The Outline of History*, H. G. Wells created a different way of looking at world events through the relatively new lenses of evolution, sociology, and anthropology; and it is from his approach to history that I have taken my cues in penning *Mapping Security*. In this first part, "Charting a Course," I first establish the foundation for the part's structure and navigation (Chapter 2), and then directly focus on six keys to success for your corporate information security program (Chapters 3 through 7). Delivered sequentially, these keys serve as foundational elements upon which any global company needs to focus for the best *return on security investment* (ROSI). Through them I present a holistic view of how to enable and secure business through the calculated use of security, and present a framework for creating the agile global security posture needed to comply and compete around the world.

After your course is charted, read on to Part 2, "Reality, Illusion, and the Souk," where these keys to success are contextualized within showcased countries on every continent. It is here that an "anthropological" approach to business is brought to bear through first-hand accounts from leading practitioners, experts, and me. Part 3, "Whose Law Do I Break?" ties it all together. I conclude with a strong summary that offers experienced, actionable advice designed to help you succeed, while providing real solutions from experienced global business experts. Part 3 focuses on solving the "real-world" conundrums that always come about when implementing what you have learned in Part 1, in all of the countries of Part 2. For Part 3, I turned to people who deal with these types of issues every day—in each of three different sub-disciplines. Overall, Part 3 provides a framework that you can rely on long term as you devise, implement, and manage security.

Wells is quoted at the beginning of each part of this book. A talented historian and futurist from a century ago, his ideas and methodology apply prophetically in the current business environment. Today the convergence of information technology with the global economy results in impressive promise for nearly any business, but also potential calamity. Therefore companies of all sizes must reexamine a previously minor or isolated component of their operations: corporate information security (or what I term *global corporate security*).

Wells has inspired my own take on how to evaluate and implement global corporate security, a perspective that I share in this book. For example, Wells observed that growth comes after tragic happenings. Even now, most of your organization's corporate security is probably busy reacting to any one of the viruses, exploits, or attacks that gain the attention of "the boss." Furthermore, Wells understood that drastic change, which in his day surfaced through the Industrial Revolution and World War I (I used Great War as its international name), required an all-inclusive view for readers to synthesize. Again, following his lead, *Mapping Security* conveys a holistic approach to your global corporate security that understands today's global business setting, leverages the hidden strengths of security, and incorporates the geographic realities of the world in which we live.

1920 Becomes 1990

Seventy years after Wells used history to foretell our future, I was helping convert a traditional defense contractor into a security services provider. I had a meeting scheduled at a large U.S. defense organization on the banks of the Potomac River. It housed some of information security's best minds. I arrived a bit early and was asked to wait in the main lobby until my appointment time. Making the best of this delay, I reached below my chair and plugged in my trusty GRiD laptop. I was astonished to find two sockets—one for power and one for the organization's *local area network* (LAN). When asked why they were offering open access to one of the most secret defense computers in the world on a wall of their lobby, the security personnel—shocked—realized that these LAN ports must have been mounted in concert with power outlets by the building's maintenance crew. Although this organization employed some of the world's savviest security personnel, who readily grasped the situation, the organization as a whole failed to leverage this understanding, creating the risk. (To its credit, the organization fixed this problem on the same day and changed its LAN architecture to manage against the security risk.)

My GRiD moment reinforced Wells's futurist voice. It continues to reverberate today. Berlin and Sun City have given way to a global business environment that requires a *common knowledge of the general facts* that enable corporations to leverage *swifter means of communication*. An escalation in war and terrorism provides graphic examples of *tragic happenings of the past few years* that, when combined with technology, illustrate just how much closer humanity is to one another for the carrying out of *good or evil*. The results of both are customarily unpredictable and, as exemplified by my visit just shy of the Potomac's placid current, alarming.

You might know first hand that at no point has business been more global and poised for significant market and profit expansion. However, did you know that at no point has business been more vulnerable to risk and fraught with an array of vastly different threats, regulations, and demands—its destiny inescapably linked to understanding global corporate security? This is a moment of inflection, when solving global security challenges will empower our greater and safer use of modern technologies. The alternative—continuing to look at security as an add-on reactive cost—will force you to reject the use of windfall technologies of all types, such as broadband in your home, WiFi in your office, and PDAs or convergent cell phones in your pocket. More importantly, you will risk taking advantage of the growth and cost efficiencies of global sales, offshore outsourcing, and cost-effective supply chains.

PART I

CHARTING A COURSE

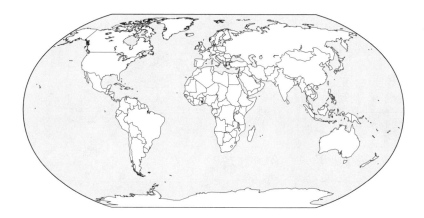

Chapter 2

Why You Picked Up This Book

Because you've picked up this book, the current business climate I just described in the opening must resonate with you. You have probably experienced how the potent combination of technology, people, and processes can lead to unprecedented business enablement. That's because you have found ways to leverage the Internet and new forms of communication to lower costs, increase profits, and encourage growth. If so, chances are that your company is doing business in more than one country. Consequently, you run more efficiently and economically than ever, looking for new opportunities. You're not alone.

Running the operations of a global leader in electronic payments has had its cross-border challenges, and we've had to really focus on getting the security just right. We needed to provide a trusted environment for our customers and ensure compliance with all of the regulations and standards that come into play in the Americas and Europe. Reactionary security would never have worked for us—we needed a plan that covered building our policies and infrastructure, optimizing and enhancing our systems and services, and monitoring and evolving our operations to stay current with the ever-changing business and security requirements around the world.

—*Scott J. Nelson, Group Manager—Client Implementation Group, Paymentech, Dallas*

Continents and countries are aggressively marketing local expertise and jockeying for position. Look around you now and pick up an object—any object. Chances are that all or some part of it was manufactured in China. China is a manufacturing powerhouse. Software development and virtual customer service are finding homes in India and the

7

Philippines. Meanwhile, robust markets exist in the Americas, Europe, and Asia Pacific where commodities and services flow at unprecedented levels. As technology evolves, traditional jobs are being moved around the world—just as boxes have been for generations. Depending on where you are headquartered, these changes could be seen as a challenge or an opportunity. Either way, this next wave of global trade is already beginning to crest.

The Business Shift and the New Global Security Equation

Global trade has catalyzed a dramatic shift in how business gets done, and facilitating its advance is global corporate security. Those of you who have failed to recognize this point may already feel the vulnerabilities of new technology and business methods that accompany a move off your home turf and the expansion of your organization.

Perhaps someone within your company downloaded an e-mail attachment that significantly slowed your ability to fulfill customer orders. Some critical intellectual property might have possibly made its way to a competitor when an executive outside your country resigned. You might have discovered that your manufacturing warehouse output slated for 1,000 units of a part this month emerged with just 900. Maybe your supply chain came to a standstill when a hacker was able to co-opt your server for his or her own nefarious purpose, or your legal department says that you can no longer back up your customer and Human Resources databases because doing so violates some other country's privacy laws!

It's How—Not How Much

Companies have been focusing on how much to spend on security, rather than focusing on how best to spend it. The 2004 survey from the Computer Security Institute (with the FBI) reports that companies spend between $110 and $334 per employee on security, and my experience shows that security budgets range between 3 percent and 13 percent of a total IT budget. Wide berths indeed, so this book helps you with actionable recommendations on how best to spend your security dollars, whatever they may be.

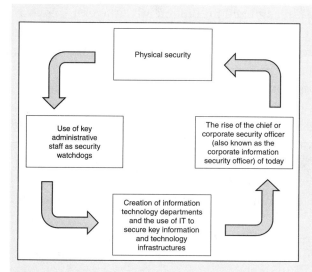

Figure 2.1 The evolution of the security officer.

The Corporate Security Officer: An Evolution

Within this book, I use the term Corporate Security Officer (CSO) rather than Corporate Information Security Officer (CISO). This is an intentional bias based on my belief that CSO more accurately reflects the convergence of global security oversight that includes information security as one in a myriad of factors.

You can find a more detailed account of this role's evolution at www.MappingSecurity.com.

In the past, these issues weren't even a factor. Company security concerns were dispatched to your *information technology* (IT) team. The help desk served as a base of operations when viruses emerged, and there were no *Corporate Security Officers* (CSOs). Security was usually in the background and first dispatched to security guards for physical concerns or to key administrative staff such as executive secretaries for intellectual property and human resource concerns.

The Shift and Technology

In 1943, IBM's venerable Thomas Watson made a bold prediction: "There is a world market," he said, "for maybe five computers." This conventional wisdom was quickly obliterated as technology physically shrank and exponentially quickened.

Companies, including your own, have recognized and taken advantage of this evolution. Perhaps now, however, your CSO or your Chief Technology Officer (CTO) is emphasizing words such as risk and threat and vulnerability in every meeting or planning retreat, and you are wondering how seriously you should take the CSO/CTO. The shift toward global operations has concurrently expanded concerns from traditional IT sectors to a broader awareness of whole-company vulnerabilities and is challenging established security budgeting and practices, and perhaps represents a dilemma for conservative decision makers in the company. For example, most decision makers want to see the day-to-day impact that proposals for broader security will have on their business and its bottom line, because perhaps the CSO/CTO's passion for expanding security across the organization seems radical and tough to grasp.

My experience at the government agency mentioned in Chapter 1, "The Historian and the Security Guy," illustrates how this shift in thinking about security, which is becoming increasingly visible, was minimized from the outset. Doubtless, you're still laughing at such an oversight, thinking to yourself, "My company has always been smarter than that." But has it? Is it?

More Than Worms: The New Reality of Technology Threats

On August 25, 2001, Emulex, an Internet server and storage provider, placed a press release on the newswire announcing that it was revising its earnings from $.25 U.S. per-share gain to a $.15 U.S. per-share loss.

Reprinted by the likes of *DowJones, Bloomberg,* and *CBS MarketWatch,* the release also discussed the resignation of Emulex CEO Paul Folino and a pending investigation by the SEC. The company's shares tanked from $104 U.S. to $43 U.S. per share over the next quarter hour.

Mark Jakob, a 23-year-old hacker, had orchestrated the release as an elaborate hoax. He had done so to knock down Emulex stock prices and, in turn, recoup his recent $100,000 loss in a stock short sale. Because he disseminated the release through his former employer, Internet Wire, a Los Angeles firm that delivers press releases to top news organizations online, it was picked up as credible news and published without verification.[1]

---

1. *George, Annarita Giani and Paul Thompson, "Cognitive Hacking: A Battle for the Mind," August 2000, Computer.*

To what is the majority of your global security budget still allocated? Does the allocation extend beyond the simpler IT considerations? (Although IT is integral to a holistic security approach, security stretches beyond its confines and into every department within an organization.) It may not be, and it is easy to see why traditional thought about technology usually takes center stage. The shift in security concerns, if not minimized by the media, is usually portrayed as a simple IT issue and linked to catastrophic losses. Consider the following statements concerning the MyDoom virus, which emerged in the first quarter of 2004 over three consecutive days:

- The financial damage from the virus-like program—from network slowdown to lost productivity—is already being measured in the billions of dollars, according to antivirus vendors. (Reuters)[2]
- The estimated economic damage caused by the MyDoom virus has now reached $38.5 billion. (Web Host Industry Review)[3]

The BBC reported that according to London-based firm mi2g, MyDoom would cost more $49.3 billion. Unequivocally, MyDoom was significant, infecting more than 100,000 machines, but this type of media coverage, which takes a significant threat and makes it apocalyptic—in this case with projected losses of nearly $50 billion—diverts attention to reactive solutions. It feeds a misconception that there is a single source of digital threats to business that is matched by a single solution (the virus, created by a hacker in a garage or basement, that can easily be addressed). As technology evolves, so must corporate thinking about global security.

The Shift and Globalization

Technology is just one element of the equation. Although the shift has facilitated opportunities for any company wanting a global operation, this adds a new array of security risks at a technological and human level. Whether it is the outsourcing of customer service or the relocation of manufacturing, a host of cross-border challenges can prove complex and tricky. Culture-specific customs and ways of doing business vary significantly. India is not Sweden. Israel is not Australia. You have to understand what standards and regulations apply to you before you or your data

---

2. Reed Stevenson, "MyDoom Variant Emerges, Targets Microsoft," Reuters, 28 January 2004.
3. "MyDoom Damage Rises, SCO Site Hit by DDoS." Web Host Industry Review. 2 February 2004.

leave home. Some of these conventions have a ripple effect: To do business in Europe or the United States, you might consider voluntarily complying with ISO 17779 and Sarbanes-Oxley, for example; if you are about to enter South Africa, you cannot ignore the tenets of black economic empowerment or the precepts of King 2.[4, 5] If you are laying down roots in China, working hand in hand with the provincial governments and the Party leaders requires special sensitivity.

It's important to note that corporate security isn't the same everywhere in the world. One of the very important elements when it comes to corporate security in Australia, China, and Japan is what I call a wait-and-see trend. Businesses are saying, "Let's wait and see what pans out in the U.S. and let's wait and see what pans out in the EU," and the region is seeing most of this being driven by strong legislation—we don't have that type of legislation in the Asia Pac.

—Kevin Shaw, Deloitte, Asia Pacific Leader for Security Services, Melbourne

I have been practicing security for a long time, and I have spent more than half my business life outside my home country—the United States—living in Europe and the Middle East and traveling extensively in the Americas, Africa, and Asia. As a result, I know that globalization, its inherent risks and its regulations, requires a new way of examining the implications for corporate security beyond your corporate headquarters.

The Shift and Accountability/Regulatory Compliance

A final factor requiring original thinking about the global security equation emanates from the ripple effect of Enron, Parmalat, and a host of other business scandals: Corporate risk is starting to involve serious liability for officers, management, and board members. In some regions of the world, the accuracy and security of intellectual, financial, and customer-related assets within an organization are increasingly tied to the compensation and careers of the executives who lead them. Global corporate security in its broadest sense now demands accountability, and to succeed in this new climate you must grasp how your corporate objectives correlate with security and privacy. Although technology and globalization can

---

4. *For more on ISO 17779, Sarbanes-Oxley, and black economic empowerment and King 2, see the glossary of regulations in the appendix.*

5. *It is a continuing trend in South Africa to distinguish between "black," white," and "colored," in discussions of race.*

help you seize competitive advantage and new levels of profitability, new standards of corporate governance and responsibility force you to do so fairly, openly, and *securely*.

It was 9-11 that created awareness for critical infrastructure in the U.S., and Sarbanes-Oxley that's created a level of accountability. Yet now, executives kind of get lost in what all that means, what it encompasses, and how it could affect their business. Yet they have become so much more aware of the fact that if "we're not doing [security] right" it's going to be more than "shame on us."

—*Bobby Christian, Acting CSO, Public Company Accounting Oversight Board, Washington D.C.*

Charting a Course: Freedom from Reactive Corporate Security

Powered by technology, business has shifted to a global environment and is increasingly governed by accountability on various fronts. Freedom to grow while avoiding vulnerabilities associated with this shift dictates that you map corporate security across your entire enterprise and chart a course. In other words, your CSO or CTO is not crying wolf: A corporate security strategy has to become a priority for every management-level executive and board member.

Corporations are still trying to develop holistic ways of dealing with security threats at a technological and human level. Today, blended threats require complete and homogenous security solutions that start with a tailored security policy based upon best industry practices. In turn, this policy must be thoroughly implemented, smartly managed, and deftly adjusted.

—*Juergen Schultz, Director, Strategic Alliances for EMEA, Symantec, Munich*

As security has moved into the boardroom, corporate officers have had few resources to expand their thinking about their own security issues. In this first part, "Charting a Course," *Mapping Security* provides a step-by-step framework for developing a thorough, global corporate security path. Using the *technology, globalization*, and *accountability* equation factors, I discuss what type of security map you need. I then further analyze the problems plaguing existing conventional wisdom, illustrating how next-generation global security strategies must move from stratified "technology-centric" processes to a fully inclusive "business-centric" process that comprehensively assesses risk while managing threats. Understanding that you're probably not used to thinking of security as a map upon which the rest of your business is charted, this part of the book provides practical information for envisioning a corporate security strategy that integrates technology, people, places, processes, and policies.

"Charting a Course" is based on the six keys to success covered in Chapters 3 through 7. In Chapter 3, "Establishing Your Coordinates," you learn that the only constant in the new corporate security reality is change, and the only truth rests in knowing that these days it is costlier to repair damage after a security event takes place. The best global security strategy is built when you examine your own business issues, compare them to applicable standards, and invest in the security technology and procedures necessary to make it all work together. The six keys are as follows:

- Establishing Your Coordinates
- Building the Base
- Enabling the Businesses
- Enhancing the Processes
- Developing Radar
- Constant Vigilance

Significant CxO Questions

Each chapter of "Charting a Course" highlights key questions CxOs should be asking. These questions will arm you with what you need to hold your own among your board, security, and technology groups or among your management teams.

You will learn how global corporate security—once the domain of IT departments—is now a significant corporate role that requires organization-wide attention. As mentioned previously, this has given rise to the CSO, who unites all aspects of risk reduction within an organization. Chapter 3 also breaks down strategy into five easily understood components:

- **You Are Here**

  In nearly every country, new horizontal and vertical standards are emerging every day. This section provides the guidance you need to implement and test the standards and to determine which parts are best done internally and when leveraging trained professionals is the best course.

■ **Pinpointing Your Business Requirements**

Risk reduction isn't the only outcome of a solid security strategy—so is process enablement. This starts with a solid security review that can help you establish the unique requirements of your corporation, helping it to prioritize security efforts. This section examines the benefits that should accrue (and be demanded) in the requirements definition phase.

■ **Creating Your Risk Profile**

Gathering information from key stakeholders who must have a say—from the CEO to business unit leaders—and developing a risk profile based on answering hard questions about business objectives and IT capabilities results in the risk profile. This section shows you how a collaborative effort will help the company know what needs securing, while enabling you to obtain critical buy-in from all participants no matter where in the world they are.

■ **Charting Your Course**

The culmination of all corporate introspection regarding security strategy, this portion of *Mapping Security* helps you understand how to examine corporate security maps and create a direction for implementing a security strategy. It focuses on the need for sensitivity to cultural differences, the lack of which could derail a plan before it ever gets moving.

■ **Turning Policy into Action Plans**

Deriving security and privacy action documents is the surest way to initiate a security strategy company-wide. Often you need a security management system to track all the documents related to the various security components (antivirus, firewalls, intrusion detection, vulnerability management). *Mapping Security* provides helpful tips about what to look for, how best to implement the various components, and points out the flaws and fallacies that can come from a false sense of security that often emerges in geographically divergent organizations.

Chapter 4, "Building the Base," covers how to build a base that enhances security, is operationally efficient, and allows for the differences that local conditions impose. Chapter 5, "Enabling Businesses and Enhancing Processes," covers how to optimize operational units within an organization, including human resources, customer relationship management, supply-chain management, and financial reporting, in ways that *make* money. You will discover ways to enhance processes to *save* money, through systems development, the help desk, regulatory and audit compliance, as well as network operations. Chapter 5 examines the hallmarks of a strong enablement program, focusing on what is possible, what to expect, and what to watch out for. It also highlights the best places to invest, critical success factors, peer group analysis, and what to expect when these internal systems are all over the map.

Chapter 6, "Developing Radar," and Chapter 7, "Constant Vigilance," are the final keys to success discussed in Part 1. These keys enable you to monitor global security both internally and externally. Internal monitoring of each element of a security strategy represents the only way to confirm whether new security processes succeed, and Chapter 6 discusses how to build internal monitoring into a global security strategy. It also examines whose buy-in the strategy requires (and how to make that happen). The chapter also identifies critical differences regarding reporting, examines the need to adhere to local customs, and discusses how to separate the good from the bad (even when you don't speak the same language).

Chapter 7 examines how to identify new threats, changes in technology, countermeasures, and business risks (new rules, regulations, and location-specific business considerations); the identification of which is necessary to stay on course. Finding the path that works is essential for long-term success, and this chapter focuses on what to watch, how to watch it even when it is far away, and what you can safely ignore.

Overall, Part 1 examines how each key to success enables you to develop and implement an enterprise-wide security strategy that effectively increases productivity, minimizes risk, and maximizes your *return on security investment* (ROSI). For companies that are already established in more than one country, Part 1 provides the blueprint for revisiting internal corporate security. For corporations that are just now expanding, it affords a ground-up view of what you must anticipate as you assess risk and expand your venture. In both cases, it frees you as an organization to run more smoothly and securely.

"Charting a Course" will help you to understand the universals involved with a comprehensive global security strategy. Then you will be ready to move on to Part 2, "Reality, Illusion, and the Souk," which examines how what you have learned in Part 1 applies to various regions and countries around the world.

Chapter 3

Establishing Your
Coordinates

Building a security strategy requires that you forget traditional notions of risk; after all, the least obvious or seemingly minor vulnerabilities are sometimes the greatest. Identify weaknesses and measure those weaknesses in each area of your organization before you start strategic planning. Overlooking this exercise, what I call *establishing your coordinates*, is foolhardy—just ask American space agency NASA. In January 2004, NASA and its *Jet Propulsion Laboratory* (JPL) successfully launched and landed the "Spirit" and "Opportunity" rovers on Mars. The spacecraft revived dreamy interest in space exploration, and except for minor technological glitches the journey seemed no more difficult than hobby rocketry.

Sadly, this mission's success was borne out of an unthinkable oversight during a similar endeavor five years earlier. The Mars-bound Explorer 98 "Polar Lander" tumbled into the planet's atmosphere and was never heard from again. Its companion, "Climate Orbiter," mounted to the same rockets, veered past its entry point. During a single day, four years of dedicated work by a team of NASA engineers and scientists evaporated, and the mission budget of $400 million was wasted.

NASA forensics found that as it strived to deliver missions under the "faster, cheaper, better" mantra, a decision was made to bypass writing certain code in favor of off-the-shelf software for every computer deployed in the spacecraft. Fatefully, the least-expensive, most-risk-free module caused the mission to unravel. As the spacecraft neared Mars and the two capsules emerged to split from their carrier, the store-bought software incorrectly tabulated a simple math equation—there was a bug in the 14 lines of code. It failed to correctly convert inches into centimeters. The Lander shattered on the surface of Mars, and the Orbiter careened into the umbra.

Mars Explorer 98 underscores the importance of establishing your coordinates and properly assessing risk when deciding to do business on more than one planet, yet its implications are very down to earth. This mindset must continually inform you as you build a global security strategy. Just like that sixth sense that discovers a new profit center, your understanding of applicable standards, specific business issues, and the security technology and procedures necessary to make it all work together must be correlated with an intuitive sense of where vulnerabilities lie. This requires significant investment. If you are aiming to build a strong and flexible security strategy, understand the full price up front and expect to invest the time and energy to create and implement it. Over the long term, it will prevent you from having to pick up the pieces of a corporation that has crashed or a career that has vanished. And even if these two extreme outcomes are averted, remember that it is always costlier to repair damage.

Security is no different than any other service, and you must remember to apply the right math to the idea of fast, good, and cheap: Fast and good but not cheap. Cheap and fast but not good. Good and cheap but not fast. Choose two of the three.

—Kobus Burger, Partner, Deloitte, South Africa, Johannesburg

The endeavor increases in difficulty the more global your operation. Establishing your coordinates on a region-by-region basis may prove easier depending on how far your company extends. Rules, standards, and regulations offer an immediately accessible example. In Germany, all aspects of a contract hold the individuals in charge of a company personally liable, and this includes security. Moreover, if it is in the contract, your company will do it, and you will do it to the document's very letter. This thorough sensibility extends beyond legal writ and into social customs. Germans are more than punctual. When you plan a meeting of any sort, it is customary that you arrive 15 minutes early. This ensures you impress and never inconvenience your host.

Let's compare Germany with the United States, starting with the sociological example of punctuality. In the United States, being on time is less significant to varying degrees. In New York, lateness of 10 minutes is looked upon as normal. In Los Angeles, where freeways carry 20 million commuters all day—everyday—30 minutes of tardiness is almost expected. Similarly, a much-less-legalistic mindset applies in business. Americans tend to look for methods of getting around the law. Contracts are at times a formality and developed only should things go wrong.

Hence, in America you would read the laws very carefully, examining them for any loopholes. In many cases, because security is such an evolving field where technology and countermeasures change so rapidly, rules, standards and regulations just cannot keep pace. When you work in America, you might discover that your partners are looking for ways to circumvent those areas—especially when they lack "teeth" for enforcement. Often a legal expert will examine a regulation and think, "It would cost me a million dollars to comply with this and the penalty's only $50,000. I'll take the penalty." In the United States, compliance follows only when regulations develop teeth, and as you can see, this stands in stark contrast to Germany.

Building on the regulatory environment, let's address how the Asia Pacific addresses similar issues differently from both the United States and Europe. In Asia, there is a tendency to compare what other parts of the world are doing—especially those companies coming from Europe and the Americas who are doing business on their continent—and add teeth to a law on an as-needed basis. And in places such as China, strong central governments exert control in ways vastly different from other regions of the world. In fact, China's *National Information Security Testing Evaluation and Certification Center* (NISTECC) controls 11 aspects of security technology used throughout the country—period.

When working across borders, compliance in the form of regulations, rules, and standards is often your number one security issue, and right now it is the single most important driver in the global security business. It involves a wisely integrated approach between your CSO, CFO, and local or regional leaders in the countries where you have opened shop. Because the CSO is the glue that ensures each component of this trio stays interlocked, this chapter defines and examines the increased significance of this corporate role.

Establishing Your Coordinates Key Questions: Board Member Focus

1. What horizontal (geographically) and vertical (industry-wide) security standards, laws, and regulations apply to your organization?

2. Do you have the capability of integrating the financial, legal, IT, and audit components into your security planning?

3. Who in the organization is responsible to map solutions to the regulations you've identified?

4. How much additional risk is being assumed with each new country touched?

The CSO As a New Global Constant

While regional variations are constantly evolving, CSOs are rising in both power and prestige. That C-level designation accentuates how corporate security has moved from an IT to an executive role. Now a part of the management team, CSOs are becoming expert in all facets of corporate security and especially in that one constant: change. During this phase of the "Charting a Course," CSOs are integral cogs because they are the ones who ultimately determine the security agenda for the organizations, establishing what outcomes the corporation seeks to advance through a security strategy. Often it is preferable to obtain outside counsel to help facilitate the process. Such consultants effectively understand the art of listening, the art of not getting in the way, and the art of injecting themselves into the process noninvasively.

In this chapter, you will notice that by describing the strategic planning process, I'm really framing the long-term role of the CSO within your company. It is my belief that one day this pivotal team member's purview will encompass all aspects of risk reduction within an organization, logically linking together the entirety of a company's risk-related elements such as insurance, safety, privacy, and IT security.

You Are Where?

Reminded that business is a game of inches (or centimeters; you do the math!), you may be gravely asking, "Where does my company fit in or even start charting a course?" The answer begins with another question: "Where are you?"

Finding your position on the security map is a multilayered process that begins with understanding a few basics about where your extended organization sits operationally and geographically and then what standards apply based on those locales.

You Are Here: Three Degrees of Separation

Mapping security requires that you take stock of your own organizational landscape. Finding that "you are here" spot on the map provides context and begins to reveal early strengths and weaknesses of your existing global security posture. It starts out easily enough. Where are you headquartered and where are your field offices? Those spots on the map represent zero degrees of separation.

The First Degree: Outsourcing

Moving out one degree, now map your direct outsourcing relationships. Where are they? Maybe India is your natural destination—the country's deputy prime minister, L. K. Advani, has indicated a 10-year goal of more than $50 billion in outsourced technology jobs by 2008.[1] With its educated population, including a million new college graduates per year whose average salary is $12,000, and with more than 10 million Indians unemployed, India is very focused on doing what is necessary to be the leading outsource processor. This growth is outpacing its ability to secure the various risks that are commensurate with the types of information it handles, yet security is better than most in the region. If it is not India, perhaps it is one of the new countries betting on the outsourcing game that promise even cheaper labor, such as the Philippines, Pakistan, and Bangladesh. (Much like the Japanese manufacturing erosion that led to Korea's rise, India already risks pricing itself out of some of the outsourcing markets.) While making the important decisions about where you outsource your product manufacturing and service offerings, take great care to understand the risks involved in sending specific information assets to those countries. As you carefully consider the standards you want adopted in those countries and as your assets begin to flow, take care to understand whether their physical and technological infrastructures are able to handle them. Remember, you can outsource the function, but you always own the risk.

Physical Security

Anywhere you expand physically necessitates certain physical security measures. As I led a team scouting out Mexico City for a company's new location, some on my team were robbed or scammed just because they were unfamiliar with the territory.

For instance, one team member walking outside his hotel was confronted by a man who asked whether he wanted a shoeshine. He said "No," but the shoeshiner insisted. Intimidated, my team member complied.

After one shoe was completed, the footwear professional asked for the equivalent of $50, to which my team member replied "No way!" and began to leave.

continues...

---

1. *Jatras, Todd. "Can India Retain Its Reign as Outsourcing King?" Forbes. 28 February 2001.*

Physical Security Continued

The shiner then quickly called over a police officer from the neighborhood, and the policeman immediately took the shiner's side. "You better pay up—you don't want to go to jail or something for not paying," he said. So the employee paid, and as he walked back to his hotel, he could see the $50 being split between the two, suddenly realizing he had been scammed by law enforcement.

When the scouting trip was completed and it was time to choose a project leader for this endeavor, I hired U.S. Marine and eCommerce specialist John Borland (now with Ernst & Young), who ran my team with an iron hand and made sure everyone stayed out of harm's way. He provided typical government-based security training, informing my team of places they should avoid and what numbers to call if they were in trouble. Mapping security as you expand also requires physical considerations; this book isn't intended to provide great detail about physical security, just know that it should dovetail with global information security concerns as you operate in different countries.

The Second Degree: The Supply Chain

Now move out two degrees, and map your extended supply chains. If you think that your ownership and responsibility begins at your border's FOB site, consult your legal teams and reread your contracts. In most countries, your liabilities and responsibilities reach much deeper into the product lifecycle, and broadening the supply chain can prove challenging as you run up against certain physical and technical constraints or regulatory issues.

Supply Chain Times Seven

As you saw in Chapter 2, "Why You Picked Up This Book," many things that weren't supplied globally now are. On average, retail products sold in the United States have been *bought and sold* seven times from the time they are created to the time they reach store shelves. All of those transactions are supply chain linked.

I once facilitated the development of an extended, online supply chain for a large, Latin American-based telephone company. As I worked with the organization to design the supply chain from a security perspective, we remained relatively low tech because we couldn't rely on users having the latest laptops or recent versions of Web browsers to run intricate SSL equations. Further complicating matters, the banking laws in Mexico mandate that financial institutions must always be involved in transactions. Every deal at our supply chain's Web site—instead of brokered between a buyer and seller—had to insert the financial institution and become brokered three ways. This created a number of security issues that we never anticipated.

Moreover, although the phone company had many state-of-the-art data centers, none could be set up separately to enforce the security policy that we required. I ultimately built one from scratch 50 miles outside of Mexico City. Completely autonomous, it housed its own power and security scheme. This may seem like an elaborate step, but it completely obviated many of the technological and personnel risks inherent in using existing offices. The new building proved attractive to a host of tenants, and it allowed for the furthering of a number of the phone company's business interests.

In many countries, a single rule applies to the previous two degrees, but these can be sliced and diced even further depending on the nation-state in which you're operating. It is always important to discern clues that could lead to more significant local nuances. Full country names afford natural guideposts. For example, consider my latest place of residence: the Federal Republic of Germany. The word *Federal* should give you a big hint. Germany today is a federation of smaller states, and the rules and customs of Hamburg in the north are very different from those of Munich in the south. Acceptable global security policy in one city is not acceptable in the next, and even more importantly in Germany, rather than a country-wide convention, security is typically handled via business contract, with each contact being different depending on the city of origin.

Of course, there are exceptions. In the United States, for example, when it comes to standards, the word *United* is somewhat of a misnomer. Rules and customs in the state of California (California Privacy Act, for instance) are vastly different from those of Minnesota (Minnesota S.F. 2908; an act relating to data privacy and regulatory electronic mail solicitations).

The Third Degree: Customers

The third degree—represented by your customers—can prove thorny. More than likely they are all over the world; depending on where the business is actually transacted and who your sales agents are (employees, contractors, independents), however, the ways they interface with you differ. Determining where your customers are, and therefore which rules/regulations/standards apply to how you interact with them, adds shades of complexity that bring new meaning to the term *the third degree*. Adding a single customer from France may require you to change how you back up all your data files worldwide.

Accountability in the third degree moves beyond physical, in-person transactions with customers. The movement of information digitally through other countries can subject you to accountability if you have servers housed there. Most people don't even know where equipment such as this is housed and what routes their information takes; they risk considerable liability now and through future regulation just by virtue of the fact they didn't discover where their data lives, where it stops on its journeys around the world, and what networks it travels through. Your technology groups will have this information, but they won't know that it is significant unless you identify it as such while creating a holistic security strategy.

Akamai and the Third Degree

Boston-based Akamai, a company described in Chapter 4, "Building the Base," and Chapter 5, "Enabling Business and Enhancing Process," has created a service that enables companies to circumvent servers used in the United States or Europe that would otherwise make information traveling through either place subject to privacy laws.

Think of your information and its travels in terms of ancient trade routes. At that time, folks in your position would have to consider what waterways you navigated and what tariffs you owed at what ports when you stopped to purchase supplies. As boats once negotiated the Rhine River from the top of Germany to the bottom, every big bend featured a castle where massive chains were set over the water. Boats couldn't gain passage unless they paid a tax, homage, or toll to whoever owned that castle. If they didn't pay, the castle might even lob cannonballs at them. The same issue applies on virtual trade routes, except now castle dwellers can come after you retroactively. They'll start looking at what towns you've been in and start sending you the bill.

Correlating Degrees to Standards

Here is a small sample of standards, rules, and regulations facing companies in today's global marketplace:

Table 3-1

Standards, Rules, and Regulations

British Standards Institute (BSI) (BS 7799)

Bundesamt (BSI Germany)

Common Criteria (CC) (IS 15408)   International Standards in information security are developed by the Security Techniques Committee of the International Standards Organization: ISO/IEC JTC 1 SC 27 (SC27). There are three Working Groups (WGs):

   WG 1: Security Management

   WG 2: Security Algorithms/Techniques

   WG 3: Security Assessment/Evaluation

Digital Signatures (IS 9796, IS 14888))

Elliptic Curve Cryptography (WD 15946)

Encryption (WD 18033)

Entity Authentication (IS 9798)

ETSI Baseline Security Standards

The EU Privacy Directive (EU)

FISMA (U.S.)

Graham-Leach (GLB) (U.S.)

Guidelines for Information Security Management (TR 13335)

Guidelines for Intrusion Detection Systems (WD 18043)

Guidelines for Security Incident Management (WD 18044)

Guidelines on Trusted Third Parties (TR 14516)

Hash Functions (IS 10118)

HIPPA (U.S.)

ISO 13335 (International)

ISO 15408 (International)

ISO 17799

Key Management (IS 11770)

Message Authentication Codes (IS 9797)

Modes of Operation (IS 8372)

NIST Computer Security Handbook (SP 800-12)

Non-repudiation Techniques (IS 13888)

The Patriot Act (U.S.)

Rules and regulations facing companies in today's global marketplace:

Sarbanes-Oxley (U.S.)

SWIFT (Worldwide)

Time Stamping Services (WD 18014)

With a clear idea of the physical locations wherein you operate as viewed through the three degrees, your attention can turn to your organization. This first step in mapping security begins to unveil significant differences as you move beyond your headquarters and begin developing a country-by-country profile. Now that you've geographically located your "degrees" of operations, it is time to start linking each of them to their corresponding horizontal and vertical standards.

What Applies to You

As the saying goes, "The problem with standards is there are so many to choose from." Standards, numerous and intricate, can be harrowing. However, they cue you to the baseline requirements for security in your company, and this is why you should use them to jumpstart your security strategy development. Depending on your industry and the countries where you do business, a different mix will apply. Rest assured that as you look at the list, your organization sits at the intersection of at least two of them, and probably more.

Horizontal Standards

As mentioned previously, executives are increasingly being held responsible for the security and purity of their information, systems, and people, no matter the industry. Horizontal standards and regulations are responsible for this. They outline the steps you need to take for baseline compliance while providing the certification that reflects it. Noncompliance jeopardizes your reputation in countries where standards hold sway. Increasingly, equal jeopardy exists in regions where compliance wasn't previously thought of as mandatory or even necessary. That's because the global village is taking hold and its influence is growing. Be aware:

Various business-related triggers lead to changes in legal and regulatory requirements on an international basis. This could include economic conditions of a given country or even business-related scandals. You must identify and ensure that you understand them and have a plan for dealing with them.

—Jean-Pierre Garrite, Partner, Deloitte, Belgium, Brussels

Among horizontal corporate security benchmarks, the *International Organization for Standardization* (ISO) 17799 provides a "standard of standards." Evolving from the UK's BS 7799, it attempts to deliver an all-encompassing guideline for corporations. It is been adopted by Australia, Brazil, Japan, the Netherlands, Sweden, and the UK. It is probably the most quoted security standard in existence.

ISO 17799 clarifies how businesses should manage corporate security. It also lists a number of "critical success factors" that should be envisioned and followed. Although the standard itself catalogs more than 100 controls that are discretely sliced into 12 headings, the most-quoted elements of the standard deal with the following:

- Having policies that reflect business objectives

- Using an approach consistent with organizational culture

- Maintaining a commitment from management

- Understanding of requirements

- Practicing effective policy promulgation, suitable training, and education

- Offering feedback to ensure continuous improvement

The Standard That's No Standard at All

The newest horizontal standard is not a standard at all. However, section 404 of the U.S. Sarbanes-Oxley corporate governance act requires that very specific IT and IT security controls are in place, and this is driving more security change than any standard today. This act is discussed in greater detail in Chapter 11, "The Americas," whereas this chapter just briefly describes a way to help ensure that you comply with the controls and reporting required by the act, and its sister laws popping up around the world.

The *Information Systems Audit and Control Association* (ISACA), which has been around since the 1960s, focuses on helping computer auditors do their job. ISACA has more than 60 country chapters, and members in more than 100 countries worldwide, and those chapters provide member education, resource sharing, advocacy, professional networking, and a variety of other benefits on a local level.

Most good computer auditors will be members, and almost all will follow a framework for controls that ISACA publishes called COBIT. The *Control Objectives for Information and Related Technologies* is a six-volume set that contains an IT governance model as well as management guidelines for determining how effectively a company controls IT and improvements that could be made. Used around the world, it has recently become famous as the single most-used framework for Sarbanes-Oxley section 404 compliance.

Standards Are Everywhere: Who Makes Up the ISO's Security (SC27) Group?

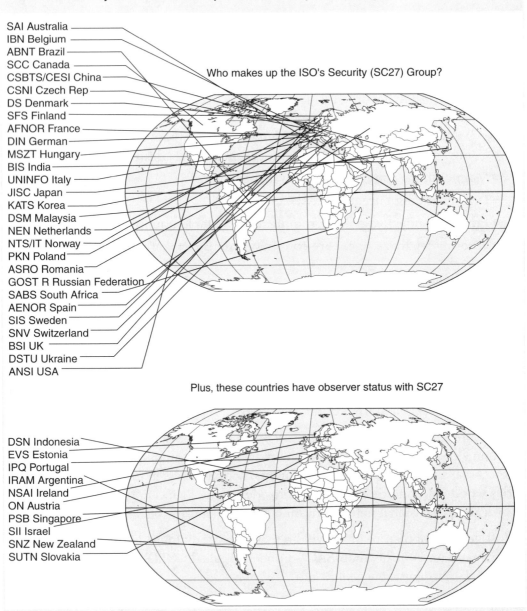

Figure 3.1 The countries that make up the ISO's Security (SC27) Group.

Vertical Standards

This section provides two examples of vertical standards. Understand for your company, however, that there are several you should hunt down. Vertical standards require patient research that assesses the legal, executive, and financial branches of your company along with industry and trade groups for each of the markets you serve. Don't rely on an old printed list, and make sure it is a living, constantly refreshed document (see Chapter 7, "Constant Vigilance").

Because they are prescriptive and customized for your industry, a vertical standard can potentially enlighten you to immediate risks that lurk inside your organization. Often times they are created to address very specific vulnerabilities that have already been exposed and focus on elements most relevant to you. One great example of a vertical standard is the financial industry's gauge known as *Basel II*.

Be Prepared

I have met too many American bankers who have ignored European standards because they are... well... European. But standards leadership can come from anywhere, and you must be prepared to comply, even if the standards are not from your own backyard.

The Basel Committee on Banking Supervision is composed of members from 13 countries. Basel designed a single document, known as the *Basel Capital Accord*, that provides an industry-wide framework. It usually makes additional recommendations through reports that deal with issues such as "risk management principles for electronic banking," "best practices for credit risk disclosure," "sound practices for the management and supervision of operational risk." Although it holds no legal force, its recommendations are extremely influential throughout the banking community.

Although Basel represents a solid guide for financial sector companies to use, be aware that as of mid-year 2004, Basel II has no teeth. European banks, like most other corporations, will wait on costly compliance until there is more bite to the regulations. When there is a penalty for noncompliance—either a fine or a business barrier—this entire sector will rally around Basel II. I project this will be in the 2005 to 2006 timeframe, but I also advise you to track the adoption rate carefully. Remember, the best security is the right security at the right time.

Another recognizable vertical standard is health care's *Health Insurance Portability and Accountability Act* (HIPAA), and it emanates from the United States. HIPAA mandates for electronic medical records and privacy are the most sweeping in health care's history. Those servicing the health-care sector are crying "HIPAA, HIPAA, HIPAA." In reality, however, most health-care facilities are only giving it lip service. Most companies I have worked with in the medical sector, from manufacturers to providers, are all nominally compliant at best.

When in private conversation with leaders of these entities, they admit that it is something they'll do when they have to do it and when everyone else in their sector does it. It is a fine set of standards, but again, there's no business reason to becoming a first mover. It is costly. It is carries a lot of extra policy and procedure, and there are no real penalties for noncompliance.

Don't Try This at Home

If you have identified some potential standards that your company needs to follow, your reflex might be to call a meeting with your CSO, CTO, and CIO and begin the process of seeing to it that you comply. I have worked on corporate security from the inside of corporations, and as a consultant; I have also worked from the outside. In security standards compliance, my ideal structure for compliance involves your CSO working with one of the larger consultancies that are expert and trustworthy in this area to map what is applicable. Why? Should you try it yourself, you may be lured into a false sense of security that could leave you more vulnerable to attack. And although this regime proved a hard task before globalization, it is made exponentially more difficult afterward.

The speed with which standards change and evolve with the risks they seek to mitigate requires experts in the respective standards du jour. In fact, I also recommend legal help, especially as you navigate between borders through your business. A slip-up in a standard or regulation can cost you time and money.

For those of you who want to courageously press on and attempt this on your own, make certain that you not only have the specific, unadulterated version of the standard, but also make use of a proven tool that will make compliance manageable. For instance, the oft-referenced BS 7799 contains more than 100 specific items to be checked, from dozens of different points within an organization, over multiple periods. Try to do this without an automated tool, and you will fail, and such attempts are often the sign that an organization is only giving lip service to the standards, and not really using them to enhance their overall risk profile as intended. However, beware of poorly constructed tools, and before deployment follow four important verification steps:

1. Determine the real use of the tool and compare it with given documentation.

2. Determine the real use of the tool and compare the results against benchmark databases obtained through similar tools.

3. Identify and analyze the side effects of the tool through the interception (sniffing and so on) of network traffic produced by the tool.

4. In the case of open source tools, review the code to detect possible malicious activities or side effects and ensure its validity.

Pinpointing Your Business Requirements

Establishing your coordinates also requires introspection. As security moves into its new corporate moorings, it is also progressing to the forefront of business operations. In this way, it becomes a process enhancer—a point Chapter 5 deals with comprehensively.

Yet to pinpoint your business requirements demands attention to your operations right up front, and a security review can help you determine and evaluate threats to your infrastructure in light of other factors. Whether you conduct it internally or enlist an external third party to work with you, this internal audit is critical to understanding where your particular risks lie today—and to help you prioritize exactly where you want to make your full investment tomorrow—to start fixing what's vulnerable. Through it, you should do the following:

- **Define Your Business Requirements**

  What's important for your business to function? What are the priorities affiliated with these requirements? This could include issues of productivity, your systems, and the whole of your infrastructure. Based on these requirements, set holistic management objectives.

- **Classify the Importance of Your Assets**

  Take stock of all your assets, including the building/facilities, equipment, contractors, products, services, personnel, information/intellectual property, and even reputation, as well as the IT infrastructure, taking into account possible threats and exposure from employees, contractors, suppliers, and others. In assessing these assets, ask yourself three questions: What can go wrong? What will most likely go wrong? What are the consequences if something goes wrong?

■ **Ensure That Proper Controls Are in Place**

Controls are a prelude to creating effective security policies. When creating them, look at confidentiality, availability and integrity. Think, for instance, if something inappropriate or private was to be told to someone else: That violates confidentiality. Think again if your business were shut down and your systems were no longer available. This is what I mean by availability. Finally, and most insidious: What if someone changed one number in your spreadsheet? This is what I define as integrity. All three areas must be considered when formulating a strong, global security strategy. Leverage the COBIT framework, or the COSO framework from the Treadway Commission, which was created by the accounting and auditing industry in 1985 to help monitor the factors that can lead to fraudulent financial reporting, to ensure that all of your controls are covered.

■ **Confirm That Information Assets Square with Your Business Risk**

Your information assets must correlate evenly with your business risk. It is one thing to say that you can provide a return on investment, it is another thing to demonstrate it. Calculate the basics, such as how much you pay your staff, how many systems you have, what your backup policies are.

Upon completion, the internal audit carries several positive intangibles that can be realized only as you remain attentive to global corporate security's critical success factors:

Intangible Benefits

Stability

Time-to-Value

Integration

Scalability

Flexibility

Global reach

Single point of accountability

Proven best practices

Strategic alignment

Strategic redeployment of resources

Critical Success Factors

Schedule

Organizational alignment

Labor resources

User acceptance

Compatibility

Integration

Although this assessment is executable in-house, I recommend employing the help of an external vendor who has a trustworthy ROI calculator tool available for your customization and use. Beware the phony calculator! The security product industry is rife with garbage calculators that always report a 40 percent cost savings over time if you buy their product. This result, with minor variations for "believability," occurs no matter what the input! However, don't let this harsh industry fact scare you away from a good calculator, which can save you time and money and be a tremendous asset for bringing your project in on time, on budget, and with the expected results. Calculators from some of the less-dependent (I hesitate to use the word *independent*, because everyone is trying to sell you something) firms such as the Metas and Gartners have proven to be both more expensive and more helpful.

Creating Your Risk Profile

Requirements in hand, the next step in the pinpointing process necessitates excellent communication. To take inventory of all potential risks, assess their probability, and prioritize them based on the potential impact on your organization, you need input from all key stakeholders within your company. First, the executive team should collaborate to decide who needs to be considered in this process, designating key board members, management, and...

"Business owners" or those individuals who are running various parts of the corporation. Security concerns must be addressed at the CEO and boardroom level of every company and by political leadership at all levels... awareness about security issues is still low.

—Jerry Rao, Chairman, National Association of Software and Service Companies, New Delhi

Sitting down with each of these parties is a time-consuming, yet valuable process that enables you to synthesize each area's business objectives with risks of importance. It requires that you ask questions about the critical factors to the business: What impacts sales? What impacts fulfillment? What impacts your job? From there, it is critical that they fully appreciate the idea of risk. When comprehended and after key pressure points are discovered, you walk through the process with the priority business owners one at a time in an interview setting until they are comfortable with their area's/the company's level of risk tolerance.

An obvious cost-benefit analysis surfaces through this process and, consequently, they can choose full security or no security. The secret formula for glue might not need to be "Fort Knoxed." The secret formula for Coke might. Most assets fall into the middle. When each stakeholder is comfortable with the levels of risk, signing off on it, the outcomes are fed back into the auditing team and then pushed up. Ultimately, the full summary is fed into the team and then pushed up to develop an overall picture of the company.

Listening 101

Bobby Christian is serving as acting CSO of a new U.S. government agency called the Public Accounting Oversight Board, which ensures compliance with Sarbanes-Oxley. How did he get the job? By listening. When his firm, True North Solutions, was thrown into the mix of the government's bidding process, he was the only one who went to each stakeholder in the organization and listened.

He spent hours discussing each owner's objectives for the coming year. Then he took time to synthesize various global corporate security needs that could match their objectives. On the day he was to present his master plan for the organization, he asked for a blank white board and mapped each owner's objectives back to the organization's overall goal array.

"They were wide-eyed and shocked because no one had come in to listen—previous firms had offered a bunch of product or single-point solutions for information security, but this comprehensive method of listening and synthesizing is the important first step to success in the creation of any global corporate security strategy—it creates the environment for sell-in that's so important and gets everyone excited."

Ideally, this process will at once enlighten and vest stakeholders with respect—they have helped create the risk language. It also serves as a critical sell-in opportunity as you anticipate creating and implementing a strategy company-wide. Assessing risk also provides you a significant opening for defining an internal "information security organization." Its components would include the following:

- **The Information Security Council**

   The information security council is designed to provide a top-down management structure for the implementation of information security within a company. It will serve as the mechanism through which high-level control is exercised. It will also promote good security practice and monitor the enterprise-wide security condition.

- **The Information Security Officer**

  The company's ISO has the delegated responsibility for all aspects of information security management, including planning, budgeting, monitoring, and reporting. He or she would also coordinate control implementation.

- **Information Security Function**

  The information security function actively fosters good practice in the implementation of information security across the organization.

- **Business Custodians**

  Business custodians are individuals who are best placed to manage the infrastructure that the information depends on. This role will typically belong to the IT stream managers. Their responsibilities revolve around ensuring that the business requirements are met and that the controls are implemented in ways that—in line with business risks—protect information assets.

Charting Your Course

With benchmarking data collected from standards; the key business requirements and the objectives of your business and their correlative risks identified, prioritized, and agreed upon; and a cohesive structure for creating ongoing dialogue and reporting set into motion; it is time to chart a course. You can do it yourself, or you can buy it (again) from a consultancy, depending on the level of experience at the CSO position. Strategic planning must focus on relevant, practical, and proportional recommendations. After it is drafted, it should be refined based on operational and financial constraints and, in turn, safeguard alternatives and a risk-reduction strategy are developed.

The Significance of Benchmarking

CSOs throughout the world tell me their single largest problem surrounds their inability to get enough budget approved. The CSO has typically thought through the issues, can figure out where the ROI will come from, and is able to understand that security needs are holistic, but has been unable to get that budget.

I tell these CSOs that they should revisit their most recent projects. Have they made gains for the company? Have they helped? Even though all of them will say "Yes," they usually cannot prove it. They cannot demonstrate to me or to

continues...

The Significance of Benchmarking   Continued

their internal or external auditors or, most importantly, to their executive team that the value of the security that they have implemented to date has paid off. What I suggest as a "step-one" element of any future engagement is to do the following:

- Benchmark where the operations are at that moment.
- Implement the engagement.
- Reexamine operations and measure the change.

Then the CSOs can point out that they've helped performance by 2 percent, throughput by 3 percent, or sales by 4 percent. However, they cannot do this until they benchmark. Any of the good internal or external auditors and rigorous security consultants will advise them in the same way.

Then the whole of the strategy, including each course of action and recommendation, is cost-justified and rationalized based on the critical nature of the asset and the level of exposure to the external forces uncovered in the pinpointing exercise. The key to your success at this phase is identifying and supporting actionable recommendations and associated implementation plans. Its main objectives are as follows:

- To qualify the degree of risk reduction and performance improvement you want to realize over time
- To understand how you can reduce or eliminate risk and achieve superior performance levels through prudent, innovative, and cost-effective application of controls (both technical and procedural)
- To understand the costs, benefits, and "lessons learned" associated with these controls

It is crucial that after a course has been charted on paper that you take this strategy back to each of the stakeholders you interviewed when you pinpointed the business requirements. They must buy-off on this strategy and they must understand what this will do for their business. In view of that, they will want to adopt the strategy and make the right security decisions for their portion of the business.

Right decisions at this point are important because the relative size of security teams at even the biggest corporations is tiny. One of the world's largest oil companies carries a staff of nine security personnel—*nine for a company of hundreds of thousands of people*! But they are making security work because each one of those nine individuals is pushing the security agenda back to each of the company's business units, serving as trusted coordinators and advisors. It is security that's being deployed judiciously and in the right place. Also ensure that all security products and services help you directly comply with the rules and regulations that you work within. Do not buy something that will cause you to translate what you have into a report. Buy one in which the output can go directly to an auditor, and remember to make the vendor do your work for you on this front.

Chapter 4

Building the Base

With coordinates established, you are ready to begin implementing a security map, and to do so you must take great care to maximize your global security investment. Expenditures must be matched with efficiency, which in this case means the ratio of money to true risk reduction. When harmonized with your freshly derived policy documents, you will see that the most fiscally responsible and securest infrastructure is driven from the top with clear strategic justification, prioritization, and timing. *Building the base* is a key to success that jumpstarts this process. It means using a step-by-step, phased approach that unifies common elements of a corporation's security by thinking through where those elements exist. It will help you realize the strongest global security structure, one that is ultimately more cost-effective. Although it has been in frequent use of late, I have used the phrase *return on security investment* (ROSI) to describe this ratio for more than a decade, and I use it frequently throughout this chapter and the rest of the book.

The process of weeding out the boxes and organizing the enterprise from a security perspective across the board—this alone can be the best return on security investment. Let me at any company for time to find the shared applications, assets, and resources, and I'll go to town, because once there is a base from which to work, the whole organization is that much more secure.

—Bobby Christian, Acting CSO, Public Company Accounting Oversight Board, Washington D.C.

In most cases (and just like a global business or marketing plan), your global corporate security strategy contains several elements that can and should be shared across your entire organization with varying degrees of ROSI. I call these cooperative security elements that are most logically shared across the whole of any company *maximum ROSI*. Other security functions, when implemented across the board, will offer medium ROSI and may be necessary for your particular situation. Elements that deliver minimum ROSI may still be needed for specific groups, but are not ideally applied across the organization's entirety.

The Rule of 3

Establishing the perfect mix of ROSI elements for your base can be challenging, but I have made the prospect simple with my "Rule of 3." The Rule of 3 mandates a search for a trio of distinct operational units within your corporation that could use one of the typically medium or minimum ROSI components. Find three "buyers" within your existing organization(s) who will "pay for" a base-level rollout—the idea being that each buyer would pay for a third of the element. If found, the given security element is generally base-worthy.

For example, identity management is hot right now; but because it is often deployed for a single task—usually as a network logon tool for employees—ROSI might be difficult to demonstrate. However, applying the Rule of 3 can change everything. In this case it is easy—potentially, ID management can be integrated with *customer relationship management* (CRM) and used to secure virtual private networks.

ROSI grows exponentially when using the Rule of 3. Business-owner signoff on given security elements tends to run more smoothly because you clearly meet justified needs. Because the security element is useful in three areas, you will also enjoy greater breadth and depth for measuring its effectiveness. ROSI is apt to blossom, and soon, more of your operations will want to jump on board to deploy it.

Now that you understand "the base," ROSI, and how to effectively account for ROSI through the Rule of 3, this chapter provides the overview you need to ask the right questions and help you envision how global corporate security is appropriately developed throughout an organization.

Establishing Your Coordinates Key Questions: CIO Focus

1. What are your baseline metrics (that is, number of computers, users, licenses)?
2. Which systems process and store your most critical intellectual property?
3. How much does "on-boarding" truly cost your organization in time and money?
4. What organization-wide software and hardware standards are in place that can be better leveraged?

The Base

Chapter 3, "Establishing Your Coordinates," discussed how business owners have their respective sets of objectives. Through the security audit, business owners correlate the amount of risk they are comfortable accepting to those objectives. These audit results are compared to applicable horizontal or vertical security standards and defined via a strategy.

When building the base, you and your security group or a qualified third party scour the strategy and begin to assert base-worthy security elements for implementation. By assigning maximum, medium, and minimum ROSI to these elements, I have started to familiarize you with a quantitative navigational device for the many security considerations you will confront. At this juncture, examination of global security's rudiments and their ROSI becomes invaluable. The base must be thought through definitively, and you need to be conversant in these mechanisms that will routinely play a role in the overall security of your company.

When we develop policies, the policy directly translates into a technology standard. We say that if you can't measure it you can't manage it. So there is very little value in dwelling upon stuff you cannot measure. Focus on the stuff you can measure, manage that, and then worry about the other stuff.

—Kobus Burger, Partner, Deloitte, Johannesburg

Sample ROSI Grouping for a Mid-Size Cross-Border Organization (Your Results Will Vary)

Maximum ROSI Across the Base

- Unified training
- Patch management
- Identity management
- Intrusion detection/prevention

Medium ROSI Across the Base

- Monitoring
- Business continuity
- Privacy

Minimum ROSI Across the Base

- Baseline security
- Application integrity

Maximum Base-Worthy ROSI

When leveraged together, these components of global security can provide ROSI that can be realized powerfully and immediately.

Unified Training Is Base-Worthy

Imagine walking into one of London's office buildings and, upon taking an elevator to the corporate headquarters of a major financial institution, you pass by its conference room. Glancing up, you notice a list of employee names and personal access codes labeled "logon" and "password." Or envision standing in line at a Tokyo bank where you see that each customer at the teller windows has his or her bank account clearly visible on desktop monitors turned out toward the lobby. Both of these anecdotes are true—recounted by Los Angeles-based global security trainer Easy-i from team members in different parts of the world, but it doesn't take a global corporate security training guru to recognize such security lapses.

I was once seated on a plane next to an executive who shrouded his laptop monitor as I slipped into an adjacent seat. Before he arose to visit the lavatory, he powered the unit down and turned it over on his seat cushion. I took a look at it and noticed that he had written all of *his* usernames and passwords on a memo sheet and taped it to the computer. Security education is rarely invested in throughout the whole of organization, but instances such as these reinforce its importance.

A unified training program that can drive awareness and understanding sets the tone for implementation and ensures maximum ROSI. Training is serious—it is not a checklist item that becomes a marketing tool to ensure customers or clients can be relieved or pacified by your organization's level of awareness. Quality training should present base policies and expectations to the corporation as a whole and then apply them to specific business units via relevant scenarios. Employees must understand what's happening in terms of the security base—not simply be informed of it.

A lot of clients we talk to think they do training, and they obviously don't. A company that has published its policies, procedures, and guidelines on the Web for their employees and customers to see thinks that it has done training. Or they will have quizzed employees on going through a policy and compliance tool and then have them confirm at the end whether they are compliant. This is auditing—not training.

—Terry Hancock, President, Easy-i, London

Security training will bring your security investment down to the level of the individual, making each person in your organization a vital steward of corporate assets and productivity. It is best done by an outside agency that has a strong grasp on your strategic direction and a working knowledge of your base. They should also have a proven track record in delivering the material in an incisive, interesting way that will be relevant to every piece of your business, no matter the language they speak or the cultural differences they exhibit.

Patch Management Is Base-Worthy

All computer systems contain bugs—inherent flaws that can interfere with their smooth operation and that expose them to outside threats. Patches fix bugs and must be faithfully managed because unpatched bugs can pose a significant hazard. Think of them as minor cracks that open up leverage points to outside attacks. (In fact, the vast majority of threats that could attack you were not invented to attack you—they were invented to attack en masse or to attack someone else.)

Patch-Free Could Mean License-Free

The number one reason that companies around the globe do not patch their Windows operating system is because it is stolen. A legally purchased operating system is simple to patch, but many global organizations know they have at least some bootlegged software and do not want the likes of Microsoft to find out.

When you think of a typical attacker, picture a "script kiddie"—a low-level hack, usually between the ages of 12 and 20—who copies preproduced, hostile software code, makes a small change or two (such as inserting your Web address instead of someone else's), and sends it back into the ether. Automated updates of applicable, tested patches in advance of known threats arriving at your system's door is the best way to reduce your risk from viruses, worms, and system-vulnerabilities attacks launched by said "kiddies." Differences between the prepared and unprepared are significant. Those who are patched simply feel such attacks as a minor annoyance. The "unpatched" remain vulnerable to what can amount to a lethal intrusion. Therefore, patch management can do two things: It keeps your technology running at maximum security, and it minimizes risk caused by outside attacks. An effective patch management program includes the following hallmarks:

- A high degree of automation. Setting this up is relatively easy; many manufacturers make real-time updates available that are executed on an as-developed basis.

- Extreme automation means that you must own registered and licensed copies of all software.

- Readiness of patches presupposes advance planning and deployment. (Reacting overnight might result in the shutdown of your vital services at peak times.)

- Patches require ongoing testing. Patches on one piece of software must be tested against the rest of your technology. Therefore, having a complete testing environment is essential. It ain't cheap, but it contributes to the "real" costs of total software ownership.

- Finally, it is essential that you stay current with the threats that could affect *you* and the countermeasures available to thwart them. (For more on this, see Chapter 7, "Constant Vigilance.")

Patch management is grueling, time-consuming, and important. Building it in to the base ensures its efficient and accurate employment. Similar to human organ transplants, new patches will interact and affect other software in different ways and need time to "settle," which could potentially leave you more vulnerable to threats. This acclimation period demands that any patch management program must include vigorous testing. If your security group seeks to keep this in-house, make sure it has a dedicated testing area that ensures easily assimilated patches that weave seamlessly into your system-wide software. If you outsource patch management, make sure your third party is qualified and tour their testing facility.

Identity Management Is Base-Worthy

Because nearly everyone in your global operation will have some kind of access to your network, developing a sound identity management component into your base offers significant protection. Generally associated with your technology group, its function can include dispatching user IDs and passwords, allowing/prohibiting computer-based resource access, or controlling who enters specific rooms inside a building.

Identity management can increase productivity and security. It reduces recurring operational costs. Often the number of IDs a typical user needs for connecting to a company's technology resources can discourage usage while increasing corporate vulnerability. When installed as an automated system that works across the organization, identity management serves as a potent, efficient design element because it consolidates business structures and streamlines business processes. It also reduces support overheads and relieves the burden users place on help desks when they cannot gain access or have an identity need (for example, a new password). Identity management benefits include the following:

- **Decreased risk**

  For example, the number of unused accounts on key systems can be reduced and effectively managed if employees leave or change roles within the company.

- **Money saved**

  By reducing unnecessary software licenses caused by a proliferation of unused usernames, identity management significantly decreases the cost and upgrades control of application access, allowing for greater control and monitoring of an individual's behavior within an organization's IT environment.

■ **Consumer and client access control**
Users can be tracked, and presented information can be customized for different types of users with different types of user privileges or needs.

When considering identity management, take stock of your existing software and be ready to map it from an "identity-centric" perspective. Too often, technology takes the front seat with elaborate interfaces that are not met with organizational depth. Create a culture wherein the use of an identity is built in to the organization. This comes heavily into play especially in terms of process alignment. In addition, if rules governing access control are not clearly laid out, the likelihood of success is low. The more planning that goes into this design element, the better.

Intrusion Detection and Protection Are Base-Worthy

Intrusion detection (ID) senses trouble on computer systems, and *intrusion protection* (IP) deals with it. If executed group by group, ID/IP will prove significantly too expensive and will usually result in failure—group A's system mistakes group B's system as an intruder, and vice versa, and the two begin squawking at one another. It must be built in to the base.

The toughest issue surrounding ID/IP rests in the fact that corporations come under "attack" thousands of times a day and to the unlearned nearly anything can seem like a meltdown. Excessive "false positive" attacks can overwhelm the group handling ID/IP implementation (not to mention create a cynical atmosphere), and the process of narrowing down intrusions to true positives is akin to finding a needle in a haystack. Although not ridding you of the challenges surrounding the volume and identification of these intrusions, building ID/IP into the global security base can eliminate one level of potential wasted effort while creating a streamlined network and system architecture.

ID/IP is increasingly a necessary part of a global security strategy because attacks only continue to increase—both purposeful and glancing—among companies that are deploying technology worldwide and that rely on the Internet. Executed correctly, ID/IP that can find that needle will prove to be the vital cog in enabling your company to prevent malicious intrusion. Often, hiring outside help to deploy such a system is the most feasible course. Chapter 6, "Developing Radar," discusses ID/IP in depth because once ensconced within the base, it becomes an important monitoring tool that, although necessary, is hotly debated within the industry.

Medium Base-Worthy ROSI

If maximum ROSI elements are best shared across the enterprise, medium ROSI elements need to be carefully considered when building the base. Again, we are discussing the R on I of performing a function in a single unified manner and not whether you should do it or not.

Business Continuity

When disaster strikes your company—either physical or technological—business continuity is the plan that keeps you up and running, making sure that each element of your business assets is mirrored (and works) in an alternative, safe location. This especially important contingency is vital to your overall security posture, but it may be best executed on a location-by-location basis. Again, if you are operating in countries where technological or physical threats are acute, it is essential; and if you're in a region routinely plagued by natural disaster, it is even more essential. Build business continuity in to your base with a flexible, light touch—creating a single, detailed, and unified plan across the base may be less efficient. Provide inclusive, easy-to-understand guidance. As you think through business continuity, examine the terrain of where you do business—its infrastructure and external landscape—and then judiciously design and implement the element with specific components that trigger the people and systems needed when disaster strikes.

In the United States and around the world, 9-11 provided an amazing, if tragic, case study in business continuity. Through it, I found that companies did a great job duplicating their systems through the use of backup tapes; often, however, when they arrived at an alternative location to use the tapes, they found unmatched protocols. Perhaps their tapes were backed up using DAT and their backup technology would only recognize optical, rendering the tapes useless.

In other cases, companies outsourced their entire information technology operation, but they had not outsourced the people—they did not have an alternative location for people to start working again—rendering a running server useless. Often Manhattan-based employees sat at home saying to themselves, "I wish I could help," even as the company's backup servers—fully operational—ran in some remote locale such as Idaho. (Had they set up something like a *virtual private network* [VPN] that was poised for deployment in an emergency and accessible via home computers, maybe these same employees could have telecommuted to their backup site, making it work.)

Another main lesson learned through 9-11 was that in business continuity, the most often overlooked issue is the literal practicing or drilling of employees and business units. As mentioned previously, ignoring human logistics can quickly make working backup systems irrelevant. Finally, if system tapes or CDs are made, it does no good to place them in the basement or the attic or anywhere else in the same power/telecommunications grid. These backups need to be physically disparate.

To that end and post–9-11, Manhattan's financial institutions cooperatively purchased huge parcels of land in middle America and built some massive backup centers. They shared the cost, and they are better prepared for terrorism, weather, power outages, labor strikes, or anything else that would jeopardize their business.

Additionally, more companies now test their business-continuity plan. Similar to "war games," they simulate floods and other natural disasters in a live setting. They set goals for nominal and fully functional operations in a matter of hours, and they drill their teams on how to get back up and running. Business-continuity planning and testing proves more important the more scattered a business becomes. The reality of most organizations today is that different business groups have different backup needs (for example, real-time versus 24-hour recovery), and most are not ready for a one-size-fits-all plan yet.

Monitoring

Monitoring your infrastructure from a base-building perspective should merge existing monitoring tools inherent in the software and hardware you already use to afford you an early-warning system. Instead of creating a be-all, end-all system that individually scrutinizes each bit and byte (a Mercedes, if you will), let the parts of your system designed to monitor themselves do their job (a Toyota). Use those existing tools to get a read on your systems in a digestible manner. (Chapter 6 extensively covers monitoring.)

Note that monitoring outcomes must be delivered in digestible form to business owners in business terms they (and you) understand. As you will see, it is relatively easy to coordinate with your technology team, and they can synthesize data from your systems through easy-to-acquire software such as Crystal Reports, a Windows-based report-generation software developed by Seagate Systems that enables you to create customized intelligence from different sources in minimum time. The ensuing data can be integrated and published in a way that is consistent with the elements of the infrastructure you want to monitor. In larger organizations, there is less cost benefit to forcing all departments in the company to use the same monitoring systems.

Privacy

Privacy is a global security poster child. Its increased fame results from significant media coverage surrounding consumer identity theft and fraud. This attention has resulted in a rising tide of regulation that differs wildly from region to region. In Switzerland, privacy is the gold standard of global security, and among financial institutions it is so copious that bank officers who travel outside the country must often leave their laptops at home. (There have been instances when they have actually been confiscated at border crossings!) In nearly *every* country today, however, laws are being enacted that concern privacy, access to information, and the regulation of communication intercepts. Traditionally Europe has led this charge, followed by North America. Europe's Data Protection Directive gives consumers the right to decide what happens to their information, and they must provide explicit consent every time it is used. The United States and the rest of the world have yet to adopt an equally stringent policy.

If you are doing business away from home, a base-wide privacy element may prove unfeasible. Penalty avoidance drives privacy measures within corporations, and the consequences of a breach can result in lost customers and, in some cases, even your business. When developing the privacy element of your global security strategy, enlist the appropriate technical and legal expertise. In many parts of the world, companies are forming entire privacy committees and sometimes even appointing privacy officers.

Building in privacy to any corporate security base may seem efficient, but a case-by-case approach may prove more effective and, in some cases, is the only legal recourse depending on where in the world you operate. Be aware of the legislative and regulatory requirements involving privacy that apply to you. In addition, think through the existing agreements and corporate contracts in light of privacy regulations to which your organization must adhere. This process will help you determine whether privacy should be a unified or customized element of your corporate security posture.

Minimum Base-Worthy ROSI

Design elements that deliver minimum ROSI should not be built in to your base, because how you approach them may vary depending on how and where you function.

Application Integrity

Software applications are usually the single largest IT expenditure made by multinational corporations and most closely touch their most sensitive and protected assets—financial, customer, and employee data. Originating from a handful of huge companies such as Oracle, SAP, or IBM, such applications probably run huge chunks of your own company. Applications are usually many years old, and written, augmented, or changed by hundreds of people in dozens of companies. Patching is rife, and occurs through periodic major and minor releases. Do not assume that because it was purchased from one of the "big boys" that it automatically enables you to manage the security mandated through your strategy. Once more, it is up to your company to test what the application does, to tweak how it works, and, in many cases, augment how it works with various security products and techniques that you deem necessary after reviewing your operations.

The Reverse Compiler: One Scary Test!

Reverse compile a few of your older, trusted applications running on your systems and watch the often-convoluted path they take and how they often access information in ways never intended or "allowed."

Although it is often the single largest security function, I have found that application integrity is not necessary on a company-wide basis. You do not use multiple CRM systems—just one. Go study it and justify security based on its value to the company and the amount of risk the business owner is comfortable shouldering per your strategy. Do the same for your remaining major systems.

Quantify to Justify

CSOs consistently complain to me about an inability to secure budget for what they know their company requires. Overcome this by establishing your baselines so that you can then prove your dollars, yens, euros, rands, pounds, and rubles in quantifiable terms (ways that CFOs, CEOs and CIOs will understand without having to be security experts). Then you will be much more likely to get the budget you need.

Information Asset Baseline

Although it is important to establish general information asset baselines, you generally do not need specific directives and do not need to build the guidelines in to the base. Chapter 5, "Enabling Business and Enhancing Process," examines how certain elements of a global security strategy provide tangible profit gains and cost savings. Trying to measure a global security strategy outside of specific elements and against regulations across the board is a waste of your investment.

When you do measure, look at things such as productivity as well as response times from the past and into the future. Also each respective business owner should understand the general elements of compliance for his or her area and be held accountable for measuring against them.

Security is so amorphous and so reliant on *fear, uncertainty, and doubt* (FUD) that you have to be wary of consultants touting FUD as a core element of your strategy. The rationale for such a move is usually laid out with a PowerPoint slide that by now has become universally pasted and ridiculed. I can independently verify the repeated sighting of one particular slide that depicts this topic. It features five interlocking pieces that spell out its importance. When you see it, ask them where they got it, and then simply say, "You cut and pasted this, didn't you?" (Words that strike fear into any consultant's heart.) To see a copy of it, visit mappingsecurity.com so that you ready yourself for a conference room chuckle.

Go Forth and Secure

Building the base requires care—it is the most critical step in developing your corporate security infrastructure. Doing it well depends on your openness to a new mindset catalyzed by a global and virtual business reality that measures efficiency in terms of a money-to-risk reduction ratio that I call ROSI. By matching your business requirements and objectives as discussed in Chapter 3 with the mix of corporate security elements covered in this chapter, you can customize a security base that will afford you a solid foundation and serve you well for the long term (that is, if everyone in the organization understands and works from it).

Your teams need to understand this overall integration effort. Involve everyone, keeping no one in his or her "silo." Develop sustainable and controlled processes and make sure your security groups integrate with the business and technology groups. Buy them lunch together and get them to share information. Importantly, emphasize the impact of people—not the technology—in developing a fortified base. As your business hops on board, you can move on to the next phase of charting a course, where business is enabled and operations enhanced.

Chapter 5

Enabling Business and Enhancing Process

The best shared security elements we reviewed in Chapter 4, "Building the Base," must be married to business services, which leads to our third and fourth keys to success—*enabling business* (leading to raised, top-line revenue) and *enhancing process* (lowering real costs of operations).

Solely focusing on the risk-reduction aspects of a security system is just half the picture. Using security services to improve business is often overlooked. Repeated fire fighting might overshadow the simple question, "How can we use security to improve our business?" This chapter focuses on business enablement in terms of large-scale enterprise software and process enhancement as reflected in internal operations. In both cases, hard work on corporate security elevates it beyond a necessary evil to a powerful, silent partner.

Enabling Business and Enhancing Process Key Questions: COO Focus

1. Which business processes (that is, supply chain, customer relationship management, finance) that you operate are your four biggest budgets?

2. Which internal business functions (phone, network, and so on) are your four biggest budgets?

3. Which of these eight would be most impacted by drastic reduction in communications costs?

4. Which of these eight would be most impacted by drastic improvements in real-time information?

5. Which of these eight would be your best choice to improve with security?

Through the clever business integration of security, there is real money to be saved. I have sat in countless executive sessions, listening to lines such as these:

- Yes, it would save us a lot of money to do it that way, but it is not secure.

- Yes, we could reach more customers that way, but it is not secure.

- Yes, we could save the money here, but it is not secure enough to go outside the country.

In each case, business owners should have taken the time to understand how security could improve these processes, save money, and permit them to do more with less—all in a secure fashion. If they had, they could have realized the following benefits:

- Reduced redundancies in major systems

- Fewer workers

- Shared usage of open networks such as the Internet—as opposed to using your own pipe

- Lowered real infrastructure costs such as office space and phone lines

For instance, are your operations in Mexico City, Paris, or London? If so, many of your employees could be spending at least five hours a day commuting. Increasing worker productivity and satisfaction (by letting them work from home over their own high-speed Internet connections, tapping into a *virtual private network* [VPN]) and streamlining operations are real-world examples of enabling and enhancing your business through security.

Now start asking about the technology that directly supports operations. What is the cost to the organization if your HR or finance system goes down for eight hours? Suppose, for example, that a hacker figures out that he or she can visit your home page, click your Online Jobs directory, type a few (less than 10) random-looking characters into the URL line, and gain compete control over your database?

It is too easy: A small child or trained circus animal could break into the most proprietary company networks by just typing unexpected characters into a Web browser when it is aimed at some part of a company Web site that is driven by a database. (My five-year-old son Will is an expert at typing these unexpected characters on the computer.) Online job listings are an obvious choice, but to a practiced eye the list is long.

Believe it or not, it can happen despite the strongest firewalls, the best intrusion detection/prevention, and a world-class consultant advising you. Buried in the thousands of lines of code that you call your infrastructure, some programmer forgot to tell a program what to do if it encounters unexpected characters. Had the programmer just keyed in "if it is not what we expect, then clear and try again," the intrusion could have been prevented. Instead the program just stops, and the hacker is left there, staring at your network, and he or she will have access to your most sensitive files. Your technology group will spend at least eight hours reversing the damage, rebuilding the server, and reloading yesterday's data from backups. Of course this is days before you actually find and repair the poorly written (and usually poorly documented) subroutine that was exploited.

So what will it cost you? That's time dependent (the day and the hour), but let's say it happened during your payroll cycle. That would cost substantially more than at 2 a.m. on the eleventh of the month. In both cases, these are the types of questions you should be asking and getting answers to. Then, and only then, should you decide how much to spend on reducing that risk.

Not Either/Or: It Is Both

You want this new security that will enable and enhance, but you do not know how to pay for it. Your predecessor probably thought that security could be had for a price—a price they could not pay. Plus, they "knew" that security would impair business functions, making its deployment all but impossible. Finally, everyone "knew" that security simply slows things down.

This drumbeat of security-as-business inhibitor has stuck for decades. Top people within organizations—probably a lot like you—have ongoing concerns about getting the business online or sharing data, and security has only impeded that progress. Instead, it is a nice-to-have if you finish with some extra budget money and extra project time, but let's cut to the chase: That never happens. Ultimately, you are not as concerned about the underlying operations and how efficiently or securely they are running. However, take note: In the new global business reality, your business focus on security can be rewarded if you pause to understand the larger issues of your company's security posture and whether it is working for or against you.

Pausing should prompt another question. Does your global security provide the strength of a transparent, easy-to-use, and systemic strategy, or does it prove a weak and bitter add-on that is too complex and cryptic for anyone to leverage? Systems must be designed properly so that the business remains efficient and in use. Remember, of course, that insecure, compromised systems lead to unavailability and downtime, which can affect sales and productivity. Hacking and vulnerabilities that temporarily shut down a company to customers or key partners diminish credibility and, ultimately, profits.

Pausing should happen early in charting a course. After a common base has been built, the security and technology group works with the business owners, finding out what their productivity needs are and enabling business and enhancing process. Timing is everything. A good time to rework to enable and enhance arrives with new hires and whenever you undergo technology upgrades. (Of course, the most common time is usually after you fail a security audit or get hacked!)

Business Enablement

To illustrate security's ability to deliver productivity and efficiencies across an enterprise, let's quickly review one of the security countermeasures in your arsenal—identity management (those ways in which you are identified so that you can gain access to information within a distributed organization)—can work for you in a secure setting. Imagine having only one password to access all your business applications. Imagine only logging on to your office computer once in the morning and not having to log on again for the rest of the day or until you leave your desk. Imagine your customers navigating from a business partner Web site to yours without the need to revalidate their credentials. Imagine your technology group controlling access to users, customers, and partners from one central point and a couple of mouse clicks. Such a simple, light touch from security can become a meaningful tool for your company's growth and output.

Enabling your business to run more productively and efficiently can make you money. Security facilitates ROSI if there is agreement up front and careful deployment throughout an organization. As I have alluded to repeatedly, this preliminary work and care must be agreed upon at a business-owner level, which makes certain that security is an effective enabler at the most critical points of a business, holding the business owners accountable from where they function.

Taking business enablement a step further and for the sake of simplicity and memory, this chapter focuses on the following four critical, common, and large-scale software systems tied to any business:

- Human resources
- Supply chain
- Financials
- Customer relationship management

Human Resources

Traditionally, human resources serves as an exponential catalyst or a significant drag on corporations. HR can become a transparent trigger point for maintaining security across the company. By consolidating and automating key moments of employee orientation, you can jumpstart careers in just a few keystrokes. In addition, HR affords a natural entry for security, because it is here that your physical and technical processes meet.

Suppose, for example, that an individual joins your company and you begin giving that person access to the Internet and to networks, you capture all of his or her personal data for payroll, you enroll the new employee into an insurance plan and make good on all the perks that have been promised. A strong, well-conceived HR system tied to identity management sets into motion a whole set of other processes that can provision user access for your new employee. It parses information on that person's role within the organization, developing a user profile and deciding which systems and applications that person can access. Thus, as a user moves through your HR department's orientation, that user's information can feed into your larger centralized system, which then updates all of your other systems and populates various access requirements the person has. It is important to note that HR can also ease transitions within the company. If a user moves to another department and his or her access privileges and rights change or expand, a centralized HR system can enable this more effectively.

Access and Denial Reflection

The most security-savvy companies can routinely provide all IT access (on an employee's first day) on day one and remove all IT access on the employee's final day. How long does it take you?

Of course, such a model also works well on the back end as an employee leaves. Once notified, HR can easily transition that employee off payroll. (It doesn't always happen, believe me.) It will also ping the centralized system so it can revoke access to various technologies inside the company. It can also create limited access, cutting off an employee's Internet or network availability as merited and then shutting down and deleting the employee's identity when he or she finally leaves for good. In the past, this has proven to be a huge security issue because dramatic holes exist when an old or unused account belonging to ex-employees stays on your systems, furnishing needless entry points for threats.

If you connect to another infected network, chances are you will be infected, so supply chain security is much like protecting yourself from a flu virus. You must begin by recognizing that anyone you connect with externally could be carrying a virus, and if you don't take the measures to protect yourself, you'll be infected and you'll wind up infecting others.

—*Ryan Rubin, Security Expert, Deloitte, London*

ROSI related to human resources can be dramatic. For example, getting an employee up and running used to take a week—automation can decrease that time to a day. Those who transition can start a new role more quickly, too. And when an employee leaves, the employee can be shut out of your systems quickly, protecting you and your assets.

Supply Chain

Communication links between suppliers and you have been revolutionized through information technology, but the rush to connectivity has created numerous challenges that could become serious threats to your organization. Of priority is making sure that one supplier with whom you connect cannot see another supplier's details. Also the advent of viruses and worms makes it important for companies to protect themselves from those on the outside with whom they connect.

As you protect yourself from those types of threats, you must also ensure that suppliers cannot gain access to details about your own proprietary assets.

In the supply chain, you must maintain contact with suppliers to dialogue and place orders, and even develop an online inventory management system for your warehouse; therefore, connectivity that guards against infection is critical. In situations where a company might have three or more suppliers, your security team must also create ways for each supplier's information to remain mutually exclusive. If your organization uses a common network or application among its suppliers, and they see what you're paying for from another vendor, this could obviously become detrimental to your posture—they can effectively leverage that information. Therefore, if the supply chain is to remain a productive part of your organization, creating a secure system that keeps threats at bay and information secure is of utmost importance.

Financials

Anyone who worked prior to the mid-1990s will remember when end-of-period (or in the United States, end-of-quarter) reporting used to take more than three full additional periods to complete (or another quarter in the United States). Because management has focused on the business benefits of implementing a more modern solution, secure computing environments and powerful software have reduced this lag time to a single day.

Today, not only must financials be reported in a timely matter, your financials must be secure, open, and verifiably accurate based on horizontal and vertical regulations that affect companies in a variety of regions. Secure technology quickens reporting and creates the automated checkpoints that correlate data with regulatory compliance and make sure that the finished product is bona fide, cradled in truth. In some cases—for instance, among banks in Australia, Hong Kong, Japan, and Malaysia—financials reporting is sealed with a legally recognized digital signature.

Customer Relationship Management

Customer relationship management (CRM) can help you effectively tailor a user experience to those whom you are trying to sell or maintain as customers, and secure, centralized systems can help you do so in innovative ways. Ryan Rubin, a Deloitte security expert for security services in London, holds extensive identity management knowledge as it applies to CRM. He once worked with a large media company in the UK that sought to provide a single, customized face that would cater to users who called, visited a Web site, or tuned in using their cable television set-top box.

Users signed up online or via telephone and in doing so, their account information and registration were entered into a single system that spanned every medium through which the company communicated. When customers made queries about their account using any one of the three mechanisms, they received a consolidated, personalized user experience. Not unusual anymore by any means, this identity management system consolidated data for what they requested by phone, and it tracked what they watched on television and visited at the company Web site. This gave the organization a better viewpoint from which to communicate with and market to that customer.

Security technology can enable this level of customization through the power of centralization. When a customer calls or goes to the site or is offered something via a set-top box, data is pulled from an array of systems at once that identifies that person as a football watcher from Manchester. The Web site displays the Premier League standings and links to relevant sports affiliates. The phone makes available a pay-per-view offer to that customer for the European Cup. The set-top box runs specials on the TV screen that remind the user of an upcoming friendly between Manchester United and the Real Madrid.

Process Enhancement

Augmenting business enablement is a host of internal processes that run businesses. Tight budgets reign worldwide. These processes have had all the extraneous costs wrung out of them—or have they? Approaching the cost-reduction problems without factoring in security is like trying to move through a Cairo bazaar with a coupon book. Security will unlock an array of hidden costs buried within your core processes. Suddenly you will be able to spend less on your physical plants and infrastructure while delivering better performance with lower risk. The interoperational units of a corporate technology landscape and its support must have the proper security fundamentals in place to run smoothly and efficiently—these fundamentals must then be fully integrated into the processes.

ROSI through process enhancement means that technology systems must be created and evolve with security firmly in place to guard against newly and unconsciously created vulnerabilities. It is also caught in time savings and staff reduction, where money is to be saved and efficiencies gained. This chapter explores process enhancement through the following four distinct, fundamental components of any corporation's internal operations:

- Systems development
- Technology group's help desk
- Regulatory and audit compliance
- Project management

Systems Development

It does not matter how your company is structured or in what industry you function, technology systems are helping you to operate and grow. As new software and hardware is either created or installed on your networks, your technology group is usually writing code to bridge systems or create new capabilities throughout your enterprise. This creative process requires that your group either write or buy a lot of software code—usually short blocks—that are obtained at the last minute under demands that might sound familiar: "I don't care how you get it to work; we just need to be up and running." Many times this code is inserted without documentation, and many times, if organizations were to reverse engineer their own systems, they would be horrified to see the patchwork that is in place. Moreover, if code is allowed to be implemented on-the-fly without checking for security and integration issues, it can leave gaping holes for hackers.

Often systems developers aren't thinking of a hacker; they're thinking of the demands they're under. However, they should also be thinking about hackers. Anytime your systems developers work to change or augment your technology, good security practices and development strategies that work uniformly can significantly benefit the company.

Such a strategy often includes the use of strong workflow management software that tracks code development and monitors exacting specifications. Change controls can also prove useful. They allow adjustments to be made only after proper approvals under the authority of a development lead. Moreover, many corporations are moving to comply with Microsoft's Trusted Computing model, which advocates centralizing the whole of a system to one computer in order to keep it safe. This means the need to assign code will become more important so that the end system that runs the code knows that the code comes from a valid source. The assigned code will carry a digital signature that divulges your sanctioned developers' identities and, with it, your applications will run the new code while keeping rogue or unauthorized code out of your systems.

The Help Desk

Your friendly help desk can become a focal point for process-enhancement ROSI, especially help desk operations can be reduced or outsourced. Your help desk might be fielding employee calls all day—more than 40 percent of those conversations will deal with one subject: forgotten passwords.

Effective solutions exist on the market to address this operational lead weight. By diverting your help desk to an automated solution where you pay by the call or users conduct a do-it-yourself password reassignment, you could conceivably reduce your staff in the United States, Europe, and other parts of the world, and you can reassign that staff to more productive projects within the company.

Even greater savings can be realized by fully automating your help desk. A typical, popular system has been developed that allows users to answer security questions if they have lost a password, allowing them to assign a new password. Of course, great care is required when developing security questions. Obviously, the Monty Python-like "What is your favorite color?" can lead to hackers guessing at a finite spectrum of hues that will lead to an intrusion (green, no blue). Educating users on how to create a password, and then a strong security question, is a key to success when the help desk becomes automated.

Regulatory and Audit Compliance

Global corporate security streamlines controls and audit compliance linked to increasing regulations that govern access to corporate data and its incumbent due diligence/good practice guidelines. You cannot achieve compliance unless you have systems in place that track who a person is, what time the person logs in, what role the person plays and what access he or she has or doesn't have.

Usually such stipulations are handed down from the highest levels through policies and written controls. However, when you descend through your organization and find applications set up and running disparately with little or no supervision of access, it is apparent that often theory is not practice. Stored customer information data or sensitive financial details of your company might exist on separate databases—or those databases might be replicated or backed up across an organization. Enforcing access regulations and audit compliance on these various layers is tough to achieve.

Regulatory and audit requirements are driving corporate security-process enhancement. Companies have started to force users through a single channel such as a unified enterprise portal that effectively vets them and verifies their access before shuttling them on to a back-end system. Application access clearly demonstrates efficiencies at work—users hold specific user IDs that give them access to a customized database of applications and are tracked—and it is invisible to the user. All they see at the database level are those applications and resources relevant to their role within the company.

This requires that you fuse all the architecture of your system together; when it comes to audit compliance, this is especially true. The threads of your architecture must be on display and visible to ensure you do not get snarled in compliance issues. As your CSO begins turning your company toward voluntary adherence to an array of regulations, it will be important that the operations of your company are built in such a way that they are working openly and in compliance. ROSI will be evident in the time, money, and potential legal issues it saves you. Although security-process enhancement is on the upswing around the world, room for improvement remains.

A strong case in point surrounds data-protection requirements in the EU. If data is carried across the ocean from the United States, certain concerns and different regulations and stipulations are placed on that data. Therefore, companies must do a better job of defining what happens to the data after it travels across company borders, tracking it through each of its waypoints, so that by the time it reaches its final destination, there is a comparable level of applied security.

The rest of the world can learn from the EU's commitment to moving ahead of the curve when it comes to regulatory and audit compliance. Asia closely follows the EU's global leadership, and the United States tends to follow soon after. This strong compliance sensibility in the EU is backed by its own protocols and by a strong sense of responsibility and sincere desire to avoid scandals similar to Enron and WorldCom.

Track Broadband

Track broadband penetration in the countries with which you work. If it is high (as in the United States and UK), you should be figuring out how you can leverage the fact that most of your employees already have their own broadband connection. Also note Internet savvy. In Chile 70 percent of all companies file their taxes online. By contrast, neighboring Argentina enjoys just 15 percent of online filings; even the United States lags behind at 40 percent. This level of Netizenry can prove helpful as you decide on sites for your South American operation, and around the world.

In a European IT audit, security is crucial, and without security in place, a company will fail. Contrast this with the United States, where such standards barely exist. U.S. companies generally are given a stern look and asked to do better next year. Unlike Europe, however, U.S. management teams rarely fail or lose their jobs over noncompliance.

Network Operations

Processes are significantly enhanced when security-managed services are blended into your network operations, and help you as you literally move across borders or find yourself just caring for your branch of the Internet.

In many parts of Germany, you are not allowed to use the Internet to gain access to the company network. Why? It is not secure. Even though many people have high-speed Internet connections in their home, they cannot use them to access the office. They can only dial in at slow speeds or drive to work. The rationale generally proffered is that companies cannot run a private network to everyone (they cannot), but were they to put in place a VPN, the load on their main network would be lighter and it would be more secure.

Enabling and Enhancing Pay Off

Anytime a security base is built, it must effectively seep into the depths of a business, filling in nooks and crannies and helping you achieve ROSI. Through business enablement, you have seen how security can play out, taking all the great technology you have placed to grow profits and make them even more productive and profitable—all by ensuring that key areas are secure. Process enhancement assists you to run at peak efficiency so that you are secure, accountable, and compliant. These operations that function across your enterprise will save you time and money. They can also help you reduce overhead or to divert talent.

Enhancement and enablement are the engines of your security strategy and must be functioning well at all times. Internal and external monitoring complement enhancement and enablement, as discussed thoroughly in the following two chapters.

Chapter 6

Developing Radar

Every company that positions security technology within its business units has two critical areas of consideration:

- The parts that are controllable: the systems and security technology itself
- The parts that are uncontrollable: threats that are flowing into your systems

Threats—perceived and real—constantly try to enter (ping) your system. What do they mean? It is impossible to understand a ping unless you can see it, correlate it to millions of other pings, and feed that ping (if it is a serious threat) through to a common reporting point that I advocate should be constructed like a dashboard, converting technical data into business vocabulary in real time. I call this *developing radar*.

Developing Radar Key Questions: CFO Focus

1. How much of the security reports do you understand, as opposed to simply trusting the people involved?
2. What is the return on your security investment so far?
3. What are you basing your decisions on when you sign the quarterly compliance documents?
4. With what security and privacy regulations are you in compliance?
5. Which security and privacy regulations are you out of compliance with, and what are the penalties?

Kofi Annan Wants a Green Light

Over 90 days in 1999, a groundbreaking project called NetAid was created. Taking its cue from the 1980s LiveAid, which brought worldwide musical talent together to assist with famine relief in Ethiopia, NetAid was founded as a joint venture between Cisco Systems, KPMG, and the United Nations Development Program. The goal was to "combine innovative programs with new technologies and work in partnership with the United Nations and the private sector [to build] a network of everyday people committed to working for a world without extreme poverty" (www.netaid.org).

The Internet debuted as a powerful force that, along with big business, linked to the global diplomatic community in an attempt to cut world poverty in half by 2015. NetAid was poised to launch and included high-profile support from America's President Bill Clinton, Secretary General of the UN Kofi Annan, and then-President Nelson Mandela of South Africa—together with a host of international music stars such as Puff Daddy (now P. Diddy), Sting, Bono, The Counting Crows, Jewel, Mary J. Blige, Wyclef Jean, The Eurythmics, and David Bowie. What most people did not realize, and even those of us who were intimately involved still find hard to believe, is that the entire event was created in exactly 90 days from conception. The secretary general liked the idea, and to keep it alive he knew it must coalesce quickly. Talent, technical, and logistical teams were delivered in an ultimate timeline in the sand. If ever there was a push to skip over normal development practices in favor of meeting a business deadline, this was it.

NetAid's global Web was to launch through a series of blockbuster, simulcast concerts rolling back to back from Europe to North America. At the time, it represented the largest Webcast ever attempted. I had been tasked to deploy and secure the online payments that would roll in from in-person and online donors as the music started. My work crossed paths with Boston-based company Akamai, which was brought on to NetAid because it has the technology that helps companies keep their vital Web operations up and running in the face of traffic spikes, emergencies, or shutdowns. Obviously, this was an important issue anticipated by the NetAid team, who had watched in horror as the previously largest Webcast—by U.S.-based lingerie giant Victoria's Secret—failed miserably. (They now enlist Akamai.)

Victoria's Secret promised sports fans a peek at its new line of women's underwear during a halftime runway show adjunct to the Super Bowl. At the appointed halftime moment, hoards of viewers began pointing their Web browsers to victoriassecret.com in anticipation of the event. Before 12,500 individuals could log on, however, the site crashed. The company lost millions and reeled from embarrassment.

To avert a similar disaster, NetAid's tech team began doing its research and enlisted Akamai. Because it distributes a given client's Web applications over a global network of secure servers, Akamai ensures 100 percent availability of vital applications. That means if something goes down in Hong Kong, it is fortified by mirror versions in Tokyo, Brussels, Nairobi, and more than 10,000 other locations.

However, the right technology was just one answer. The NetAid tech team had to find the right way to communicate and translate what was happening on its network to the important parties involved—many of whom were not tech savvy. In response, Akamai rigged a simple red/yellow/green signal that let key personnel know whether necessary data was streaming to facilitate the concert's appearance online or whether there were problems brought on by a variety of issues such as hackers, bandwidth crunches, or both.

As the first act readied from UN headquarters in Geneva, I was standing in the wings alongside Secretary General Annan, Cisco CEO John Chambers, and Akamai President Paul Sagan. While the fans and the media focused on the talent, we huddled around Paul's pager that delivered the signals. When the music started, the pager lit up and stayed green and the Webcast began. Champagne flowed that evening as Akamai's system worked to perfection—each of concerts played from the Palais des Nations in Switzerland, Wembley Stadium in London, and Giants Stadium in New York streamed uninterrupted. Millions were raised, and a wonderful new charity was launched, which continues to flourish.

Akamai's network of distributed services pushed the video out to more than 125,000 simultaneous views around the world without fail. Importantly, we developed radar that enabled everyone—from the tech and security groups to the business and UN stakeholders—to be on the same page simultaneously through an easy-to-read alert system. This is rare, but equally necessary in global business.

Why It's Rare

Creating an apparatus to monitor your internal and perimeter security creates a potential conflict for any organization, especially companies that have gone global. At the conflict's center, the technology and security groups begin to strangely separate from the business owners and their respective units. It is a counterintuitive division that is not in the best interest of either party, but it happens in too many companies all over the world. Solidly translated monitoring is rare because security personnel often create monitoring in a vacuum. Only recently have companies evolved to look at such indicators as part of their company's lifeblood, proactively seeking ways to place technology and security in business terms. Why? Technology became compulsory even in the world's Luddite havens.

For example, as recently as 20 years ago, many Arab countries were not interested in computers. I helped create the first word processor that enabled Arabic characters. It went nowhere. The average businessman in an Arab country disdained computing—the keyboard looked like a typewriter, which was solely the domain of women. Arab states' pursuit of globalization has been hampered by this cultural bias against personal technology.

CSO As Bridge

Elevating the SO to CSO gives him or her the political power to unite these two sides. Failing that, a wise executive team, an empowered board committee, or even the external auditor can push to make this happen.

Today's global business environment requires a connection between the business and innovation vernaculars, finding a common language and working together to ensure that business units function in concert with the technology and security groups. This reenergized combination can ensure that security, regulatory compliance, and the bottom line remain profitable. Both sides hold responsibilities that developing radar brings into high relief. Business owners must be willing to add a security gauge to how they measure business performance. Technology and security groups must deliver well-analyzed information that translates its respective, specialized languages into viable business terms. Businesspeople need to move beyond yesterday's thinking—security as a specialized technical thing—and become better educated about the fundamental security issues that can be the difference between success and failure. That is what we are honing in on. To effectively manage the security map you have built and deployed across your organization, you must have radar that, through a real-time reporting device (the dashboard), informs you of your company's security in relevant ways. Just as you routinely check your stock price, sales figures, and productivity, security must join this suite of indicators; but even if envisioning radar is easy, pulling it off is difficult. As business reaches beyond your home borders, it has never been more necessary.

Akamai's Andy Ellis on Developing Radar

To many people, security is a black art. In the technology group of a company, everyone knows what the software people are doing, but the security people are in the shadows, unknown and unknowable. That has to change.

For me it started with my management committee, and it is because of them that I'm building my very own, customized real-time system especially for reporting to management. It is based on ISO 17799—the gold standard—and it is correlated to the domains of the organizational chart and labeled red, yellow, and green. I will update it every six months. Going into meetings, I will know the reds and the yellows, and we will fix the yellows beforehand. I am developing it because I do not want to hear executives say, "You're doing it wrong. Why are you focusing your time on this issue or that?" Moreover, it is so I can report that "the fact we're not doing enough is not my fault."

For a CSO, what is needed most is positive visibility (a dashboard is a great help) throughout the company all the way to the boardroom. In many big companies, doing security well requires that the CSO's visibility increase—this will ease security's uphill battle in the office of a nonengaging CFO who is scrutinizing the budget and making the CSO argue for every single item.

As a CSO asserts him or herself, the CSO should not spread FUD—fear, uncertainty, and doom. No other part of the business is run this way. Walk in to reporting environments with a top five list—tell them what's happening, and when they're not interested, keep telling them. They have a short attention span; if they do not know you are solving a problem, however, they do not know whether you are doing your job.

Beyond reporting, remember that you must make friends and take baby steps. In security, when somebody is imperfect, you must implement perfect security to foster change. You must make friends step by step—make sure you enhance performance and security on little things—one at a time. Then say, "Let me show you the next step." If it is good, they will come back for the second step.

Do not, however, accept responsibility for decisions—a business owner is ultimately responsible for his or her decisions. If a business owner comes to you and says, "Here's this thing that's horribly insecure and I want to do it anyway and you will secure it, right?" educate the business owner. Tell the owner you will not do this. If it is not security postured before it goes live, you cannot do it.

Developing Radar Is Like, Well, Developing Radar

When I talk about developing radar, I mean it in every sense of the term. Think of a ship's command and control center where that giant, rotating antenna surveys the ocean, capturing dots of information revealed on shimmering green screens. These dots are translated by skilled technicians and developed into sound analysis for the captain, who carefully makes decisions. It is at the screen-meets-technician level that global business can break down. Indiscriminate or improper use of monitoring radar can reveal nothing but danger—not just potential threats in the water, but a school of fish or a tired, old fishing boat. How to tell the difference between fresh alarms and false alarms means the difference between managing your risk or an expensive pile of junk that everyone resents.

The key to successful eBusiness is safeguarding it against security breaches.

—*Alan Wong Chi-kong, Director, Information Technology Services of the Hong Kong Government, Hong Kong*

The pings themselves are not the threat—they are just indicators of what exists in the outlying area. These mean nothing to the ship's safety, and in any good movie about naval warfare the technician who is at the scope never looks to the commander and yells, "Captain, a big fish up ahead 40 meters off starboard." Likewise, that same technician will take a genuine hazard on the monitor and make it real for the captain in terms the captain understands: "An oscillating granular green dot is impinging on our short-term safety" gives way to "An enemy destroyer off our port bow."

Just as radar technicians work closely with technology to decipher and relay important information to superior officers, so must technology groups and security personnel synthesize myriad correlations that are able to decode real threats that matter to the business. Whereas a busy radar screen might show dozens of simultaneous blips, the average security monitor tracks and evaluates thousands of real-time activities. The unlearned or indiscriminate placement of system monitoring by global companies often leads to a dearth of activity. The radar is saturated with dots that could be a nonthreat, a nonserious threat, or a menace of devastating proportions. Every day, thousands of events on technology systems could be unimportant—for example, an employee forgot his or her password and repeatedly typed the incorrect one. Such activity could legitimately arise as a dot on a monitoring tool, but its emergence would appear with the same level of severity as a targeted hacker fishing for consumer data or an employee who is quietly siphoning off intellectual property to his or her home.

In a typical business setting, this level of activity might lead the technical group to scale back the monitoring sensitivity. Although commonplace, this is precisely the wrong move. The radar is then weaker, and the company is more vulnerable. In today's global environment, this scenario is the norm. Events that are real threats have gone forth and multiplied, and they hide in the millions of nonthreatening lookalikes. Developing radar calls for a wiser approach to monitoring that is not less aware—just more focused so that human intelligence and algorithms can relay the most important information to business owners in terms they understand. This wiser approach will lead to business owners who grasp and are happy with the ROSI the technology or security group provides, and it enables technology or security groups to get budgets approved by the business owners with whom they are attempting to work.

First Things Are First

So far, every chapter of this book has emphasized the importance of mapping business requirements to regulations and threats that each business owner must weigh with the amount of risk they want to take on. This same principle applies to developing radar that secures your perimeter and technology applications.

You don't deploy monitoring and then say to yourself, "We're going to fine-tune this over time." It just doesn't work that way: you'll end up tweaking your system ad infinitum. But if you take a step back and take stock of your system, how it works and where it all leads, then you can have everything pristinely organized and deploy monitoring the right way.

—*Bobby Christian, Acting CSO, Public Company Accounting Oversight Board, Washington D.C.*

Bobby Christian, CSO for the Public Company Accounting Oversight Board, has a long history of deploying monitoring systems in organizations. His company, Netrex, was acquired by ISS systems, creating the leading monitoring and intrusion protection provider worldwide. He says that some key elements must be in place before any monitoring system ever goes live within an organization. He also points out that he has usually been tapped for this kind of project when (you guessed it) an organization has been hit with a major attack that makes the need for monitoring that much more real. When developing a monitoring strategy, Bobby recommends four steps for companies endeavoring to develop radar.

Step One: Know Your Environment In Depth

What systems do you use as an organization? Has each business owner worked with your security and technology groups to assess environments at the business unit level? Do you run on UNIX or Microsoft? How many each do you have? What about your *enterprise resource planning* (ERP) software—SAP, Oracle, PeopleSoft? Who makes your hardware? Hewlett Packard? IBM? Cisco? Hitachi? What applications run on those systems, and what do they do? This deep examination is absolutely essential to making a monitoring system to deliver ROSI.

Step Two: Understand How It All Works

When you understand the environment in which the business units work, it is then time to weed out and clarify how respective applications work and interface across the networks. This enables you to match the security policies of the business units with the business operations. It can also fully weed out any redundancies and inefficiencies within the system. Often you end up finding and fixing problems here, even before active monitoring starts.

Step Three: Only Apply Monitoring to Necessary Systems

Monitoring is often likened to finding needles in a haystack because no preplanning is in place that effectively begins minimizing the haystack in the first place. After that is taken care of in the first two steps, haystacks can be further minimized by monitoring only those that are absolutely necessary and based on the security policies of each business unit. Watch out for the overly aggressive security salesperson—monitor critical systems only.

Step Four: Make Sure an Effective Filter Is in Place

As your company begins placing monitoring hardware and software within the organization, make sure that there are filters in place that automatically weed out the fish and the fishing boats so that humans working on your end can effectively identify and ignore them.

Taking Monitoring Outside

Relaying the meaning of a monitoring event to a business owner becomes the primary concern of technology and security groups, and therefore companies generally tend to hire an external firm such as Symantec, IBM, ISS, and a number of country-specific monitoring firms. Often it is more effective than taking it on yourself because third-party providers harvest the entirety of clients' threat data at one time and can deliver necessary information based on this scope combined with a solid combination of human and technological skill. This alchemy is a must when you are looking for a monitoring firm. You want to give business owners just the information that the company should really care about, and leave the reading of hundreds of millions of attack points throughout the world to informed automation. With effective automation and a skilled professional to deliver the synthesized relevant information to the business owner, you can achieve this goal.

A great example of such a managed solution is Symantec's RipTech. Inside its command center, there exists a giant map of the world that showcases hundreds of threats aggregated with tiny pulsing dots that get bigger and brighter based on real-time information, such as which tier-one providers are getting clogged and what throughputs are beginning to back up. They examine this with human brains and apply it to your company better than any single piece of technology and certainly better than any one company could on its own.

Third-party providers can step in at any point to deliver value. They can help you audit your environment as outlined by Bobby Christian. They can also be tapped to deliver dashboard information for either the whole of your system or just specific components of your system.

External Monitoring Counterpoint

The outsourcing of monitoring and intrusion protection is popular in business right now, but it is important to consider realistic counterpoints. Some believe that the biggest secret in corporate security is that no one is ever happy when outsourcing monitoring to a security provider. It is expensive, and the company that enlists the service never believes the monitoring is of high enough quality. Many security professionals admit that is true—third parties are stretched too thin because they are servicing more than what is reasonable.

One security provider set up monitoring agreements for one of their clients, but the monitoring service kept making significant mistakes. Repeatedly, they mistook the policy of a company for the provider's client and inadvertantly shut down its entire global online storefront. This happened five times. Accordingly, the vetting of monitoring providers thoroughly is important. It is also important to remain realistic when you enlist a monitoring provider. A service contract is going to deliver about half—or in some good cases three quarters—of what it is promising.

Despite these challenges, monitoring is still important. The forensics it yields are valuable because the data collection is often thorough and well aggregated. When thinking about the outsourcing of your monitoring, remember two things:

- Pay for no equipment. Tell the third party that you just want service and that the service should come bundled with the equipment and there is just one price—period.
- Get them to audit you and work with them to discuss how you are going to integrate the new equipment into the whole of your system, and be direct— do not be afraid to challenge them.

Intrusion Detection Versus Intrusion Deflection

The future of the external monitoring business is moving from passive to active. In the past, you were notified about an attack, and you adjusted your defenses accordingly. The next wave of this industry rests in systems that actively fight back when they meet an aggressive attack. Although it is starting slowly, look for more automated counterpunches from these systems in the near future.

ROSI and Monitoring

Well-tuned radar must flow through your internal reporting systems. Monitoring cannot just replace or stand beside your existing systems—it must also feed into your systems. Again, the key to success is for business people to understand the business impact of security events in real time. If the technology or security group reports incorrectly and ends up flooding the system with data that is irrelevant or does not pose a business danger, monitoring will be written off forever. If done correctly, the path to ROSI for business owners and the path to new budget monies for tech and security groups will remain smooth.

Security-specific measurements must be explained by very talented individuals who can paint a picture in meaningful ways that matter to the lot of business folks.

—Adel Melek, Partner, Deloitte, Toronto

In bridging this gap, the onus generally falls on the technology and security groups to make the sell. Consider a relevant example from the automotive industry. Suppose that a design engineer wants to ask for more money to redesign a bumper for a leading model. He argues that by retooling the bumper line by 32 millimeters, the tensile stress will be stronger. He requests the money, but the request is denied. He cannot figure out why. Perhaps if he had put this in business terms, equating the retooling to a stronger bumper that would improve crash test performance by 12 percent—meaning it would make the manufacturer eligible for a tax break or would increase sales and decrease the number of lives lost through the lifecyle of the vehicle—perhaps his request would have received immediate approval.

After the need has been assimilated into a business vocabulary, technology and security personnel must make certain that they report information on security monitoring directly to the business owner. It should not be passed off to someone who holds no power. Monitoring must be in the hands of the owner, who can then make the decision should something arise—just as he or she would do with other line items discussed earlier (stock price, sales).

Monitoring at Work

Real-time dashboards mentioned throughout this chapter continue to evolve. One such system has just emerged from IBM through a strategic alliance with Cisco Systems; it attempts to deliver data that matters to technology and business groups simultaneously. Dashboards work best when they unify technology and business issues and when they bridge the gap between perimeter defense (firewalls and antivirus), the control layer of an organization (who gets access), and the assurance layer (compliance, audit reports, and so on).

IBM's Paris-based Jean-Charles Cointot suggests that next-generation global security technologies will do a better job of taking intrusion detection/prevention functions and correlating them to security policies to determine whether a threat is real. He also points out the trend of security companies continuing to refine these products that marry the business owner and technology group's priorities. He asserts that the *piece de resistance* will come from security systems that automatically respond when intrusions deemed real threaten companies. This real-time provisioning of resources in one area of a system if another is in trouble will be able to quickly and effectively illustrate return on investment. This fully instinctive system, where the business rules and risk management are coming together with reactive technologies that report in CxO terms, will begin helping businesses to further quantify the return on their monitoring strategies.

Developing Radar in Review

Developing radar for monitoring your internal systems requires that you take great care in getting both the business owners and technology/security groups on the same page and speaking the same language. Ignoring monitoring or making it less sensitive could make your business much more vulnerable. Practice monitoring, and in doing so coax business owners into adding a security gauge to their overall roster of key business indicators. At the same time, force the technology team to create a meaningful gauge that will report on security by delivering only business-relevant information in business terms.

Upfront planning when creating this dashboard will pay off in significant ROSI because you will effectively organize your environment, business requirements, systems, and networks to focus specifically on those elements that require monitoring. Filtering correctly will catalyze success even further, because the deeper you go, the more superfluous threat data you can weed out. Make sure that your monitoring runs through (not beside or on top of) your system.

Remember, too, that bringing in a third party might be the best way to develop radar, especially if you determine that the third party's breadth of experience and the scope of its client base can work powerfully on your behalf. When choosing a third party, make sure you weigh the merits of keeping monitoring in-house, and screen potential third parties comprehensively. Bargain hard for a single, fair price that does not include needless options. Understanding and having a thorough knowledge of monitoring technology on the market will make you that much more ROSI savvy. That is what the next chapter focuses on: constant vigilance. Before you turn to it, take a charitable moment and check out www.NetAid.org, which has lots of innovative ways for you to donate your time or money for a truly important global cause!

Chapter 7
Constant Vigilance

- Ten years ago, the biggest threat to your company's information came from your own employees.

  Not anymore.

- Ten years ago, an external hacker actually had to sneak onto your property to steal something valuable.

  Not anymore.

- Ten years ago companies bought firewalls and felt safe from hackers.

  Not anymore.

- Ten years ago, to prosecute a perpetrator you had to nab him or her on misuse of a telephone or some tangential law.

  Not anymore.

- Ten years ago most of your data was in one place.

  Not anymore.

- Ten years ago your corporate officers were willing to accept technology risk because it wasn't "their job."

  Not anymore.

- Ten years ago, I had just finished bringing out the top-selling PC security device—Centel's Net/Assure—and was moving to help launch secure eCommerce on the newly public Information Superhighway. I too thought that security products were the answer.

  Not anymore.

Ten years ago, the most important commercial asset on the Internet was reputation. Early Web sites were just electronic copies of annual reports or product spec sheets. The biggest damage came from someone hacking in and defacing one of two pictures on a home page. (Sometimes companies did this to themselves. When IBM launched its first Web page, they put up a "large" picture of then-CEO Lou Gerstner. However, the image was so large that most people couldn't even load the page, and if they did, their browsers could only display a feature or two—an ear or a nose or a chin.)

Constant-Vigilance Key Questions: CEO Focus

1. How has your infrastructure matched the changes in your business these past 10 years?
2. Who (besides you) is responsible for managing your corporate risk?
3. What changes do you track proactively that could be affecting your business?
4. What security-related changes are you tracking, and what do you do with the results?
5. Who on your board understands and cares about your risk governance?

Even though this may seem like a pointless exercise in nostalgia, I do have a method to my madness: We are not through the cycle of change brought about 10 years ago. Rather, we are right in the middle of it. Without maintaining constant vigilance, no security is safe. And now that operations, threats, and countermeasures quite often cross borders, you suddenly need to be vigilant on a lot more information in a lot more places. To do that, you need a system.

Not Anymore, Continued

Constant change is relentless in global corporate security; overtime regulations, threats, countermeasures, and the technology facilitating all of it morph to higher levels of magnitude and complexity. This inexorable progression needs to be figured into your company's global corporate security strategy. Five years ago you might have been more willing to take risks. Why? Risks were less significant than today. In 1988, there were roughly 100 reported security incidents via the Internet, and by 1996 there were nearly 350 in just the third quarter. Today incidents per year are in the millions, and these intrusions do not even begin to touch the issue of piracy. Nearly 40 percent of all the world's software is pirated, and in countries such as Pakistan and China those rates eclipse the 80 and 90 percent marks, respectively.

A typical organization with 100 servers and 3,000 PCs behind a firewall will generate 10 million security events a month. Of these, 500 to 600 require human intervention, only 50 will involve some malicious intent, and just 2 will have caused a problem.

—*John Schwarz, President, Symantec, San Jose*

Every element of charting a course—regulations, personal liability, corporate governance, greater awareness of the damage caused by threats, and greater reliance on computer networks to function as a business—have significantly evolved. In the past year, you might have asked your CFO about a potential violation of Zimbabwe's data privacy act, and he or she said not to sweat hiring a lawyer to descend upon Harare, but check this year and see what she says. Regulations are in constant flux.

To outpace change and to realize ultimate ROSI from your global corporate security strategy, remaining constantly vigilant on the following four fronts is critical:

- Threats
- Countermeasures
- Regulations and legal frameworks
- Technology

Threats are evolving fast, but by the time you read about them in your morning paper or news brief, you are already behind the curve. You need to have some insight into what is around the next corner (and the one after that). And given the very nature of the threats, it is mandatory to call your security package complete.

Luckily for you, countermeasures are quickly evolving. Not only do the biggest names in security products and services develop new tools, but there are also numerous smaller companies scattered around your world that will save you time, money, and significant headaches (or worse). Regulations and their various legal frameworks are written in sand at best right now. Not only are the "regs" different in every country you do business in, they also differ in the same countries, from day to day. Compound that with the evolving legal frameworks that you are relying on to protect you, which change from court case to court case, and from political leader to political leader. I know of one company that relied on one-year-old business intelligence for some operations in Bolivia, only to arrive to a changed government and legal system that disallowed everything they had planned to do there. The biggest mistake is assuming that *your* laws will work where *your* data goes—an assumption that could cost you significantly.

Finally, your COO will say that the only thing remaining constant from your technology providers over the years is the brand. Software is rewritten, acquisitions and mergers are common, and suddenly you are running a completely new information system after an upgrade. This can and does offer real challenges to your organization, and the best way to turn these changes into positives is to gear up with advance warning, advance copies, and advance planning. Do not be fooled by the sticker on the box or the logo on the startup screen; your technology is changing as you read this.

Constant Vigilantes: Where to Find Them

- **Technology**—Your tech group
- **Threats**—A trusted third party
- **Countermeasures**—Your security group
- **Regulations**—Your legal group

Even as you consider the people you will need, it is also critical to remember that the four fronts of constant vigilance, which are changing today, tomorrow, and forever, are out of your sphere of effective control, but they are within your sphere of adaptive control. However, you must know what is happening in each of these areas, and ROSI within constant vigilance is gauged by how cost efficiently you acquire this knowledge.

Deputize to Realize ROSI

You should be aware that in many cultures it is not appropriate to question authority. Doing what you are told and following orders is still the preferred management style in some countries in Europe, the Middle East, Africa, Central and South America, and the Asia Pacific areas. People are more used to questioning orders from a security perspective in places such as the United States and Canada. This questioning of the status quo is critical after your corporation

continues...

Deputize to Realize ROSI   Continued

and your global security strategy are distributed throughout the world. There are too many nuances at work for you to maintain a handle on them all, and you need people who will come to you and say, "This won't work because of this." You need to go the extra mile when training and managing and find ways to specifically solicit the input you are going to need based on this cultural difference.

Ideally, these sectors are delegated, with specific reporting reaching up through the CSO. I have enjoyed success delegating each of the four to different members of my staff. For instance, in nearly any company, there are staffers who scour the chat rooms, list serves, and Web sites of technology companies. I would just create a process whereby I alerted them of information I wanted or needed and information that could be discarded. Although it takes some back-and-forth dialogue at first, soon you will have initiated a reliable, free-flowing channel of information.

Identify someone in your technology group, deputize that person as your information asset, train him or her as you want, and then let that person do what he or she loves to do. Each month, hold a pizza party in the evening to debrief and share information. It is fun, everybody learns something, and those you have deputized have a vested interest and role in helping the company adapt.

Tracking threats necessitates a more exhaustive route, and this cost is best shared with others—lots of others. Imagine trying to staff a team tasked with watching the development and deployment of every threat around the world. The bill for pizza and Coke would raise the eyebrows of your CFO. Luckily, there are a precious few companies that do this on behalf of hundreds and thousands of clients around the world, and this allows them to employ a large enough staff, vast enough technology, and deep enough experience to provide the right information at the right time and in the right manner. After you have deputized your information asset infrastructure, these considerations must be correlated with your business requirements. It demands a routine loop back to department heads and business owners to let them know what has changed. In turn, they should report on what has altered for them and, in light of the latest global security intelligence, what level of risk they are now willing to live with. Ultimately, they are the ones who stand to gain or lose from the process. This virtuous circle, comprised of trend spotting, reporting, adapting, and correlating is what I call *constant vigilance*.

Threats

In a global corporate security stance, keeping an eye on threats correlative to which ones are relevant to you is extremely important, and here's what you need to know. Threats come in two varieties:

- General attacks
- Targeted attacks

Both demand awareness. This does not mean that you need to become a regular at Black Hat or Def Con conventions or read *2600* magazine. In fact, you do not even need to know that the *lingua franca* of the hacking underground is Portuguese—the most active hacking collectives are located in Brazil. However, your global security team does need to stay current. If you run UNIX BSD and there exists a new UNIX BSD threat posted by rya (Rooting Your Admin), you will need to act.

Newest Hacking Threats in Business Terms

- **DoS attacks**

  Hackers are now using "standard" viruses to launch *denial-of-service* (DoS) attacks on specific companies or industries. Computers by the thousands are being turned into unwitting zombie machines, ready to launch coordinated attacks against anyone who is targeted by the latest hacker. Examples include MyDoom and Slammer (the latter of which targeted banks).

- **Black holing**

  Another type of hacker attack is black holing, which I call *corporate identity theft*. Someone completely out of your control can issue a command to many of the routers that make up the backbone of the Internet. Anyone who tries to link to your site through one of these routers will be *redirected* to the hacker's site—either a black hole of empty space or a fake site that looks just like yours that was designed to entice customers into typing their ID and password.

- **Mail spoofing**

  Mail spoofing is the forgery of an e-mail *header* so that the message appears to have originated from someone or somewhere other than the actual source. Distributors of *spam* often use spoofing in an attempt to get recipients to open, and possibly even respond to, their solicitations.

  continues...

> **Newest Hacking Threats in Business Terms   Continued**
> - **War driving**
>   The use of wireless technology is a great timesaver, and easy for companies to use. A lot of companies have it without even realizing it. War driving enables people to drive down the street with a $100 antenna and tap right into your organizational lifeblood, tap right into your intranet and your internal networks. It is like dropping a wire outside your office window down to the street with a big sign that says "Plug In Here."

Known Vulnerabilities and Known Exploits

If you knew that your company's warehouse door was often left unguarded for three minutes during a daily shift change, would you do something about it? A better lock? Change the shift schedule? Maybe add a video camera at the door? Perhaps. Or you might think, "It is only three minutes, and cameras are expensive"—no one will know that you are supremely vulnerable for those 180 seconds. Then, after the inevitable happens, and you have lost your property, you would overspend to make sure that the specific door would never be compromised again. That is the real world.

When you factor in the Internet, the question begins to look even more ridiculous to the uninitiated. I'm talking gaps of milliseconds on one open, internal password-protected port among thousands. Yet to a hacker, these types of commonplace vulnerabilities represent more than a three-minute open gate, and hackers capitalize on them every minute of every day, in every country in the world. Even though crime fighting is growing—among EU member nations, groups such as the UK's National High Tech Crime Unit sniff out and investigate cybercrime—hacking is still a favored pastime for the 12- to 20-year-old set.

Known vulnerabilities are weaknesses inherent within existing technology of all types. Exploits are hacker attacks on those known vulnerabilities.[1] Keeping tabs on what vulnerabilities exist in your hardware and software and discovering what new (or previously undiscovered) ones apply in both legacy and upgraded systems is absolutely vital to the ongoing security of your company. Keeping up with these threats is paramount.

---

1. *Definition of "exploit," n.d., searchsecurity.techtarget.com/sDefinition.*

As your global security team prepares for new hazards, it should also master the technology hardware and software you run, knowing what its strengths and weaknesses are. All team members should have a card by their desk that literally lists this exhaustive roster so that it is easily referenced when threats are anticipated and dispatched.

One of the best, least-expensive ways to maintain constant vigilance on threats is by joining your country's *Computer Emergency Response Team* (CERT). CERTs were born in the aftermath of the world's first virus—the Morris worm—which infected fewer than 100 computers worldwide, when it was found that the world's collective of Web administrators knew only e-mail addresses. (What was needed was a list of phone numbers. With no computers working, they had no way to contact each other!) Its founders understood the long-term ramifications of threats and developed the very first CERT on Carnegie-Mellon University's campus in Pittsburgh. These individuals knew that a clearinghouse of confidential, yet available contact information must be readied and shared for the next-generation Web.

CERT Alerts Require Translation

Always translate CERT alerts for your CxO of choice. Tell me, how could they understand it if you quickly IM them this recent CERT high alert?

A Cross-Site Scripting vulnerability exists in the 'index.php' script in both the 'admincp' and 'modcp' application directories due to insufficient sanitization, which could let a remote malicious user execute arbitrary HTML and script code.

The original CERT was a simple phone tree, and it evolved into the safe place to report threats, bugs, break-ins, and thefts so that information could be analyzed and redirected. CERTs have since grown, country by country, into independently run, cosmopolitan organizations. If you do business in Singapore, you would access SingCERT through the country's Information Development Authority (www.ida.gov.sg). Thailand runs a ThaiCERT, and Malaysia boasts a MyCert. You get the idea. If you are a legal, certified business, it is generally free to subscribe. CERT will help you put your own process in place for vetting exploits by delivering ongoing alerts and offering insight on how to create a threat-readiness posture.

CERTS are so successful, an international umbrella organization was created called FIRST (www.first.org). FIRST stands for the *Forum of Incident Response and Security Teams,* and it coalesces security-incident response teams that work in government, commercial, and academic organizations throughout the world. It "aims to foster cooperation and coordination in incident prevention to prompt rapid reaction to incidents and to promote information sharing among members and the community at large."

One indicator that new information-sharing links with federal governments are strategically important to top corporate executives can be found in the 13 *Information Sharing and Analysis Centers* (ISACs)—one for virtually every key vertical sector of private critical infrastructure. The companies participating in these ISACs constitute a who's who in their corporate world. For example, those looking for the Information Technology ISAC will find it at IT-ISAC.org. ISAC's are built around trust. It started with the financial services industry, and most major industries in major countries followed suit. You must be invited to join by another, trusted ISAC member. There are almost no vendor members—just security personnel who are trying to do their job well.

Targeted Threats

Although known exploits target known vulnerabilities, there are also threats that act against software in perfect working order. It is not a mistake or a bug that will victimize you. Instead, a targeted attack is launched using an exploit that only requires a way into your systems. Hackers are using well-known exploits that target specific businesses.

During the summer of 2003, a targeted threat materialized aimed at financial institutions. BugBear.B, discovered on June 5, 2003, was the first instance wherein a known virus proved increasingly harmful depending upon the specificity of the target. If you had updated your patches, BugBear.B would be detected by antivirus scanning and removed from your system. If it attacked you and you were not prepared, however, you simply lost all your data. If it attacked you and you happened to be connected to one of about 1,200 financial institutions that were hard-coded into the virus, it would deploy in your system and wait for your employees' keystrokes to reveal usernames and passwords. After the sensitive information was collected, it would forward it on to 1 of 10 e-mail addresses written within the virus.

Share and Share Alike
Wherever you do business, ISACs can be your friend. Join as many as apply to you.

This trend is worsening at this writing and will continue to on an array of fronts. A targeted threat could be industry specific. It could arrive via a dissatisfied customer or a disgruntled ex-employee. You need to be on top of targeted threats. Threats that are either well known, or that piggyback themselves on well-known attacks, are easy to stop with the proper foresight and planning.

Critical Systems and Threats

Solid, big-picture data from your local CERT will assist in combating known exploits and targeted threats. At a granular level, you can enlist customized products to forewarn you. One such service is Symantec's Deep Site, which gives clients raw data and customized security alerts about all threats. Before deploying either mechanism, you must prioritize your technology, mapping it to critical systems at critical times. Note that labeling a system as critical takes discernment. If you use Linux to print the company newsletter, it would not be categorized as a critical system. If Linux processes payroll every month, that's a different matter (especially at month's end—if payroll goes down for a day on the last week of the month, it is a crisis).

Make sure to give your global security team ample time to stay current. Threats have changed since you last worked on your security plans, and they will continue to change. You cannot stop it, but you can track it and adapt accordingly, and honestly; to do less would be shirking your fiduciary responsibilities.

Countermeasures

Usually, for every threat there is a pretty effective countermeasure. Some countermeasures are built in to your regular software and its patch regime. There are multiple third-party countermeasures that save you time and agony, and security technology is evolving on the hardware, software, systems, and managed services sides. It pays to have a policy in place that is designed to stay fresh on all fronts in an organized way. Moreover, you should consider how countermeasures can boost ROSI.

Instant messaging provides a handy object lesson in how countermeasures can provide ROSI. It also exposes a problem symptomatic of companies that do not yet practice constant vigilance. In any work environment, instant messaging can offer a handy mechanism for employee theft of intellectual property, enabling the attachment and sending of it wherever the employee wants. Moreover, it can be a huge time waster.

I have seen instant messaging at its worst, and I have worked with companies where it was used to make fun of management in real time during corporate conference calls. I have also seen employees send company-sensitive data to their home or to their friends because they knew that even though the corporate e-mail was monitored, there was no system in place to track instant messages.

On the flip side of such flagrant abuse, I have also run a global business where instant messaging was a critical time- and money-saving tool. With the time zones around the world, instant messaging is a cheap and easy way to get real-time information passed around the world. I had all my leadership teams use instant messaging at the office and at home so that they could be reached as needed. It was a lot cheaper than provisioning global Blackberrys to everyone, there was no training required, and it was deployable around the world within an hour of our decision to use it. People who say instant messages do not have a place in the office are probably the same ones (or their children) who told us that desktop PCs were just toys and would never become a workplace solution.

It is tough for a company's existing, global security system to track instant messaging, and because of this internal threat, an instant messaging backlash has persisted in many corporations. In many organizations, the technology group might see someone using instant messaging on a network port (say port 64) and think, "Ha! Shut it down." This is generally considered to be a solid practice. However, instant messaging has figured this out, and in response, it has installed a clickable option that asks users whether they would like to hunt down another available port in a network through which to get access. A user clicks, and instant messaging zooms up and down the company firewall, looking for a way in. When it finds one, previously closed "port 64" is dumped in favor of wide open "port 2048."

Taking it a step further, when the technology group discovers instant messaging operating on its new port, it might decide it is time to take an extreme countermeasure—it shuts down IM throughout the entire organization. Seems logical. However, in the current global business environment, this action could prove Draconian. Remember, technology is supposed to enable productivity and enhance communication. In this instance, wouldn't it be great to let the right people use IM for the right reasons and stop the wrong people from using it for the wrong reasons?

Countermeasure constant vigilance ensures that you understand what innovations exist that can map back to your business requirements while delivering fiscally responsible solutions that reduce risk. In the case of our instant messaging dilemma, a countermeasure does exist. Developed by British-based HyperScape

Security, netREPLAY is a tiny appliance that you attach to your network that enables you to track every system that is unscanned by your existing, major security systems. If netREPLAY finds anybody using instant messaging, it will lock on it and look for sensitive information being transmitted through it, automatically shutting off access should it detect suspicious activity. This small appliance will cost you a few thousand dollars. Over time, however, it could you save you millions by allowing your organization to re-enable instant messaging and communicate in real time, increasing productivity and the bottom line.

External threats—those that originate outside the company—require another form of countermeasure vigilance. In February 2004, one such menace—the *distributed denial-of-service attack* (DDoS)—afforded an effective contrast in constant vigilance related to external threats and their countermeasures. MyDoom was a targeted virus that carried a DDoS aimed at international software provider SCO Group, Inc. A variant known as MyDoom.b—bug-plagued but no less serious—carried the same attack to Microsoft. In late January, both companies braced for the storm and commented on their respective countermeasures in veiled, yet revealing terms.

SCO spokesperson Blake Stowell spoke to the technology tabloid eWeek: "Every security expert talking about this and the ones we are talking to say this is really real and needs to be taken seriously. This will probably be the biggest test our company has seen from the Web site standpoint ever."[2]

In the same article, a Microsoft spokesperson commented, "While [we are] unable to discuss the specific remedies [we] are taking to prevent the reported DDoS attack, we are doing everything we can to ensure that Microsoft properties remain fully available to our customers."[3]

On February 1, MyDoom slammed into SCO, and, according to *eWeek*, "The SCO Group Inc. confirmed that by midnight EST, a large-scale, DDoS (distributed denial-of-service) attack had rendered its Web site completely inaccessible."[4] SCO.com was useless, and service interruptions began. The article continued, "SCO will not be defending itself against the attack though until Monday.

---

2. Matt Hicks, "SCO, Microsoft Prepare for MyDoom Battle," 30 January 2004, www.eweek.com/article2.
3. ibid.
4. Steven J. Vaughan-Nichols, "SCO's MyDoom DDoS Hammering Begins," 1 February 2004. www.eweek.com/article2.

Spokesperson Stowell explained, 'We don't expect many real site visitors on not only Sunday, but Super Bowl Sunday.' Stowell goes on, 'We have seen this coming and do have plans in place to address it on Monday morning. If Plan A doesn't work, we're ready with Plan B, and then with Plan C.'" It is important that plans not be created in real time or days before the threat, and SCO seemed to have been caught with its guard down.

Two days later, MyDoom.b careened into Microsoft. *eWeek*'s lead read, "Microsoft Corp.'s main Web site showed no ill effects from the scheduled denial-of-service attack generated by computers infected with the MyDoom.b virus."[5] The company would not reveal its countermeasure in the article, but its message? Microsoft hadn't sweated the attack. Somehow, it thoroughly understood the level to which they needed to be prepared for attacks of this nature. It had deployed the correct countermeasure to address MyDoom.b.

The suspense is killing you at this point. You want to know what I think the killer "anti-Doom" was. I will say that Microsoft, as a part of its global corporate security strategy, is a customer of—you guessed it—Akamai. When Microsoft chose Akamai to host some of its Web presence, it had done its homework. It knew that Akamai gets more than 30 billion hits a day and controls more than 10 percent of the Internet's traffic.

The SCO and Microsoft contrast underscores how your global security team must identify, evaluate, and apply new countermeasures that can keep you running smoothly and securely.

Regulatory Issues

The global environment necessitates an acute awareness of regulations in any country in which you do business. Just like your technology, you should map your organization's literal geography and all the geographic regulations—countries and locations—that apply. If you are a Swiss company, you might not know the whole of German law. If you are headquartered in Brazil, you cannot be expected to have a working knowledge of Dubai regulations.

---

5. Dennis Fisher, "Microsoft Unfazed by MyDoom's DDoS Attack," 3 February 2004, www.eweek.com/article2.

Regulations represent terrain on which your global security team, your technology team, and your legal department must have a strong and close working relationship. This team will expand as your business expands. That way, if you move into the United States, you can figure out that each state has its own regulation profile: California has more regulations, for example, and Oregon has fewer. Having a legal team in place on the ground or at home that has a strong working knowledge of the laws that apply to you both geographically and vertically is critical to any constant-vigilance plan.

The World Economic Forum's Little Black Book

At the 2002 World Economic Forum in Davos, Switzerland, HP wanted to introduce attendees to its latest palmtop device that was replete with Windows CE and a wireless card. The Forum outfitted these new beauties with all the attendee information and personalized codes for finding places to eat and, when loaded with your credit card number, you could use it to scan and purchase books.

That year's Forum was met with antiglobalization demonstrators who showed up in person and virtually. One of them war drove the conference and was able to hop onto the wireless network provided by the Forum's host. There was no security, and soon the demonstrator had the information of every attendee in his or her computer. This included the addresses, private cell phones, credit card numbers, and exclusive e-mail addresses of the world's power brokers, including the likes of Bill Gates, Al Gore, and a host of others. This experience quickly illustrates how constant vigilance can even be missed at the highest levels.

Note that war driving is illegal in some spots around the globe, and hackers can be cited in interesting ways. In the United States, a man was arrested because he tried to access a corporate WiFi net while standing in the company's parking lot. He was found guilty, because he did it from their property—had he sat across the street, there would have been no law with which to prosecute him. In most countries, there are still no laws covering this new technology, so each case is handled differently. Look for these laws to evolve quickly, matching the rise to prominence that wireless is making around the world. Understanding what rules are in place will help you lay out the distribution of your WiFi repeaters and help you plan your WiFi policies accordingly.

Technology

Your and every company's technology—the bread and butter that has enabled you to go global—shifts throughout its lifecycle before it is retired and replaced. These movements range from subtle to seismic, and they occur in phases. Once a quarter, patches pop up and are added. Every year your Oracle databases are upgraded from X.1 to X.2. Every handful of years you have to consider major upgrades as Oracle moves to 9.0 and you decide to outfit the entire company with WiFi-enabled laptops. Okay, so what do you do when WiFi becomes WiMAX?

You must maintain constant vigilance regarding technology. At the writing of this book, a bevy of legacy systems are giving way to newer, faster, and potentially more *secure* technology. Your global security strategy must account for what technology you need as it relates to the risk and business requirements of each business owner.

Suppose, for example, that data is important and it travels on myriad laptops out the door of your company. If your concern is losing that data through theft, perhaps you want to consider the new IBM Thinkpad that carries a built-in encryption chip inside. If your concern is damaged or potentially lost data, you might want to consider the Thinkpad that devotes 20 percent of its disc space to making a mirror image of all your data. Even if you get hit by a virus and your data becomes toast, you can bring the Thinkpad to the office, boot it up, and boom!—you have your data back. These new machines, which cost about $500 more than a typical notebook, might prove more expensive in the short term, but the total cost of ownership could prove dramatically less if your investment properly accounted for the risks your people face outside the office. However, if your business owners do not even know they have the option, then that is a correctable fault.

A Word About the Long Term: IPv6

If I had a nickel for every time a business executive told me that he didn't need to buy my security stuff now because the next generation of the Internet protocol, called IPv6, would be available "next year" and have built-in security... Back in 2000, when I was at IBM, I briefed the U.S. secretary of commerce on IPv6, and what it would be able to do. Although we spent more time trying to convince him that broadband would become commonplace and that wireless was a reality, we did focus on the additional security that would be available when there was full adoption of IPv6. (Today we run under IPv4. No one knows what happened to version 5. It is like that weird uncle who just disappeared and is never talked about at dinner.)

IPv6 is here now. Can you feel it? Do you use it? Does it matter? If you use Microsoft XP or newer, you can select version 6 as your protocol. But the key to my message to the secretary was that it needed to be "fully adopted." It is not today, and it will be a while until it is. Also, like much new technology, it won't live up to its hype. Just like Dean Kaman's Segue did not "revolutionize human transportation around the world, changing the way cities of the future are designed," IPv6 will not automatically make the Internet a safe place to work. Just as Segue turned out to be the adult bicycle of the scooter set, IPv6 will be just the next protocol. It will not be the answer to all your prayers, and waiting for it is no excuse for poor security today. That's not to say IPv6 isn't necessary and won't help. Today only 10 percent (600 million out of 6 billion) of the world's humans are online (and the world is adding 79 million new people a year—and IPv4 is already running out of address space). Compound that with the coming "always on" broadband evolution, wherein each human will require dozens of individual network addresses. IPv6 will give us an almost limitless supply of these addresses, and this is the key driver. Also, IPv6 has security built in, whereas IPv4 needs to add security on top. IPv6 also has built-in privacy capabilities.

Some countries are betting big time on this next generation. Japan has invested in IPv6 more than any other country, and its companies are best positioned to enjoy the future fruits. Companies such as Sony have met an "All IPv6 Compatible" pledge, and these companies stand to be a prime supplier to European countries such as France and Sweden. Although the United States has many IPv6 product companies, look for them to export more than is used domestically for a while, despite a strong Department of Defense mandate to purchase. High-population countries that came late to the Internet, such as China and India, will benefit most from IPv6, because their address space allocation under version 4 is highly fragmented and prone to breakdowns and workarounds. And countries trying to leverage mobile communications such as Sweden, Japan, and Germany will see early rewards.

What does all this greatness-to-come mean for cross-border companies today? One piece of advice, from a trustee of the Internet Society and the president of the IPv6 Forum Latif Ladid, is to "look for 'IPv6 aware' on all the communications products that you purchase today, and expect to be buying new security technology from new security vendors over the next five years, to leverage the different security capabilities that will be available to you. Although it will have many new security capabilities available to us, it will still be up to the companies that use the Internet to ensure their own safety."

Internet Protocol (IP) has become a cross-border natural resource. It's up to all of us to increase its capabilities.

—Latif Ladid, President, IPv6 Forum, Luxembourg

IPv6 Security Benefits to Come
- Greater address space provides for greater granularity.
- Built-in header authentication, which will stop current spoofing.
- No need for *Network Address Translation* (NAT) boxes, which have raised risks.
- Built-in end-to-end security functionality.
- Slower spread of viruses because of longer address lengths. (IPv4 = 10 hours and IPv6 = 2 billion years to scan address space.)
- Built-in privacy protocols.

The Organizational Security Posture

Within this chapter, you have seen how keeping tabs on threats, countermeasures, regulations, and technology creates an effective virtuous circle of awareness. To maintain this posture, your IT team must stay current and aware by having a keen grasp on what's out there, and communicating it to business owners in a clear, business-relevant manner.

Having your IT and global security teams scour the Internet for online tradeshows and conferences represents an easy-to-cull intelligence. They should also join key professional organizations such as the *Information Assurance Advisory Council* (IAAC.Org.UK) and begin immersing themselves in the constant-vigilance circle in person and virtually.

At times, it will be wise to send your teams to tradeshows in your country or region to see the latest innovations first hand. These gatherings showcase relevant tools for counteracting threats. Teams should approach them with a critical eye, looking past "brochureware" and custom testimonials and asking for the contact information of at least three CSO or CIO customers with whom they can talk who support the product. If they get the "If I told you, I would have to kill you" treatment, it is time to move on. The CSO and CIO community *will* talk and share with peers—just not in public.

As they become steeped in knowledge, create opportunities for raising constant-vigilance issues within your business owners' units. Host an after-work pizza gathering where everyone has a chance to share—and listen—to new threats, countermeasures, regulations, and technology that might affect each unit. This should roll into a formal audit process that occurs yearly and is figured into the following year's cycle of security planning.

What Parts of Constant Vigilance Should I Outsource?

As constant vigilance begins to seep into a corporate culture, it, too, is evolving. In a recent conversation with Marco Plas, security chief at Netherlands-based broadband provider nlTree, we talked about this evolution and where it is headed.

Marco illuminated three stages of global security constant vigilance that companies tend to work through, and in each stage, more control is given to third-party providers. This change has been catalyzed by (you guessed it) the growth and complexity of threats, countermeasures, regulations, and technology.

- Basic Monitoring Packages
- Adding Infrastructure-specific traps and traces
- Allowing Remote Control

Stage one—general information security—is usually outsourced to monitoring companies such as Symantec. Specialists in below-ground bunkers in London or Berlin spend their lives tracking viruses throughout the world and providing patch-level updates. By outsourcing this portion of constant vigilance, you will receive updates such as "MyDoom is headed your way; update your patch."

In the second stage of constant-vigilance outsourcing, a company moves to handing the blueprint of its technology to a third party. In turn, that third party examines what levels of threats, countermeasures, regulations, and technology you should pay attention to based on the customized needs of your organization, sending you alerts and updates accordingly. Still, the company takes the action to secure itself from harm or legal action while executing disaster recovery. This second stage is where most companies in Europe are today.

Moving beyond the blueprint and giving a level of control is the third stage of constant-vigilance outsourcing. At this stage, the company hands over the blueprint and select scripts that enable a third part to take control of your systems when you are not there, so if a patch is needed or a portion of your system requires shutdown, it can be done remotely. This effectively ensures a more thorough form of constant vigilance. This is happening more and more throughout Europe because the need is increasing.

Marco Plas on the Consequences of Intermittent Vigilance

In the recent past, I worked to put together a constant-vigilance program for a bank in the Netherlands. After deployment, and on a Friday afternoon, we alerted the bank that a patch was needed for an incoming virus. We saw it, and we said, "It is coming to you; we need you to take your firewalls down for the patch install." We sent it to them, and they began to install it.

By that evening, the patch was in place, and we called the bank to bring the firewalls back up, but no one was there to do so. Now this was a pretty big bank with many ATM machines. With their firewalls down and their system vulnerable, they lost 2 million euros over that one weekend.

Scenarios such as Marco's are propelling many European companies to take the next step in the outsourcing evolution curve—providing a third party with full access to a company's firewalls so that the third party can leverage even more control over serious threats. This final stage will ultimately evolve into the full outsourcing of constant vigilance at a network level.

What to Keep

When outsourcing, it is important to remember that you are mainly offloading fault—not risk. Although you have someone to blame should something go wrong, you must also arm yourself with unparalleled constant-vigilance resources and keep some elements of the process. When giving your constant vigilance over to a third party, remember to maintain control of the security policy that you created, which maps regulations and business requirements to threats and delivers a process whereby your organization reviews its constant vigilance in the virtual circle discussed earlier. In addition, you should routinely audit your third-party provider for response times and other key factors that figure into your program.

Who to Seek

Constant vigilance is best undertaken by a party that has significant scale and that maintains a client base that spans your industry and the parts of the world in which your extended enterprise does business. On the technology side, there are some good local shops, but I recommend the strength in numbers and working with a Symantec, Redhat, or ISS. On the consulting side, going with a big four such as Deloitte, PWC, KPMG, or Ernst and Young, or one of the global consulting firms that has a strong security area (not just a pretty brochure, but lots of people and lots of R&D) is advisable, because they all have very structured approaches to security. In both cases, again, make sure that policies remain in your control and conduct an internal audit of your business requirements and an external audit of your third party at least annually.

You Have Just Charted a Course: Let's Set Sail

In Part 1, "Charting A Course," I spelled out the six global (and universal) security keys to success that cross all borders:

- You need to design a clear policy—or **global security strategy**—that is embraced by the global organization by listening to and working with business owners, who are ultimately responsible for the amount of risk they do or do not mitigate.

- Understanding that a **security base** tied to the concept of ROSI as it relates to what components are base-worthy or best executed independently can prove potent to your organization as threats increase in magnitude and intensity. Although base-relevant ROSI varies from maximum to minimum, understanding and applying my Rule of 3 will help you determine what kind of a return any one of the components I discussed could be realized within your organization. By using this rule of three, you can also drive greater adoption of security services throughout the organization.

- **Business systems enhancement** (finance, HR, CRM, supply chain) presupposes that the deployment of security can and will deliver money savings and time/productivity efficiencies. Similarly, **functional process enablement** (operations, networks, call centers, development) posits that security, if prudently applied, can drive profitability and prove the worth of a strategy.

- **Developing radar** that effectively integrates monitoring into the flow of corporate vital signs when reported in business terms to the business owners can ensure that a strategy deployed remains strong, successful, and legal.

- **Constant vigilance**, that step you take to deputize key people within your organization to stay current on the changes to technology, threats, countermeasures, regulations that will at once vest them with a sense of responsibility and accountability when it comes to security, will ultimately prepare your organization and keep it in a potent security posture.

Now that we have addressed some universal truths in global corporate security, it is time to set sail and begin visiting local security environments in *Europe, the Middle East, and Africa* (EMEA), the Americas, and the Asia Pacific regions. Here we step off our boat and walk the streets that might already comprise your map, examining local rules, regulations, customs, best practices, and conventions. I do so in Part 2, "Reality, Illusion, and the Souk," with an eye toward helping you succeed in countries beyond your own.

PART 2

REALITY, ILLUSION, AND THE SOUK

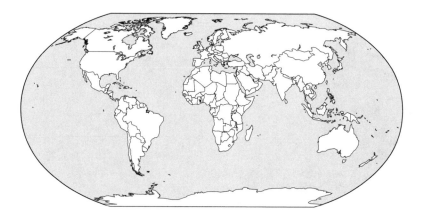

Chapter 8

Wells and the Security Guy Travel the Globe

I am constantly gratified by flattering untruths about English superiority which I should reject indignantly were the application bluntly personal. This habit of intensifying all class definitions, and particularly those in which one has a personal interest, is in the very constitution of man's mind. It is part of the defect of that instrument.

—H.G. Wells, *A Modern Utopia* (1905)

I find Wells's self-criticism in A Modern Utopia refreshing, and I wish more business people could examine their own attitudes and biases with equal candor while factoring in some cultural sensitivity along the way. It is this posture that I bring to Part 2, "Reality, Illusion, and the Souk," where you will get a glimpse of how global corporate security can be tailored to a country other than your own. Part 2 provides a broad-based view of how security is practiced across borders. As we travel to every continent and learn from security professionals worldwide, my goal is not to fill you in on every detail. Instead, I seek to supply you with an arsenal of knowledge that can possibly make or break your global security's implementation of the keys to success outlined in Part 1, "Charting a Course."

Tied to each covered country is a *Mapping Security Index* (MSI) score. The MSI combines a host of indicators to provide you with some measurable way to determine how you should perform your security business in a new country—it is described in detail later in this chapter. To be complete, the MSI's quantitative data and cold facts are married to qualitative, first-hand stories that take you inside culture—perhaps the most important aspect of the section. Hopefully, I convey enough information to help you make your own decisions based on locales that matter most to your global organization.

We begin with the region known in global business as EMEA (Chapters 9 and 10). Comprised of Europe, the Middle East, and Africa, we cover it from pole to pole, including Russia and the Nordics, the UK and Ireland, through western, central and southern Europe, on to India, the Persian Gulf, and the Middle East, ending on the tip of South Africa. We visit the Americas (Chapter 11), beginning in Canada and the United States and diving into Latin America. We then move west and visit four representative countries from the vast Far East of Asia and the Pacific Rim (Chapter 12). Finally, because it will endure as a global security concern, we examine how Part 1 and Part 2 connect through the topic of outsourcing (Chapter 13).

"Those" Americans

Can you believe those Americans? They have an uncanny knack for thinking their way is best, that their country is somehow responsible for most useful innovations in modern life, and that their way of existence is somehow God's gift to the globe. They call the championship of baseball, their national sport, the World Series. They believe in an "Americanization" that is manifestly destined for global adoption. They relentlessly export their own forms of popular culture with little or no understanding of how it is interpreted on the global stage. They believe their business style—often very direct, efficient, and bottom-line oriented—is best. You have probably encountered your share of these arrogant, imperialistic loudmouths before, haven't you?

My Fellow Americans

Americans take note: If you are outside the 50 states and everyone in the room is agreeing with you, they are either internally livid or externally lying. Please, for the sake of us all, take time to listen before you talk.

I am an American. I love my country and am proud of its idealistic moorings, work ethic, and the opportunities it offers its population. I have also lived abroad and been exposed to its weaknesses reflected in other countries' perceptions of our less-cosmopolitan edges. Importantly, I have witnessed the challenges arising out of the American "our way or the highway" mentality.

I wish I could say provincialism and nationalism were exclusively the property of my country, but I have seen it everywhere—from Paris to Punjab. Citizens in most quarters believe their nation and way of conducting business is best. This creates certain biases that can skew truth, fashioning unfathomably difficult situations when outsiders import their operations.

Effects within the global corporate security milieu are particularly acute. Even though much of security's vocabulary and processes are universal, it is naïve to think that each country views global corporate security in the same way. Disparate motivations and cultural customs driving security practice render ideas of homogenous implementation absurd. When your global security strategy moves off your home turf, rest assured that your security, if informed by superficially uniform operations abroad, is an illusion.

Moreover, when multilateral cooperation is required between a single organization and its branches located across multiple borders, the biggest differences materialize from the least-expected places. I once worked on a project that required two parts of a newly merged financial institution to upgrade and standardize their security in respective countries—Germany and Switzerland. I entered the scenario thinking there would be noteworthy disagreement on security standards, that perhaps teams from the two countries would have diametrically opposed ideas of which international benchmark they worked against.

Nothing was further from the truth, and the security teams of both nationalities were strongly attached to the well-known ISO 17799. I was pleased, thinking our work would proceed smoothly. Not so. My thinking that ISO 17799 leads to some sort of a standardized security utopia was an illusion. Again, uniformity is seductive.

Your technology is only your tool, but it still must be aligned with the policies of the market that you're in. Don't be fooled by titles. While you need to make use of roles and classes, a VP in Prague can have vastly different roles than a VP in Peoria. A title might look fine from 5,000 miles away, but you need to understand the people behind the title to deliver the best security.[1]

—Dan Pietro, Professional Staff, Select Committee on Homeland Security, U.S. House of Representatives and International Affairs Fellow, Council on Foreign Relations, Washington D.C.

---

1. *The views expressed by Mr. Prieto are solely his own and do not reflect the views or positions of the House Select Committee on Homeland Security or its members.*

The Swiss financial institution believed through its interpretation of the guideline that front-end deterrence, which in their minds rested in flashier forms of newer technology, was clearly the order of the day. It would create a formidable barrier to the outside. The Swiss wanted to search for fiber-optic taps along the kilometers of underground fiber cables laid in Germany that might carry its traffic. Conversely, the Germans contended that all the data is encrypted, that the fiber is buried and protected, and that the only company that even would be in place to conceivably tap the fiber would be Deutche Telecom itself, and they were trusted... but not as much by the Swiss. It turns out that Deutche Telecom holds most of the world's patents on tapping fiber-optic cable. The Germans, vehemently opposed to the Swiss perspective, repeatedly emphasized their specific method, emerging from a copious analysis of ISO 17799, and followed the standard to the letter—their letter. These differences took significant time to iron out.

Going Deeper

Geneva-based Marco Ricca discusses how privacy is everything to the Swiss in Chapter 9, "Europe," and Hamburg-based Stefan Weiss lends perspective to Germany's commitment to corporate accountability.

Sometimes such discrepancies are never resolved, to the detriment of both countries' operations. I have observed a South African consumer goods company take over an American-based firm and then attempt to integrate security. The South Africans tried to run an operation headquartered in the U.S. rural heartland and it hit a wall. The Americans stubbornly refused to set aside what they considered to be its vastly superior "made in the U.S. of A." security architecture. Even though the South African corporation held appreciably advanced expertise based on stringent international security standards, it eventually gave up trying to negotiate with its Yankee counterparts. Unfortunately, this lack of cooperation has caused the company to become more vulnerable in both countries and around the world.

Going Deeper

Find out about South Africa's unprecedented racial reconciliation in the boardroom and how that is affecting security with Johannesburg's Kobus Burger in Chapter 10, "The Middle East and Africa." Then visit Adel Melek's takes on the ongoing struggles in the United States in the post-Enron-meets-outsourcing era in Chapter 11, "The Americas."

The Lessons of the Souk

My time in Damascus, Syria was nearly over, and I wanted to take home a memento of my journey. I paid a visit to the world's oldest continuously operating shopping center, the world-famous Grand Souk (*souk* means marketplace). Soon I found just what I had hoped for: a pillow dealer. I caught his eye, and he waved me into his stall. I smiled and looked at his pillows and admired them aloud. I complimented the dealer on his inventory variety.

"It is a lovely day, too," I said. "This country is remarkable and wonderful, and I've enjoyed my time in your city."

The dealer asked whether I would like some tea, and I expressed gratitude. He brought out the pot and some cups, and I told him the set looked beautiful. He poured, and I let him know how absolutely tasty it was. He asked me where I was from, and eventually we talked about what it was like in my country. Then came the moment of truth, and I decided to test my abilities as a souk negotiator:

"These are really lovely pillows," I said, "They are very valuable to me, and in reality they are worth so much more, but for me, I'm willing to pay X."

"I can tell these pillows are perfect for you," the dealer replied, smiling. "You find them precious and you deserve them, and I'm willing to let you have them for Y."

This complex ritual continued for about an hour. If you do it well (as I did), you will have a very positive experience and, believe me, a fine set of pillows. This type of negotiation is a high art, and I have only been successful with it after watching for several years and learning from the well-qualified Lebanese. I mention my time in the souk because in creating global corporate security strategies outside your home country, you must be sensitive to the cultural customs that exist in regions throughout the world. If you are a fellow American, imagine entering the pillow dealer's stall and thinking to yourself, "This is a bazaar, and they want me to haggle." You stride in, nab a few decent-enough looking pillows, and say, "Hey there, here's what I want and I won't pay more than X for it." You've become a cultural bull in a pillow shop.

Going Deeper

In Saudi Arabia, the law states that government contracts in corporate security can only go to Saudi Arabian companies. Find out why that's a good thing in Chapter 10, "The Middle East and Africa."

Similarly, as you enter work environments in different parts of the world, this colonial missionary style of business could, again, literally break you abroad, leaving you open to increased threats, a lot of wasted time, and vaporized money among masses that are seemingly converted (yet who are quietly resenting you). In Part 2, I'm seeking to provide you with a starter map from which you can draw your own. It is a rendering of cultural topography married to global corporate security practice focused on local rules, regulations, customs, best practices, and conventions. It holds the anthropological mantra of "participant-observer" in high esteem, meaning that when you enter a new culture or environment, you must observe it, learn its ways, and then adapt your security to it—preferably with the help of an indigenous guide. This does not mean you sacrifice your standards. You simply adapt them, becoming open to how new people in new places do what you do best in their backyards. It also alerts you to the different types of threats that can emerge and that you must watch even as you cross borders.

Going Deeper

Learn from Melbourne's Kevin Shaw about how Novell executives arrived at a user group meeting in China only to be greeted by 2,000 people who didn't have licensed versions of its software in Chapter 12, "Asia-Pacific."

Traversing Your Map: What to Remember

Before we take the plunge into respective countries, it is very important to reflect on some issues that you will face when crossing borders. Jean-Pierre Garritte, former head of the International Association of Internal Auditors and a fellow traveler I admire and have worked with often, is perhaps one of the most well-trekked executives in the world. He frames the discussion well.

"You have to know why you want to go, correlative to the type of talent you need and the customs you'll need to account for," he said. "When scouting out a location, make sure you go covertly so as not to draw attention to yourself or your company and receive a misleading tour of the prospective country." I have taken these considerations and expanded on them below, and I invite you to reflect on them before you take your business abroad:

- **Why do you want to go?**

    Is it because there is a market for your product or service? Or do you want to go there because it is considered to be a low-cost country? If it is an outlay issue, remember that this will not remain a low-cost country. Take, for example, India: They were once the "low-cost leader" in terms of labor, but now even they are outsourcing to Pakistan and Sudan. So you won't see that same cost benefit, but you will be operating in a country that could be vastly different.

- **Where are the hardest workers?**

As you think about moving, match your need for human resources with talent that shares your strong work ethic and strong values of personal responsibility. You want people who can make a difference for your organization—who are creative and can think on their feet. Look also for a spirit of entrepreneurship. You will find a lot of these qualities in smaller countries such as Denmark or the Czech Republic.

- **Travel to that country on vacation: Be anonymous.**

If you scout out a country on business, you will come home and report, "They were so good and so nice to me! They wined and dined me!" Of course they did. You were there holding out the carrot of investment and jobs. This is especially true when moving into developing or rebuilding countries—if you were to visit one of the Baltic States, their values are not the same as those in the United States or Western Europe: They need and want money as they strive to catch up. They will be sizing up your cash—not for the country, but for themselves. So there won't often be a long-term vision. (Why should they have one?) You, as the investor, will bring the money, the know-how, and some of the technical assistance. So travel first for pleasure and second for business.

- **Pay attention to the new culture.**

Even though France and Belgium may seem 90 percent the same, it is that crucial 10 percent comprised of local laws and customs that will differ enough to merit attention.

- **What will make my project successful or unsuccessful?**

Know the talent and limitations of the new country inside and out. Know the laws and the legal infrastructure. Know how companies really work, and map these back to your critical success factors.

- **Decide on an indigenous venture partner.**

An American doing security in Europe is crazy. A Brit doing business on the continent is nuts. A German in France, a Frenchwoman in Spain—just doesn't happen. It is accepted in developing countries, because they do not (yet) have sufficient local resources. Of course, a few countries are more welcome on foreign soil: the Dutch, the Nordics, and the South Africans work across borders more easily. Ultimately security is about trust, and usually people only really trust their own citizens. For example, most executives I have met in EMEA assumed that I would feed info back to the U.S. *Central Intelligence Agency* (CIA) and that it would not be a risk if they hired one of their own. (By the way, I don't.) My point is that you should involve locals, but be practical and balanced in the way you empower them.

■ **Create a team of expatriate and local experts.**

If you do not have a local expert, it will be very hard to succeed. You will always be viewed as a "colonial" presence. Remember that you must take care when choosing a local expert.

These seven considerations have served me and many other successful global business executives very well for a long time. They have saved us countless headaches. When applied to the security space, they will lower your risk in each country and maximize the overall enterprise gains.

The Mapping Security Index: MSI

As you travel from continent to continent, you will notice that I have included a score designed to help you determine which countries are best for cross-border business as they relate to your own objectives and global security needs. This MSI combines four quantified components to deliver a measurable result amid a difficult landscape.

The MSI leverages metrics that examine *communications throughput, risks* and use of security, actual *threats*, and *culture*. The actual results of each component are then rank ordered for our 30 target countries. Details of the MSI components follow.

First, to get an accurate read on the communications throughput you will experience in each target country, we have gone to Internet bandwidth scalability leader Akamai, which has tabulated a new throughput scoring system generated through its EdgeScape service, which maps IPs to locations and throughput. Specifically, EdgeScape is comprised of country code, throughput, and *classless interdomain routing* (CIDR)—the new addressing scheme for the Internet that allows for the needed growth of IP addresses through sharing. Akamai then assigns a score to the throughputs, 1 to 4 for each classification of EdgeScape throughput levels (low/med/high/high).

For every EdgeScape CIDR, Akamai then multiplied the throughput score by the number of IPs and then added that onto the running total for each country. What does this mean? A 100 percent scale is relative to the total throughput on the Internet to every end-user IP in each country.

The second component of the MSI, risks, is sourced to the Terror and Political Stability Index of global insurer AON Corporation. AON has developed a Terrorism Risk Assessment that measures terror from negligible, low and medium risk to high and extreme risk, based on geopolitical circumstances, war, terrorist incidents, and threats.

The third component, threats, is based on actual security attacks by country. This historical data has been mined from the Symantec DeepSite security database and is rooted in long-term measurement of security threats and incidents and from where they emanate. It is an especially important score for understanding the threat level and vulnerability of each country.

The fourth and final component of the MSI is the *Mapping Security Cross-Border Index* (CBI). The CBI is based on my and other expert views researched for this book. It identifies the degree of cultural difficulty for a U.S.-based company to do business internationally. Obviously subjective, it is no less important. Culture contributes to the success and failure of global security operations, and I thought it important to develop such a factor. Also I am keenly aware that not all readers of the book will be focusing on the "U.S–Abroad" country pairing. I hope that in reading the details given throughout this part that you will be able to approximate your own culture scores from your home country.

The CBI is based on cultural differences that range from the simple (language barrier and local customs) to complex (security emphasis and corporate culture). That said, it accounts for a comprehensive cross-border business inventory that assigns country scores from 1 (least-favorable cross-border business environment) to 10 (most-favorable cross-border business environment).

The MSI is the mathematical amalgamation of each country's/region's rank order within each of the four components.

MSI = Throughput + Political Risk + Threats + Cultural Differences
The highest possible score is 100.

Figure 8.1 The highest possible score is 100; here, we have used the Czech Republic as an example.

Use of the MSI is for comparison purposes and obviously subject to change over time. The data used to create this version (MSI 2005) is based on historical data and information from 2003–2004. Updates for this score will be posted on this book's interactive companion Web site (www.MappingSecurity.com).

Chapter 9

Europe

Figure 9-1 Europe

EMEA, an acronym that stands for *Europe, the Middle East, and Africa* and comically simplifies a vast region long categorized in this manner for the sake of business, is the focus of this chapter and the next. The EMEA areas—covered here in the order they appear in the acronym—comprise a landmass whose cultures have been inexorably linked for centuries. Trade, conquest, and colonization have pervaded all three territories, and as we travel we will discover that vestiges of history still play a role in how global corporate security is practiced. Do not forget that even the term *security "arch"itecture* traces its roots to ancient Rome's invention of the arch.

Even if locales appear the same, strong undercurrents of security dissention and difference move with invisible swiftness. In places that may seem unfathomably foreign, you will find many links to your own understanding of security. In each case, strong focus on "impedance matching" of your business, security, and cultural beliefs with those you engage is necessary.

Look for security anomalies in terms of what is normal in their country not yours. In some countries, traffic spikes at certain times is normal; in others, it's a risk.[1]

—Dan Pietro, Professional Staff, Select Committee on Homeland Security, U.S. House of Representatives and International Affairs Fellow, Council on Foreign Relations, Washington D.C.

First we make stops in Europe and see the potentially dangerous misnomer of the *European Union* (EU), and how it is comprised of fiercely independent sovereignties that hold divergent ideas about how global corporate security should be practiced and what influences of the past and present figure in to this mix. In each region—as throughout Part 2—we scrutinize the local rules, regulations, customs, best practices, and important conventions of each country.

---

1. *The views expressed by Mr. Prieto are solely his own and do not reflect the views or positions of the House Select Committee on Homeland Security or its members.*

Europe: Cannon, Queens, and Customs

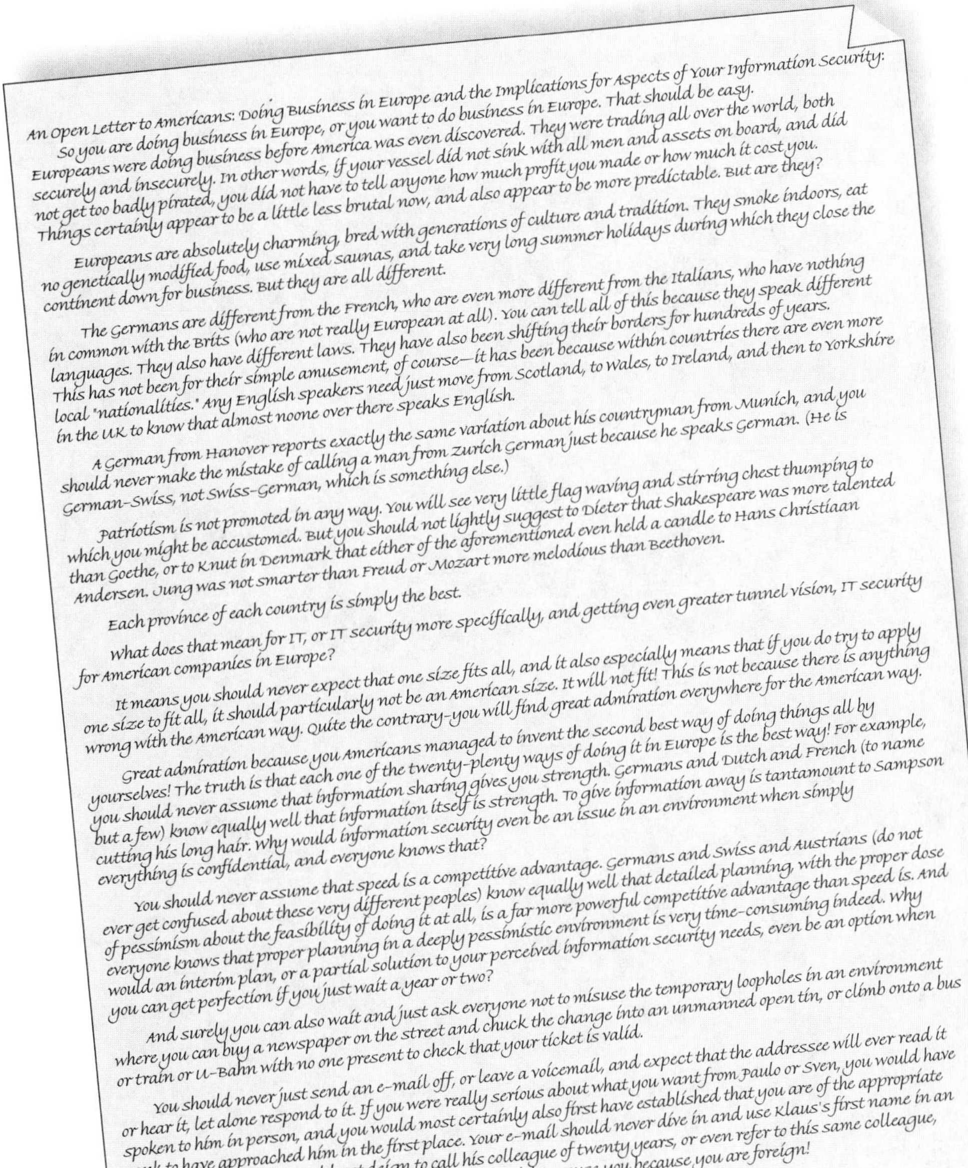

An Open Letter to Americans: Doing Business in Europe and the Implications for Aspects of Your Information Security:

So you are doing business in Europe, or you want to do business in Europe. That should be easy. Europeans were doing business before America was even discovered. They were trading all over the world, both securely and insecurely. In other words, if your vessel did not sink with all men and assets on board, and did not get too badly pirated, you did not have to tell anyone how much profit you made or how much it cost you. Things certainly appear to be a little less brutal now, and also appear to be more predictable. But are they?

Europeans are absolutely charming, bred with generations of culture and tradition. They smoke indoors, eat no genetically modified food, use mixed saunas, and take very long summer holidays during which they close the continent down for business. But they are all different.

The Germans are different from the French, who are even more different from the Italians, who have nothing in common with the Brits (who are not really European at all). You can tell all of this because they speak different languages. They also have different laws. They have also been shifting their borders for hundreds of years. This has not been for their simple amusement, of course—it has been because within countries there are even more local "nationalities." Any English speakers need just move from Scotland, to Wales, to Ireland, and then to Yorkshire in the UK to know that almost noone over there speaks English.

A German from Hanover reports exactly the same variation about his countryman from Munich, and you should never make the mistake of calling a man from Zurich German just because he speaks German. (He is German-Swiss, not Swiss-German, which is something else.)

Patriotism is not promoted in any way. You will see very little flag waving and stirring chest thumping to which you might be accustomed. But you should not lightly suggest to Dieter that Shakespeare was more talented than Goethe, or to Knut in Denmark that either of the aforementioned even held a candle to Hans Christiaan Andersen. Jung was not smarter than Freud or Mozart more melodious than Beethoven.

Each province of each country is simply the best.

What does that mean for IT, or IT security more specifically, and getting even greater tunnel vision, IT security for American companies in Europe?

It means you should never expect that one size fits all, and it also especially means that if you do try to apply one size to fit all, it should particularly not be an American size. It will not fit! This is not because there is anything wrong with the American way. Quite the contrary—you will find great admiration everywhere for the American way.

Great admiration because you Americans managed to invent the second best way of doing things all by yourselves! The truth is that each one of the twenty-plenty ways of doing it in Europe is the best way! For example, you should never assume that information sharing gives you strength. Germans and Dutch and French (to name but a few) know equally well that information itself is strength. To give information away is tantamount to Sampson cutting his long hair. Why would information security even be an issue in an environment when simply everything is confidential, and everyone knows that?

You should never assume that speed is a competitive advantage. Germans and Swiss and Austrians (do not ever get confused about these very different peoples) know equally well that detailed planning, with the proper dose of pessimism about the feasibility of doing it at all, is a far more powerful competitive advantage than speed is. And why would an interim plan, or a partial solution to your perceived information security needs, even be an option when everyone knows that proper planning in a deeply pessimistic environment is very time-consuming indeed. Why you can get perfection if you just wait a year or two?

And surely you can also wait and just ask everyone not to misuse the temporary loopholes in an environment where you can buy a newspaper on the street and chuck the change into an unmanned open tin, or climb onto a bus or train or U-Bahn with no one present to check that your ticket is valid.

You should never just send an e-mail off, or leave a voicemail, and expect that the addressee will ever read it or hear it, let alone respond to it. If you were really serious about what you want from Paulo or Sven, you would have spoken to him in person, and you would most certainly also first have established that you are of the appropriate rank to have approached him in the first place. Your e-mail should never dive in and use Klaus's first name in an environment where he would not deign to call his colleague of twenty years, or even refer to this same colleague, by anything other than his title and surname. He might excuse you because you are foreign!

Figure 9-2 An open letter from Miles Crisp.

You should never set up your information security management reports in a manner that could be seen to belittle one branch at the expense of another. Your cunning plot to get Copenhagen or Luxembourg to outperform London by pitting one against the other using the age-old competitive ploy is not only clumsily transparent, but could lead to a demeaning loss of face. This crassness would simply serve to highlight your own American ineptitude—because you will have designed inappropriate performance criteria that imply patently incorrect ratings of your branches. Any more normal manager would be able to see that Copenhagen is the best, regardless of how you choose to measure. "Just say what you want, and we will do it because you can trust us, and we always do it correctly."

There are many, many differences and lessons for any company getting going on foreign soil. The most important thing is to listen, understand the drivers, and then do not try to be European yourself. After I have chaired a meeting, I always thank my non-English speaking colleagues for speaking English throughout for my benefit. When I attend a non-English speaking meeting, I try to give them my full attention and concentration so as to understand as much as I can (which is sometimes very little!). This is sometimes incredibly hard work, but always appreciated. Many of my American colleagues return e-mails or play with their Blackberries during meetings if the language changes (or even if it doesn't). This seems to be quite acceptable in United States, but it always elicits quiet comments afterward from many Europeans who consider this to be bad manners. Remember, many Europeans do not necessarily return e-mails at all, and certainly do not consider noninstant turnaround to be bad form as you do.

Good luck in Europe!

Sincerely,

Miles Crisp

Partner in charge, Enterprise Risk Services
Europe, Middle East, Africa
Deloitte
Johannesburg

Figure 9-2 An open letter from Miles Crisp. *(Continued)*

Our security journey through Europe begins with a story about... the United States. Remember Enron and WorldCom? These two, fraudulent giants fueled a law-making frenzy that resulted in U.S. legislation titled the Sarbanes-Oxley Act of 2002. If you are European, you may only know it as SOX. Early on, as Congress passed the act and the *Securities and Exchange Commission* (SEC) hinted at compliance standards reaching around the world, Europe became outraged. In the media, the tack was strictly business—editorial and organizational opinions were followed by strongly worded suggestions to the SEC and heavy lobbying to work around the new law. Behind the scenes, European disgust for American business policies played out in rather unsubtle ways, right in my American business face.

At an exclusive meeting of 100 top executives from continental Europe, dining at a long table in an ancient German castle atop a snow-covered hilltop, a high-ranking EU commissioner rose to address our collective. His remarks quickly turned to the United States and differences in business standards and corporate governance. With fury, he laid into Sarbanes-Oxley and the arrogance of the SEC. He contrasted the greed-mongering Americans with a storied tradition of integrity-rich business on the continent.

"It's the Americans," he said. "The American standards, American frauds, American regulations, American leaders!"

As the speech reached its climax, he triumphantly announced how even in his Belgian neighborhood, a historic park's cannon had been symbolically aimed at the United States to repel "the demons." Indeed it was the Americans who were in moral decline. Conversely, Europe had forged ahead in an environment of accountability. Further, he stressed, if Harvey Pitt, then-head of the SEC, were to land in Europe, he would be handcuffed on the tarmac and thrown in jail. Attendees (me excepted) shouted and pounded their palms on the table in delight and agreement.

I tell this story not to create a divide (of course, after Italy's Parmalat and Holland's Ahold, there's very little of a divide left). Rather, I hold it up as an example of how the European community is equally proud of what it brings to the global corporate table—even at the business standards level. I offer it to demonstrate that what others tell you may belie deep-seated passions. If Americans hold certain stereotypical characteristics that create for it certain challenges on a global scale, so do Europeans. However, much like the America I love, there is the Europe I love, too.

What Matters Most? Everything!

In 2004, security specialist Evidian surveyed European firms in various countries to determine the biggest threats to companies in their respective homelands that should be considered when moving across borders. France, Spain, and Germany saw viruses as their top risks. Nordic countries believed that accidental damage by staffers was theirs. The UK cited corporate databases as the most vulnerable of company assets. The lesson? Establish your coordinates in the new country and get solid third-party perspective to see whether these risks hold merit when building your base.[2]

A case in point: I was once with a *Member of Parliament* (MP) enjoying bitters at Westminster Palace's "Friends" pub, an outer-sanctum drinking establishment for the House of Lords and Commons. It is where most MPs retire after Prime Minister's Questions to continue debate in a jollier setting among their colleagues and guests. After quizzically referencing the nearly constant ringing of bells and chimes, which were audible codes to go vote on this or that, I had been enlisted by my friend to create a centralized matrix of computer monitors that would inform MPs on upcoming votes, results, and the week ahead within this bar and its storied backroom cousin, the "Members" pub.

It was decided that upon surveying the environment, running simple Ethernet cable through the building would provide the least-invasive technique. I gathered a team to conduct the work, and as we were about to drill the first quarter-inch hole in the floorboard, a loud, shrill "Halt!" stopped us dead in our tracks. There stood a stern-looking MP who fervently informed us that no modification could be made to any royal property without the direct approval of the Queen. Years later, my brush with British royalty paid off, and an official declaration of permission to lay simple Ethernet cabling in Westminster Palace from Her Majesty, Queen Elizabeth II was delivered and work began.

E–Who? The List Continues to Grow

The European Union has admitted 10 new members, most of which come from the formerly communist East:

- Cyprus

continues...

---

2. *"Europeans Are Far from United on E-Security."* 23 July 2001, *www.evidian.com/pres.*

E-Who? The List Continues to Grow   Continued

- The Czech Republic
- Estonia
- Hungary
- Latvia
- Lithuania
- Malta
- Poland
- Slovakia
- Slovenia

From a cross-border security perspective, these newest EU inductees all carry cheap labor that is relatively untrained yet imbued with a strong work ethic. Legislation is generally weak. Infrastructure varies in both scope and reliability. Nevertheless, these nations will eventually become partnership-worthy, and some, such as the Czech Republic, can make for a potentially solid security collaborator even now.

For those of you who are already clutching a world atlas, we start this security expedition in Germany (the banking capital of Europe), working our way clockwise through France (the banking capital of Europe) and the United Kingdom (the banking capital of Europe). These three countries are bundled together because they account for more cross-border business in Europe and therefore deal with more cross-border global security concerns, and even they cannot decide on who does what to whom. From there, we move to Ireland, and then we sweep back across the English Channel to Belgium, home to the European Union (used to be the EC, or EEC, but now it is the EU—stay tuned!) capital, Brussels. Moving north again, we visit Russia and the Nordics, whose governments have facilitated unique ways of approaching security.

Our last stops move us south toward the Mediterranean and to Switzerland, another cross-border hub. We land in Spain and Italy to discuss these two language-centric trade routes that require unique cultural perspectives when creating a security strategy. We end our pilgrimage in central Europe to see how the new EU states in the east are experiencing tremendous growth and how, as these economies develop, significant security issues ensue.

A World of Different "Best Practices"

Did you know that 73 percent of Spanish small business companies update virus definitions on a weekly basis? Compare that to 51 percent of German companies and 39 percent of British companies and you can quickly discern that significant difference is a constant when it comes to best practices in Europe. Countries make the best use of global security technology when language is not an issue (read: virus definitions). Use professional, tech-savvy translators who deliver the best results in a timely fashion. Do not expect some staffer with free time to be as cost-effective or correct.[3]

On the Ground in Europe

Europe represents one of the most technologically savvy territories on the planet. The Internet is an extension of nearly every business throughout the continent. Connectivity among the general populace is high, and according to a recent EU report, more than two thirds of its citizens use a wireless phone.[4] Wired schools/ universities and electronic government continue to grow. Critical infrastructure (utilities and public works) is increasingly facilitated through the use of computer technology. Of course, with the advent of technological adoption there is an increased awareness and understood need for global corporate security.

Bigger Than ABBA: SMS

You probably know text mobile phone use is much higher in Europe than other regions such as the United States, where mobiles are termed *cell phones* or in Germany where they're called *handys*.

European mobiles usually come equipped with *Short Message Service* (SMS), which enables users to send and receive messages of up to 160 characters. More Europeans use SMS for instant corporate updates, which is unheard of in the United States. Does your security policy leverage SMS, or even allow for it?

---

3. Matthew Broersma. "Europe Wide Open to Virus Attacks: Concern Doesn't Translate into Company Action." *Techworld.* 1 April 2004.

4. Christina Okoli. "A Call to Arms." *The AnswerBank.* 28 July 2004.

Individual governments have responded, and as you will soon see, their foci are dependent upon the security emphases in respective countries. However, there are overall concerns on the European-wide agenda that have begun to receive attention by various European Union collectives. The EU Commission on Network and Information Security was established early in this century to enhance and promote great Member State security in the EU. It launched its own awareness campaign to foster cooperation between Member States as it relates to what it calls market-oriented standardization and certification of security. This led to a European Council resolution, passed in 2002, that acknowledged further steps were necessary for information security to be "addressed appropriately at the European level," something which had previously (and in many respects still has) proven unfeasible.[5] It paved the way for the commission to initiate a cybersecurity task force that "will enhance Member States' ability, individually and collectively, to respond to major network and information security problems." The commission has also prompted the European Parliament to issue an opinion that has "requested a European answer to the increasing security problem."[6]

Reactions of Member States have been disparate and not sufficiently coordinated to ensure an effective response to security problems. Due to the technical complexity of networks and information systems, the variety of products and services that are interconnected, and the huge number of private and public actors (you!) that bear their own responsibility, a consistent security response at Community level has not been developed yet. A particular problem has been the lack of interoperable security products and services, thereby jeopardizing the interoperability of the networks concerned. Equally, these characteristics have made the effective application of Community measures subject to rather complex technical analysis and understanding.

In 2003, the EU facilitated the creation of the *European Network and Information Security Agency* (ENISA). ENISA is a next-generation organization that works on draft legislation surrounding security, mediates cross-border disputes, cultivates security awareness among the public, and functions as a CERT. Looking forward, ENISA faces tough challenges because the stick of influence it wields is small. Yet to European and global corporations considering doing business in the EU, it can be extremely helpful.

---

5. *Commission of the European Communities Proposal for a Regulation of the European Parliament and of the Council Establishing the European Network and Information Security Agency. 11 February 2003. Page 3.*
6. *Ibid.*

Eavesdropping Happens—Get Used To It.

Governments aren't purely philanthropic as they help businesses navigate their laws and compliance issues. The oft-reported-on ECHELON project was designed and is coordinated by the United States and certain allies "to intercept ordinary communications throughout the global telecommunications networks." ECHELON is a cooperative service of the UK, the United States, Canada, Australia, and New Zealand. It monitors nonmilitary targets, such as governments, organizations, businesses, and individuals. The reported goal of the system is to intercept large quantities of communications and analyze the gathered data using sophisticated processing to identify and extract messages of interest. The ECHELON processing equipment searches through huge amounts of intercepted communications for keywords. Those keywords may contain concepts, names, locations, subjects, and individual personal data. Be aware that it could be put to use on you or your organization as you move abroad.[7]

Education and awareness throughout Europe is being fortified with an enhanced legal framework. In 2004, the *European Arrest Warrant* (EAW) took effect, which covers security breaches and computer crimes. At this writing only Belgium, Denmark, Finland, Ireland, Portugal, Spain, Sweden, and the UK have adopted it. Defined by the Framework Decision on the European Arrest as drafted by the EU Member States, the EAW enables these countries to extradite suspected terrorists and criminals with ease and the warrant will cover any offense that holds a sentence of one year or more. Importantly, this includes any computer-related crime.[8]

European Law Enforcement and Your Data

The Council of the EU is supporting demands from law enforcement officials for the recording and storage of all telecommunications data—including e-mails and Internet traffic—for up to seven years. The initiative, which would increase police powers to intercept communications data, is contained in a European Commission draft proposal on the processing of personal data in the electronic

continues...

---

7. *"ECHELON UKUSA Alliance." No date.*
8. *Council Framework Decision of 13 June 2002 on the European Arrest Warrant and the Surrender Procedures Between Member States. 13 June 2002.*

communications sector. If adopted, it would increase the data-retention responsibilities of network operators and Internet service providers. Ministers involved in the council have agreed to back the police on the issue.[9]

In the United Kingdom, the Regulation of Investigatory Powers Act (RIP) was enacted to give law enforcement agencies the power to view data communications. Privacy advocates claim it will go much further and would require changes to the EU data protection and privacy directives. "It seems police officers are overturning the data protection directive, turning the Internet into their spy system and bizarrely claiming that privacy protection decreases consumer confidence in using the system," said David Banisar, deputy director of Privacy International. "Europe has been at the forefront of protecting individual privacy. It would be tragic to turn it into a law enforcement directive." Since 1998, the European police enforcement group ENFOPOL has lobbied for authority to intercept Internet and wireless communications. ENFOPOL proposals have recently gone through the EU Justice and Home Affairs Council. This will help legitimate businesses in Europe and around the world.[10]

Computer security-incident response teams (CSIRTs) are blossoming throughout the continent. CSIRT teams typically have from 3 to 15 members. Most work closely with the Internet's academic side, protecting the computer networks of institutions and universities. Every country in the EU has at least one such team, as do many of the bigger private companies. CSIRTs raise awareness about threats and vulnerabilities surrounding insecure networks.

On the regulatory front, the EU has created a series of "directives" that represent its parliament's first steps toward continent-wide security and privacy laws. Dealing mainly with consumer protection and privacy, the EU parliament has built its regulations upon measures taken in 1997 within the telecommunications milieu. Its most recent, titled 2002/58/EC, has outlined privacy measures to be taken by Member States that "ensures the rights and freedoms of natural persons with regard to the processing of personal data, and in particular their right to privacy, in order to ensure the free flow of personal data, and in the Community."

---

9. *Ibid.*

10. *"Europe Considers Net Traffic, E-mail Archive." 17 May 2001. CNET. news.com.com.*

This was revised to deal with how companies handle specific parts of consumer information. When you collect from anybody, you have to let that person know how you collected it and what you did with it. Although it is jumpstarting European dialogue about the issue, this directive has few to no "teeth" and few are implementing it.

The EU directive on privacy says that any information you collect from anybody must be disclosed to that person and further, what you do with it must be disclosed to that person. This is a major issue for large, global companies because they must implement more complex data collection, protection and data management processes to comply with these regulations. For example, a company operating in the EU now has to inform each and every client before they use their data for purposes other than those for which it was originally intended. Recently, one issue related to the EU regulation became a discussion on the highest political level between the EU parliament, the U.S. government, and airline carriers. The EU parliament finally gave in to the request for passenger data to be transferred to the U.S. authorities because of political issues. Yet, the airline carriers are basically under violation of the EU data-protection directive. As long as no one cares and sues the businesses for invading their privacy, the data-protection measures to be taken are too complex and costly to be implemented.

—Stefan Weiss, Security Expert, Deloitte, Hamburg

Personal data processing systems that do not meet the *European Commission's Directive on Data Protection* (ECDDP) threatened to impede the flow of information between EU and U.S. organizations. So complementing the privacy directive is the EU's Safe Harbor law. To help U.S. companies continue their European business dealings, the U.S. Department of Commerce (with the European Commission) developed a "safe harbor" system that "allow(s) continuing data flows between the U.S. and the E.U. and ensure(s) privacy protection for E.U. citizens' personal information." Approved by the European Commission in 2000, the safe harbor principles essentially enable U.S. companies to do business in the EU by establishing an "adequate" level of privacy protection. In its simplest form, Safe Harbor prohibits trade between countries unless personal information can be "adequately protected" from start to finish —but *adequate* is never defined. At its best, it provides aid to countries attempting to navigate various European nations' privacy and data-protection laws with the least resistance and potential slowdown. However, one-year exemptions are easy to apply for, receive, and renew, so to date there is much transatlantic privacy ado about nothing.

U.S. organizations can comply with the Safe Harbor by either "self-regulating" using the seal program, using the "Standard Clause" to set up an interorganizational agreement, getting an exemption (a political process), getting covered under a local privacy law, or gaining each and every EU customer's consent (not likely).

No Safe Harbor?

Safe Harbor rules focus mostly on customer data protection, but be aware that in many countries there are also strong employee data controls in place. France, for instance, bars the transmission of French employee data across its borders. So do not plan on doing all your HR system backups in your American HQ, or you will be in clear violation.

The most significant new European-wide security effort is the European Convention on Cyber-Crime, which was first signed in 2001, and has been ratified by the majority of old and new European countries in recent years. Its intent has been to pursue a common criminal policy on cybercrime in Europe, and to assist in managing some of the cross-border issues from the member countries. Title 1 relates to "Offences against the confidentiality, integrity and availability of computer data and systems." Title 2 relates to "Computer-Related Offences." Title 3 relates to "Content-Related Offences." Title 4 relates to "Offences Related to Infringements of Copyright and Related Rights," and Title 5 relates to "Ancillary Liability and Sanctions," which includes important aspects of corporate liability. As a convention and not a law, it compels convention countries to enact laws that address these issues, but it is not a law in itself. However, as a method of understanding where "Europe" comes down on computer security issues, it is a must read.

Along with regulations, the EU's standardization of business practices is slowly leading to surface homogeneity—again, this masquerade shouldn't prompt delusions of sameness. It is incumbent on outsiders in any one of these environments to consider why they are laying down roots in a new country and then actually do so only by partnering with someone on the ground in those countries.

Corporate Governance, Security, and the EU

This newest security driver in Europe has quickly risen to the level of fixation among senior management, board, and CxO types. World markets have surged and plunged in the past five years. In the aftermath, we have all gazed upon the exposed underbelly of paper empires.

Emerging governance regulations have us asking the same old security questions: Who creates the information, who processes it, where is it stored, and how does it get there? Pressure rests on the executive leadership of companies to fully understand and attest to the accuracy of their information lifeblood. So these same old questions take on a fresh significance. Executives can no longer attempt to shirk or veil answers. Information swept under the rug will be subject to the Hoover. Again, using the international term "hoover" is meant to be an easy device to remind the reader that they are part of a big world out there. I'd like to keep it, but if you hate it or want to explain it, I'll bow to your experience.

Many among us know who is next, and that has led to a quick reevaluation of business practices in an attempt to right wrongs that save ourselves, restore investor confidence, or both. Chapter 11, "The Americas," analyzes Sarbanes-Oxley. However, in EMEA, there are several corporate governance initiatives that have or will become law. Each of these will impact the way you manage your global security when it passes a European border. Although it is an age-old concept, it has a bright new light shining on it, and therefore a standardized "corporate governance" definition is rare. Here is an overview pulled from a variety of organizations and laws across the region:

Corporate Governance relates to the internal means by which corporations are operated and controlled. While governments play a central role in shaping the legal, institutional and regulatory climate within which individual corporate governance systems are developed, the main responsibility lies with the private sector.

—Organisation for Economic Cooperation and Development (OECD)

Corporate governance describes the legal and factual regulatory framework for managing and supervising a company.

—Germany

Corporate governance is the system by which companies are directed and controlled.

—United Kingdom

A code of conduct for those associated with the company—in particular, executives, Supervisory Board members and investors—consisting of a set of rules for sound management and proper supervision and for a division of duties and responsibilities and powers affecting the satisfactory balance of influence of all the stakeholders.

—The Netherlands

Stakeholders and their commensurate priorities vary. Yet corporate-wide issues surrounding risk management, power and control, auditor credibility, or top-management liability are undergoing relentless inspection as these laws/guidelines are authored and put in play. They are sourced from different bodies that range from investor groups and governments to industry organizations and ad hoc committees. The legal grounding of these regulations comes through nearly as diverse means: via law, from voluntary compliance pressures, or as a part of a "comply or explain" cycle. Importantly, corporate governance laws are a unique beast because there are instances where a single mandate may not be fully mandatory. As we look at corporate governance country by country, it is first helpful to examine what has happened within the EU. Here, the combined efforts of bodies such as the IMF, OECD, and other organizations have yielded guidelines and principles (outlined in the appendix) that have begun to coalesce and surface in European Commission thinking. In turn, the EC has drafted two significant reports worth mentioning:

- **The Commission's Action Plan**

  Developed as a way to strengthen shareholders rights, the Action Plan "reinforces protection for employees and creditors and increases efficiency and competitiveness." It hopes to "ensure adequate coordination of national CG codes without implementing a European CG Code. Though several laws are planned."[11]

- **The 10 Audit Priorities**

  Created to "improve and harmonise the quality of statutory audit within the EU," the priorities seek to initiate a "possible change of law mainly covering the education, approval and registration of persons who can be approved by Member State authorities to perform audits."[12]

---

11. *"Company Law and Corporate Governance: Commission Presents Action Plan." European Commission Online Pressroom. 21 May 2003.*

12. *"Audit of Company Accounts: Commission Sets Out Ten Priorities to Improve Quality and Protect Investors." European Commission Online Pressroom. 21 May 2003.*

Just as the U.S.'s new governance law, Sarbanes-Oxley, has its section 404, which directly impacts the security of all corporate information as it is processed, transported, or stored, each of the individual European countries has enacted or will enact law in this same area. You, your lawyers, your financial officers, your auditors, and your CSOs must study each of these laws as they evolve, mature, and are enforced. Links to each of these are detailed in the appendix, "Local Security Resources by Country."

Even as the EU seeks ways to standardize corporate governance through the introduction of legislative dialogue, respective European countries are drafting guidelines and laws.

Germany, France, and the United Kingdom

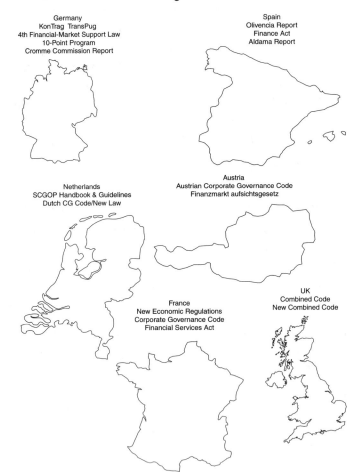

Figure 9-3 Key corporate governance rules by country.

This north-central section of Europe provides an example of how business practices are becoming more similar in the EU while maintaining a unique, geographic sensibility upon which history has made indelible marks. When we begin examining what these countries value in terms of information security, national characteristics emerge. Germany, rational and purposeful, combines rigor with thoroughness in the way it approaches and legislates security. France is much more individually focused in its security posture and places a high premium on personal protection and freedom. The UK, an island unto itself, has taken its lead from strong government and university programs.

Germany/Deutschland (.DE)

Figure 9-4 Germany

MSI = 73

Pros: Security-friendly, skilled talent pool, strong infrastructure, cross-border savvy

Cons: Cultural and legal nuances significant, security often second priority, highly fragmented business environment

Germany is both good at and comfortable with global corporate security. Its volume of cross-border business and corporate multinational presence brings with it a top-quality security talent pool. The country is a noteworthy purchasing market that is built on strong infrastructure, and it has everything you would expect of a trading partner. Nevertheless, when entering Germany, caution is advised, and creating a positive security experience necessitates that you be aware of the country's corporate interpretations of laws, regulations, and contracts. Contract law supersedes legislation and other directives when dealing with security, and you must realize that often security is prioritized below the overall success of the company and must be managed appropriately.

On Holiday

Europe's "August" holiday can be anywhere between mid-July and mid-September. In general, the farther north you are, the earlier the month-long holiday starts. Without proper scheduling, this can potentially mean *two months* of downtime. That might be okay in accounting, but it is disastrous in security!

Straightforward cultural issues complicate any German corporate security mix. A sometimes-stereotypical (yet usually beneficial) obsession with rules plays out differently when moving into this federation's respective states and towns. The government is decidedly employee oriented, layoffs are unheard of, and, usually, hires are for life. This strong work-life balance also necessitates calibrating the German calendar, filled with a host of different holidays, with your global security calendar.

On the Ground

I have lived in Germany twice—once in the mid-1980s and then again in the early twenty-first century. Both times, I based myself out of Frankfurt on the Main River. I make this distinction because upon reunification, there are two Frankfurts in Germany. Frankfurt on the Main (a/M) sits on the western side and contains most of the international banks. To wit, it is often called Bankfurt, or MainHatten. Frankfurt on the Oder River (a/O) is on the eastern side, and is lovely, pastoral— the fairytale Germany you may have read about as a child. Frankfurt a/M is a bustling financial nerve center and a crossroads of Europe. Few know there is a great town that lies beyond its famous airport.

During my two professional stints in the country, its people-empowering social framework came into play with interesting ramifications. Near the beginning of my first tenure my administrative assistant stopped by my office and informed me quite directly of her peculiar need: "I want to get pregnant, and I need your help." Needless to say, I was intrigued. I asked her to go on.

She reemphasized her call for help, claiming once more that I was the person she needed. The story then took a turn. She and her boyfriend needed time at a resort to unwind so that they might conceive. I was shocked as she calmly (and with a straight face) explained to me the German *Kur* or spa culture. Through it, the state paid her expenses for extended convalescence at a spa of her choice, and in this case, she had already picked the Bodensee. In turn, my organization was responsible for approving her paid leave. I had no choice. We allowed her to take 30 days beyond her annual, government-mandated month of vacation.

This anecdote reflects a form of socialism that directs corporate guarantees of human well-being. It is this type of human resource issue you will confront when you arrive in Germany, and it is just one of the pressures placed on corporations and their top executives: Germany combines strong socialist underpinnings with some of the most stringent CxO accountability legislation in the world. The government's "10-Point Program" increases top-management's liability for the success or failure of the business. Reputations and careers are on the line every day. This is why German executives view global corporate security in such efficiency-based, systems-availability terms, carving out for security a secondary, yet potent niche.

Once you hire somebody in Germany, forget about it. It's for their lifetime and you will take care of them and their families forever.

—Jean-Pierre Garitte, CIA, CISA, CCSA, Partner, Deloitte, Antwerp

Similar philosophies are reflected in larger German companies such as Deutsche Telekom, Siemens, and DaimlerChrysler, all of which navigate myriad cross-border issues and in doing so have adopted strong business-continuity strategies and systems to make sure their clients and employees have uninterrupted access via technology. Ask the typical German business owner what they invested in the past 10 to 15 years, and they would probably say, "mechanisms that keep our business up and running." Somewhere, they have experienced downtime and other obstacles that hamper operations. This prompts swift measures required to shore up the business before it gets out of hand and they lose their company.

Germans Do Text Messaging

In 2004, the Global System for Mobile Communication announced that Germans were the world's foremost text message senders, dispatching a whopping 200 million messages a day, nearly three times as many as the Finns (75m) or Britons (69m).[13]

During its maturation, German corporate security has shifted from the technology group's domain into areas of quality control and quality assurance. Some corporations have even reconfigured roles, placing security under the CFO rather than the CTO. According to Hamburg-based Stefan Weiss, "German businesses have always been more skeptical and thoughtful, adopting new security technology more slowly and strategically. The performance of new technology is typically being tested in length and the return for every investment is being calculated in detail before implementation—so security falling into the CFO's hands is a logical step."

Messe Mess

Germany is famous for its tradeshows (fairs) held at their various *messe*. You have probably heard of the venerable CeBit show in Hanover. However, CeBit—huge and international—is not a good place to see German security on display. Instead, head to the annual SYSTEMS show for the best of local, federal, and governmental security that is truly German.

Key Regulations

Germany's potent laws, reports, and regulations must be examined by anyone doing business there. Remember, they are augmented by uncommonly comprehensive business contracts that typically contain a majority of both security and managerial liability language between companies or between a company and senior management. Here are ones with which you should be familiar:

---

13. *"UK Exceeds 2 Billion Text Messages in March." Pierz Group Newsletter. 25 April 2004.*

- **The KonTraG (1998: Law)**

  Dealing with the responsibility of the business owner for his or her business, the KonTraG mandates that owners must do everything in their power to manage the business in a risk-averse way.

- **The TransPuG (2002: Law)**

  By correlating accounting standards and company management/control standards to state-of-the-art international criterion, the TransPuG tightens accounting standards, risk management responsibility, and auditor accountability.

- **The 4th Financial-Market Support Law (2002: Law)**

  With a focus on shielding shareholders while developing better market opportunities of capital market participants, the 4th Law seeks to regulate the adjustment of share prices and financial analyst liability while making transparent a company's directors' dealings.

- **The Cromme Commission Report (2003: Guidelines)**

  A government-originated commission that was appointed by Germany's justice minister, the Cromme Report summarizes how increased transparency and liability can improve company performance, competitiveness, and access to capital.

- **The Datenschutz (1994: Law)**

  This German data-protection act protects employee and consumer information. This should be examined in concert with the EU privacy directive because implementing security that deals with data becomes extremely complex when the two intersect.

Bundsebar!

Germany's eGovernment initiative—bundonline2005.de—is set to go online (you guessed it) in 2005. It will house more than 100 authorities and offices that deliver 450+ services to the populace. This is one in a series of European governments that is going virtual and sparking extensive, local security debate.

When considering German regulations, notice that the country's federalist framework is formed by 16 states. National law is intertwined with state-based laws and ministries. (You can find more information about such in the appendix.)

Legislation is fortified by the country's ministry of information security known as the *Bundesamt für Sicherheit in der Informationstechnik* (BSI). The BSI creates countrywide guidelines and standards for corporate security.

Best Practices

As a rule, German-headquartered global businesses follow ISO 17799 as their horizontal best standard practice of corporate security. If more than 50 percent of their business remains in Germany, corporations will generally opt for the BSI-issued IT Grundschutz. IT Grundschutz is a more detailed version of ISO 17799, and Germans argue over which came first—Grundschutz or the British BS 7799. They see theirs as the more stringent, realistic approach to a baseline. It is heavily focused on infrastructure and architecture. A 2003 update to the IT Grundschutz accounted for more aggressive outsourcing of security operations.

Tailoring for Germany

Germany's lack of a pure business center and its scattered populace may mean that you have a country-wide presence requiring an accordingly tailored security strategy.

On the industry front, recent buzz about creating vertical standards emerged for specific sectors, but little has materialized. The financial services and manufacturing sectors have shared information among themselves. In the former, they pool expertise especially among larger financial institutions while following Basel II to the letter. (For more on Basel II, visit Switzerland in Chapter 9, "Europe").

BSI vs. BSI

Think you know your BSI? Did you realize there were two? The German BSI, detailed here, focuses on German-wide security standards. In the UK, the British Standards Institute, which describes itself as "the national standards body of the UK, and among the world's leading providers of standards and standards products."[14]

---

14. *"About the BSI Group." n.d. www.bsi-global.com/News.*

Predictably, security is portrayed as a natural extension of business and simply a function of good management. This reasonableness combines with a strong sense of duty and accountability that are written into law and contracts. They export this sensibility to other countries, particularly to places such as India where they have invested mightily and hold sway.

When doing business in Germany, find a local (state-specific) data protection officer. For each state in Germany and at the federal level, there are data-protection contacts. They will help you in informing you about important legislation and support you in setting up the necessary requirements. Of course, be aware of the EU directives and legislation regardless of where you do business in the EU. In fact, if you take the EU directive, the strongest legislation on data protection that exist today, as your yardstick to go by, you will basically comply with data-protection legislation around the world. That is what most multinational companies do.

—*Stefan Weiss, Security Expert, Deloitte, Hamburg*

In nearly every country we visit, security incidents will have catalyzed some level of security implementation. Germany is no exception. Stefan Weiss confirmed that incidents hit the papers occasionally, but he would not characterize these events as moving industries to adopt stronger security postures as much as a rational understanding of the accountability and expectations placed upon senior management.

Final German Thoughts

You can succeed with your security operations in Germany. You will find a vast amount of skilled human resources, many strong university programs focusing on security, a strong understanding of the local German security standards and requirements, and a bilingual populace. Hire in a specific city, because most Germans would rather commute three hours than relocate, and note that each city and state has its own business rhythm that will affect security. When hiring security personnel in Germany, you will find some of the best at the smaller firms. This is in recognition of its federalist nature, because firms in one city have trouble winning business in another city, and leads to smaller-sized companies.

The skilled resources come at a price. Employees are hired for a long time. Carefully choose employees. Expect longer ramp-up periods for your projects, and get used to the fact that you will be required to "carry" some existing employees who will need to be completely retrained. This not only costs time, but it could also sacrifice security if the training lacks a cultural awareness or is done inappropriately. The majority of the actual work involved in carrying out a security plan will be done in the German language. It is a mistake to expect German staff to be functional in English or French, and security rules are not the place for a simple mistranslation. Have true bilingual leadership in place to avoid staff-level mix-ups.

Again, the German calendar also takes some getting used to. Staff holidays tend to coincide with school downtime, such as winter holiday, ski holiday, all religious holidays, spring holiday, and of course, the European mainstay of August off. Finally, know which state your offices are in, because they celebrate many holidays specific to regions. Hesse (where Frankfurt a/M is) observes some holidays not traditionally followed in Bavaria (home to Munich), and vice versa. These staff accommodations are a good trade-off for their business infrastructure, which is among the best in the world, with information highways the equal of the famed Autobahn system. Power and communications backbones are equally solid.

Germany's legal system is reliable (although some have complained that it too often favors the German side, I have not found it to be a problem) and leans toward over-regulation. For instance, in my German hometown we were limited to two backyard barbecues per month, with a maximum of six per year. This is important to note for your compliance with security rules, because even as your neighbor will turn you in for that third luau, your employees or competitors will blow the whistle on your company's security miscues. Everyone looks after everyone else's compliance (even crossing against a crosswalk light will get you a scolding from anyone else there), so do not expect to get away with skirting any local laws. When dovetailed with the accountability premise in Germany, such legalism has an upside: You can bank on contract law.

France (.FR)

France
MSI=71

Figure 9-5 France

MSI = 71

Pros: Strong partner (especially in banking and consumer products), well-trained security personnel

Cons: Legal system skews nationalistic, infrastructure differs regionally, reactive tendencies

Like Germany, France has proven itself a perennially strong global security partner for multinational companies. Banking and consumer products stand out as stronger sectors, and this mirrors the country's corporate strengths. In France, it is crucial to leverage the working infrastructure, all of which resides almost exclusively in Paris. Eclipse its metropolitan boundaries, and it can become hit or miss. France's legal system holds nationalistic tendencies, and this needs to be monitored if you are establishing a presence there. Also be on guard for any monitoring that may be trained upon you. You may be familiar with the 1993 account of French agents bugging first-class seats on Air France to unearth hush-hush business conversation. The next year, a study by Richard Heffernan and Dan T. Smartwood exposed "a French intelligence plan to target 49 American defense firms."[15]

Corporate Espionage

France's escrow rule has required that companies give private key encryption to a *trusted third party* (TTP) that has the blessing of the French government. In addition, using more than 40 bits of encryption data must by preceded by direct government authorization. Fishy? Yes, but the French are not the only ones engaged in government assistance to corporations for national interests. As previously mentioned, The United States and the UK have allegedly collaborated on ECHELON, an eavesdropping system that's a popular story recycled among journalists. It now has coverage of an array of countries throughout the world, including France. ECHELON's existence has become significant enough that the European Parliament has drafted a report that sets in motion a resolution that will adequately protect its citizenry and corporate sector against such intelligence gathering.[16] For more on Echelon, turn to Chapter 11, "The Americas."

The security workforce is well trained, but culturally a number of factors make finding a partner imperative. Although English is the language of business, French is the language of respect and productivity. Parisian business differs from the outlying countryside and other metropolitan areas. The workforce has often taken labor matters into its own hands, and routine strikes directly affect business continuity and security. Engage a French connection who can navigate these issues.

On the Ground

"Liberté, Equalité, and Fraternité" has served as a national motto since the country's third republic, and this ideal courses deeply within the French psyche. Even the creation of France's CNIL—the *Commission National de l'Informthatique et des Libertes* (the Committee for Information Technology and Freedoms)—includes an article in its founding tableau that reads, "Information technology must be avail-

---

15. *Bill Day. "The spying Game: Staying Competitive Takes More Than Tracking Competitors' Products and Prices." Business Record. 17 July 1995.*

16. *"Report on the existence of a global system for the interception of private and commercial communications (ECHELON interception system) (2001/20987(INI)). European Parliament Session Document. 11 July 2001.*

able to each citizen. Its development must take place within a context of international cooperation. It must not infringe against human identity, human rights, private life, individual or public freedoms."[17] France especially values the rights of its workforce, perhaps more dearly than any other nation in the world. Although this has led to significant freedom of expression—aforementioned weekly strikes and peaceful demonstrations—it has also hampered the economy's growth, and you may find it problematic for your security.

French business culture is divided into two camps: those in Paris and those who are not. The countryside's business community would almost prefer dealing with foreigners than Parisians, but Paris is where the action is, making it tough to go elsewhere even if it is made attractive and correctly marketed.

Sophi-Antipolis demonstrates such an instance where French businesspeople and local politicians made a bold move to locate a business complex outside Paris and near the nation's coast resort city of Nice... to mixed results. The idea? Bring in the major technology players from throughout the world and house them near St. Tropez and Cannes so their teams could work and play hard. IBM and HP moved into the complex, and soon more than 50,000 new residents were pouring into the region. Now an outpost in a lovely region with non-French multinational neighbors, it is not Paris, so it is not where the French do business. Consider this issue as you think about where and why you house your operations in France.

Key Regulations

French corporate security regulation is generally guided by EU directives and the Safe Harbor law. Indigenous privacy and data-protection laws are some of the oldest in recent history. In 1978, the country passed the Act on Data Processing Files and Individual Liberties (simply known as "the act").[18]

I had a Frenchman once tell me, "The problem with the Internet is that it represents the second U.S. invasion of Europe." He was alluding to World War II as the first invasion. "If we could mandate a quota for surfing for the inclusion of French content, much like we do for TV and radio, it could be workable, but as of now, it's killing our culture."

—Stephen Rose, Security Expert, PriceWaterhouseCoopers, Washington D.C.

---

17. *Commission Nationale de l'Informatique et des Libertes. n.d. www.cnil.fr.*
18. *Charles Franklin. Business Guide to Privacy and Data Protection Legislation. (New York: ICC Publishing, Inc., 1996). n.p.*

The act created the CNIL. This independent agency keeps a close eye on data processing in the country and works in an advisory and administrative capacity for the government and the judicial system. The CNIL also informs citizens about their rights and duties related to the processing of personal data. It testifies annually before the president and parliament on its duties and publishes periodic reports. The act offers guidelines for data processing, protects personal identity and freedom, and ensures privacy. It applies to both the public and private sectors. Pertaining to computers, personal data files, and the rights of citizens, breaching this law is punishable by up to three years in prison and a fine of up to €45,000, even in cases of negligence.[19] This makes it one of the few European cyberlaws with teeth!

Financial dealings have also risen in significance. France's *Insitut de l'Audit Internel-France* (IFACI) has put together a task force that includes chief audit executives among France's publicly held players to study a draft law on financial safety, which will ultimately become the French Sarbanes-Oxley. It places special focus on how internal auditing assists the CEO in creating a given organization's report on internal control.

Best Practices

France's recognition of laws and standards—domestic and EU driven—its high degree of professionalism, and its steadfast following of national regulations make it a better-than-average place to do your security business. Again, the French legal system is at times exploited for national advantage, but it is clear and rooted in centuries of practice. You will find skilled players in big business, and there is no shortage of talent thanks to fine local universities.

Remember culture. Artificial business ghettos such as Sophi-Antipolis, although attractive from afar, will be a more difficult place to locate personnel than in Paris. Almost all security business will need to be conducted in French by the French. Expect to be taken to lunch if you fly in, but do not expect to be taken seriously. Employ locals from other large companies rather than small shops. Know that the French will be ambivalent about other EU citizens working alongside them, and they abhor the American policies that Americans represent.

People with French government experience can also prove to be a big help. Do not anticipate foreign rules or regulations to get more than a passing shrug—most are irrelevant. If you are trying to implement your corporate security policy, you

---

19. *Ibid.*

will do well to "translate, not transliterate." Put it into terms that make sense locally. Understand that because the French do not do fire drills, they will not automatically comply with your disaster-recovery testing schedule either. (You might not find out about this until you ask.)

Technologically, cutting-edge hardware and software can be found in most offices here. Communications systems are sufficient, but just as the Parisian roads are often clogged, so too are the country's networks. Use SMS for real-time communications, and to do that, ensure that you have everyone's mobile numbers directly linked into your security-notification systems.

Bear in mind that France is slower than most at adopting security technologies. Translating threats for C-level executives is the best way to ensure that such adoption takes place.

—Mikaela Cavarec, Security Expert, Symantec, Paris

Many of the more expensive (read American and British) security services are being put off until some future when money is not a problem. That leaves some French firms and divisions at a greater risk in unnecessary ways; but just as it took the Montparnasse Tower to catch fire before a national fire drill regimen could exist, many companies here will wait (and ultimately pay) for reactive security.

French Final Thoughts

Look at France as yet another security-savvy nation that works more for you than against you. However, working securely can be a tough sell. Remaining vigilant while taking care to understand regulations that lean France-ward and a business undercurrent that runs nationalistic can make a careful placement in France possible. Prepare for labor strife that could affect you negatively and deploy French professionals to assist you. Then uncork a Bordeaux and hope for the best.

The United Kingdom (.UK)

United Kingdom
MSI=75

Figure 9-6 The United Kingdom

MSI = 75

Pros: Easy to work with, top personnel and technology, strong and stable government

Cons: United States synergies overrated, not a steppingstone to Europe, you can pay the price for oft-compulsory compliance with UK-specific laws

Typically thought of as the optimal European partner for American business, several factors need to be understood before jumping onto the British Isle with both feet. It is in many cases, and certainly when it comes to corporate security, still considered very separate from continental Europe. Its great security knowledge reflected in top security staff and top security technologies work very well in-country, but they do not export nearly as well as many Americans tend to believe (this despite the fact they involve themselves in collaborative security measures with the EU, including recognition of the European Arrest Warrant that covers a host of security-relevant crimes).

Other considerations should be factored into any decision to settle in the UK. Its stable and powerful government sector leads the country's security purchasing and drives much of its security industry. ECHELON was codeveloped here and remains a factor if you decide this is the place you will settle. The country's strong legal system dates back centuries. Even though its larger cities are a target when it comes to both domestic and international terrorism, it has a fine infrastructure and supports well the companies working there.

Security Breaches in the UK

The Department of Trade and Industry conducts an annual Information Security Breaches Survey.[20] The 2004 version found the following:

- 74% of all businesses (94% of large companies) had a security incident in the last year; Malicious incidents (such as viruses, unauthorized access, misuse of systems, fraud and theft) have risen dramatically. 68% of companies (and 91% of large ones) suffered at least one such incident in the past year, up from 44% in the 2002 survey and just 24% in 2000. Virus infection and inappropriate usage of systems by staff were the cause of most incidents, with the former resulting in the greatest number of serious breaches.

- The average UK business now has roughly one security incident a month, and larger ones around one a week.

- The average cost of an organization's most serious security incident was around £10,000 (or £120,000 for large companies). The impact on availability was by far the biggest contributor to this cost, with some organizations suffering a major disruption to their operations for more than a month.

- 75% of respondents rated security as a high or very high priority for their top management or the board. More companies than ever have a security policy in place; however, many businesses do not fully appreciate the risks they are running. Three quarters of companies are confident that their technical security processes are sufficient to prevent or detect all significant security breaches. However, less than half of these businesses have robust security controls in place, so this confidence is likely to be misplaced.

continues...

---

20. *"Information Security Breaches Survey 2004." PriceWaterhouseCoopers and DTI. 27 April 2004.*

Security Breaches in the UK   Continued

- There is a clear skills gap. Only 12% of respondents were aware of the contents of the internationally recognized standard for information security, BS 7799. Only one in ten companies have staff with formal information security qualifications.

- Although spending on information security has increased, it is still relatively low and seen as a cost rather than investment. Companies spend an average of 3% of their IT budget on security compared with 2% in 2002, still well below a reasonable 5% to 10% benchmark level. Less than half of all businesses ever evaluate their *return on investment* (ROI) on security spend, almost no change from two years ago.

The UK possesses unique security and privacy laws. Account for them even if you merely land there or your data passes through. New laws and regulations that have recently emerged will afford you some degree of protection. Stay on top of it—often compliance requires annual renewals, and noncompliance can lead to heavy fines or full-fledged shutdowns.

Overall, the UK is a very easy place for American companies to work. However, if your end game is on the continent, it is certainly not the only country in Europe with whom you should be working. Instead, you must determine which country on that side of the channel can most effectively deliver security that is well received across borders and that can assemble a more universally accepted strategic approach.

On the Ground

The United Kingdom has become a literal island and, of late, has taken its business cues from the United States. It continues to be a post-colonial center, drawing upon world citizens who reside and work there. Sociologically, there is what London-based security expert Ryan Rubin has called a "strong blame culture. Security professionals face intense pressures. If something goes wrong, the guy who made the mistake is going to get fired." It fosters conservative decisions and a late-adopter mindset, which has led to significantly more secure corporate environments. It is also a boon to third-party security providers who capitalize on companies seeking to outsource their strategies and any potential blame.

Madonna Loses Truth or Dare

In 2004, the UK's *Sun* reported that Madonna attempted to "trick" fans who downloaded music from Madonna.com without paying. The prank went awry when a hacker found her out. The complete 11-track set from her American Life recording was posted as available for download. However, when the files were played back, listeners only heard the Material Diva's voice saying, "What the f*** do you think you are doing?" *Sun* reporter Simon Wheeler recounted that "one angry computer buff got revenge by hacking into the Web site and adding his own message, saying: 'This is what the f*** I think I'm doing.'" The online tagger forced the site to shut down while the virtual graffiti was removed.[21]

Don't Be Like a Virgin

Don't read too much into stories like this that are publicity driven. The phrase "any publicity is good publicity" is ever-present.

When I came to the UK from South Africa, I noticed two things. The weather was lousy, and I couldn't believe the banking technology! It was four years behind South Africa. Yet it was also much less vulnerable from a security perspective, and that's one of the great lessons I've learned about the British psyche: Their caution has traditionally served them well.

—Ryan Rubin, Security Expert, London

In 2004, the UK's *Register* reported that call center staff for a UK bank in India had received bribe offers from Indian organized crime who promised a year's wages in exchange for financial and credit card details from the institution. Engineers who held unrestricted access to the networks they serviced were primary targets because their annual salary topped out at approximately £4,000. The government and business sector are reevaluating these relationships as outsourcing on the whole undergoes increased global scrutiny.[22]

---

21. *Simon Wheeler. "Madonna Anti-Download Prank Backfires." 22 April 2003. www.thesun.co.uk/article.*
22. *John Oates. "Indian Call Centres Pose Security Risk." 5 April 2004. www.theregister.co.uk.*

Beware the nuance of London's commute. It is usually at least an hour, so people like to work efficiently and then get on with family or social life. This requires a "VPN mentality." Your security scheme must leverage broadband to the home and GSM mobile technology. It will increase your productivity but need not raise your risk, and it leads to a main feature of British social and business life—the pub. I have often been in London and in the midst of discussing a key issue in a meeting when an executive will suddenly suggest, "Let's talk about this after work at the pub." Although tea may spring to mind as a daily, interfering ritual, it is not as faithfully followed in recent generations. Much of informal business takes place in pub settings, and all-hours alcohol consumption is allowed. Even lunch will be served with a beer—something absolutely taboo in some regions of the world.

International standards are another arena wherein the UK continues to assert global influence. The British Standards Institute pioneered BS 7799, which became the ultimate security baseline and was adopted internationally, essentially becoming ISO 17799. The ISO version omits one section of the BS 7799 that underscores how security strategies should be organized within an overall information security management system. Standards such as BS 7799 make certain that the UK will remain a significant figure on the global corporate security stage.

On the European front, the country definitely acts independent of the EU, but a local referendum issue by Prime Minister Tony Blair will more closely link the UK to the EU through currency and participation. Look for eventual integration with continental standards such as the euro, but expect that the security standards to be followed in Great Britain to be very British for a long time.

Key Regulations

A reputation for following U.S. influence has been re-ignited in the era of Sarbanes-Oxley, which is driving a lot of activity on a host of business fronts, including security. The country's Financial Services Authority, an independent body that regulates the financial services industry in the UK, describes its aim as "maintain[ing] efficient, orderly, and clean financial markets and helping retail consumers achieve a fair deal." Increasingly the FSA is dealing with issues of money laundering and terrorism related to consumer data. The EUDDP's Safe Harbor law—EU legislation that heavily regulates the shielding of personal information as it passes through different countries—applies in the UK. Two other British-based laws/directives of note are the following:

- **UK Data Protection Act (1998)**

  Companies that process information about individuals must do so in a responsible manner. They must also provide a guarantee that if they use consumer information for marketing and other purposes, they will receive consumer permission to do so.[23]

- **New Combined Code (2003: Guidelines)**

  This Financial Reporting Council guideline, based on the initial code that was developed in 1998, attempts to outline board structure, independence levels of senior management, control and risk management considerations, financial reporting, and internal/external audit practices.[24]

Best Practices

Although caution has generally prevailed in the adoption of technology and its commensurate security, the UK is starting to implement certain technologies more quickly. The laggard adoption curve has begun to diminish. Wireless is a prime example. Increasingly, security services are falling upon third parties in this country as wireless technology rapidly grows throughout the nation.

If you're going to do business in the UK, check to see if you need to apply with the FSA. If you do, you'll have to demonstrate your own best practices in a number of areas including security policy, data protection, disaster recovery, and business continuity. If approved, you'll receive a license to do business.

When on the ground in the UK, it's extremely helpful to list a larger third-party consultant and/or lawyer than going directly to the FSA yourself. Also, think carefully where you'll be located. There is much cheaper land in areas such as Manchester, Cardiff, and Birmingham, yet think about where your customers are or what size data center you might need.

—Ryan Rubin, Senior Manager, Deloitte UK, London

Threats are driving security practice, as well. Although Slammer and MyDoom did not directly affect true operational security (but a nuisance? yes), their impact on organizational and systems availability has drawn new attention to patch

---

23. *"Data Protection Act 1998." Her Majesty's Stationary Office. 1998.*
24. *"The New Combined Code on Corporate Governance." The Financial Services Authority. 23 July 2003.*

management and other security processes. Moreover "phishing," that methodology whereby hackers set up branded Web sites that look authentic in order to gain personal information of visitors, is a growing threat in the UK, and incidents are driving public awareness.

When practicing security, history illustrates that the British do not necessarily need to be in the spotlight (unlike Americans). In World War II, Britain very quietly developed advanced security technology that broke codes of the German forces. When revealed years later, it wasn't made into a big issue by the people involved. This same stealth applies to the quiet application of corporate security, with the focus fixed on the best solution that is deployed anonymously and via BS 7799. It is a fact recently fortified by the formation of the UK's own *National Infrastructure Security Co-ordination Centre* (NISCC). Created to evaluate the security readiness of companies in the UK, it can be an indispensable source, because NISCC will actually send a team out to test your security posture free of charge. I strongly recommend that companies doing business in the UK avail themselves of these top-flight people and their services.

British security personnel are unsurpassed and can be drawn from multiple sources, including Her Majesty's Government, a stellar university system, from large companies, and throughout smaller consultancies. Because most American firms mistakenly use the UK as their leverage point for all Europe, there are many security outlets with quality people available for hire. Beware that although they will serve you well in the UK and many of Her Majesty's former subjects such as India, they are as welcome on the continent of Europe as an American (read: when spending money only). England is a big market unto itself and carries the requisite infrastructure for security. Scotland has some great tech areas (Silicon Glen, between Edinburgh and Glasgow), and Northern Ireland maintains good security growth potential, but it arrives with higher risk factors.

Beyond personnel, London has some of the best computer security gatherings and periodicals anywhere in the world. This makes it easy to stay current on local resources, including people, technology, partners, and events. Britain's www.silicon.com will keep you abreast of these for free and throw in a bit of England tabloid-style gossip to ensure that you know they're British!

Technologically, even though you will find as many smart card readers in the UK as in other European countries, do not expect a national smart card anytime soon. Most British subjects equate any type of national ID card with war preparations, and so they have constantly rejected any call for one. But look for this to change as pressures to develop cost-saving eGovernment systems gain ground.

Constant Vigilance Revisited

Here's yet another need for global constant vigilance. Did you know that UK firms could be breaking Sarbanes-Oxley regulations by failing to track and archive *instant messaging* (IM) conversations among workers? According to the *Register Newsletter*, just 22 percent of mid-sized to large UK corporations monitor IM and only 9 percent claim to archive IM data—this could "run-afoul" of Sarbanes, which continues to influence countries outside the United States at a rapid pace. Think back to my example about the little company that let you manage your instant messages. With a constant vigilance program in place, you will be better able to keep pace with global security requirements.

Public awareness of security measures isn't in sync with the country's smart card sensitivities. An annual experiment surrounding one security tradeshow amply demonstrates as much. The show's staff members stand with clipboards at Tube (American = subway) stops near the "City," which is London's financial center. Well dressed and cheery, they inform Tube riders that they are doing a survey, and promptly request inappropriate forms of personal information, including passwords to critical Internet and intranet accessibility. More often than not, they respondents tell all. In the experiment's first year, show staffers simply asked for the information. Then the exchange became more sophisticated. In year two, a cheap pen was offered. In 2004, riders were lured using a chocolate bar. Of course, this story isn't revealed to make an example of the British—it simply illustrates that they can have fun with their security!

The British Final Thoughts

Often mistaken as the ideal European ally, the UK makes for an easy—if separated—partner in global corporate security. Despite its passwords-for-chocolate populace (it would take less than chocolate in the United States, believe me), the UK has distinguished itself as a proven, major player. There is little to no language barrier, but remember Winston Churchill's witty aside—The United States and Great Britain are two countries separated by a common language—and be aware that assimilation to unlearned words and phrases can take time. The number and depth of nuanced laws that are UK focused, and a security strategy framework that functions well indigenously, make it somewhat harder for companies that seek to extend themselves continentally.

The North

Northern Europe is a hotspot for global corporate security and continental governance. In Ireland, we will look at a unique tool in global corporate security known as a honey pot. Then we pop back across the channel to discuss how Belgium, as the EU capital, is evolving and growing into a main continental security center. Traveling north once more, we visit the Nordics, providing general comments on its highly advanced technology, business, and security environments. Finally, we sweep through the Netherlands, where some of the most trusted cross-border players in Europe live in a diverse, open society committed to strong global corporate security.

Ireland (.IE)

Ireland
MSI=68

Figure 9-7 Ireland

MSI = 68

Pros: Not a significant target, strong legacy of global security infrastructure, talent

Cons: Little cross-border business, island mentality

Although geographically small, Ireland has a rich security history. This stems from a strong university system and a renowned history working with cryptographic codes and code breaking. Commercially, such skill gave rise to the once-famed Baltimore Technologies, which was once a major contributor in the global security arena.

Legal, power, and communications infrastructures are solid, and like the UK, Ireland recognizes the European Arrest Warrant. However, they do not usually register as typical target. Some notable companies are based there, but they have yet to become as obvious a mark. Despite the fact that Northern Ireland and Ireland are connected, the terrorism threat in the country is minor. This secure environment is offset by the fact that the country's volume of cross-border business, although growing, is relatively scant. Again, similar to the UK, it is an island in more ways than one.

On the Ground

Ireland's environment from a corporate security perspective is similar to the UK. It deals with increased threats that have arrived with wireless technology's maturation, which is especially acute in Dublin. Gerry Fitzpatrick, a Dublin-based risk management expert, says his nation is navigating its host of challenges. Wireless has taken over the country, and the use of hotspots has begun to reveal a lack of security for Blackberrys (a popular e-mail palmtop in Ireland and the United States) and other PDAs. Wireless networks are not properly configured to handle secure wireless traffic, either. In Dublin especially, there is easy access from the outside to wireless LANs.

Another concern surrounds the lack of a clearly defined security officer in Ireland. Today it is typically cradled in the technology group or under the vice president of finance. Executives and board members have yet to understand the ROSI of adopting company-wide security strategies.

Ireland's rich tradition in the technical aspects of security is evidenced by some of the globe's top encryption algorithms and security companies based here. It has a small pool of security resources, but talent is usually well schooled. Look for staff from other multinationals that are based in the country. Ireland's support of the BSI standards over the ISO gives a push in a more secure direction, but actions speak louder than standards, and to date, security groups here will need to be shown the return on *their* security investment prior to implementation.

Regulations

EU directives are tracked here, and the European Arrest Warrant, which covers corporate security crimes, is honored and Safe Harbor is in effect throughout Ireland. Keep in mind that the country also has some regulations of its own. The National Standards Authority of Ireland developed a baseline technology standard known as the I.S. ISO/IEC 17799 Information Technology Code of Practice for

Information Security Management. It fortifies relatively early legislation surrounding eCommerce. Taking EU directives surrounding digital signatures and electronic commerce, Ireland passed the Electronic Commerce Act. Enacted in 2000, it is the first legislation of its type in the EU.[25]

Ireland's Data Protection Act of 1988 was recently updated through a 2003 amendment. It sets forth how data controllers"—people or organizations holding information about individuals on computers or in structured, manual files—must comply with certain standards in handling personal data, and individuals have certain rights.[26]

From a computer crime perspective, Ireland has two key laws—the Criminal Damage Act of 1991 and the Criminal Justice Offences Act of 2001. The Criminal Damage Act covers hacking and other computer crimes in its section 5. It has been proven to be broad enough to convict even when nothing was stolen or damaged, but simply trespassed upon.

Finally, Ireland has signed the European Convention on Cyber-Crime, which goes further than many of these existing Irish laws. The European Convention, as it was created very recently, addresses computer security with more current definitions, making prosecution easier and better integrating itself into the European approach to cybercrime.

Best Practices

I have taken this Irish side trip to discuss a component of corporate security that is certainly not unique to this country—a honey pot. However, the level of success and notoriety that this particular honey pot has received demonstrates well how partnerships in the private and public sector can work beyond bodies such as a CERT and provide new levels of global security intelligence. Begun in Dublin by Espion (an Irish security provider), Irish ISP Data Electronics, and Deloitte Ireland, a honey pot was developed. An unadvertised network of computers connected to the Internet that uses only basic firewall protection, honey pots assist companies and security professionals to understand the nature and number of threats that networks can undergo in day-to-day use. It is usually constructed with a variety of popular operating systems, including Linux and Windows, which replicate day-to-day operations at a typical company.

---

25. John Gaffney and Vincent Nolan. "Electronic Commerce Act: Ireland Leads the Way." International Business Lawyer 28, no. 11 (2000).

26. Charles Franklin. Business Guide to Privacy and Data Protection Legislation. (New York: ICC Publishing, Inc., 1996). n.p.

Once online, the honey pot is designed to attract "bears" who might be interested in exploiting such a vulnerable system for their own devices. Because it is unadvertised and there are no lures used, it typically attracts proactive, suspicious visitors. Built in to it are sensors that capture all the system's activity.

This particular honey pot, known as the Irish Honeynet, went live using an .ie IP address in 2002 and became a haven for blackhat activity. Soon, an Internet relay was set up from the outside and a chat room was opened. A hacking toolkit was uploaded to the network, which was traced to a known hacker in Russia. No legal action was taken: the honey pot was doing its job.

A default installation of a Windows system that has been left on the Internet unprotected will be discovered by the blackhats in a matter of hours. The blackhats are extremely proficient at scanning and discovering vulnerable systems on the Internet very quickly. To put this in perspective, it is feasible for an individual to scan every single Internet-connected computer in Ireland in a 12-hour period.

—Gerry Fitzpatrick, Risk Management Expert, Dublin

By the middle of 2003, attacks spiked to more than 1,000 in a single month—25 percent of which came from the United States. Another 34 percent came from Asian countries, including China, Taiwan, South Korea, and Japan.

Still open, the Irish Honeynet discloses how unconfigured technology remains vulnerable if not correctly deployed. It also exposes how patches and fixes, when not properly secured and tested, open new areas of vulnerability within a network. Having proven its worth quickly, the Irish Honeynet is affording an invaluable glimpse at the scope and frequency of attacks. Currently, it is being expanded for use in academic and professional settings, further enhancing its usefulness for the whitehat world.

Irish Final Thoughts

Ireland is a secure sleeper for cross-border business in Europe even though its multinational traffic is minimal. It is a solid partner for those who can leverage its best attributes: solid infrastructure, skilled labor, and strong global security awareness tied to partnerships such as the Irish honey pot wherein the best of the corporate and university sectors collaborate. Like the UK, do not mistake it for a good stepping stone to the European continent.

Belgium (.BE)

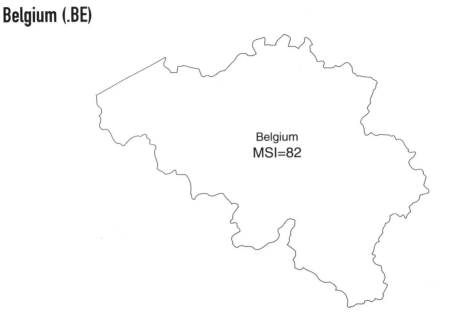

Figure 9-8 Belgium

MSI = 82

Pros: Crossroads of Europe with an appealingly high level of multinationals, security savvy and committed to empowering business through it

Cons: Closer scrutiny

Boasting the EU capital, NATO headquarters, and a burgeoning corporate sector, Belgium has enjoyed ever-increasing significance as a European security crossroads and is a multinational darling. Situated in Europe's most densely populated corridor, this small nation has a market of more than 320 million affluent consumers. It has assimilated much of the EU's aggressive global security posture, including a new commission on security and Directorate XIII, which oversees technology.

As the EU has raised its profile, Belgium has become an increasingly popular choice for cross-border security business. It has led to country-wide demand for robust security systems that have resulted in a brawny infrastructure matched by one of the strongest legal systems in all Europe. Here, international laws are enforced and the European Arrest Warrant is accessed. These security and legal backbones are paralleled by quality power and communications networks.

On the Ground

Brussels is the EU's nerve center. Here, security guidance can be your best friend, giving you a clear map to follow, or your worst enemy because of that roadmap's vulnerability to strict enforcement (even if it doesn't agree with the rest of your global security strategy). Brussels has a specific business quality that is comparable to Washington D.C. and its famed "Beltway bandits." The "bandits" are companies so named for their proximity on the U.S. capital's city-circling motorway (the Beltway) and their tendency to leverage the government's deep pockets for business.

Brimming with an expatriate and diplomatic community that is forging the destiny of a mostly united Europe, Brussels and the whole of the nation vibrates with an excellent work ethic, and nearly all employees are bilingual or even trilingual. Global security is European-centric and adheres closely to prevailing European standards, laws, and the common application of those laws to companies doing business there.

Security services will be important as the Brussels sphere of influence only expands. With the many newly formed security committees of the EU, and because it serves as NATO headquarters (another big security buyer), Brussels will provide all the requisite security staff, technologies, and partners needed for any project. Be aware that operations are scrutinized to a greater degree, because it is the source of most European-wide legal direction. It is a town where your own staff or your competitors are likely to report any violations of security or privacy acts.

In most cases, something must go wrong inside a Belgian company before they are willing to invest in corporate security.

—Chris Verdonck, Risk Management Expert, Brussels

According to Chris Verdonck, a risk management expert working out of Brussels, the EU's eGovernment initiative has taken hold. Urgency around getting the Belgian national government online dominates the local agenda. Belgium has just started online invoicing for tax e-filing and license renewal. Additionally, the country is concerned with privacy and data protection. These two issues—eGovernment and privacy—will ultimately converge as Belgium works toward a national identity card. Viruses and spam are also key security and privacy challenges that corporations in Belgium are working hard to tackle.

Key Regulations

Belgium's regulatory environment is similar to the rest of western Europe. The European Arrest Warrant, your teeth when attacked, is in effect. The Safe Harbor data law is enforced and sits beside the country's own Privacy Protection in Relation to the Processing of Personal Data as Modified by the Law of 11 December 1998 that offers guidance on how to properly handle consumer and personal information.[27]

The nation is also examining and applying portions of Sarbanes-Oxley, including section 404, which covers computer security, to companies that are touched by or touch the United States. Additionally, Belgium is home to SWIFT. To best understand SWIFT's origins, you will need to look decades into the past. It was then that banks were using a technology known as TELEX to communicate with each other. In 1973, a group of more than 200 financial institutions compared notes and realized that TELEX wasn't a very secure medium for communicating sensitive account data. They thought perhaps new technology could be used for creating a proprietary messaging system. Accordingly, they formed the *Society for Worldwide Financial Telecommunication*, and SWIFT was born.

Beyond French

Belgium has two official languages and yet four language regions as based in a 1935 "language law": Dutch, Flemish, French, and German. Every security rule and e-mail must be translated into at least Flemish and French. Plan ahead, allow time, and use pros.

Today SWIFT describes itself as "the industry-owned cooperative supplying secure, standardized messaging services and interface software to 7,500 financial institutions in 200 countries." It serves "banks, broker/dealers, and investment

---

27. *"Consolidated Version of the Belgian Law of December 8,1992 on Privacy Protection in Relation to the Processing of Personal Data as Modified by the Law of December 11, 1998 implementing Directive 95/46/EC." Privacy Exchange. 11 December 1998.*

managers, as well as their market infrastructures in payments, securities, treasury, and trade." SWIFT certifies communications deployment to third parties such as Big 4 firms on a country-by-country basis.[28] This accreditation allows for the education of SWIFT experts and free attendance at workshops for implementing the standard.

It is important to do so. Over the next few years, thousands of banks around the region and the world will be spending hundreds of millions of dollars and euros, pounds, and yen to make the way they communicate more secure. Why? I was at the 2002 SIBOS conference (the annual SWIFT gathering that happened in Geneva that year—it is more user group-esque and not a traditional tradeshow), where security was rated SWIFT's top priority. Every member bank must switch from the old x.25 connections to the new FIN, required by SWIFTNet. This is a massive project for all banks around the world.

Best Practices

Negative incidents and clear ROI drive Belgian security strategy development and implementation. A sense of urgency is increasing even though Belgian business is still operating under the "preshift" notion that global corporate security is still the technology group's main responsibility. Except for its largest companies that employ CSOs, the most senior security executives usually fall under the CIO's jurisdiction.

Although regulations fall in line with the EU directives, baseline security is usually created through guidelines provided by the British standard BS 7799 or ISO 17799. Brussels-based Verdonck is an ISO 17799 expert who is trying to perfect the first ISO 17799 certification program in Europe. He believes that when companies embrace security, this standard provides the ideal roadmap, affording 127 best practices and practical methodologies that help distinguish security priorities for a given company's needs.

Belgian Final Thoughts

Belgium's corporate security growth curve is steep and combines security awareness and preparedness with a strong legal system and an able workforce. Cosmopolitan and multilingual, it is a sound choice for opening a European business—unless you disdain increased scrutiny and greater enforcement. Conversely, if you are Belgium-ready, more than likely you will be Europe- and global-ready.

---

28. "Company Information." n.d. www.swift.com.

Nordic Focus: Denmark, Norway, Sweden (.DK, .NO, .SE)

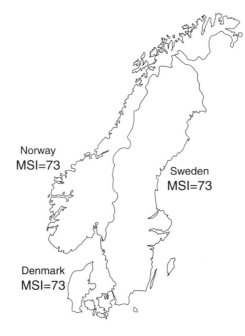

Figure 9-9 The covered Nordic Nations.

MSI = 73

Pros: Security aware, open society, laid-back and trusting citizenry

Cons: Heavy government control leads to more regulated countries with separate nuances, open society and trusting citizenry

Despite being lumped together, the Nordics' individual countries maintain a fierce, nationalist pride. From a corporate security standpoint, enough similarities surface to assert overall cultural-meets-security perspectives that filter into country-by-country specifics.

The Nordics share dark frigid winters, and their northerly proximity lends itself to astronomical differences brought about by longer summer days and longer winter nights. It can affect when your workforce arrives and leaves the office, and you must ready yourself for different ideas about when to work hard and when not to.

Within each Nordic nation, governments and national law overshadow EU legislation. Denmark, Finland, and Sweden recognize the European Arrest Warrant. Norway doesn't. The Nordic citizenry is generally trusting, and its respective societies emphasize an equality that surfaces in global corporate security practice. Privacy and consumer information are led by an opt-in mentality. Do not mistake this presupposition of trust for naiveté. The populace is bright, and each nation's infrastructure is strong, serving the business community well.

On the Ground

Comprised of Denmark, Finland, Iceland, Norway, and Sweden, we have chosen to focus on three of the Nordic nations that are pursuing some of the most aggressive security strategies in the EU. Closely regulated, most public services are run by the government, including hospitals and educational institutions. Economies are healthy and diverse. Sweden is built on multinational brands such as Volvo, IKEA, and great telecoms. In Norway, 95 percent of all private enterprise has fewer than 100 employees. Denmark is an entrepreneurial hotbed. Governments in each country are the driving force behind security.

Culturally, the Swedes are formal, more politically correct and the most heavily regulated. Danes are shrewder businesspeople. And the Norwegians? We are the youngest nation of the three (barely 100 years of independence in modern history). We were amongst the poorest European nations until 1900. Now we are amongst the richest.

—Jørn Arneson, Security Expert, Oslo

Nordics worry about security, but surprisingly, it is not just a matter of external threats. Instead, internal processes receive the most scrutiny and public attention. Oslo security expert Jørn Arneson related the story of a Norwegian bank transaction payment center that was switching platforms and became dogged by internal carelessness on an inopportune week. A technician working on the transition repeatedly received an error message when deleting backups of data over several hours.

Tired of it, the technician said, "No more error messages!" and began deleting them until they were all gone. However, instead of erasing the backups, he was actually deleting the hard drive of a transaction center that maintained customer access privileges and balance information. It took 72 hours to revive the center, but in the process, nearly all ATMs throughout the country were down, and some individual and corporate data was lost. It came at a time when many Norwegians were on week-long holiday. Skiing without Visa cards became no laughing matter.

The technician and the entire senior management of the bank were fired, and Jørn, also on vacation, became a ski resort folk hero by dolling out loans from his unaffected account.

Scandinavians focus on quality. Its large middle-class is fairly well off. There are few extremely rich people and little poverty. Each country is intentionally designed that way, and locals term it "equal sharing." Known worldwide as the Scandinavian model, it is defined by larger governments that provide citizens with a free education more or less to the university level, free health care, and equal salary. Taxes are high. Security staff workers are paid better (therefore, globalization is hurting them), and security managers are paid less.

Egalitarianism is a business mentality, and there is an air of informality (more prevalent among Norwegians than the Danes and the Swedes). Therefore workers expect respect for the jobs they do, and a manager would be very reluctant to pull rank. This has both positive and negative repercussions, especially when your policy calls for background checks and comprehensive information.

Regulations

Executive accountability runs high in the Nordics, and regulation drives security. According to Jørn Arneson, who has worked on Norway's security legislation, "Companies have to be driven by regulation in order to adopt stronger security postures and our governments recognize this." All three countries abide by EU directives and have created specific ordinances for critical infrastructure and privacy. I expect both the EU's Safe Harbor law and European Arrest Warrant will soon take full effect in each Nordic country.

Respective populations are increasingly aware that the extent to which private enterprise and the government uses personal information is increasing all the time. Enterprise is seeking the information for its own devices and the government harvests personal information to keep its countries secure. Consumers are more reluctant to give up their personal info and will query you in depth as you request it of them.

Denmark

The Danish Act on Processing Personal Data takes its cue from the European Commission privacy directive and became law in June 2000. It applies "to the processing of personal data wholly or partly by automatic means, and to the processing otherwise than by automatic means of personal data which form part of a filing system or are intended to form part of a filing system."[29]

Denmark, although small in size, has a rich and astute business tradition. It is helpful in the auditing of security systems and other compliance-based security activities. Expect push back on the use of expensive new security technologies, and pull through on the use of auditors (both internal and external) to help manage your security processes.

Norway

Norway's Processing of Personal Data Act protects "natural persons from violation of their right to privacy through the processing of personal data." It ensures that personal data processing respects privacy," including the need to protect personal integrity and private life and ensure that personal data are of adequate quality. Interestingly, in the wake of 9-11, the government is reconsidering the amount of privacy citizens are entitled to, and it may revise this act in some way to further deter potential terrorist activity within its borders.

Norway has passed a thorough critical infrastructure law. Included is Penal Code, Paragraph 151b, which will send offenders who inhibit information gathering or tamper with/destroy critical links such as power plants or broadcast and telecom entities to a maximum of 10 years.[30] The Critical Information Infrastructure Protection Handbook asserts that Norway's laws "generally tend to place blame firmly with the operator in cases of accidents such as rail crashes and [natural disaster]. However, systematic errors and poor leadership have become apparent as the underlying causes of many accidents."

Norway's agencies that oversee regulations related to privacy, cybercrime, and information security include the OKOKRIM (the National Authority for Investigation and Prosecution of Economic and Environmental Crime), which also has a unit dedicated to *Information and Communications Technology* (ICT) crime. The country's VDI (Intelligence Services Initiative) enables "intelligence and security professionals to chart the extent of the threat to vulnerable information infrastructure."[31] VDI will "alert clients to breaches and attempted breaches of computer networks."[32] The *Center for Information Security* (SIS) provides a repository of

---

29. *"Act on Processing Personal Data." PrivacyExchange. 8 October 1998.*

30. *Andreas Wenger, Jan Metzger, Myriam Dunn, ed., International CIIP Handbook: An Inventory of Protection Policies in Eight Countries. (Zurich: Swiss Federal institute of Technology, 2002), 65.*

31. *Ibid. 69.*

32. *Ibid.*

shared information about threats, countermeasures, standards, and general knowledge. It serves public- and private-sector legislators, security practitioners, and government offices. However, it is independent of the government and does not deal with privacy.

Sweden

Sweden's Personal Data Protection Act of 1998 augments and adjusts the Data Act of 1973 by considering and assimilating the EU privacy directive. It effectually covers all areas of personal information processing—automated or semi-automated. Individuals who use their own private data are exempted.[33] Additionally, the Swedish Data Protection Board is a clearinghouse for licenses for collecting and processing data. The government is also looking to update telecommunications acts and penal codes to account for new threats to critical infrastructure and information.

To combat computer crime and "information warfare," the government has formed the Swedish Cabinet Working Group on IO-D. According to the CIIP, it "identifies threats and risks due to information warfare, the dissemination of knowledge, proposals for sharing responsibility, and guidelines for strategy."[34] Since its founding in 1996, the group has expanded to include relevant organizations from the private sector. Sweden is also home to numerous public clearinghouses that address critical infrastructure, disasters, and the securing of information technology and potential information warfare. They include the following:

- **The Swedish Emergency Management Agency**

  Created in 2002, it is tasked with all information security within the country. A national form of constant vigilance, it fosters public/private partnerships and pools data on threats and countermeasures for information technology and critical infrastructure.

- **The ICT Commission**

  A general body that balances the analyses of information technology on society while promoting innovation. It actively pursues ways in which technology can securely enable all walks of life in the "information society."

---

33. Ibid. 78.
34. Ibid. 74.

- **The National Center of Information Operations**

  A defense-related entity, the National Center of IO/CIP is the Sweden National Defense College's main liaison for customers surrounding IO/CIP— information operations and information warfare.

- **Information Security Technical Support Team**

  This agency has been created to set up all certification and evaluation systems as they relate to information security within Sweden.

- **Swedish Security Service and National Criminal Investigation Department**

  Both of these entities report to the National Police Board and serve as the country's intelligence agencies. Both oversee "protection of sensitive objects, counter-espionage, anti-terrorist activities, and the protection of the constitution." This includes information security.

- **National Center for Reporting IT Incidents**

  Similar to a CERT, it will join the preexisting Telia CERT (telecom) and SUNET CERT (university) that has been constructed under the auspices of the Swedish National Post and Telecom Agency.[35]

Best Practices

Nordics have not only adopted the EU privacy directive as their own when it comes to privacy legislation, they have also consistently chosen BS 7799 as their baseline approach to security, which takes a control and quality assurance approach to creating organization-wide strategies.

Opt In

"Opt in" is a best practice supported by regulations in some European countries, most notably the Nordics. Opt in is usually demanded by the populace and supported by industry. The concept is simple. Consumers are deemed to own all rights to their most important personal information that may be given for a specific use such as ordering a product online, but they must further "opt in" before that info is allowed to be used by that business for anything other than the purpose of an order. Conversely, opt out means that consumers have an opportunity to opt out of giving companies free reign over this potentially sensitive data. Your global corporate security scheme must be flexible enough to account for the properly moral and ethical stance, no matter the country.

35. Ibid. 75–80.

The post-9-11 terrorist threat has surprisingly affected the Nordics. Oil-rich Norway is obsessed with redefining how it secures its derricks and in doing so has reconsidered how it creates processes for security within key infrastructures. Security is top of mind in other industries, too, mainly due to central government mandates. Arneson has pointed out that each of the Nordic countries requires a yearly internal audit of security as it relates to annual management reviews. Nordic technology groups are increasingly worried about the magnitude and number of threats that have begun to dog them locally and globally.

For the most part, security within the smaller Nordic states has remained in the hands of technology groups who largely rely on outsourcing its management to third parties such as the Big 4 and other, smaller suppliers. Although you would find teams of dedicated security personnel at larger companies, you would not find an information security officer—you would need an internal auditor. Arneson recently penned an article on the topic that declared the CSO dead in the Nordics—his way of saying that security had to be folded into the overall management milieu.

Nordic Final Thoughts

Depending on your organization and its specific needs, note the key differences in representative countries. Enter the Nordics assuming that you will encounter heavy government regulation that delivers burdens and benefits in equal measure. The society is open and trustworthy, and it will be a much-better-than-average place to work in a cross-border setting. Although the United States shares some of these same values, they play out and are interpreted differently by the Nordics. (Think collective vs. the individual.)

The Netherlands/Nederland (.NE)

Netherlands
MSI=90

Figure 9-10 The Netherlands

MSI = 90

Pros: Everything you need, as well as respect and acceptance by nearly every other European country and other continents

Cons: Purchasing power continues to limit the deployment of top countermeasures

The Netherlands could be your very best friend on the European continent. Its physical infrastructure—power and communications—is ideal for any global security operation, and there are few security events targeted against its companies. There is only a minor threat of violence, with the exception of potential eco-terrorism against some of its oil operations. The legal system is among the best in Europe.

Culturally, the Dutch are universally accepted throughout Europe and other regions of the world. Home to a diverse, multilingual (strong in English) citizenry, this tiny country has become a friend to nearly everyone. Augment this openness and acceptance with a well-educated security talent pool, a country-wide positive legacy in developing corporate security strategies and technology, and it is a perfect locale for multinationals who seek to set up shop in Europe. Without hesitation, the facts point to the Netherlands holding the biggest potential ROSI in Europe.

On the Ground

When you think of the Netherlands, you will probably call up stored images of Van Gogh, a cannabis bar, or a long canal that ends on a street corner with red lights in the windows. Known throughout the world as an open society with a casual flair, the Netherlands is home to corporate giants such as Shell Oil, KLM Royal Dutch Airlines, Heineken, Philips and Unilever, and, of course, Ahold.

Marco Plas, security chief of rising Dutch broadband star NLTree, believes that at their core the Dutch work hard from nine to five and then enjoy a lot of free time. "We're a laid-back country with a lot of principles, and, because we value our free time and 25- to 30-day holidays, we sit around, philosophize, and have an opinion about absolutely everything," he said. "We're a small country and not an exporter, so we invest heavily in knowledge, universities, and test environments. We also know how to get along with people."

The Netherlands is a multicultural society and one of the few that is widely accepted as a cross-border security partner. Nearly everyone speaks at least three languages—English, Dutch, and French or German.

In the Netherlands, security drivers pull the masses. It's like a game of follow the leader: follow the government, follow my industry peers, follow best practices, follow the standards. Like the Nordics, the followers are focusing on internal threats. A typical example is the University of Utrecht, which runs an ongoing study that asks the question, "Can wireless really be secured in a corporate environment?" This is a place where security is serious business.

—Marco Plas, CSO, NLTree, The Hague

When compared to other countries, the Netherlands is favorably similar to Scandinavia, Germany, the UK, and France. Internet usage is high, and technology is driving security awareness. Gateway security and a focus on internal systems that are vulnerable to external threats in the form of hackers, viruses, and even spam also prove to be priorities. Security still tends to be looked upon as a cost—not a business enabler. However, as in many parts of Europe, one enabler, wireless, is emerging as a new innovation that can be exploited and needs to be secured. Ahold's recent troubles and Sarbanes-Oxley have moved corporate governance to the fore. The government is framing its own corporate governance laws.

Regulations

Given that EU directives are taken seriously and provide guidelines for companies in the Netherlands, the Ministry of Justice is an influential body that is committed to "building a safe and just society." It administers the country's *Wet bescherming persoonsgegevens* (WPB) (its Personal Data Protection Act of 2000) that "regulates how companies, authorities, and institutions are to deal with personal data which they gather, store, keep on file, compare, link, consult, or provide to third parties."[36] It should be followed in concert with the Safe Harbor law. Additionally, the European Arrest Warrant, which can be a relevant appendage to global corporate security law, is in effect.

Corporate governance guidance is emerging through two main initiatives:

- **The *Stichting Corporate Governance Onderzoek voor Pensioenfondsen* (SCGOP) Handbook**

  SCGOP is the Foundation for Corporate Governance Research for Pension Funds. Its handbook provides voluntary guidelines aimed at facilitating accountability to and protecting shareholders.[37]

- **The Dutch CG Code/New Law**

  Designed to help corporations reinstate trust and confidence as integrity-ridden, transparent in their doing business, the New Law aims to fortify checks and balances, define powers and responsibilities within company management, and outline the roles of any external auditors.[38]

Best Practices

International standards such as ISO 17799 influence baseline global corporate security strategies in the Netherlands. Among financial institutions, the Dutch Central Bank is very involved in the Bank for International Settlements, the "bank for central banks," and is a key supporter of Basel II. Both subjects are detailed in "Switzerland," later in this chapter.

---

36. *"Act of 6 July 2000 containing rules for the protection of personal data (Personal Data Protection Act) (Wet bescherming persoonsgegevens)." Bulletin of Acts, Orders and Decrees of the Kingdom of the Netherlands. 6 July 2000.*

37. *"Corporate Governance Committee Presents Definite Dutch Corporate Governance Code." European Corporate Governance Institute. 8 December 2003.*

38. *"Dutch Corporate Governance Code: Principles of good corporate governance and best practice provisions." Dutch Corporate Governance Committee. 9 December 2003.*

With a focus remaining on internal threats, it has traditionally been tough for Dutch companies to make a business case for corporate security because it is still viewed as a cost center. However, quantifying risk in the face of new technology such as the proliferation of WiFi is leading to more proactive security postures throughout the country. In the process, business enablement that carries with it stronger security is on the rise nationwide.

If you are thinking about crossing the border into the Netherlands, Plas recommends local help. "The cultural mix and the business community nuances require that you find someone here that can help you begin to build your security profile," he said. "I'd go with a Big 4-type company such as KPMG, PWC, E&Y, or Deloitte. They represent one-stop shops that are just a door-knock away." They have, and need to have, offices in the dozens of small towns that make up the domestic security market.

The Netherlands is a great place for the Americas to partner while doing security on the continent. English is both common and functional, even at staff levels. Dutch subjects are welcomed in many countries in Europe, more so than Americans, Brits, Germans, or French. There exists solid infrastructure, a good rule of law, and a history of international law. (The Hague is a beautiful beach town on its west coast.)

Systemic and professional appreciation for corporate security is high. The Dutch hospital system and other slightly indirect aspects of the government have become strong proponents of security, driving its development and use. Universities are pumping out qualified staff who are exported throughout Europe on both long- and short-term projects.

Final Dutch Thoughts

If you are doing security business here, expect a very professional global-centric view of the issues, and a strong adherence to international laws and standards. If you seek a strong European partner that affords you unfettered representation across the continent, the Netherlands could be your answer. Its openness, global security savvy, skill, and multicultural/multilingual populace can help you get a Europe-centric operation off on the right foot. Its well-built infrastructure can ensure it stays there. Upon entrance, make sure you seek help from someone on the ground who can become that trusted envoy in and outside the country.

Switzerland, Spain, and Italy

Moving south and through the heart of Europe, I have chosen to focus on three countries and an entire region. Switzerland merits inclusion because of its global banking renown that is closely linked to misconceptions about its resulting security posture. Italy and Spain are two countries that are commercial centers and pose unique challenges and opportunities for those anticipating a border crossing to either nation.

Switzerland/Suisse (.CH)

Figure 9-11 Switzerland

MSI = 77

Pros: Strong rule of law and solid infrastructure, wide acceptance due to neutrality

Cons: Potential blind spots due to privacy obsession, increased vulnerability to outside attack

Switzerland's neutrality has made it a trusted haven for the world's money that involves an uncommon pledge to confidentiality. This has created a privacy fixation that could be either beneficial or risky if you are anticipating a Swiss component to your cross-border business and global security plans. Security is a hot topic in boardrooms and bedrooms. Physical infrastructure for power and communications is solid, although it is creeping up terrorist target rosters. Note, too, that the International Red Cross and other global organizations headquartered in Switzerland have come under increased attack.

Switzerland's historically verifiable privacy mania has translated into unusual biases related to Swiss regulations, its legal system, and Swiss-exclusive components of security strategies. Therefore, privacy breeds blind spots—especially when you go about establishing your coordinates or building the base of your global security plan. If you settle here, it is best to confront this issue clearly and immediately instead of assuming that because of its formidable banking industry, the basics are covered.

On the Ground

Switzerland's neutrality has made it a trusted haven for the world's valuables. So it isn't surprising that financial institutions are driving security. Because it is the world's repository, and because so much of Switzerland's wealth comes from the banking industry, the most prized security asset is secrecy.

Lingua Suisse

Switzerland is comprised of two unique linguistic regions, and business people are trilingual. In the east, a complex German dialect is spoken. French is spoken in the west. To compensate, the two regions conducts school in the non-indigenous language so that all children become fluent in both. Everyone in the country's business sector speaks impeccable English.

Marco Ricca, principal of Ilion Security in Geneva, believes that secrecy—not security—is almost a single-minded priority. "Our customers are not as much worried about their data being erased or corrupted or money being stolen. Their real fear is information getting out; and if you work in the banking centers in Switzerland, you will find that secrecy is of utmost importance."

Some Swiss bankers cannot cross borders with a corporate laptop, and if they do, they are subject to harsh penalties from their organization or the state. For companies doing work with financial institutions, signing a banking secrecy agreement is mandatory. These agreements are so strict, the rest of the EU has pleaded with Switzerland to relax them—to no avail.

In Switzerland, precision and rigor are necessary. You must reach into your industry of choice and from there take the time to be involved in that community. Build relationships over the long haul. Secrecy requires trust.

Regulations

It should come as no surprise that the Swiss city of Basel houses the *Bank for International Settlements* (BIS). The BIS serves as a "bank for central banks." It strives to be a monetary and economic research center. It serves as a "prime counterpart for central banks in their financial transactions." It also acts as "an agent or trustee with international financial operations." Finally, it provides a forum for dialogue and main facilitator of decision-making processes by banks. It does not serve the public or corporate sectors.[39] It is out of the BIS that the widely used Basel II Capital Accord originated. Basel II mandates that all global banks, size not withstanding, must adopt the same risk-management practices for tracking and reporting exposure to operational, credit, and market risks. To that end, Basel II has demanded that banks develop, deploy, and monitor a full program of global corporate security embodied by prevention, detection, analysis, and management of risk. Compliance must be achieved by 2006.[40]

In addition to Basel II's influence over the country, Switzerland does have a data protection action that was suggested by the Federal Council of Switzerland and ratified by parliament in 1992. The Federal Law on Data Protection went into effect in 1993. It has sought to "protect the personality and fundamental rights of those individuals about whom data is processed."

Best Practices

Swiss security is marked by privacy above all else. Network security that focuses on intrusion protection is integral to best practices and is based on ISO 17799. Employee awareness of security issues has recently begun to gain momentum. These two factors represent the heart of current Swiss wisdom. Global corporate security is still a technology group function in Switzerland, and this may account for such an emphasis on monitoring.

When setting up in Switzerland, having a trusted Swiss third party beside you will be crucial. Assimilation is tough, and therefore you must consider your partner very trustworthy if you are to be successful; and although Switzerland may seem a good choice for cross-border security partnerships, a few factors need to be weighed. Salaries for top professionals are higher due to the strong demand from the country's many profitable banks and insurance companies. With their national identity so closely linked with *absolute* privacy, it is sometimes too difficult to

---

39. *"About BIS." June 2004. www.bis.org/about/index.htm (5 August 2004).*
40. *"Basel II compliance fears grow for UK banks." AccountancyAge.com. 9 August 2004.*

implement the "reasonable" privacy that you might deploy in the rest of the world. Finally, the Swiss have tended toward flashier (but often less-effective) security measures. In one instance, a bank insisted on building tiny GPS chips into their employee laptops to ensure that data wasn't being downloaded outside Switzerland. With more proven technology, this could have been done equally effectively (not perfect, either way you do it), while integrating with the rest of the banks' security structures for a lot less money.

Final Swiss Thoughts

Secrecy, privacy, and confidentiality are the bedrocks of the Swiss security psyche. When a flashy GPS is deployed here or a multinational executive is stopped at the border, you will understand that working closely with the Swiss is the only way to develop a bulletproof base. Switzerland's muscular infrastructure and a strong justice system can help you; and if you have someone on the ground who can bridge indigenous wants with your needs, you should have a good experience. Like many other countries, the Swiss really only trust other Swiss. Find locals you like and keep them.

Spain and Italy

I have focused on a combination of two countries in southern Europe that are similar in an important way: To some extent, both are committed to their native languages, and for conducting cross-border business, it is challenging. Both countries are security savvy—in Spain it is motivated out of the strong banking and telecom industry influence, and in Italy it is strong commercial ties to the rest of the world.

SPAIN/ESPANIA (.ES)

Spain
MSI=66

Figure 9-12 Spain

MSI = 66

Pros: World class security practices and market segments, strong work ethic

Cons: Spanish is the language of choice, and this alienates the country from multinationals

Except at its highest levels, Spain has yet to make English its language of business, and this makes it a problematic security partner to multinationals from Europe and parts of North America. The country awaits programming, rules, and training to be translated into the country's common Castellano Spanish dialect or its "cousins"—Basque, Galician, or Catalan. However, upon translation, they implement security at a world-class level. Obviously, Spain matches well to Mexico and most of South America.

Legal Piracy Spanish Style?

The Register Newsletter recently reported that "a Spanish judge has ruled that modifications to games consoles to allow them to play DVDs and games from other countries 'are not illegal.'" According to *El País*, the ruling comes after the Guardia Civil charged Barcelona video games shop Innovagames with offering its clients "alteration of Play Station 2 and X-Box games consoles to allow them

continues...

Legal Piracy Spanish Style? Continued

to read games from other parts of the world or download directly from the Internet... by carrying out modification of their components as per diagrams found on the premises." It is moves such as these that illustrate why attention should be paid to local laws and customs when establishing your coordinates on a global level.[41]

Spain is a linguistic island, and therefore the country is often misperceived by the rest of Europe as a laggard outpost. Historically, Spain also endures domestic terrorism that directly affects business. Foreign companies are treated well, and incorporation can be your ticket to doing business. If the locals are who you are after, it could be one of your top security outposts.

On the Ground

The Spanish enjoy unprecedented work-life balance. Two business styles dominate: the Barcelona/Castellon style, which tends to be more informal; and the pulsing stylings of the country's commercial center and capital city, Madrid. The country works hard, if at unconventional hours. Heading out to a bar or restaurant at 5 p.m. and then back to the office at 10 p.m. to conclude the day's business is perfectly normal.

When the Spanish have the technology and training they need, they do a great job of implementing a corporate security base, and it is a country full of talented security professionals. There are superlative high-tech domestic industries such as finance and communications that make advanced use of security, and this makes some of its banks and telecoms absolutely world class from a domestic perspective.

Regulations

Between 1994 and 2002, Spain decreased domestic piracy of software from 74 to 42 percent. It has done so by taking its cues from EU security directives, and it is one of the eight countries currently recognizing the European Arrest Warrant. It

---

41. Lester Haines. "Spanish judge rules X-Box mods 'legal.'" *The Register.* 27 April 2004.

also abides by the Safe Harbor law regarding personal data. In 1999, Spain passed the Ley Orgánica de Protección de Datos (LOPDAT) (Ley 15/99) "to guarantee and protect the public liberties and fundamental rights of natural persons, and in particular their personal and family privacy, with regard to the processing of personal data."[42]

Best Practices

ISO 17799 serves as the main guideline for building the base in Spain and a vigorous security community, but a locally focused community demands that whoever you work with on the ground has a thorough knowledge of local best practices. Most new mindshare emerges from Madrid's *Securimatica: The Congreso de Seguridad en Tecnologies de Información y Comunicaciones.* Securimata is the country's definitive, three-day event that shouldn't be missed by those doing security there on your behalf. Topics range from certifications to large-scale security projects. *Seguridad en Informática y Comunicaciones*, which is really the default periodical of the entire Spanish security sector, covers well the issues facing the Spanish security sector.

Spanish Final Thoughts

Spain is a great place to practice security, leveraging their business infrastructure, work ethic, and adherence to global standards. What they lack is due in large part to slow or incomplete translations of global security thinking, and a more limited local budget for deployment. Spain is probably not a first choice for multinationals entering Europe in hopes of continental success. It is relatively stable, highly secure, and technologically skilled. Settle here if there is a local market opportunity, if you are able to garner local support, and if you can overcome the language barrier. Of course, it is also a great destination if you have significant Spanish-language operations in other Spanish outposts such as Mexico, Central and South America.

---

42. *"La Ley Orgánica de Protección de Datos Personales" n.d. www.alaroavant.com/AlaroAvant.*

Italy/Italia (.IT)

Italy
MSI=69

Figure 9-13 Italy

MSI = 69

Pros: World-class security practices and market segments, strong work ethic

Cons: Italian is the language of choice and—although less serious than Spain—this alienates the country from multinationals, purchasing power limits and delays adoption of new countermeasures

Although Italians prefer to do security in Italian, they will speak English and they are more open to cross-border business than Spain. The country works from a single, well-established legal system. It is the country's infrastructure that has shown enough vulnerability to merit caution for cross-border business. Because of a hard-line prohibition of domestic nuclear power plants, more than 50 percent of Italy's power is imported. Alternatively, Italy funnels power into the country from French nuclear power plants just across the border. Many joked that one tree falling in France could turn out the lights in Rome. This was substantiated in 2003, when a tree falling on the Swiss-French border overloaded the power lines that flowed into Italy and lights in nearly all Italian cities faded to black over a 24-hour period. Communications, when not disrupted on a massive scale, are relatively reliable.

The legal system is historically strong and internationally fair, and Italy supports the power of business contracts. Italy is also "brand central." Names such as Gucci, Ferrari, and Prada have given it a global voice on intellectual property law. Corporate governance issues have become a priority following the Parmalat scandal. Because nearly every Italian in the country had money tied into the corporation's stock, nearly every Italian is outraged by its actions. Also, organized crime may seem like a traditionally important concern, but its old-school feel is much milder then new-school mafias that emanate from Russia and other parts of eastern Europe. It should not figure as prominently in your corporate security approach.

On the Ground

Relative to its European neighbors, Italy seems like a Shangri-la, and at first glance, it may strike you that its approach is apparently not businesslike. Deregulated, security is a voluntary exercise, and this is problematic. Imagine trying to mesh your German security posture with your Italian security posture. Could there be two less-compatible frames of mind? Using Italy as a continental hub will force you to conduct culturally sensitive training programs that prepare the Italians for your approach.

Regulations

Italy's 1997 Personal Data Act (known as the act) "is designed to 'ensure that the processing of personal data is carried out by respecting the rights, fundamental freedoms and dignity of natural persons, especially as related to privacy and personal identity....'"[43] Its Law n. 675 requires that companies attempt to secure data with antivirus and firewall devices.

---

43. *"Protection of Individuals and Legal Persons Regarding the Processing of Personal Data Act." PrivacyExchange.org. January 1997.*

Presidential Decree number 318 (1999) provides some specifics that cover the minimum security measures that corporations must take for the protection of personal data. Specifically, it covers the following:

- Who are the responsible parties
- Categories of data and information
- Identification methods
- Data security schemes
- Object reuse
- Storage of data (long term)

Other law is scant, but it is my belief that the Parmalat scandal will catalyze a bevy of new security regulations in the near future.

Best Practices

Italian companies conduct a fair amount of global trade, and have the fourth highest Internet usage in Europe, and in doing so usually adhere to ISO 17799 and European guidance, such as the European Convention on Cyber-Crime. Additionally, articles 7 and 9 of the Italian Law 675 (above) state that you must notify the government in advance of using any Italian-centric personal data, and must certify that you will both use it lawfully (Italian law) and keep it safe.

Italy's law number 513 essentially makes the use of digital signatures valid in the country, and the official register is the *Authority for Information Technology in the Public Administration* (AIPA), with the INFN the obvious choice for a local certificate authority. If doing electronic business in Italy, it is recommended that you at least cross-certify with this site, which will provide local revocation lists, and make any future transactions simpler and more secure from a local legal perspective. And despite what your global backup plans may say, duplicating the private keys, either electronically or within devices, is illegal in Italy, so ensure that you get local legal advice.

Current best practices do not hold Internet service providers liable for content that their users submit, but watch this area closely in the coming years.

Final Italian Thoughts

An Italian-language business sector, slightly vulnerable infrastructure, and lack of current specifics in a formidable regulatory framework make Italy more work as a cross-border partner than some, but these issues do not mean that you should rule out Italy. Telecom Italia is a world leader, and well recognized as a major player in the security and information economy.

Italian law enforcement have a strong track record of international cooperation in the information security world, and are used quite successfully in the prosecution of domestic and international cybercrime. They are high-profile members of the G8 High Tech Crime Network.

With its long history of global trade; strong domestic markets; and smart, hardworking, and well-trained security staff, Italy could be a southern destination you.

Central and Eastern Europe

Move farther east in Europe, and business turns dicey. Central Europe and the Balkans are recovering from civil war, ethnic strife, and occupation. There is plenty of organized crime in previously communist states, and the general economic outlook is clouded by glacial growth and widespread poverty. It is a region steeped in the unknown and opportunity.

Mob Renaissance

Organized crime was often the only functional commerce under communism, and too often it remains so during this uphill transition to a free market. Ethical and even criminal lines are blurred here, so maintain constant vigilance.

There are glimmers of hope. Of the last ten nations admitted into the EU, eight came from central and eastern Europe. Regulations are growing teeth. Romania has passed some of the world's toughest tech-related laws to ensure that it can continue as a talented, low-cost programmer hub for Western corporations. Almost as quickly as it went into effect it was tested. A local hacker was caught morphing the original Blaster virus into what is known as Blaster.F. The catch was a source of national pride. A recent Forbes.com article quoted Mihai Radu of Romanian antivirus provider BitDefender as saying, "I do not think he realized he could be tracked down. He played with fire and got burned."[44] Another new member state, Bulgaria, has recently approved an additional chapter to its penal code on fighting computer crimes and is expected to soon ratify the European

---

44. *Antonio Oprita and Bernhard Warner. "World's Toughest Cyber Law on Trial in Romania." Forbes.com.*
   23 March 2004.

Convention on Cyber-Crime. All this bodes well for the future of security in this important region. Central Europe is still finding its way, and I spend some time characterizing this situation while focusing on the Czech Republic.

We focus subjectively on this part of Europe and visit some of its largest and smallest countries. We start with Russia. Still an unwieldy giant, it has become a poster child for cross-border inhibitions. We discuss why that's so. Then we make a 180-degree turn and visit the tiny yet strategic Czech Republic, which is blossoming into a cosmopolitan commercial core that has made it the hot cross-border security partner in a new Europe.

Central European security funding flows from regional sources outside the country and is correlative to EU membership and the merging of their banks into the European Central Bank. Note that as of this writing, most countries are still doing the absolute minimum to participate in these regional structures. Be glad that these international security requirements exist as critical path items for growth; otherwise, there would be a much less secure region to work in today.

Russia (.RU)

Russia
MSI=26

Figure 9-14 Russia

MSI = 26

Pros: Strong technical outsourcing potential has lured some U.S. multi-nationals

Cons: Legal and technical infrastructures lacking, most routine business services not yet on a par with the rest of the region

Russia is a nation in flux. Its people struggle to rise above adversity that has plagued them for centuries, and post-communist reconstruction has proven a hard prospect. This northern mammoth's transitional confusion has incubated a haven for international terrorist organizations even as it comes under attack from within. Economically, it is struggling under the weight of organized crime, and so much separates a razor-thin upper crust from the struggling impoverished class.

Russia's infrastructure is inconsistent depending on the region. Vulnerable, it is an increasingly convenient target and launching point for cyberterror. To get an idea of where things stand, think early 1990s intrusion detection, no on-site supervision and yet plenty of computing power being exploited by a 15-year old Slovenian who has broken into a "dormant" series of Siberian servers. Transformed into zombies, they become easy foundations for malicious aggression. It has happened. Just ask the Pentagon or myriad banks who have suffered from such attacks. Within the country, the technology that controls critical infrastructure, from water systems to nuclear reactors, are also potentially at risk.

Computer crime is spiking, as well. According to the Computer Crime Research Center (www.crime-research.org), Russia's Ministry of Internal Affairs of the Russian Federation saw the number of high-tech crimes double in 2003, logging more than 11,000 cases. And based on information collected from IDS companies around the world, I would say that those known cases are just a tiny tip of the iceberg. Targeted attacks, piracy, and unauthorized access to systems lead the activities roster, but companies still cross its border because labor is cheap and talent is plentiful. Despite Dell, Motorola, and Boeing investing there, I cannot recommend such a move from a global security perspective without a very long-term domestic agenda and a hardened security shell.

From Russia, With Love

The *Arabian Electronic Jihad Team* (AEJT) launched itself in 2003. Their goal? Conquer the Internet and destroy all Israeli and American Web sites. Its servers are housed in Russia.[45]

continues...

---

45. James S. Robbins. *"The Jihad Online." Computer Crime Research Center. August 2002.*

From Russia, With Love   Continued

In late 2003, Maxim Kovalchuk, a 25-year old Ukrainian, was arrested in Bangkok after receiving an underground blackhat nomination for "best hacker." As is the tendency of media outlets, he was described as one of the most prolific and dangerous hackers in the world. True to form, these same journalists report that he inflicted more than $100 million of damage on U.S. companies.[46]

On the Ground

After nearly a century of isolation from the West, Russian cross-border business is not for the timid. Here's a taste. Just days following the Soviet Union's collapse, a client of mine set up a presence in Moscow using the office of a separate—but loosely related—company that they bought out. After a while, there were so many obvious internal problems in Moscow that the firm decided to send in an American to oversee the operation. After about a week on the job, he realized that the two Russians running the office were stealing the company blind. He fired them, but they refused to leave, saying that they didn't recognize his authority. Finally, more company officials backed up the American and eventually the duo left... with their corporate cell phones and company limos. Over time, the company paid them more to get the limos back. It never could recover the phones. This is common and turns worse the further you drill down.

There is a small subset willing to work very hard to international standards and leverage new opportunities to better themselves. There is also a larger group that lived under an entitlement umbrella and they simply won't show up for work. Such a transitional array of workers has made it difficult to set up a reliable and secure operation within the country, and you should never rely on a security scheme that doesn't involve a complex set of checks and balances. Look for advances and adherence to international security standards to come first from the energy industry, heavy manufacturing, and mining.

Amid the chaos, there is potential. Russians are proud of many technical firsts that have gone largely unknown in the West (space exploration, television), and talent is profuse. It can and will be tapped when the society believes conditions are better than communist rule and firmer allegiances to ethics become distinguishable.

---

46. *Timofey Saytarly. "Ukrainian Hacker Appears in Court." Computer Crime Research Center. 6 April 2004.*

If Russia were to shore up its criminal element, it could potentially challenge India as an outsourcing destination for development (not call centers, however, due to language issues). Gradually, questionable commerce will evolve into more legitimate business, a la Gazprom—another post-Cold War phenomenon. During the Soviet disintegration, organized crime allegedly took over Russia's natural gas fields and declared ownership. Within days of the fall, the gang bought the rights to the entire industry for rubles on the dollar. Today, it is the single largest company in Russia and it is already going through a restructuring since the government "discovered" this crooked past. Again, this is typical.

It is important to note that Russia is trying to polish and market a new technical image. One president of a software firm, Alexis Sukharav, said that any U.S. company shipping programming work to Russia stands to save between 40 and 60 percent—the average Russian programmer makes $12,000 a year. Although true, additional costs—extensive background checks and a supplemental security infrastructure, when matched with an eavesdropping government, a language that is extremely hard to learn, and generally poor quality control standards—outweigh the investment. Russia has also undergone a nationwide brain drain. Some of Russia's best are in Silicon Valley or Glen, waiting out their homeland's storm. Time will tell if they return.

Regulations

Significant regulation of technology and data/privacy is nonexistent in Russia. In 1993, the Constitution of the Russian Federation contained spotty provisions addressing data protection. In 1995, the Information Computerization and Protection of Information of 1995 and the Participation in the International Information Exchange of 1996 were both ratified by the Russian Duma. A law on personal data has been pending in the Duma since then.[47]

In response to the plentiful cybercrime that riddles the country, a new Web site has been created at www.cyberpol.ru. It tracks information security and cybercrime throughout the country.

Best Practices

Be circumspect. Be thorough. Be willing to invest a lot of money to settle in Russia. Anticipate the unexpected as it applies to your industry.

---

47. *"National Omnibus Laws." PrivacyExchange.org. n.d.*

Final Russian Thoughts

When this new quasi-democracy continues to find its footing, restabilizes after the fall of communism, dismantles (or evolves) its Web of organized crime, subdues its domestic and international terrorist ties, and creates a secure infrastructure, it will become a fantastic cross-border partner.

Czech Republic (.CZ)

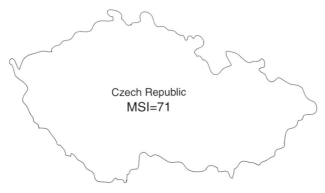

Czech Republic
MSI=71

Figure 9-15 Czech Republic

MSI = 71

Pros: World-class security practices and market segments, strong work ethic

Cons: With anything this new, you have unproven systems that need extra attention

The Czech Republic could be viewed as a glass half full or empty. If you studied it based on where it was yesterday, comparing it today, you can quickly ascertain which way the glass tips. Looking back a decade—a newly birthed country that has lifted itself up by its bootstraps—and seeing that it now has an MSI in the 70s, I would bank on its continuing to trend up. The Czech Republic is a great place to house European security operations. You will find an ever-improving infrastructure and a legal system that's headed in the right direction. A strong workforce is boosted by a culture that has traditionally worked well with other countries. They are not a prime security target. In short, the "CZ" is open for business.

Be aware that on its surface the country may not appear to be easy to embrace. Czech corporate security pros may seem overly rigid and country-centric. Over time you and they will usually settle in well, as their understanding of the global business flow and the need to securely interact with their partners takes center stage. Remain patient with your business relationships, and know that breaking the ice comes with the territory.

On the Ground

Driving east and talking my way through border crossings with an eastern European rarity, citrus fruit, I made it to Prague's Wenceslaus Square in late November 1989. I had noticed people gathering at its heart as I checked into the Hotel Europa. As I made it to my room, there was a crush of humanity—later, I found out numbering nearly 200,000—facing an opposing hotel balcony. Vaclav Havel—in the throes of leading the Velvet Revolution (or what is called simply "November" in the Czech Republic)—spoke a simple message: The communists must leave. Near the speech's conclusion, he exhorted the masses to symbolically jangle their car keys as a bell that would toll for the old regime. The keys shook in unison, and an ocean of impromptu ringing resonated off the enclosure of centuries-old buildings. By year's end, the communists were gone. Just 14 years later, in the spring of 2004, the fledgling country was admitted into the European Union.

It is no surprise that optimism runs deep through the country (especially since its football team stunned Euro Cup fans), and this moment redeemed that day 35 years earlier when Soviet tanks rolled through the city and massacred demonstrators. The Czech Republic houses a well-educated talent pool best characterized by a New York-styled attitude—they work hard and smart and then play hard. A country-wide business model is focused on attracting foreign investment at a steady clip. If you have specific global security requirements, they will meet them. If there are treaties that need to be followed, they will follow them.

Regulations

As the Czech Republic continues to take shape, the country is working hard to develop proper regulations related to corporate security. The Federal Assembly of the Czech and Slovak Federative Republic passed the Act on Protection of Personal Data in Information Systems (the act) in 1992. This was amended in 2000 through the Act of 4 April 2002 on the Protection of Personal Data and on

Amendment to Some Related Acts. This newest iteration "regulates the protection of personal data concerning natural persons, the rights and obligations in processing of these data, and specifies the conditions under which personal data may be transferred to other countries."[48]

Through the European Convention on Cyber-Crime, which the Czech Government supports, Prague-based companies tend to support relevant international instruments on international cooperation, and they have the backing of the centralized government to enforce reciprocal legislation with trading partners. Although it is too early to be banked on, the enthusiastic support of global security standards that I have witnessed, even where not specifically mandated by local laws yet, has been encouraging to me, and is a harbinger of future success for security in the Czech Republic.

Best Practices

With a freshly minted membership into the European Union, the Czech Republic is adaptable to EU directives and guidance. International security money rules here. Import your security strategy, train locals thoroughly and sensitively, and build your posture on ISO 17799 or similar standards.

Final Czech Thoughts

The Czech Republic is the security star of central and eastern Europe. It illustrates how a small, resourceful country can band together and create lasting economic change through a commitment to cross-border business that's aligned with the proper infrastructure, positive legislation, and a commitment to global corporate security. It is a wonderful place to set up your security shop!

---

48. *"101 Act of 4 April 2000 on the Protection of Personal Data and on Amendment to Some Related Acts."*
   The Office for Personal Data Protection. 4 April 2000.

Chapter 10

The Middle East and Africa

Figure 10-1 The Middle East and Africa

Moving through various regions of the Middle East, we cut into southwest Asia via India, Saudi Arabia and the Gulf States, Israel, and North Africa and the eastern Mediterranean. Then we continue on to South Africa, where our EMEA journey concludes.

Southwest Asia

Perhaps the security gem of this region is India, and we cover it here as the region's representative state. Other developing countries such as Bangladesh, although gaining momentum and investment, are not beginning to vie for cross-border security partnership. Clearly, however, India is cultivating an escalating outsourcing business that is lifting up the country and creating opportunities that are greeted with enthusiasm by its intelligent, eager populace.

India (.IN)

India
MSI=65

Figure 10-2 India

MSI = 65

Pros: Self-starting workforce that is matched with brightness, best choice among inexpensive outsource-welcoming countries

Cons: Physical infrastructure and legal system are sketchy, personnel risks still high, costs rising relative to others

India is a frontier land that continues to entertain more questions than answers on the global corporate security front. The country's infrastructure is sketchy. You will find power systems evolving, but they are still much more of a risk than Indian companies will lead you to believe. Communications is spotty, and the nation is devoid of a major trunk line, but it is all trending in the right direction as more multinationals move in. India's legal system is also evolving in the right direction, but it can be somewhat hazy. Contracts are supported with a rule of law that is enforceable. From a cultural perspective, you will find a willingness from Indian companies eager to work with you on security strategy.

India's Commitment to Growth

NASSCOM, India's *National Association of Software and Service Companies,* is saying that Indian demand for corporate security personnel will eclipse 77,000 by 2008, with most sliding in from Asia. "This specialized manpower will become a major requirement for the Indian IT sector," NASSCOM said, quoting *International Data Corporation* (IDC) research.[1]

This nation's gifted personnel are still a high security risk that must be integrated into your total cost of ownership. Terrorist activity and political instability are constants. A continual threat of war with neighbors has not yet ended. Business continuity will be an issue.

Nevertheless, among the outsourcing countries available to date, it is probably the best, with a complete package that outpaces cheaper rivals such as Bangladesh or the Philippines, but it is still not on par with European counterparts. It is crucial that your own people stay on-site full time to monitor your situation.

On the Ground

For many of us, the world's largest democracy conjures visions of palatial estates draped in greenery and a society tinged with marks of British colonial rule commingling with BBC1 footage of sari-wrapped women pounding laundry along the banks of the Ganges. Today India's population is highly educated, highly motivated, and hopeful. As the country's economy has rocketed through a worldwide outsourcing binge, growth is exponential, and this is a country that is living a "get online now, secure later" credo.

However, the UK's legal system and train lines aren't the only elements holding sway—Germany has been leveraging India and with the Germans has arrived a requirement for regimen and thoroughness that is historically based. The country's

---

1. *"Information Security Manpower Demand Estimation." NASSCOM Report. February 2003.*

business climate has matured because of these strict requirements. Because of both European influences, India has been transformed into a very flexible business setting that usually adopts the highest common denominator.

The populace averages three languages per person. There is an extremely high level of personal responsibility. In India, integrity and family name mean a lot. On the one hand, this inhibits nefarious activity—if someone is caught doing something criminal—especially at a corporate level—his or her name will be pretty much mud, and that will effactully blacklist that person from doing business in that culture ever again. The country also values education to the level of some Asian cultures (for example, Japan). Sending a child to university is of utmost importance, and almost any given Indian would much rather put money toward a college fund than any luxury. Ten people wait behind whoever is doing a job, waiting for their chance. Although depth and breadth of talent pools in India are staggering, income has not kept pace with competitiveness.

While you may have heard stories about India's rolling power blackouts, there is now rolling Internet access throughout the country, courtesy of ingenious, indigenous innovation. For the many towns and villages without constant connections, enter the Internet rickshaw: These locally created microbusinesses are bicycles with a satellite dish mounted to the steering wheel, a generator attached to the back wheel, and an Internet WiFi hub slung below the seat. The rickshaw entrepreneur then peddles into town at the agreed hour, kicks his bike onto the stand, and starts the peddle power that connects dozens of locals to the Internet for a time.

Know Indian Nuance

Soft-spoken Indian programmers may remain quiet even when they notice problems, and subtle differences in gestures can cause confusion (shaking the head up and down means no in some areas, yes in others).

Any company wanting to move across its border would pack its bag at this description, but remember that these same elements can be a two-edged sword. Disgruntled employees know what to do. Turnover at companies is high. Background checks are tough to verify. Job sharing among staff is common, with relatives filling in for a sick worker so that the sick worker does not lose his or her valuable job. One country's norm is another company's security nightmare.

And then there's the growth. Imagine the Wild West colliding with an economy that's expanding at a rate seldom seen in world markets. New money has flooded the country. In addition to natural EU neighbors, the United States has poured in millions and delivered a whole new echelon of requirements and technology, which includes application security. The first signs of an upsurge in educating Indian professionals for security certifications are apparent.

India recognizes its need for global corporate security. An upsurge in immigrants from Europe and North America who are eager to earn combat pay abroad to help secure organizations, all the while experiencing estate living, is bringing with it security-awareness expertise.

Find a Trusted Partner

In India, do not rely too heavily on the host country when moving there. Make sure you go with someone who has been there before, and focus on finding a strong, trustworthy liaison who can play a connector role between you and a potential Indian partner.

Outsourcing is obviously a major concern to those setting foot in India who seek to secure their organization—it seems like risky business, but the Europeans and Americans seem to be relocating operations at a rate that merits special consideration. We further explore this issue when I revisit India and discuss outsourcing Chapter 13, "Outsourcing and Your Map."

Regulations

India is in the process of creating privacy and data-protection laws. Currently, none of consequences exist, and this is a rather well-known fact even though the likes of Microsoft and a host of other major, global players are investing millions. Local law is less of a concern, and the rigor with which debate and interpretation occurs on the creation of corporate agreements is much more crucial. This vulnerability and a lack of any teeth-rich law to punish violators are concerns. As with security in all outsourcing havens, enter with caution and take my advice: Find someone you can trust, and through that person begin building a secure organization.

Lufthansa has proven to be one of the biggest influences in maturing the local, domestic companies of India as to the expectations and requirements of first-world powerhouses. In addition, with close ties to the UK's legal system, it's been easy for India to adapt to the BSI standards and Basel II. The culture understands and absorbs it. Now it's time for India to develop its own standards.

—*Royal Hansen, Vice President, AtStake, Boston*

India does have an array of agencies that are starting to deal with global security issues. NASSCOM is the leading professional organization in information technology. At its most recent annual gathering, corporate security took center stage, dealing with key issues such as corporate governance, early-warning systems, consumer awareness, technical standards, and security across software development.

The country also boasts its own computer society—the Computer Society of India. Founded in 1965, it has more than 2,000 members and it includes a data-security wing. In 2004, an India-wide CERT-IN was developed—as Information and Technology Minister Arun Shourie said, "To guard Indian computer networks that represented the 'acupuncture points of the economy.'"[2]

Best Practices

The only strong security in this immature market is imported by the UK (read BS 7799), Germany, and the United States. However, if you are able to follow the steps outlined in the opening of Part 2, "Reality, Illusion, and the Souk"—finding the right people and places to be for the right reasons—India can enable and empower your business. There is an unaccounted-for human factor: Turnover at outsourced companies is high. Intellectual property and consumer data is vulnerable. Security measures—until stronger local law is developed—might be impotent.

Final Indian Thoughts

India is abuzz with outsourced business and the boundless optimism of an exponential economic growth curve. A governmental mandate is committed to establishing whatever security is necessary to attract and retain U.S. and European outsourcing contracts. But security is not something you snap your fingers and get,

---

2. *"Indian Cyber Security System Unveiled." Sify News. 19 January 2004.*

and changing cultural norms is often a fool's errand. The nation is evolving toward mapping a first-rate global corporate security—just not quickly enough to keep pace with the growth. These are heady days, and the air is thick with threats. Be aware of them and send someone you trust to stay there full time, making sure your technology, processes, and people are safe.

The Gulf States

The Persian Gulf may not be a logical first thought for mapping a cross-border business, but there are some countries and emirates that are impeccable when it comes to creating secure business environments. Perhaps the greatest example of Middle Eastern progressiveness is the United Arab Emirates' Dubai.

Gulf Neighbor Oman Gains Certification

In 2004, Oman's Doha Bank became the first Middle East financial institution to receive the prestigious British standards certification for information security. The bank demonstrated preparedness with "any emergency arising out of possible external interventions in its information systems through virus-inducing or hacking attempts."[3]

---

3. *"Doha Bank gets BS 7799 Certification." Dohabank.com. n.d.*

Dubai (.AE)

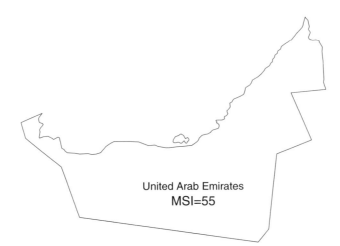

United Arab Emirates
MSI=55

Figure 10-3 United Arab Emirates

MSI = 55

Pros: Progressive and a strong security partner for the Middle East

Cons: Terrorist threats toward Western interests are growing

Dubai, the business jewel of the United Arab Emirates, has built a tremendous reputation for cross-border business that could work in your favor. Its unmatched eGovernment program is a good example of this—the electronic business community can interact directly with the tiny emirate's administration in a secure manner. It has cascaded into a greater understanding of security awareness and technology. Therefore, Dubai-based companies have more advanced security postures than companies in other parts of the region or even the whole of the developed world.

Dubai's forward-thinking business leadership has been successful in maintaining its historic way of life and standards while fitting in nicely with the rest of the world. The port is free and tax-free—coming or going. Dubai figured it could make money outside port taxation, and the global trade poured in. Multinational law firms, financial institutions, and packaged-goods firms have headquartered themselves there. There is a security infrastructure that's supporting it all, driven by trade, staffed by a skilled expatriate workforce and supported by royalty.

Israel (.IL)

Israel
MSI=66

Figure 10-4 Israel

MSI = 66

Pros: Security that is battle-tested and talented personnel

Cons: Top terrorist target, infrastructure

Israel has a fine-tuned appreciation for corporate security stemming from a hostile environment that has existed since its modern founding. Israel understands that its survival depends on global markets and remains generally accessible to the United States. Domestically, the Palestinian conflict has developed security competency that flourishes in the military and corporate sectors. Companies are the highest consumers of security. Either of the two large security companies in Israel are great to work with—just make sure you check individual personnel's pedigree.

At the writing of this book, the situation does not yet allow for Israel to conduct cross-border security trade with its immediate neighbors, but Israeli security firms are busy in other parts of the world, including the Americas, Europe, and Asia. Israel has a flourishing technology sector that is marketed heavily through a national reputation in physical security, and the country's two main security firms are augmented by several great small ones. These petite players sell well in the local markets, and many are supported by state-sponsored venture funds that will help them grow.

Infrastructure is still a risk in Israel, with power reliability falling below the five-nines (99.999 percent) uptime level. Communication is also less reliable than in most European countries. The legal system has been shown to favor Israeli companies, so it is important to craft security contracts that specify whose laws will be used in a dispute. I have not found that most companies are regularly confronted with scenes from the six o'clock news, but terrorism is likely to be a factor in human or information availability over the life of your business.

On the Ground

Israel. The word is received with either full support or a host of problematic issues when doing business across borders. For some, it represents a critical link to many of the brightest minds in technology and corporate security. Others recognize it a nation rich in history or a modern underdog that has beaten the odds to survive. Some believe its present incarnation poses ethnic, political, and even religious issues that can hurt you abroad. Perhaps this is why the United States has allowed its citizens to hold two separate passports: one for Israel and one for everywhere else, so that an entry stamp from one country does not become a "no entry" stamp for another.

From a global corporate security perspective, Israel is day-by-day case study of security amid an array of physical-meets-technological concerns. Because nearly everyone in the country serves in the military at some point in their lives, security awareness is high. Often, militaristic approaches to security segue into the corporate sector. This has only intensified over the past few years. In Israel, defense resources go into building corporate strategy. Most high-tech companies can trace their roots to defense.

Avi Brenner, managing director of local security leader AvNet, says that this is a live environment where threats are real. "In Israel," he said, "the physical security is a main concern, and we're experiencing how the physical and the logical are two threats that really become one for the CSO. We have a strong measure of classification and inspection: Supervision is the same."

Don't get me wrong. You won't get the flavor that we're philanthropic. But you know, there are many projects we take on because of terrorist reasons. It won't get you wealthier, but we're doing it because it's the right thing to do.

—Avi Brenner, Managing Director, AvNet, Rishon Lezion

Since the upsurge of reciprocal attacks between Palestinians and Israelis in 2000, the country has become a cauldron of physical threats, but the battle has also hopped from the physical world and onto the server. Here, targeted sorties against Israeli technology are routine. For example, the Israeli government's Web site experiences daily attacks from the outside.

The government is thorough in its prosecution of computer crime, but one instance of an attack came from within and was ruled legal. Israel's daily *Ha'aretz* reported that Avi Mizrahi, who had been arrested in 2003 for gaining entry into a Mossad recruitment Web site, did so ethically. "Internet surfers who check the vulnerabilities of Web sites are acting in the public good," said the judge. "If their intentions are not malicious and they do not cause any damage, they should even be praised."[4]

Availability is a significant challenge facing Israeli business. Denial-of-service attacks are frequent and can often be interpreted as information warfare. Firsthand stories from the inside are infrequent. The atmosphere is tense, and defense is in many ways linked to the private sector. Nonetheless, Brenner is upbeat, "We hope that the people we've been struggling with today become our eventual, peaceful neighbors."

Regulations

Israel's regulations vary. Its Protection of Privacy Law covers the processing of personal information. Outlining 11 types of activities that can be interpreted as law breaking, it is enforced by the Registrar of Databases within the Ministry of Justice. The registrar maintains the register of databases and can deny registration if he/she believes that it is used for illegal activities. In addition, a Digital Signature Law was passed in 2001, which regulates signatures on electronic media.

Because infrastructure is vulnerable, Israel also follows the U.S. National Cyber Security Division's CERT closely. Among the medical community, HIPPA is receiving attention and compliance.

Best Practices

Israeli business most often follows the BS 7799 standard, but importantly, threats and intensity of threats to Israel usually carry more than a technological component. Brenner has said, "With the rise in terrorist activity, the first consideration in

---

4. John Leyden. "Mossad Website 'Hacker' Walks Free." *The Register*. 1 March 2004.

Israel is always physical security—then technological and logical." Increased awareness and protection of critical infrastructures becomes a part of this equation, too, in both the public and private sectors.

In building a security strategy, Israeli companies examine five distinct circles, as follows:

- Physical security
- Detection
- Emergencies
- Recovery
- Insurance

The first circle is a physical security concern. Because of it, the CSO undertakes both elements of security simultaneously (marrying, so to speak, the physical to the technological). This saves time and creates a high level of awareness that is organization-wide. It also enables the elimination of redundancies. In some respects, however, it can also reduce corporate investment in information security, leaving systems more vulnerable.

Second is the circle of detection: If physical or front-line security has given way, a bell should sound or an alarm should reveal a breach. This second sphere is one of the most critical because, again, when you combine the physical and the technological, the idea of "false positives" discussed in Chapter 6, "Developing Radar," increases considerably.

Beyond detection, the third circle is emergency related. Each company must ask itself what emergency procedures are in place that can control a situation or a person who carries out emergency-relevant activities. For example, has he or she been shot, separated from their work area, or otherwise compromised?

The fourth circle of security in the Israeli environment deals with recovery—whether physical or logical, recovery is necessary for moving the whole of the organization forward, and a strong business continuity plan is a must-have.

Finally, to carry out business continuity, there is a need for the fifth circle: insurance. As companies begin to figure out their security investment, they must examine the benefit of protecting their entire infrastructure and technological assets, weighing its ultimate destruction against proper protection.

"The major conclusion we've reached in all of this isn't really a solution: If you want to protect the system from the outside world, don't connect it to the outside world," says Brenner. "Defense is never connected to the outside world, and it works hard to secure resources from the public domain. This is my major conclusion, but this conclusion can't be applied to business."

Final Israeli Thoughts

There are two large security service companies in Israel, and a host of good smaller ones. However, similar to stories you will hear in Saudi Arabia about all of your partners being "closely related to the royal family," the corporate security trade in Israel is riddled with those who are "former Mossad" agents. Although this is more likely to be true here than in the rest of the world, you should still beware of the old "if I told you I'd have to kill you" response when checking backgrounds. Network with the community, and you will have a head start in sorting out the good players from the James Bond wannabes.

Many large companies, such as IBM, have long-standing security operations based successfully in Israel, and you can, too. Follow their lead by hiring smart locals from the top universities and well-trained staff recently retired from military or intelligence services. Just remember that passions run deep, rumors become reality, and security means the difference between life and death.

North Africa, the Eastern Mediterranean, and Saudi Arabia

North Africa is a very difficult place for international cross-border security operations. There is very little rule of law—contract or regulatory—that is enforceable. Do not leave things to trust. Most North African states are ruled with a shaky degree of political and technical infrastructure, a higher degree of terrorism, different cultural work ethics, and anti-Western biases in the workforce. A great many local companies, which have been passed down through generations, are thriving. Over time, they have learned to work in sync with the flow of power, trade, and terror. Do not mistake your difficulties working in their environment with theirs.

In the Eastern Mediterranean, you will experience something wholly different. In much of Lebanon you will again find a trilingual populace that is Western-leaning and that is guided by strong leadership. Vetting local personnel will still pose an underlying risk to your global security operations. As you move further up the coast into Syria you will find a provincial mentality that does work domestically, but do not expect a jumping-off point into the rest of the territory.

Should you choose this region, I recommend using local partners in Cairo, Egypt, because of its size and stability, as your stepping stone. After Cairo, I suggest that you look to Amman, Jordan, because although it is smaller than Cairo, it has a very pro-business environment. Finally, my third choice (and first with my heart) is Beirut, Lebanon, because it has made so much progress toward reclaiming its historic leadership role in regional commerce.

Saudi Arabia (.SA)

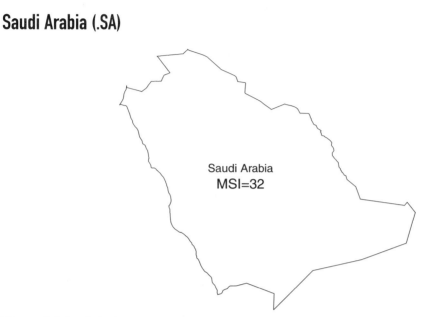

Saudi Arabia
MSI=32

Figure 10-5 Saudi Arabia

MSI = 32

Pros: Burgeoning domestic market that houses many multinationals, security savvy

Cons: Difficult security partner, low Internet penetration, practically no cross-border activity

A vast marketplace, Saudi Arabia is where many want to do business in the region. And then there's the oil. Aramco, the American Arab Oil Company, is the world's largest, and it is based in Saudi Arabia. Most major Western countries do business here. However, Saudi Arabia does not function as a cross-border business hub to the rest of the Arab world. You can come here if you are invited by a member of the extended royal family or by an officer of an established Saudi business.

The days of the Saudis abandoning their Rolls Royces on the side of the road when they run out of gas is long over. Global corporate security is taken very seriously in Saudi Arabia. Trade is the country's lifeblood, and they do not want to be taken advantage of. Do not underestimate their intelligence or veracity. Expect them to have the highest understanding and insight into a global security scheme.

In turn, the Saudis are highly effective global business people, but do not expect a sea of progressives. The culture is not readily accepting of women in authority, and that includes security officers (sorry Patty). It would be unwise to send a woman to do your negotiating. I know one female president of a software firm that lost an already-awarded Saudi contract after she showed up to a ceremonial signing—only then did the Saudis realize that Gray was a woman's name. Her company lost a software deal for the world's largest airport located in Riyadh. Surrendering gender equity is simply the cost of doing business in Saudi Arabia.

So is surrendering intellectual property—piracy is a perennial menace, and laws prohibiting it are inconsistent. The Saudi legal system "protects and facilitates acquisition and disposition of all property rights, including intellectual property." Although the government signed on to the Universal Copyright Convention in 1994, implementation is incomplete, but seizures of pirated goods—especially U.S.-made goods—has been stepped up in recent years. Trademarks are protected under the Trademark Law. Trade secrets are not protected by law and must be written clearly into contracts.[5]

Baksheesh

The first word I learned in Arabic was *baksheesh*, which loosely translates to "bribe." It is not a bad word in this culture. In fact, it is a way of life that is quite different from a bribe. For a U.S. company that is covered under the Foreign Anti-Corrupt Practices Act, it is not a matter of trying to skirt the law. It is a matter of understanding fully how business operates here before you make decisions. You must be firm in your business ethics all over the world, while still being polite and respectful of age-old traditions.

Saudis put a lot of stock in security, and they aren't afraid to invest. When working with a major oil company there I found a strong emphasis on information security and database security. One of the big drivers is confidentiality and privacy, and I'd have to say that because the whole country is run by a small family, privacy is a main driver, the crown jewel. This extends into the security environment. Don't think you'll get access to a Saudi company's firewall or access control. They'll refuse you no matter how much they trust you.

—Mike White, Security Expert, Johannesburg

---

5. *"Saudi Arabia." Middle East Diversification and Defense Market Guide. n.d.*

If you do enter Saudi Arabia, it should be purely for the domestic market. You must get an invitation, and it must be stamped by the Ministry of Commerce. This invitation qualifies you for a visa application and paves the way for finding a local partner. Make sure you pick the right one. That's not as easy as it sounds. Know that many will say they are of royal or kingly descent to get your business, because that's how business gets done.

Saudi Arabia records one of the lowest levels of Internet use in the world; it is still highly restricted by law. Concerns over how best to censor non–Saudi-acceptable content is causing its people to be held back in terms of learning the latest security technology. Although there is a high level of computer network usage, the packets all stop at the proxy server. Just like Western magazines often take three extra months to hit the newsstand (it takes a while to Sharpie over all the offending pictures and words), e-mail is often delayed for similar reasons. Although this makes it easier to secure against viruses, working within these restrictions for companies that have a legitimate need for electronic interactions is best left to local security professionals.

Trust Works Both Ways

All visitors to Saudi Arabia must have a Saudi sponsor in order to obtain a business visa to enter Saudi Arabia. Visas tend to be for only one entry and for a short duration. The Saudi who agrees to act as a sponsor accepts certain legal obligations, including personal liability for the actions of the visitor. Therefore, a Saudi rarely assumes sponsorship unless he has a personal interest in the proposed visit.[6]

Just as you receive regular scam e-mails from Nigeria that plead with you to open your bank account to a widow's hundreds of millions of dollars, so will royal family members spring from the woodwork when you seek them. Many really are royalty and simply want a piece of your money. Here, all Saudi contracts go to Saudi companies, and you will probably need that royal leverage. Just prepare yourself: You will be a subcontractor here, period.

6. Ibid.

South Africa (.ZA)

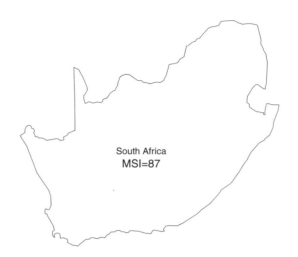

South Africa
MSI=87

Figure 10-6 South Africa

MSI = 87

Pros: Smart personnel, universally accepted and desired

Cons: Limited connectivity, 12-hour flight from Europe

If not for the 12-hour flight from central Europe to Johannesburg, South Africa might very well be the highest MSI-ranked nation in EMEA. From experience, it is easier than the trans-Atlantic flight simply because there is no time zone difference, but it is still tucked at the bottom of the region and tough to reach.

South Africa's sophisticated corporate security professionalism, education, and training are impressive. Corporations make very good use of security internally, especially among some of the largest global companies in the world (most of whom maintain a very low profile).

Apartheid's end has rekindled national pride that is at once fervently engaged in the country's athletic squads such as rugby or cricket and yet able to adapt with perfect chameleon-esque skill on the world stage. South Africans are by far the most sought-after talent pool in EMEA. They are welcomed everywhere. They have significant expertise, and they are relatively inexpensive; just compare the rand to the euro. South Africa has yet to (but it could certainly become) an outsourcing haven. Salaries can remain low, and people will still be very happy in their jobs. Power is sufficient in the big cities. Communications can be risky, because the African north-south trunk line is *it*, but satellite has alleviated this concern in recent years. Local crime exists, but usually does not affect foreign business staff as much as natives, and it is usually low tech. Terrorism threats are moderate but rising. Because South Africa's democracy and its entrée to the community of trusted nations is so new, it can be difficult for South Africans to get foreign visas.

Since the dismantling of apartheid, black empowerment has become job one in South Africa. Security is number two, and choosing partners accordingly is critical. Also, computer security is new, and it is one of the first sectors that black-empowered business has leveraged because it doesn't require a long track record.

On the Ground

At the bottom tip of the continent and nestled amid some of the earth's most diverse, striking landscape, the South African experiment continues. More than 10 years after apartheid's fall, the country has taken on the courageous, difficult task of dismantling, reconciling, and reconstructing a state from minority white to majority black rule.

With this upheaval have come significant economic, intellectual, and security obstacles. Educating a new generation of blacks, many of whom are just now pulling themselves from unthinkable destitution and oppression, is a tall order. In addition, the AIDS epidemic that has torn through the entirety of the continent has not spared even this developed country, but South Africa presses on.

Glue and the Manufacturer's Floor: Business Evolves in South Africa

Still, the change in South African is heartening and is producing some amazing results. Mike White, a partner at Deloitte, recounts a story wherein a division of one of the largest manufacturing concerns in South Africa called him up one morning and said, "Mike, we have to talk to you—we need a new computer system."

According to Mike, this had happened a lot of times in his career and he wasn't that surprised—something is always happening in the DNA of the organization that requires such a move. But, then they told him what the problem was...

"We're having a stock issue that could be security related. When we take stock every month, our physical inventory of metal coils is way up compared to what we have in our books—that is what our computer's telling us."

continues...

Glue and the Manufacturer's Floor: Business Evolves in South Africa   Continued

The problem was significant—these weren't tiny springs, they were massive coils that were resulting in about 300,000 rand of write-off per month, which, at that time and in that place, was very important to the company. So, Mike suggested that they get together to begin theorizing what could be causing the issue, which by this point Mike didn't think was computer related. He recounts the rest of the story as follows:

There we sat in the boardroom with the management of this manufacturing concern, putting our minds at work on behalf of the issue, when I said, "We need to get everyone up here that has anything to do with these coils—from the people who touch the raw material to everyone on the line. We want everybody in the room and we need to know what they think the issues are to see if we can't connect the dots."

This is where the glue part begins. We brought people upstairs from the manufacturing floor—including black people, which was unheard of, who had never been in a boardroom in their entire lives. They'd only worked on the factory floor and the management was quite nervous. "Why do you want those people up here?" they asked. This was all seen as a bit odd and strange, but nonetheless they decided to follow our lead.

So, we get all these folks up there and while they're bemusedly looking at the posh furniture and paintings and so on, we laid out the problem and asked if they had any clue as to what might be happening. I'll never forget it: One of the first people to talk was one chap—he became our glue man—who said, "I'll tell you where the problem starts. It starts with my area. I get these coils and they all come with labels printed out and they come into my receiving area and, quite simply, the labels fall off."

Well, obviously, the labels were everything—you couldn't track the supply chain without them. Our chap wasn't done though.

"I can solve this problem," he said.

"What do you mean?" we asked.
"You need better glue," he said. "I have a friend who has this great glue and I bet the labels won't fall of once you get this glue on them."

continues...

Glue and the Manufacturer's Floor: Business Evolves in South Africa Continued

So, one of the first implementation recommendations is that we need to get this glue, and there were a series of recommendations that I ended up writing into our report, and this one—need new and more glue—was the most unorthodox of any recommendation I'd ever made on a formal report, but they implemented new glue that very same month.

And I'll tell you what, at the end of that first month, when we first implemented a labeling system that involved this different glue, there was NO write off. It disappeared and the manufacturer was glowing.

"You guys are geniuses," they said.

In reality, we just listened to their people. We gave a collective of workers who had never sat in a boardroom a voice, and they solved the problem in the most effective, cost-efficient, practical, and meaningful way. That solidly reinforced to me that people are important up and down an organization and, as we celebrate the 10-year anniversary of apartheid's end, this is a powerful example of how communication in the security function led to business process enhancement, which under previous rule of law would have been impossible just because of skin color.

Critical to the transformation of South Africa is the notion of black economic empowerment. Various charters ensure that a certain minimum of industry needs to be in the ownership hands of black people so that economic power can become more equally dispersed. This affects business in significant ways. If you are seeking government work in South Africa, you must do so with an appropriate percentage of black involvement.

Although medicine, economics, and various sciences have been areas significantly enriched by black empowerment, the tech sector as it relates to security has yet to benefit as much. Because audits on percentages in terms of race can penalize firms heavily for noncompliance, it is a challenge; take heart, however, because it is a comprehensive percentage that's measured—all of your stationery could come from a black provider, for example, whereas all your security could come from a white provider. Kobus Burger, a Johannesburg-based security expert, has said that major effects of black economic empowerment have had little effect on business, but he has seen government sometimes choosing newer, and thus less-qualified security and accounting consultancies based on the legislation, but knows firsthand that progress is developing.

South Africa's economy in general is experiencing very deliberate growth of about 2 to 2.5 percent per annum. There is no economic boom, and a special focus on cost-cutting and rand-counting has followed, affecting security spends by companies, which have traditionally gone toward less-holistic means of protection such as firewalls and virus protection. That said, the Middle East has opened up to become a growth market for South African companies, with both private and government opportunities beginning to flourish.

Wireless represents a growing, nascent sector that is posing a host of new security challenges throughout the continent, and they are also very acute in South Africa. Its ease and flexibility have catalyzed a quick up-tick. Companies are pushing its functionality. Many security service consultancies are trying to promote guidelines for its usage and highlight the inadequacy of native security features.

War Driving and You

War driving is *illegal* in many quarters of Europe and the United States. Make sure you understand the laws surrounding data and privacy before embarking on your own war drive.

Many South African companies simply do not care about security. They would say, "We need to roll out a network as soon as possible, and wireless seems like the easiest." Myriad installers make it readily available, and same-day access is common. Burger discusses drive-bys—wherein his team cruises a location in search of wireless signals. He says there is a complete ignorance around organizational exposure:

In many cases I surprise clients. For instance I could drive by a bank, pick up a wireless network, pick up the wireless interface point identification, and gather that information—then take it to the bank and say, "Did you know you have this vulnerability?" and then the whole activity starts. More often than not, the financial institutions have no previous knowledge of a wireless install at the highest levels. Then they dig a bit, or I dig a bit, and find that inside there was an unapproved project going on. Someone obtained equipment from an IT supplier—they borrowed it to evaluate the technology—and there were no formal approval procedures in place to stop it, and the person using it just wanted to get their hands dirty with it. Yet, they've just exposed the entire financial institution's network and, in turn, customer data, to anyone driving by who could pick up a wireless signal and had minimal hacking expertise. Know that we embarked upon this ethically, and we just gathered information. We didn't evaluate how significant the find was, but we were able to do that without any legal repercussions here. I'm not sure I would do that in Europe.

South Africa Awakening

The *Cape Times* recently reported that "A South African digital security company has successfully traced a group of young Brazilian computer hackers who have defaced Web sites for the past month—purely for fun and to 'punish' Webmasters they consider sleepy."[7]

Even though this story highlights financial institution ignorance surrounding its own technology, the financial sector is probably the most attuned to security needs and has gone to great lengths to secure itself, spending more than most segments in the country. Significantly, at the other end of the spectrum sits manufacturing.

Manufacturing's claim that it doesn't care about its information remaining insecure in the face of competition underscores one of the most significant issues in global corporate security facing South Africa: ignorance. It's a global game, and they don't know it.

—Kobus Burger, Partner, Deloitte Security Services Group for Southern Africa, Johannesburg

Certain manufacturers have said their information just isn't important. They are very infrastructure-cost capital intensive. They say even if competitors get this information, it is very difficult to do anything useful with it. Furthermore, manufacturing simply tends to be lax in maintaining internal monitoring functions at peak levels. One company fired employees for e-mail abuse—sending attachments home and carrying on too much personal e-mail during hours of business. What the company didn't bargain on was that the employees would go to court and then start to prove that management was in violation of the same policies used to fire the employees. The situation cost the company millions in terms of severance

---

7. *"Hackers Deface More Than 70 Websites in Weekend Raids." Cape Times. 1 June 2004.*

packages. This starkly showcases how an inconsistent application of policies affected a company. They used the right policy in the wrong way even while they were themselves guilty of infrastructure abuse.

Regulations

South Africa is still developing laws related to information and technology as it continues to rebuild under its newest constitution, penned in 1996. That landmark document discussed the need for a privacy act within the country. Further, 2002 saw the South African Law Commission initiate a draft of a comprehensive privacy act. Additionally, access to information laws, regulation of interception to communication laws—all these are maturing quickly in a drive to avoid having to fall under EU data-protection directives.

As of now, businesses considering a move into South Africa should consider the following two regulations:

- **Black economic empowerment (BEE)**

  In a concerted drive to redress the stifling economic effects of apartheid, the democratic South African government has adopted a policy of black economic empowerment, which is broad based, inclusive, and part of the country's overall growth strategy; it was signed into law in 2003. Public-private partnerships are being strategically aimed at substantially increasing black participation at all levels in the economy. BEE seeks to substantially and equitably transfer ownership, management, and proportionate control of South Africa's financial and economic resources to the majority of its citizens. It also aims to ensure broader and meaningful participation in the economy by black people.[8]

- **King 2**

  King 2 deals specifically with corporate governance and executive roles in understanding and managing risk, maintaining open and honest lines of communication with shareholders, and serving companies in an accountable matter. An entire section of King 2 deals specifically with information technology and corporate governance. Although this is not yet law, it is important to be familiar with its precepts.

---

8. *"Code of Practice for Black Economic Empowerment in Public Private Partnerships." PPP Unit, National Treasury. December 2003.*

Best Practices

ISO 17799 and ISO 13335 serve as the baseline best practice standard in South Africa. In the financial services community, Basel II provides definitive guidance. Any companies dealing with the United States are taking Sarbanes-Oxley very seriously and creating internal stipulations based on it.

In South Africa, organizations have so many risks to manage, and they very often look at security as a technology issue. They have yet to embrace the notion that information is a business asset and is actually an asset that's integral to line management—to senior execs—in terms of conducting their business and making profits. They haven't made that mind shift.

Management thinks: "IT are the ones who process information, therefore they are the ones who should protect it. They are the ones who should assign a value to it and apply appropriate measures." This is, of course, wrong. So we also have misalignment between how internal auditors view the risk and report it up through the audit committee channel vs. what management views it as vs. what IT views it as. So that misalignment causes wrong allocation of resources, wrong levels of controls implemented in many instances.

— Kobus Burger, Partner, Deloitte Security Services Group for Southern Africa, Johannesburg

The biggest issue? Management has never really undertaken an exercise to determine the value of information assets. That value contains many components—monetary value, embarrassment value, brand value, litigation value. So when things go wrong or there is a compromise in terms of information as it relates to confidentiality, integrity, and availability, what is the consequence? Well, then you get to the real value, and South African management has no concept of what that really means to them in context of their business and industry.

However, top companies in South Africa have begun to embrace a holistic view. They really understand the value of awareness and they understand the value of culture—that the overall culture of an organization can really nullify a holistic approach around a security that a CSO or manager might have. Burger talks about a financial institution in South Africa that has a rule book and in that rule book—they're very proud of this—they have just one rule: "There are no rules." Says Burger, "That's a very anti-policy and bureaucracy and red tape posture to which the application of best practices and policies and behaviors is very difficult."

Go Big 4

In South Africa, there are few full-service consultancies of the Ernst & Young/Deloitte/KPMG/PWC variety; if you're headed there, however, I suggest enlisting one because they will afford you the advice and service and approach you will need to remain culturally sensitive and secured.

South Africa is also home to many multinational companies. They pretty much run their operations out of the country as islands. They appoint security officers in their respective countries, but there's not necessarily a vice president of security to whom they report. South African organizations are not like U.S. companies where you would have an equivalent to a security vice president. They would see the need, but they would report to their local technology group. It is very fragmented, and it makes them very vulnerable.

Final South African Thoughts

South Africa is a fine cross-border partner. Skilled and well loved throughout the Middle East and Europe, the country is known for superior global corporate security practices and low-cost labor. It would make a great security outsource match for any American or European company looking to save money while not compromising risk. Do not hesitate to partner here no matter where you plan to do business in this broad expanse of land called EMEA.

Chapter 11

The Americas

Figure 11-1 The Americas

Stretching from Canada's Nunavut Territory to Chile's Terra del Fuego, the Americas encompass the once "New World." Seafaring Europeans divided and conquered its continents in the fifteenth century. Assimilation with indigenous cultures followed. Young and vibrant on the world stage, the Americas remain historically adolescent to adult counterparts in EMEA and Asia.

Beginning in Canada and the United States, I discuss how these similar cousins are tackling different threats and corporate security challenges. In Mexico, you will see how changes in language, culture, and security awareness begin and become more pronounced the farther south into Central America you go. Starting with Columbia, I discuss variations on South America's big countries where dictators and political intrigue have long seasoned this region's iconography.

Why America?

Amerigo Vespucci discovered the "New World" seven years after Columbus, and yet he is the Americas' namesake. Why? Cross-border business savvy! Upon returning to Europe, he quickly created pamphlets that were printed in Latin and distributed widely, one of which fell into the hands of German cartographer Martin Waldseemuiller. The mapmaker ultimately named the new territory after Vespucci, including the explorer's likeness on an initial 1000-count print run. Where was Christopher Columbus? Obviously *not* practicing constant vigilance in a quickly shrinking global business environment![1]

North America accommodates the majority of global Internet users. In the 1980s and 1990s, North Americans pioneered the ARPANET and the National Information Infrastructure, both of which led to the Internet's creation. Its first-ever commercialization of the World Wide Web standard laid a foundation for the shift that has redefined global business and necessitated the use of corporate security strategies. Canada has long been a multicultural haven and international gateway to the region. The United States, as the world's lone superpower, has driven much of the world's trade, technology adoption, and some aspects of corporate security practice.

CanAm Honesty

The United States has the lowest piracy rate in the world, topping out at 25 percent. Canada's rate is also lean at 38 percent.[2]

---

1. *"Amerigo Vespucci." Encyclopaedia Britannica Online. n.d.*
2. *Robyn Greenspan. "Global Piracy Rate Rises 40 Percent." Internet.com. 9 December 2002.*

Canada (.CA)

Canada
MSI=93

Figure 11-2 Canada

MSI = 93

Pros: Cultural shift proves easiest, business climate very similar

Cons: Adoption of bleeding-edge technology and therefore security is more conservative

Canada is a federation of 10 provinces anchored by Nova Scotia and Newfoundland in the Atlantic east and British Columbia in the Pacific west. Its vast, often-frigid real estate stretches northward to the Arctic Circle. The populace is generally open. Cultural diversity is celebrated. Canadians bring a thoughtful and intelligent demeanor to bear in business. Corporate security is practiced skillfully, although technology adoption tends to be a step behind the neighboring United States, because of the lower buying power of the Canadian dollar. Security business is generally conducted in English, although it is joined by a second official language—French, which is spoken most often in Quebec—and therefore your security policies must be bilingual.

The Quebecois are proud of and steadfastly committed to French to the point that enlisted provincial language police patrol Montreal's retail districts to ensure business is carried out *en Français*. Quebec also differs culturally, and there is a distinctively European flavor.

Built on a superlative infrastructure, Canada has an equally impressive rule of security law. Prominent multinationals settle here, and most are U.S.-involved, including Ford, GM, and a host of telecoms. Canadian security personnel are embraced around the world and are welcomed for their high degree of business acumen, strong security skill sets, historically expatriate thinking, and inviting cost structure.

Mounties Upgrade

Canada's (and much of the world's) current information security infrastructure is built upon disused Y2K operations. I remember meeting with the *Royal Canadian Mounted Police*'s (RCMP) information security leadership, who along with the *Communications Security Establishment* (CSE) hold much of the jurisdiction in the country. It was in the late 1980s, and the accommodations were not posh. In fact, their offices consisted of the upper floors of an abandoned shopping center. Now, with the greater attention and the ability to leverage Y2K facilities, greater force is brought to bear on Canadian and foreign companies doing business in Canada. Its approach to corporate security is highly collaborative, with strong public/private links that work.

Doing business here requires demonstrative "Canadian experience," meaning traceable domestic successes and multileveled relational buy-in. Importantly, there is a distinct, unspoken expectation of Canadian pricing resulting in Canadian citizens paying proportionately less for goods and services at home than their counterparts shopping at home in the United States or Europe. Canada is reportedly an ECHELON partner, which allows its government to listen in on foreign business communications.

Some of the most gifted professionals in Canada drive cabs in Toronto. They have two or three advanced degrees and hold invaluable skill that our country could use, but they don't have "Canada experience," and that's absolutely necessary for them to assimilate into the business, medical, and law cultures of the country.

—Adel Melek, Security Expert, Toronto

On the Ground

Canadian business casts a conservative eye on technology, but its security talent is preeminent. According to Toronto-based Adel Melek, Canadians tend to "be swifter at assimilating the conceptual framework for security than Americans, but we're always a step behind in terms of technology adoption." However, remember that Y2K significantly helped usher in a nationwide technological upgrade.

Slower technological adoption can be correlated to a less-than-robust economy. Executives request clear articulation and demonstrative ROI before making purchasing decisions. Any CSO trying to jumpstart a security strategy must justify ROSI that is reinforced by several compelling case studies. "We don't have the same regulatory environment as the U.S.," says Melek, "And so without real teeth, it's tough to motivate security out of thin air." Lack of teeth, a recurring theme when discussing emerging security regulations around the world, simply means that repercussions for violating a regulation cost less than compliance.

Key Regulations

A sparse regulatory environment is overshadowed by Canada's first-rate corporate security agencies. CANCert provides a national constant vigilance function. Additionally, the *Federal Association of Security Officials/Association fédérale des Responsables de la Securiteé* (FASO/AFRS) "works closely with government security organizations and the security industry to organize training seminars, workshops, and conferences. It also delivers briefs on new developments and new technologies."[3] Canada's *Office of Critical Infrastructure Protection and Emergency Preparedness* (OCIPEP) is the country's main agency responsible for developing and implementing "a comprehensive approach to protecting Canada's critical infrastructure."

Light-touch regulation includes the *Access to Information Act* (AIA) and a privacy act. Passed in 1983, AIA attempts to ensure governmental accountability by providing the public with access to information about use of public funds.[4] Fines for violations never exceed $1,000. In 2000, the Personal Information Protection and Electronic Documents Act (commonly known as C-6) was passed "to support and promote electronic commerce by protecting personal information that is collected, used, or disclosed in certain circumstances, by providing for the use of electronic means to communicate or record information or transactions."[5] Although the guidelines for this act are stiff, the penalties aren't.

---

3. "Who Are We?" *FASO-AFRS. n.d. www.faso-afrs.ca/about-e.html (3 June 2004).*
4. *National Omnibus Laws. PrivacyExchange.org. n.d. www.privacyexchange.org (3 June 2004).*
5. *Ibid.*

Corporate governance has risen in priority with passage of the U.S. Sarbanes-Oxley Act (SOX). The Canadian bill C-198 mandates that any company that trades on the U.S. or Canadian stock exchange must file an internal control report along with its annual report. This will have long-term implications for corporate security practice because it closely links with corporate governance best practices.

Canada's *Personal Information Protection and Electronic Documents Act* (PIPEDA), S.C. 2000, provides for the acceptance of electronic documents (over paper based), and spells out where a digital signature may be accepted. Subsection 31 defines a secure electronic signature, and subsection 48 describes the characteristics of secure electronic signatures that have been issued by "reliable" certificate authorities.[6]

As of this writing, there are no recognized standards for accrediting reliable certificate authorities, so the regulations authorize the president of the Canadian Treasury Board to approve certificates that will hold up in court. The Treasury Board maintains a Web site that keeps a current list of approved providers, so be sure to use one for your Canadian business.

Best Practices

Canadian companies such as Entrust made a name for themselves by writing some of the world's finest encryption algorithms. Significant because the United States barred encryption exports due to its "munitions" classification within the Export Control Act, Canada became an early cross-border encryption hotbed. The country's security professionals are well trained and highly skilled.

Canada and Fast-Track Common Criteria

Common Criteria, now the global benchmark when building security products and services, has significantly leveraged the forward-thinking Canadian Security Establishment. The CSE, roughly equivalent to America's *National Security Agency* (NSA) and the UK's *Government Communications Headquarters* (GCHQ), looked at the best parts of the NSA's Trusted Computing programs and found a way to bring much of the goodness directly into the market without the crippling time lags that made the American system irrelevant to the general business user. The CSE created a fast-track "functionally equivalent" process that mirrored the security levels designated by the NSA's Orange Book

continues...

---

6. *"Statutes of Canada: 2000. Bill C-6/Assented to 13 April, 2000." Office of the Privacy Commissioner of Canada.*

Canada and Fast-Track Common Criteria   Continued

and thus was able to help security products get to market in a timely and secure fashion. It was these early successes that the globally accepted Common Criteria was built upon, and this type of thinking, which blends strong security with business realities, typifies the Canadian approach to security.

When a typical Canadian company builds its security strategy, it prioritizes international and local regulations that merit compliance. These are combined with those elements of security that either deliver business-process enhancement or enablement and that have a clear ROI. BS 7799 is the preferred standard, true to Canada's British roots. "I can't underscore enough how Canadian companies are also complying with American regulations that will eventually touch us, such as the SOX," said Melek.

Vancouver: Asian Gateway

Vancouver was expected to accept the mantle of a bridge to Asia upon Hong Kong's handover to the Chinese government in 1997. Preparations began before the formal transition of power. Then, no one anticipated that Hong Kong would continue to thrive as an open business center. Since it did, Vancouver hasn't become the nerve center for Asian business as anticipated, but it still remains the best gateway to China in North America.

Final Canadian Thoughts

Canada represents a potentially ideal cross-border partner, mainly because characteristically difficult obstacles to cross-border business—communications and customs—barely exist. Its business culture nearly mirrors that of the United States, and its combination of an eased regulatory and terror-free environment provides ample reason to settle there. Expect to find it easy to integrate Canada into your global security plans, and expect their help when working elsewhere in the world. In creating your global security strategy, I highly recommend Canada's vast marketplace and strong international ties to any cross-border business.

United States (.US)

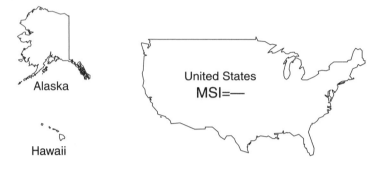

Figure 11-3 The United States

The United States is a lightning rod for derision and a beacon of hope. Its seemingly boundless affluence as the world's only superpower offers pervasive market opportunities for foreign business. In security, as in business, it is certainly a global driver. Creators of the Internet and much of the complementary technology that frames modern cross-border business, the United States continues to grapple with bringing security to the level of its powerful innovations. In 2003, it spent $391 billion trying to figure that out.[7]

Although U.S. companies face cultural challenges when moving cross border, those wanting to gain entry in the States face one of history's most imposing regulatory landscapes. Although Americans consider their security very straightforward—regulations-driven, government-led, and home to many of the security and infrastructure products that work around the world—there are twists such as state-specific rules, flaunting of regulations without commensurate penalties, and a legal system that rewards finding loopholes that will confound many first timers. It is necessary, therefore, to examine and understand American security through foreign spectacles, because successful navigation here will help you leverage a fantastic talent pool, the world's best information infrastructure (see China's 2008

---

7. *"Manufacturing and Banking Industries to Lead U.S. IT Spending in 2004, IDC Report Reveals." 12 February 2004. www.idc.com.*

claim on that in Chapter 12, "Asia Pacific"), massive domestic markets, and a strong position in the hardware and software that run the leading companies of the world today.

Federal and state governments facilitate a granularity to local laws that can be shocking to the outsider. Regionally, microclimates of culture merit mention. The Northeast is typically known for its banking and finance. The Midwest and South are agrarian- and manufacturing-driven. The West has become known for its technology and entertainment industries. Each region has a commensurate pace of life. The Northeast moves quickly and best exemplifies an American directness and sometimes bullish attitude. The Midwest and South function more slowly, and each has social customs that require an almost "souk-like" mentality. The West was the last to be settled by Europeans and combines the two cadences—here anything goes.

Global Perception of the United States

Of import to most readers are the ways the United States is perceived abroad. All stereotypes are in play and, amazingly, the J. R. Ewing/*Dallas* and *Baywatch* mindsets are still figuring prominently into foreign ideas of who we are and how we operate. So are the brands that precede Americans abroad—especially the one with the Colonel and the one with the golden arches. America is also deemed narcissistic, with its one-digit (1) country code (everyone else has two) and lack of widespread external, global awareness. Most do not expect that we will know a second language or understand geography or have a grip on politics in their part of the world. In turn, we think they should probably know everything about us.

U.S. German

I was once chatting with a very senior German executive of a consulting firm in Germany. We got on the subject of America. The man leaned very close to me and nearly whispered, "You know that if it had not been for a single congressional vote, German would be America's national language." Nodding politely, I chalked it up to a defect in the German education system. You can guess my surprise when I got back to my hotel and "Googled" it, discovering that it was a defect in the American education system. Expect these different perspectives from everyone you meet, and remember that the versions of history that you were taught are not always in sync (or even correct) with what your foreign counterparts believe. This will make its way in to security, on the delivery sides, and for the rank-and-file staff. Look for these signs early so that they do not knock your security policy off its tracks before you get out of the gate.

We are known as hardworking—usually too hardworking—but we are also considered underachieving. For most parts of the world, we do not take enough time off. We are overly litigious and overly expansionist. Our commitment to democracy has the vocal support of some and silent support of many others. We are perceived as direct in our dealings, which plays with varying degrees of success depending on the cross-border partner. There is now an opinion that we are imperialistic and arrogant in our understanding of freedom and how it should germinate.

One-Sized Password Fits All

In Chapter 9, "Europe," I discussed how the UK citizenry was tempted to give out passwords for chocolate. The United States is full of mishaps, misuse, and carelessness, and here are two prime examples.

During the Cold War, the United States had more than 1,000 Minutemen *Inter-Continental Ballistic Missiles* (ICBMs) poised to create mutual assured destruction if so ordered by the president. To prevent a hacker from gaining access to this arsenal of death, they required an eight-digit launch code to be entered before they would lift off. But as discussed previously, a password system is only as strong as the password you choose. What did the White House use for decades as said code? What many people who worked on the system could tell you—this most important password in the free world was set to 00000000.

But wait, there's more. When Wang was the leading mini-computer manufacturer, they had a problem with maintenance of their systems after they were sent out into the field. So they hard coded a field-service master password right into their operating system. Much to the chagrin of the U.S. State Department that relied on these computers in all of their embassies and consulates around the world, many folks knew that this override password was field.service.

All of these perceptions serve to help and hurt us among foreign security partners. If you are American, I exhort you to take great pains to learn about the countries in which you do business and not comically recount the travails you have had abroad. You can read article after article in American business journals that deal with "Cultural Mishaps and Mayhem Across the Pond" or "Big Trouble in Little China: When I Didn't Bow in Hong Kong." Just like establishing your coordinates or building the base, nothing will surpass the legwork and ROI of a reasoned anthropological approach and strong relationship building with your new partners abroad. It will only improve your security posture.

On the Ground

U.S. global corporate security has undergone uncommon shifts in rigor and practice since the 1990s. Pre-network security was an interesting blend of battlefield methodology trying to cram its way into the business environment. In the early 1990s, the only best practice baselines were those that came from the U.S. government. Its rainbow series of guidebooks were applied, but as networks emerged, these became quickly obsolete.

Reading Rainbow

The NSA created a series of security guidebooks for products dealing with the U.S. government. Each cover was marked by a different color, and the set in its entirety became known as the "rainbow series." Although it collectively covered myriad security topics, the tome (and shade) of choice was the "Orange Book," which focused on the three main security levels that computers could attain. The second most popular volume was the "Red Book," with its attendant focus on network security.

Each of the Orange Book's three major levels (A was highest, B was next, and C was lowest) had subcategories, with C2 becoming so often quoted that it became the near-mantra of the security field of the 1980s. In addition to spelling out what security functions were necessary to meet the C2 level, the NSA offered an excruciating process of testing and compliance. In the end, although everyone sought this "certification" for their products, most balked at the time, money, and patience needed to attain it. Imagine creating a computer in the 1980s that could not be changed for five years. No faster processor, no more memory, no larger disks. By the time it made it through the C2 process, no one would buy it because it was too slow, too small, and too old. So as an evaluation process, it failed, but as a set of guidelines for security, it was not only the U.S. standard for decades, but became the basis of many other countries' (Canada and the UK included) security criteria.

When the network and the Internet were born, business changed overnight and with nearly incomparable speed. This momentum, as I have mentioned time and again, was usually the first element considered as technology seemed a boundlessly empowering and get-rich-quick ideal. Security was slapped onto the back end. Perhaps now, you might think that reaction would swing the pendulum far to the other side. Interestingly, however, the climate in the United States is very much tied to a continual deployment of technology as an enabler—letting it do what it does best while carefully slotting security where it can be most effectively and efficiently deployed. That is not to say stringent regulation isn't driving security practice; it is—like never before. But it's happening in a culture where progress and justice exist in tension.

C2 by 92

Although 9-11 awakened the American public to issues of national security, it has not driven corporate security. For those who sell corporate security products and services, it has gone of the way of "C2 by 92," which in the late 1980s prophesied big sales for 1991 that were never rung up. Public key encryption was said to be the next boon for the industry, changing the way the world did business and making passwords obsolete. Wow, that worked, too.

What is simply known as the "Enron debacle" has catalyzed one of the biggest security drivers in American—and now global—business culture. Sarbanes-Oxley, described in detail below, has emerged as a corporate governance law that is holding boards of directors and senior executives accountable for the lives of their companies. The other large driver in America proves to be another law—the *Graham-Leach-Bliley* (GLB) Act, also detailed later in this section, is one of the deepest privacy laws ever written and makes the consequences for mishandling customer data severe. Other drivers include *Critical Infrastructure Protection* (CIP), Homeland Security (PATRIOT Act), HIPAA (health care), and outsourcing.

These drivers have far-reaching impact around the world. As laws emerge on the global playing field, there is considerable cooperation with Europe and especially the United Kingdom. The United States is one of 38 nations that signed on to the Council of Europe's Convention on Cyber-Crime, although the U.S. Senate has not yet ratified the measure. cAmerican business is also saddling up to the European Safe Harbor law—albeit reluctantly.

Law and Order

U.S. federal authorities broke up what they called the biggest identity-theft case in U.S. history and charged three men on November 25, 2002 with stealing credit information, draining victims' bank accounts, and ruining their credit. U.S. Attorney James Comey said the losses were calculated so far at $2.7 million but would balloon to many more millions as more victims are identified. He said credit information for 30,000 people was stolen, and authorities are trying to determine how many of those individuals were victimized. The prosecutor called the case "every American's worst financial nightmare multiplied tens of thousands of times." Some victims had their bank accounts pillaged, addresses changed, lines of credit opened, and new credit cards issued without approval.[8]

"With a few keystrokes, these men essentially picked the pockets of tens of thousands of Americans and, in the process, took their identities, stole their money, and swiped their security," Comey said.

The scheme apparently began about three years ago when Philip Cummings, a help desk worker at Teledata Communications, sold passwords and codes for downloading consumer credit reports to an unidentified person. Teledata, a software company, provides banks with computerized access to credit information databases. Cummings was allegedly paid roughly $30 for each report, and the information was then passed on to at least 20 other people, who set out to make money from the stolen information. More than 15,000 credit reports were stolen from credit bureau Experian, and thousands of other credit reports were stolen from a handful of other companies. Cummings pled guilty, and could receive up to 30 years in prison for wire fraud and millions in fines.[9]

In the U.S. there have always been teeth behind penalties related to noncompliance. Even before 9-11, if you were to violate a regulation, there was a specific price to pay that usually meant a stiff monetary fine and even jail time.

—Adel Melek, Security Expert, Toronto

---

8. Larry Neumeister. ""U.S. Charges 3 in Historic ID Theft Case." AP. 25 November 2002.
9. Larry Neumeister. "Feds Break Up Identity Theft Ring." AP. 2 November 2002.

The U.S. industrial environment—driven by intellectual property—requires protection. Regulatory developments are pushing it from the other side, mandating that business take more control and become more secure. A minimum baseline that started with BSI 7799 and has evolved into ISO 17799 is driving a security posture that attempts to balance the right amount of security for the business process in question.

Key Regulations

Thought you had seen regulation? The saying goes "only in America," and in 2004, New York-based analyst and research firm Gartner declared "deregulation is dead, so get over it."[10] It pointed to America's Homeland Security initiative as a very public excuse to "increase overall governmental supervision of business. Regulation will go beyond healthcare and financial services industries to affect all industries. The impact of international rules regarding money laundering, privacy and security will spread from financial services to other industries, regardless of jurisdiction." This has and will only help security and privacy as it funnels into customer and organizational fortification. American security organizations and regulations can be dizzying, and I have developed four categories to permit coherent focus on each:

- Public agencies
- Existing, important regulations
- Homeland security-driven regulation
- Accountability-driven regulation

Public Agencies

The September 11 attacks on New York's World Trade Center and Washington D.C.'s Pentagon prompted significant overhaul in the way national security is conducted. The main adjustment came with the development of the Department of Homeland Security. Although so much of Homeland Security's task is poured into critical infrastructures, it does carry three key areas that run under its auspices and that are relevant to global corporate security. The first is the Critical Infrastructure Assurance Office (CIAO). Developed in 1998, this agency's role is to...

- Coordinate and implement the national strategy.

---

10. *"Don't Get Blindsided By Privacy and Security Regulations." GartnerG2. January 2002.*

- Assess the government's own risk and dependence on critical infrastructure.

- Raise awareness and public understanding and participation in critical infrastructure protection efforts.

- Coordinate legislative and public affairs to integrate infrastructure assurance objectives into the public and private sectors.

FedCIRC—the *Federal Computer Incident Response Center*—works on computer security issues that affect civilian agencies and departments of the federal government. It is also responsible for detecting and responding to attacks while coordinating responses.

The *National Infrastructure Protection Center* (NIPC) is an agency that provides threat assessment, warning, investigation, and response for threats or attacks against critical infrastructure. It "facilitates the federal government's response to a host of mitigation and investigation."[11] Whereas the NIPC serves as the single source for private enterprise, each sector is now establishing an *Information Sharing and Analysis Center* (ISAC).[12] Importantly, both the FedCIRC and ISAC play early-warning roles as it relates to national security.

The National Cyber Security Alliance is an educational body that tries to raise citizens' awareness of the critical role computer security plays in protecting the nation's Internet infrastructure.[13]

ECHELON

The media has often focused on an international electronic surveillance network run by the intelligence organizations in the United States, UK, Canada, Australia, and New Zealand. The EU describes ECHELON as a "global tapping grid, started as a simple cooperative intelligence information clearinghouse in the late 1940s." A recent BBC report noted that in 1971, the first ECHELON network was built. Today the nations that use it are able to covertly eavesdrop on phone conversations, e-mail, fax, Web browsing, and satellite transmissions. ECHELON "captures all the traffic it can and then sifts through it for keywords or anything the intelligence services deem to be 'suspicious.'" Know that it could be a silent listener as you conduct business in each of these regions.

11. Andreas Wenger, Jan Metzger, Myriam Dunn, ed., *International CIIP Handbook: An Inventory of Protection Policies in Eight Countries.* (Zurich: Swiss Federal institute of Technology, 2002) 104.
12. Ibid., 106.
13. Ibid., 107.

As mentioned in Part 1, "Charting a Course," the world's first *Computer Emergency Readiness Team* (CERT) was founded at Pittsburgh's Carnegie Mellon University in response to the Morris worm. The U.S. CERT is a clearinghouse for information and resources on serious computer incidents that are happening worldwide. It is a part of FIRST, the *Forum of Incident Response and Security Teams*, which is the global CERT umbrella organization. Remember, CERTs are for security professionals. The typical report from a CERT would do nothing but scare business people who are not well trained in the secure arts.

Pre 9–11 Regulations

Even preexisting the changes over homeland security and Enron, some regulations proved important in the United States. The Computer Fraud and Abuse Act of 1986 illustrated the federal government's awareness of and need to move on computer-related crime. It set forth two primary felonies—the offenses of "unauthorized access to 'federal interest' computers" and "unauthorized trafficking of passwords."[14] It was augmented by the Computer Abuse Amendments Act of 1994, which served to cover the transmission of viruses and malicious code.

The Electronic Communications Privacy Act passed in 1994 sets parameters on wiretapping and other forms of electronic communication interception. The Fair Credit Reporting Act is administered by the Fair Trade Commission. It is designed to promote accuracy, fairness, and privacy of information in the files of every *consumer reporting agency* (CRA). Most CRAs are credit bureaus that gather and sell information about you—such as whether you pay your bills on time or have filed bankruptcy—to creditors, employers, landlords, and other businesses. Finally the *Graham-Leach-Bliley* (GLB) Act addresses privacy concerns by outlining an array of requirements to protect customer information. It is one of the world's furthest-reaching laws of its kind and must be studied carefully as you implement business and design the appropriate corporate security measures. Remember, too, that local law must be followed in addition to federal mandates. GLB is one of the largest drivers of corporate security action in America. Why? Because it has teeth!

Correspondingly rigorous laws around security and privacy are beginning to surface at a state level. California, which on its own has the eighth largest economy in the world, recently passed a GLB-correlative law. The California Privacy Act was signed in 2003, and prohibits financial companies from sharing the details of a customer's financial transactions with third parties without the customer's permission. California consumers will also have the right to stop companies from

---

14. *Ibid.*, 102.

sharing information with affiliated companies unless they meet very stringent criteria. Of course, this has nuanced implications. Suppose, for example, that your servers are housed in California and are hit by hacker—you would have to report it to Californians. However, if your business is in California and your servers are in Nevada instead, they are outside the jurisdiction of this law and do not require reportage. If your business is outside California and your customers are California residents, however, it does! California Department of Consumer Affairs' Office of Privacy Protection (see the appendix, under United States of America) provides a necessary guidebook for compliance, including recommended practices, who to notify, how, when, and for what, as well as sample notices that you can leverage. With the buying power of a small country, this state law immediately takes on global significance. Moreover, note that that most other states now have relevant agencies and laws to examine, or they will in the near future. In 2002, Florida created the Cyber-security Institute, which focuses extra attention on cyber crimes in that state.

Budding industry-specific regulations regarding security and privacy continues to mature. The *Health Insurance Portability and Accountability Act* of 1996 (HIPAA) affects the health-provider industry. It seeks to enforce standards of health information while ensuring security and privacy of health information. It has mandated that all providers migrate to electronic medical records, which also makes security even that much more of a priority. Although security companies will extol the virtues, until there are significant penalties for noncompliance, expect lip-service-level responses by most health-care organizations.

America is a very litigious society. Take for example the California Privacy Act. If any California resident holds proof that a corporation in any way shared information on them to any third party without permission, even if it's a security incident, they could and will sue.

—Adel Melek, Partner, Deloitte & Touche, Toronto

Homeland Security–Driven Regulation

The terrorist attacks of 9-11 awoke the American government and public to dangers that had been commonplace elsewhere in the world. As President George W. Bush declared a "war on terrorism" that same year, the country's legislative branch began working with key government officials to draft the *Uniting and Strengthening America by Providing Appropriate Tools Required to Intercept and Obstruct Terrorism* (USA PATRIOT Act [yes, it really is an acronym]) of 2001. This extensive law has several elements relevant to the practice of corporate security in the United States. In sum, it deals with criminal laws, transporting hazardous materials, money laundering and counterfeiting, investigations and information sharing, federal grants, victims, immigration, and domestic security. It also expands electronic surveillance laws.

Concerning the latter, there has been a tightening of the Computer Abuse Amendments Act of 1994 to "address the transmission of viruses and other harmful code."[15] The act imposes five years of prison for first offenders and ten years for repeat offenders who damage a federal computing system "used by or for a government entity in furtherance of the administration of justice, national defense, or national security." Damage includes any injury to the "integrity or availability of data, a program, a system, or information that causes the loss of at least $5,000 or threatens the public health or safety. To be found guilty, the person must

- "Knowingly cause the transmission of a program, information, code, or command that results in damage to a protected computer without authorization or

- "Intentionally access a federal computer without authorization and cause damage (§ 814)."

The PATRIOT Act also mandates that the attorney general develop regional computer forensic labs and support existing ones for the study of seized or intercepted computer-based evidence, to train relevant government personnel, to aid law enforcement, share federal talent, and mindshare on computer criminal law. The PATRIOT Act's affect on civil rights has become controversial, and its swift passage provoked immediate protest. Time will tell whether the act fully infringes upon individual freedoms, but proponents of the law say that it was a necessary next step in evolving the country's security posture.

Security As a Weapon

Due to its classification as a "weapon," U.S. encryption could not easily be exported... until 2000, when a new rule allowed encryption product exports to 15 nations of the European Union and 8 other trading partners, including Australia, Japan, New Zealand, Norway, Switzerland, the Czech Republic, Poland, and Hungary. So for the first 20 years of my career, I was classified an arms dealer!

---

15. *Ibid.*

Accountability Regulations

Although it sounds like a haberdashery or sauce to be served over aged beef, Sarbanes-Oxley is far from either. A critical first step in reforming corporate governance following scandal's latest poster child Enron, the act was crafted by two legislators—Maryland Senator Paul Sarbanes and Ohio Congressman Michael Oxley. SOX aims to increase the transparency, security, and integrity of corporate governance in the United States. Signed in 2002, SOX practically overhauls federal regulation of public companies' corporate governance and is the toughest such law since the early twentieth century. It turns the screws on accountability standards and reporting obligations for directors and corporate officers, legal counsel, and security analysts. CEOs and CFOs must now sign off on the security of their data and infrastructure, and if done dishonestly or haphazardly, will result in fines from $1 to $5 million dollars and jail time. It also seeks to purge shady financial dealings between corporate officers and the company at large.

A new bill in Congress that has spawn from Sarbanes-Oxley is the Corporate Information Security Accountability Act of 2003, which is intended to protect the public safety, the economy, and shareholder investments by requiring public companies to include a certification by an independent party that an assessment has been conducted of the company's computer information security in accordance with standards prescribed by the SEC. Look for this—or something very similar—to become law soon.

With Sarbanes-Oxley, companies won't be wholesale penalized for wrongdoing, but they will be penalized if they don't clearly and comprehensively demonstrate that they tracked and acted on information resulting from the faithful, full compliance to the letter of the law as detailed under every provision of the act. Moving forward, and coming out of the first audit, companies who've band-aided their security and verification compliance will quickly see that's not feasible. This puppy's too extensive.

—*Bobby Christian, Acting CSO, Public Company Accounting Oversight Board, Washington D.C.*

SOX impacts corporate security directly, because the transfer, verification, and access of information all fall under the corporate security umbrella. Tracking identities that have access to corporate data, tracking what happens to that data and tracking who authorizes access and manipulation of that data will become more copious under SOX. In general, corporate security and corresponding technology either exist or are under development to at once fulfill and communicate SOX compliance. Elaborate identity-management systems are being adopted, and smart cards are making their way into the corporate environment. Over time, SOX will transform how corporate security is done in the United States.

Best Practices

Although some global businesses in the United States follow ISO 17799 as their standards base, it has not been adopted here nearly as fully as in many other advanced countries of the world. Part of this stems from the historical reliance on the U.S. government's own standards bodies, such as the *National Institute of Standards and Technology* (NIST), which is part of the Department of Commerce. The trend exists in moving away from U.S.-specific guidance to more internationally accepted guides, but the pace is slow. Expect that as businesses expand beyond the U.S. borders via outsourcing, supply chains, global customers, or simply organic growth, that this trend will accelerate and bring more U.S. companies into conformity with global standards.

Help for Implementing U.S. Security Regulations

A helpful hint to implement complex rules such as HIPAA: Go to the NIST Web site (see the appendix under United States of America), and look for security implementation guides. They will save you a lot of time, trouble, and legal bills in getting started with compliance. Here is an example:

—*NIST Special Publication 800-66: An Introductory Resource Guide for Implementing the Health Insurance Portability and Accountability Act (HIPAA) Security Rule (Information Security)*

One new place to look for best practices is in "Information Security Governance: A Call to Action," which was a report created from the first National Cyber Security Summit. It details recommendations for identifying cybersecurity roles and responsibilities within corporate executive management structures and begins to help establish security baselines and best practices. This is a group to watch, but also watch out, because it is predominantly composed of companies that are selling security, not buying it (as opposed to the Jericho Forum, discussed in Chapter 9).

Finally, for companies involved in critical infrastructure industries, and even those that aren't but want help with heightened security postures, there is the InfraGard program (http://www.infragard.net/). InfraGard is an information-sharing and -analysis effort serving the interests and combining the knowledge base of a wide range of members. At its most basic level, InfraGard is a cooperative undertaking between the U.S. government (led by the FBI) and an association of businesses, academic institutions, state and local law enforcement agencies, and other participants dedicated to increasing the security of U.S. critical infrastructures. All InfraGard participants are committed to the proposition that a robust exchange of information about threats to and actual attacks on these critical infrastructures is an important element for successful infrastructure protection efforts. The goal of InfraGard is to enable the flow of information so that the owners and operators of infrastructure assets can better protect themselves and so that the U.S. government can better discharge its law enforcement and national security responsibilities.

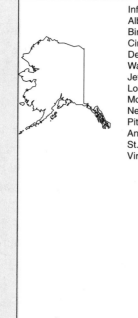

InfraGard by Location (mid-2004)
Albany, Albuquerque, Anchorage, Atlanta, Austin, Baltimore, Baton Rouge, Birmingham, Boston, Buffalo, Charlotte, Chattahoochee Valley, Chicago, Cincinnati, Cleveland, Columbia, Columbus, Connecticut, Dallas, Dayton, Delaware, Denver, Des Moines, Detroit, Eastern Carolina, El Paso, Fort Wayne, Harrisburg, Honolulu, Houston, Indianapolis, Jackson, Jacksonville, Jefferson City, Kansas City, Knoxville, Lafayette, Las Vegas, Little Rock, Los Angeles, Louisville, Madison, Memphis, Miami, Milwaukee, Minneapolis, Mobile, Nashville, New Jersey, New Orleans, New York, Norfolk, Northern Nevada, Oklahoma, Omaha, Orlando, Pensacola, Philadelphia, Phoenix, Pittsburgh, Portland, Richmond, Rochester, Sacramento, Salt Lake City, San Antonio, San Diego, San Francisco, San Juan, Savannah, Seattle, Springfield, St. Louis, Tampa, Toledo, Tucson, Vermont, Washington Field Office, West Virginia, and Wilmington.

Figure 11-4 InfraGard—city by city.

So far, the information shared among members has proven to be both useful and topical, with presentations on GLB, SOX, and other topics of the day. Membership is required, and you will need to be vetted, but once in, it is a great resource.

U.S. Drivers: At Home and Abroad

- **Graham-Leach-Bliley**

  This law is forcing American companies and companies that do business with America to get their customer data secured in short order.

- **Sarbanes-Oxley**

  Expect this to come up with a certain amount of glee whenever you talk cross-border security—be prepared to take it. Expect that Enron arrows will await you.

- **American security products**

  An ounce of prevention is worth the pound of cure—purchase software legally and implement a solidified patch-management regime. Much of the world's security countermeasures are exported from here.

Corporate security practices are led by financial institutions and are driven by ever-increasing regulations that provide extensive checklists of security policies and procedures. Although point solutions (buying a firewall, buying a virus scanner, buying a virtual private network [VPN]) are still relatively common, this wave of factors, along with increased, and at times flagrant, outsourcing practices are forcing companies to consider security as the silent centerpiece of their operations. It empowers business, enables processes, and ensures that in a time when the United States is becoming a larger target on the corporate side, that your company can function profitably and securely.

Final United States Thoughts

The United States is highly innovative and widely regulated (more so than most countries, when you add federal, state, local, industry, and national security rules together!), and the latter will prove challenging to companies outside the country seeking a cross-border partner. Recent legislation has now blanketed the corporate environment with a fresh layer of security concerns that require immediate attention and a move to more holistic security approaches. This requires Americans to create strong cross-border security strategies that balance implementation with prevailing foreign cultures and customs that are handled sensitively. Love us or hate us, the United States requires foreign businesses to follow the letter of the law, and you will need American legal advice on your security operations to do so.

Latin America

It doesn't take a survey of the Mexican border crossing from the U.S. side in San Pedro, California, to understand that you're not in Kansas anymore. The striped donkeys and bootleg commerce of Tijuana are in plain view. Here's where the Americas shift. We examine this territory as follows:

- **Mexico**

  This country, a chosen security destination because of its huge market by its northern neighbors, although security is not at the forefront of the corporate psyche, delivers interesting choices for cross-border businesses.

- **Central America**

  Here you'll find a recently stabilized land that is still finding its footing in the global economy, and this chapter briefly discusses this as a generalized region.

- **South America**

  Robust cross-border business is afoot in South America. It can prove a solid partner for U.S.- and European-based companies. Here we take quick tours through Columbia (a fast-evolving nation), Brazil and Argentina (its two largest countries), and Chile (its most advanced).

Mexico (.MX)

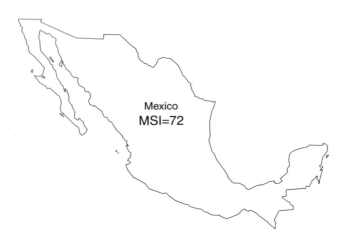

Figure 11-5 Mexico

MSI = 72

Pros: Inexpensive and cross-border friendly locale marked by decent infrastructure

Cons: General lack of corporate security awareness or emphasis within the business community, commuting

If you ask Mexico City-based security expert Manual Aceves what he does for a living, he'll immediately say to you in very soft English, "Do you know what an evangelist is? You know, someone who preaches to people who have never heard before? I am an evangelist."

This sums up well the Mexican corporate security environment. Converting the masses to a global corporate security scheme is the biggest challenge, and the "un-churched" are listening and converting, if slowly.

Laid back and friendly, Mexico's market is booming, welcoming some of America's largest brands that are hoping to attract its untapped mass market. It is still immature, and security is not a part of the business culture's vernacular yet. Still, Mexico can prove a wonderful partner in cross-border security business. The infrastructure is, for the most part, very solid. There is a great rule of law. Security knowledge is not a problem—commuting is. Take Mexico City. Because it is so massive and built on an urban plan that is circa 1000 A.D., commutes are sometimes nearly three hours each way, and the streets are jammed with Volkswagens as far as the eye can see.

Know Your Taxi

There are two types of taxicabs in Mexico City: ones that are safe; others that you enter, drive to a field, and lose your shirt. In Mexico City's airport, if you walk out straight and catch a green VW cab, you might well be robbed. If you instead turn left and ask to reserve a car for your hotel, you should expect to almost never get robbed. Your local operations should be telling you this kind of thing; in a pinch, contact the *regional security officer* (RSO) of your home country at your local consulate or embassy.

On the Ground

Security business in Mexico varies significantly from the United States. It is built on close personal relationships that must precede business. There is a strong family culture, and asking about families—wives, husbands, and children—is expected. If possible, present pictures of your own. This will begin to gain you entrée into the hearts and minds of the "few" who make security decisions here—the very top executives.

Just as you take care to build relationships, take care for your personal safety and take care of your data. When it is ready to roll across the Mexican border, configure it knowing that it will fall into the hands of any Mexican bank. Prepare its path at a very localized level, because by law, banks are a part of every business transaction in Mexico, even online.

In Part 1, I discussed how I once facilitated the development of an extended, online supply chain in Mexico for that Latin American-based phone company. It is important to note that such companies are both dominant throughout Latin America and often they drive security initiatives. In that story, I detailed how even this forward-thinking company needed to create their own secure data center from scratch to match international security standards. The experience became both a physical and information security case study because some of my colleagues were victimized by corrupt local officials who looked the other way at scams and petty crimes. That's a microcosmic example of how businesses are secured here—on an individual and careful basis. You need local partners.

Many companies have found that strength lies with big players such as Telmex and, in the manufacturing sector, CEMEX. Both have third parties they work with across industries, and with them on your side it is much easier to get the appropriate permits, regulations compliance, and access to key influencers and information.

In Mexico, the concerns become far more fundamental in nature. If you're a North Carolina company with a just-in-time warehouse in Mexico, you may find that you wanted to produce ten sets of X and end up with just eight sets of X when it makes the stockroom database.

—Royal Hansen, Security Expert, Boston

As I worked to design the exchange from a security perspective, we needed to remain relatively low tech because we couldn't rely on users having the latest laptops or latest versions of Web browsers to run sophisticated SSL algorithms. Because of the bank involvement in transactions, every deal at our site—instead of being brokered between a buyer and seller—had to be negotiated three ways, inserting the financial institution into the equation. It created security and data exchange issues that we never anticipated.

Key Regulations

In 2000, several modern security amendments to the Civil and Commercial Codes in Mexico (originally written in 1889) were published in the Official Gazette. They cover Mexican Federal Civil Code, Federal Commercial Code, Federal Civil Procedures Code, and Federal Consumers' Protection Law. Key areas include the following:

- **Integrity and authenticity**
  For electronic documents to be deemed valid, they must conform to standard rules of evidence, such that proper security has been maintained throughout the lifecycle that can reliably demonstrate its integrity and authenticity. This can be done with encryption, *message authentication code* (MAC), and even the new AH components of IPv6 packets (see Chapter 6, "Developing Radar").

- **I Accept**
  Now an agreement can be made binding in Mexico with a simple online click. Proper security must be taken to avoid fraud.

- **Privacy**
  There are four key areas designed to protect consumer privacy in Mexican electronic transactions. They are (i) the company must keep information provided by the consumer in strict confidence and not share it with third parties without the explicit authorization by the consumer (opt-in) or by a legal order; (ii) the company must use technological means to keep the consumer's information safe; (iii) the company must provide information to the consumer about where and how they can make a claim on a product or obtain

further information about it; and (iv) the company cannot try to trick the consumer. (Although this wouldn't work in the United States, it is a great rule of law in Mexico!)

Best Practices and Final Mexican Thoughts

Although it is lacking in security awareness, Mexico presents a great market opportunity for cross-border business. ISO 17799 is most often followed, but the country will usually satisfy the standards any multinational brings to bear, including the United States.

One place to look for local guidance in security is the AMECE (the Mexican eCommerce Association). Although they track online transactions in Mexico (up 400 percent year over year, reaching more than $2 billion/yr), and Internet penetration (more than 2.5 million), they also are a great group to leverage for local best practices, interpretation of local security rules, and networking with others in your position.

Although infrastructure and rule of law are both in place, make sure your contract enforces their implementation. Mexico has deployed a relatively low level of international computer security rules and guidance, but be careful not to run afoul of the laws that are there with the "no tricks" privacy rules. Solid, savvy local partners are abundant, and trying to do security in Mexico without one is a lesson in futility—even IBM does business with MBM. You should bring your standards, and then go local.

Central America

Central America
MSI=38

Figure 11-6 Central America

MSI = 38

Pros: Good university systems, political awareness, and moving toward global business relevance

Cons: New, untested infrastructure, legal systems, cultural work ethic

The seven Central American states are rich, diverse, and have come a long way since the last generation's localized conflicts and will prove to be a cost-effective way to set up shop. Focusing on these seven countries as cross-border partners doesn't make sense—yet. Although they are all moving toward greater use of the Internet (as opposed to their neighbor island to the east, Cuba, which just passed a law specifically designed to keep its citizens off of the Internet, under the double-speak name of Information Security Law), do not expect to find the physical or legal infrastructure present elsewhere in Latin American national capitols. There is a promising security capability, and universities are emphasizing its study. Most of the countries are best trained through their state universities, and those same universities (like the Universidad Francisco Marroquin in Guatemala) will make great business partners for your domestic security operations. Again, find a partner, get up to speed on what is happening at a micro-local level, and proceed carefully.

South America: Brazil, Argentina, Columbia, Chile

In South America, Brazil excepted, stay in the national capitals—do business in the city. Keep your local intelligence current. Political changes happen more rapidly in South America than in Europe and North America. Power structures differ, and titles matter little. Diverse laws are enforced in different ways at different times, depending on who is in charge.

These factors make current local intelligence of ultimate importance. Throughout the continent, wireless infrastructure is above average, and wired infrastructure is below average. Power is usually very reliable in national capitals, but it becomes sketchy once you move into the countryside. Back up data, make sure you have auxiliary power, and do not rely on main sources of power and communications. Language is exclusively Spanish, except in Brazil, where Portuguese is spoken. There are indigenous dialects. Hire in-country speakers.

Brazil (.BR)

Brazil
MSI=50

Figure 11-7 Brazil

MSI = 50

Pros: Multinational outpost, good use of Internet

Cons: Language-isolated island, piracy/cybercrime reputation deserved

The girl from Ipanema is not traveling to do business in Brasilia, the nation's capital. There's nothing there. When real estate became too expensive in Rio de Janeiro for expansion, the government (and some Lebanese land speculators) bought up all the land in a little town called Brasilia and established a new national capital there, profiting from the sale of yet more acreage. Government contracting favors Brazilian business unless no local firm in a segment exists. Partnering locally will increase your chances for success in the public sector.

Brazil is a language-locked land that contains great beauty, a large domestic market, and difficult security circumstances. If you want to do security business, head to Sao Paulo—unless you're dealing directly with the government. Sao Paulo is one of the world's great cities. Sao Paulo is built on a very solid infrastructure, and it has a wealth of well-trained security professionals who come out of the country's university system and pour into the city. It has everything but a good quality of life.

Brazilian Cybercrime on the Rise

Brazil is quickly becoming famous for its cybercrime, including identity theft, credit card fraud, and piracy. Brazil is a hacker hothouse because of the proliferation of freely available, automated attack tools that can be launched by experts and script-kiddies alike; few laws to prevent digital crime giving rise to hacking communities; and high incidence of organized crime syndicates exploiting cross-boundary opportunities. The United States is the leading victim of such crime. Brazil is a distant second, followed by the UK, Germany, and Italy. They are improving on their history of piracy (formerly number one), after losing a World Court case; the government promised not to do it anymore.

Like Mexico City and Denver, it is built in to a depression that conveniently seems to hold 100 percent of pollution from air and ground transportation, and a thermal inversion keeps it cooking. Residents often catch quarter-hour flights to Rio de Janeiro, or they drive north into the rainforest or south near the Argentine border to witness the Igauzu Falls. U.S. telecommunications and banking sectors do a thriving business in Brazil. Sao Paulo is the place, Portuguese is the language, and it is a hardship post for most multinational executives.

Brazil Fingerprints Air Travelers

In reaction to beefed up U.S. security for in-bound travelers, Brazil has initiated retaliatory measures at its international terminals, including an aggressive fingerprinting regime.

Brazilian Overview

According to *CSO* Magazine, as of 2003, Brazil led the world as the source for digital attacks, with more than 95,000 digital attacks having originated from within its borders—far more than any other country (and that's not more per capita, but more in real terms). By the way, Turkey is second on the list at 14,795 attacks, followed by the United States with 2,995 attacks, Indonesia (2,360 attacks) and Egypt (2,365 attacks). This sets the scene for your security in-country. Take great precaution, expect high awareness—but not much help—and be aware that you may be subject to various Portuguese and European laws.

Brazilian net citizens are making their voices heard worldwide, for better or for worse. They post more pictures online than any other country and dominate many message systems like the popular American site, "Orkut," where they account for more than 60 percent of all postings (marketers take note—based on their postings, they are young, single, and want to make friends!), and where they are doing their part to help change the lingua-fanca of the Internet from English to Portuguese. Also of note, on the day I wrote this page, Brazilian sites accounted for eight of the 10 most often defaced Web sites, so all of this talent is not without risk.

From a local corporate security perspective, Brazilian talent is matched by relatively diligent enforcement of contracts. Most multinationals maintain an outpost—especially American banks—that are sometimes involved in driving security. The country has a terrible track record of piracy. The government often looks the other way even as they promote a good track record. The man on the street toting multiple copies of Windows XP selling for pennies belies that. As with most South American countries, find a Brazilian and a Brazilian firm you can trust to get you started there.

Columbia (.CO)

Columbia
MSI=48

Figure 11-8 Columbia

MSI = 48

Pros: Rebounding

Cons: Kidnapping as small business venture, negative bias toward U.S./Europe

Just 10 years ago, if I were to ask you what comes to mind when I said Columbia, you wo
probably say kidnappers or perhaps the Medellin cartel. How about the leading Columbian
industry? Drugs? Well it has come along way, now touting a solid domestic industrial comple
Like Israel, its security posture has been honed in a perilous environment. It is true, like Yem
and a few other countries, kidnapping is a way of life here. After it has finally been eliminate
Columbia will be more fully participatory in the cross-border business arena. If you are an
American or European, it is assumed that you have money and your company can pay a rans
South Americans are not readily targeted—enlist them to oversee any operations you potentia
base there.

Columbian Overview

Security business in Bogotá is booming. In fact, Colombia has become the first point of entry in Latin America for many Indian IT companies, such as Aptech, Tata Infotech, NIIT, and Pentasoft. This progress is based on the internal capabilities of the Columbian security professionals and a Memorandum of Understanding (MoU) signed with India in 2002 on bilateral cooperation in IT (including information security and cybercrime). If you are trying to capture the South American market, finding a Columbian business partner is vital. You will not find a strong rule of law, nor will you find it specifically American- or European-friendly. However, uncovering a good business associate to transact with South Americans could be an inexpensive way to capture a big market. Keep your corporate security and local business intelligence up to date. Even as you do so, remember, you must still be diligent to ensure that your data isn't kidnapped while you are still safe at home.

Argentina (.AR)

Figure 11-9 Argentina

MSI = 67

Pros: Understanding of business, traditionally strong market

Cons: Recent destabilization and piracy issues

Argentina is the most European of all South American countries. Setting foot in Buenos Aires is reminiscent of Milan. Although it is scored as an MSI in the 60s, it is so ranked because of qualitative, not quantitative factors. Once thought of as an easy choice for cross-border business—there are plenty of multinationals in a historically rich market—recent destabilization of its political and financial systems combined with a legacy of piracy make it slightly riskier, but the bulk of the crisis is over. Although it has significant economic challenges ahead, the way its people, businesses, and government tie to the rest of the continent leads me to believe it will recover. Enforcement of contracts is limited and regime dependent. Impose your own standards and infrastructure when landing there.

On the Ground

In most cases, the government turns a blind eye to piracy as the corporate sector plays "catch-up" through the immoral acquisition of intellectual property. Food is more important than integrity, and although not as rampant as in other parts of the world, it is enough to pay attention to. Contracts need to be more effective here—the rule of law is not consistent enough to bank on: Import your own. No security or privacy-specific regulations are routinely enforced, but they can be used as levers against foreign companies or employees who have been otherwise targeted. Insurance can hedge against unenforceability.

Argentina does not have a great track record with large U.S. companies. The day I joined IBM in was the day they arrested IBM Argentina's head of sales on bribery charges. He still maintains he simply did what the company required of him to complete his job.

Mixing Business and Politics

From 1997-1999, IBM-Argentina engaged in a contract to provide computer systems to the Banco de la Nacion Argentina. The IBM team used a local subcontractor on the job, which ultimately skimmed off $4.5 million of the $22 million total contract. Although the SEC found IBM (the parent company) guilty of SEC Rule 13b-2 (books and records provisions) and collected a $300,000 civil fine, Argentina charged 30 senior IBM-Argentina executives with intent to defraud, and 10 of them, including the president of the subsidiary, were indicted on bribery charges.

Companies are in survival mode here. There is no money. Executives think hackers are the only threat and they constantly say, "It won't happen to me, my company." Yet of the attack and penetration tests I've done on Argentine companies I've gained access to 100 percent of the time. I'm hoping that further international regulations will begin to touch us, forcing us to be aware of an issue that could shape the destiny of our economy.

—Andres Gil, Attack and Penetration Expert, Buenos Aires

Andres Gil, a Buenos Aires-based attack and penetration expert, also reports that Argentine business doesn't even realize security is a problem. "It's a murky environment because security incidents aren't widely shared or published, and no one really knows what's going on." He said, "The financial situation has forced companies to look at the ledger more than what's affecting that ledger." Pick a security fundamental and you would be hard pressed to find it being implemented at any given company. Lack of the CSO level contributes to the lag in elevating security as a priority. Adopt standards where practical.

Key Regulations

There is one regulation of note. In 2000, Argentina passed the Habeas Data, or the Personal Data Protection Act.[16] The acts work toward the full protection of personal information recorded in data files, registers, banks, or other technical means of data treatment, *either public or private for purposes of providing reports*, in order to guarantee the honor and intimacy of persons, as well as the access to the information that may be recorded about such persons, in accordance with the provisions of Section 43, Third Paragraph of the National Constitution.[17]

Also of note is its Digital Signature Law No. 25.506, passed in 2002, which lays out the mechanisms and acceptability of using digital certificates to sign electronic documents in Argentina. Just as in Canada (you should certify Canadian), it is wise to use an Argentine CA for this purpose if you want to avoid legal difficulties.

Doing security business in Argentina contrasts vividly from Brazil. Foreign investment is encouraged and needs no prior government approval, and it is easy to import security hardware and software from almost any point on the globe. Foreign firms can engage in publicly funded research or "subsidized research and develop-

---

16. *"Principios Para La Proteccion De Datos Personales En La Nueva Ley De Argentina." Ulpiano.com. February 2001.*
17. *Ibid.*

ment programs on a national treatment basis" and are subject to the same tax liabilities as local firms. However, unlike in the United States, there is not much Argentine-funded research in the information security field, so here it is best to focus on the many small security companies that are woven into the fabric of Sao Paulo.

Final Argentine Thoughts

With a past rich in multinational business, Argentina is a relatively familiar South American choice for cross-border security. However, the struggles of defaulting on its World Monetary Fund loan sent it spiraling, and it is still attempting to recover. The battle over the Malvanis Islands (a.k.a. Falklands) seems still fresh in many minds, so "Buy American," in its broadest sense including all of two continents, is a good choice in the security area. Its revival will be a hard road, and although partnering is a possibility, its current environment requires vigilance and someone constantly on the ground. With the right political precautions for intellectual property protection, you can tap into a well-educated security workforce that will serve the domestic market well.

Chile (.CL)

Chile
MSI=74

Figure 11-10 Chile

MSI = 74

Pros: Stable with a solid capital-city infrastructure and little to no terrorist activity, the best South America has to offer

Cons: Language, isolation

Take an objective look at Chile as your South American security entry point. Maybe you have never heard of it. It's not as European as Buenos Aires, but the Pinochet regime is finished and the country is stable. Chile has a solid stock market and a Wall Street-esque business environment. There is limited English spoken here, so you will need to conduct business in Chilean Spanish (faster than anything you may have learned in school!). Bracketed by the Pacific Ocean and the Andes Mountains that run north to south, Chileans love it and wouldn't trade it. You won't either.

From Pinochet to Evita

I was once paid to visit Chile to evaluate some eCommerce investment opportunities for an American company. A week turned into a month as I fell in love with this country and its people. Through some contacts at the American Embassy, I was able to attend Chile's version of the Military Day Parade. This included a full accounting of the armed services—fighter jet flyovers, missiles, infantries, cavalries—in Santiago's largest football stadium. (Of note, Chile claims the most unique fighting force outside of Libya, one that includes an exclusively female unit. On this day, they marched with giant automatic weapons strapped to their backs, drab camouflage uniforms, and bright scarlet handbags coordinated with matching lipstick.) It happened to be the last such gathering at which former and notorious dictator (and to some, national savior) Augusto Pinochet would be in attendance. Retired and newly elected "Senator for Life," he gave me unique insight on the differences in cultural devotion to despots.

Indicted by the United States and toppled from power by his own people, he was offered an honorary seat at the event. Outside the stadium the crowd was abuzz and on the verge of pandemonium. Only invited guests could gain passage to the stadium, and here the masses teemed. Upon pushing my way in amid Uzi-toting adolescents, I found that the huge outdoor arena was in relative calm. I found my seat near the President of Chile, Eduardo Frei's reviewing stand. President Frei arrived thereafter. The crowd barely reacted.

Suddenly, the sonic boom of the jets clipped the top of the stadium, and following them six limos traveling at top speed screamed onto the pitch toward the president. They slammed brakes in unison and skidded into a perfect row of diagonally parked cars. From the middle car, a red carpet rolled from the passenger door, and out burst Augusto Pinochet. The stadium shook from the crowd's roar. This was the guy who just a few weeks earlier had appeared in a *Washington Post* story that discussed how he was universally hated in his homeland. On that day, however, his hands were raised as his people showered devotion upon him.

This story underscores the unique place of strong, charismatic dictators in South American governments. The cult of personality runs deep, from top to bottom, no matter the severity of a given leader's transgressions. The same held

continues...

From Pinochet to Evita   Continued
true with the Peron duo in Argentina and Stroessner in Paraguay and now Chavez in Venezuela. Guided by an almost Catholic sense of iconography, these men and women have risen to the equivalent of beatification among their people.

On the Ground and Best Practices

Especially since recent U.S. Senate passage of the Chile Free Trade Agreement, it is easy to operate here. There is a first-class university system. Telecommunications, wireless, and Internet services are all big business in Chile. Because it is in a state of upgrade, demand for foreign investment in these areas is high and there are little to no barriers. Domestic players will invest $3 million in the next few years. Although it is a large country, all multinational commerce—and most of the infrastructure—is located in Santiago. There is a reliable currency here, too.

Chile is marked by unusually prolific broadband penetration—nearly 37 percent of the population surfs with speed. The technology market is also growing in Chile, where there are more computers per capita than any other South American country (3.4 per 100 citizens—compare to 30 per 100 citizens in the United States).

Connectivity has led to a stout eGovernment program—70 percent of corporations and self-employed individuals filed their taxes online in 2003. Moreover, under the administration of President Ricardo Lagos, a Digital Agenda was recently announced. Through it, he seeks to connect the government's more than 12 departments on a giant intranet that is powered via a digital superhighway dubbed 5D. By 2006, government purchases for more than $500 must be made online. The agenda also seeks to embark on the high-speed wiring of at least 80 percent of the country's schools and 100 percent of universities by 2006. The drive toward this most ambitious goal has already started.[18]

Global corporate security should be conducted with your company's best interests in mind. As in all South American countries, it should be done with someone who knows the terrain and who can find the talented, indigenous people who can help you create a strategy that does not compromise your posture.

---

18. *"Agenda Digital—(versión corregida Agosto 2004)." agendadigital.cl. August 2004.*

Key Regulations

Chile is further separated from the rest of Latin America through its continental first-of-its-kind legislation regarding privacy. The Chilean Act on the Protection of Personal Data took effect in 1999. It is a major first step in Chile's protection of personal information.[19]

Final Chilean Thoughts

Because of its stability, its people, its ongoing innovation, and the nature of business in Chile, I give it the highest mark in South America. I think it is a country headed in the right direction on the global security stage, and partnering in the post-Pinochet era should be relatively easy. Security here is taken seriously, and the business infrastructure understands and accepts it. Many multinationals from around the world are "discovering" Chile's strong pro-business capabilities, and the security industry is no different. Although you may have to import some people and product, you will find Chile a great place for South American security operations now and in the future.

---

19. *"Act on the Protection of Personal Data." PrivacyExchange.com. August 1999.*

Chapter 12

Asia Pacific

Figure 12-1 Asia Pacific

Where else on earth will you find the world's oldest civilization doing business with what was once the world's largest penal colony? Asia Pacific (AP) is a vast, developing region that is anchored by China on the continental mainland and Singapore, Australia, and Japan in the Pacific. These four countries account for our tour of Asia. Do not get me wrong. The rest of the region is abuzz with activity. The Philippines and Vietnam as out-sourcing destinations, South Korea's business renaissance, the Taipei 101 building, and

Malaysia's Petronas Twin Towers—all of these are landmarks of corporate growth in the region. Yet Asia as a topic of cross-border corporate security still boils down to this quartet.

Throughout the region, expansion is enabling and empowering government and business interests. Most countries in the region are learning from the West's mistakes, and as a result they are devising strong technological infrastructures and doing it right the first time.

We start this tour in the economy that is poised to become the world's largest mainly due to government planning and control: China. We then hop down to tiny Singapore and see how government is the biggest driver in a different way. We then make our way farther south to Australia, where more than 60 percent of all AP security practice emanates, and then end up back in Japan, which is banking on new security technology to enable its future.

China (.CN)

Figure 12-2 China

MSI = 51

Pros: 1+ billion consumers, early adoption of IPv6 and Next-Generation Internet, growth opportunities

Cons: Legacy of piracy, government control, language translations

China has a special air that mixes exotic, millennia-old culture with the stolid hand of "the Party." Maybe you picture a lone, brave activist in front of a tank or Chow Yun-Fat gracefully hopping bamboo trees in Ang Lee's Crouching Tiger

Hidden Dragon. But if you plop yourself into the middle of Shanghai, you might be asking directions to the Sears Tower—it looks remarkably more like Chicago than the movies. It is all just part of the plan.

The Internet is also part of the plan. Despite the fact that Stanford University in the United States owns more IP addresses than all of China, the country has focused on this technology to help vault them to global leadership in many world markets. China has overcome the limits of IP addresses by strongly embracing the new global standard for Internet Protocol, IPv6. This gives it access not only to practically unlimited address space, but also provides for much stronger security that is built in, not "built on."

Increased use of the Internet is one of the single largest agents of change throughout China. In 2003, the country launched the *China Next-Generation Internet* (CNGI) program, rolling out more than 300 interconnected hubs connected by 30-gigabyte (really, really fast) links. And all of this is running on the increased built-in security of IPv6. The CNGI is scheduled for completion in 2005, and should combine fixed, mobile, wired, wireless, satellite, and video communications. It will help China meet its goal of being the most technologically advanced networked country in the world by the 2008 Olympics. And by leveraging the security advancements that IPv6 brings, they could well have the most secured network infrastructure in the world as well—and they will hold the keys.

Chinese Harsh

According to the official *Xinhua News Agency* in China, in 2004 new regulations were passed down by China's Supreme People's Court as part of a campaign for greater state control over the Internet. Examples include the shutting down of thousands of internet cafes, increased surveillance of individuals, greater use of filters and proxy servers, and harsh penalties The *Xinhua News Agency* states: "Cases involving pornographic Web sites that have been clicked on more than 250,000 times will be considered 'very severe,' with convictions resulting in life sentences."

China is the fastest-evolving big country in the world right now. It has initiated a fast-track, aggressive program to modernize by laying a colossal, technology-based infrastructure headquartered in Beijing. Even so, and despite the fact this upgrade is happening in all of China, Shanghai is still the place to do business. There, the rapid business evolution scheme is alive, well funded, and well thought out. It has been executed under the global radar for decades and is just now in the process of emerging. There is fantastic manufacturing capability, great infrastructure in Shanghai and Beijing, and world-class infrastructure within the protectorate of Hong Kong.

The legal system favors the state—if you have a short-term contract in place, it is fairly reliable. Long-term agreements are subject to country-wide political winds, and although the Chinese understand the value of the international contracts—they are a part of the WTO—they've shown in recent history a penchant for tearing up the papers should the deal not suit their needs.

Piracy is generally not viewed as wrong in China, and although slightly condemned by the government, I have seen it turn more than a blind eye. Government supports business to ensure the long-term stability and growth of the country. They also want to catch up and pass the West. They want to have the best information infrastructure in the world by 2008. To get there, they will continue to act in a very "pro-China" manner, and areas such as piracy, privacy, and security could well be decided in the favor of the state. While it is safer to think of your intellectual property as a contributor to their fast track, There is still a good chance of success with the implementation of appropriate security measures.

It is a huge country, and right now Europeans and Americans can live well in Shanghai and Hong Kong. In ten years, they'll be able to live as comfortably in Beijing as Boston. With the Olympics arriving in China in 2008, expect it to have hit a benchmark that will turn into a corporate coming-out party for their industries.

The story is different in terms of security technology. China has the world's largest implementation of Next-Generation Internet equipment based on IPv6. Because the security built in to these networks is vastly superior to IPv4 networks that run Europe and America, there is a great infrastructure to work with here.

On the Ground

Imagine 92 percent of the American population owning pirated software. Now multiply that by five. According to the Business Software Alliance, welcome to China![1] Although the government may testify otherwise to the World Court, actions speak louder than lawyers. There is scant penalty for stealing intellectual property, so forget about a clever contract. Again, it is this country's way of catching up. You must deploy your best security here because the government is watching and listening, and they possess world-class intelligence that is no match for "lite" operational security. The government has said openly and on many

---

1. *"Major Study Finds 53 Percent of Software in Use in Asia Pacific Region is Pirated." BSA.org. 7 July 2004.*

occasions that they will help its companies, because their companies are a part of their economic stability and growth as a country. You get their market for a short window of time, they get your IP, but it is getting better.

A Novell Surprise

Kevin Shaw, a Melbourne-based security expert, has related that when Novell first expanded into China, they wanted to jumpstart their user-group community. Having advertised the first session throughout Shanghai, they anticipated many of their 100 registered customers to show up. Upon arriving at the meeting, they were stunned to find nearly 2,000 people had arrived. Upon registration, they found that almost none of them had licensed versions of the product. Most of it was pirated.

"While piracy is rampant, it was once thought of as the only way to leap ahead. But now, even though mistrust continues, there is a new environment of enforcement that is springing up—if slowly," says Jack Z. Chen, the Shanghai-based chairman, Asia Pacific, for U.S. law firm Barrington Associates.

The Plan Set in Steel

Shanghai's BaoSteel offers a prime example of the Chinese plan. When I met the BaoSteel execs in the 1990s they knew little about managed services. At the time, I led one of the world's largest managed services groups. Bao came to America to meet with me and others about our offerings, visited, asked a lot of questions, took a lot of pictures and notes, and then left. Bao today has mastered the use of managed services throughout their organization. They've also quietly become the worlds largest steel company and they've done it in the classic Chinese way. Again, I cannot emphasize enough how in China learning from others is seen as a natural extension of business. When understood and planned for, this can be a win-win situation.

There is a fine balance struck between businesses that enter China and the Chinese government. The government recognizes that world-class standards need to be brought to bear. World-class companies understand that the growth inherent throughout the country is going to pass them up if they stay on the sidelines.

For example, Cisco Systems recently filed a lawsuit accusing Huawei Technologies, China's largest telecom equipment maker, of unlawfully copying its operating software, and after several years of negotiations, the two companies reached a settlement. On the consumer side, a pirated copy of Microsoft XP sells on the street for as low as $1.50 (with the box!), compared with the original price tag of $199 for the home version, and $299 for the professional version. Intellectual property protection will continue to be a security issue for all who trade here.

On the customs front, there is a loosening of the legalistic cultural mores that used to dog Western business in the region. In other words, bowing, while appreciated, is no longer a make-or-break gesture—nor is leaving a business card. However, note that Chinese do tend to be more relational when doing business. Cutting to the chase is not the appropriate tack.

You're seeing a convergence of customs in China, especially as it's opened up more to Western business. It used to be a politically motivated power struggle. Now people want to cut a deal, and there has been a forged middle ground that includes some Western and some Chinese ways mutually adopted. On the whole though, a Westerner is still seen as more decimal-point oriented, and any investment in people will go a long way in dispelling that perception and only help you over here.

—Jack Z. Chen, Chairman, Asia Pacific, Barrington Associates, Shanghai/ Los Angeles

Key Regulations

The Chinese government controls China. Although on its face it may seem over-simplified, consider this: If your company hosts a Web site in China, the government will sanitize your content for its citizens. They may also do so without your knowledge. There have been times when the Chinese government has been known to mirror Western sites, deleting any negatively perceived content. Say you are a Western news agency that's providing a sidebar feature on Tianemman Square—in China, it would simply disappear and the content would be blocked. So here you will find iron-fisted regulation, and often you will find that, again, any laws on the books will generally favor the country and its corporations.

Foreign companies are not permitted to directly engage in trade in China, other than marketing any goods they have manufactured there. Accordingly, Western exporters need to use a domestic Chinese agent for both importation of security products and services into China and marketing within China. Searching for an agent in China is complicated by the separation of the two elements that basically characterize international trading firms: import/export authority and aggressive marketing expertise.

Offset/Upset

China often enforces an "offset" program, requiring a percentage (usually 30 percent of the value of the imported component) of a major purchase be reinvested in commercially viable businesses in China. This can sometimes lead to strange and circuitous transactions. I have seen one that moved consumer equipment in-country, gave up key components to local competitors, and ended up having to take millions of dollars of hemp rope from Africa as part of the deal. You can imagine your CFO trying to put that into his spreadsheet!

The enforcement agency in China is the central government. There is a cost for its role—multinationals don't want to bring their best to China. Over the long haul, this will affect both the quality and security of foreign business here.

—Jack Z. Chen, Chairman, Asia Pacific, Barrington Associates, Shanghai/
Los Angeles

Best Practices

China is committed to following ISO standards. In 1998, its Zhongguo Guojia Xinxi Anquan Ceping Renzheng Zhongxin (the *China National Information Security Testing Evaluation and Certification Center* [CNISTECC]) was officially authorized to issue Internet security certification. Later, the Guojia Zhiliang Jishu Jiandu Ju (China Quality and *Technical Supervision Bureau* [TSB]) tasked it with hardware, software, and data-security certification. In 1999, the China National Accreditation Council for Product Certification Bodies and the TSB certified that the CNISTECC fulfilled the criteria set forth in ISO/IEC Guideline 65.[2]

Professor Wu Shizong, CNISTECC director, is actively working to apply U.S. and international standards to corporate security in China so that the country is brought up to speed with WTO guidelines. Encryption modules are already at certifiable levels. As you can see, CNISTECC is attempting to visibly move toward

---

2. *"China: Information Security/A June 1999 Report from U.S. Embassy Beijing." usembassy-china.org. June 1999.*

compliance on many fronts. It has been hit by criticisms surrounding its technical expertise and motivations. It is best right now to view it as trying to be both a regulator and a CERT in the same breath, taking its cues on both from above.

Melbourne-based Shaw reports that overall, Chinese security is improving for two predictable reasons. I have already mentioned the first—accruing the methodologies of multinationals. The second is what Shaw describes as an "expatriate community that is learning corporate security in the West and then applying it on their home turf, and this has resulted in some very qualified security firms springing up on the mainland."

Make sure that your corporate security best practices in China are your absolute best in the world. Pay much more attention to internal employee security. Like most countries, you need to segregate your information flow and give your local operations only exactly what they need. Take care to find security personnel in-country (and to get such contracts you will need to work with Chinese nationals and companies), who will want to step up tactics such as two-person authentication for recovery, where it takes two people to decrypt a file using two people in separate provinces who speak two different languages and who do not know each other. Control access and flow of your information by leveraging discretionary access controls within your global systems. Remember that if you send out an e-mail and accidentally cc it to a person in China, many people could be listening and you could compromise all the good firewalls you have set up throughout the rest of the world. Do your best security work here.

Final Chinese Thoughts

Although it is difficult to imagine the piracy = catch-up mentality, China still represents the ultimate brass ring. Questing for its more than a billion consumers for your consumer product or—as in the gold rush—selling your services like shovels and Levis to "49ers" who are headed to China, could greatly expand your profitability. Be extremely careful. This country has been given an MSI score in the 50s because there is a strong motivation behind Chinese business growth, and it could affect you. It wants to catch up and surpass Europe and America as the world's dominant economic power and I believe it will succeed in my lifetime. This means it is better to get involved early while the stakes are smaller. Find your local partners. Practice your best "opsec" here. Manage the diplomatic tip-toeing around where politics are quiet and attention from above is not yet focused. Do not be charmed, by the Chinese, into not doing your homework. But, do leverage the high-tech security infrastructures, highly trained staffs, and rapidly developing economies you'll find here.

Singapore (.SG)

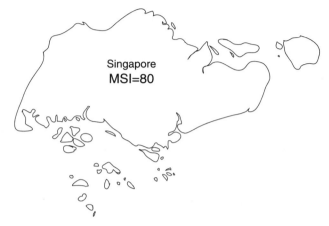

Singapore
MSI=80

Figure 12-3 Singapore

MSI = 80

Pros: Most technologically advanced country in the world, the premier Asia mainland trampoline

Cons: No significant in-country major market

I want to highlight two major elements of Singapore that I believe make it ideal for cross-border business. Singapore has made the best use of Internet computer technology in the world so far—bar none. Because it has been an international port of call for centuries, it is the most Western-friendly spot in this non-English speaking part of the region, and English (or Singlish as most locals call it) is its first language. Rule of law is strong and fair. It is characterized as the perfect place to "dabble" in Asia. It has also been called the "gateway to Asia." Believe it all. The cultural adjustments to be made here are few. It caters to Western tastes and it is a beautiful spot that's great for business—the "livin' is easy."

Singapore Justice
Kendrick Tan Cheng Kang, an MBA graduate and product development officer, overran Singapore's Housing Board with 7,500 e-mails in the span of 2 1/2 hours to speed his purchase of an apartment. He was arrested, charged, and tried. Found guilty of "interfering with the lawful use of the Board's e-mail servers," he was fined $30,000.[3]

3. Adam Creed. "Singapore Man Fined Over Mass E-Mail Anger." Newsbytes News Network. 22 May 2000.

Singapore is also one of the first countries in the world to wrestle with the significance of technological change. I was involved in the bidding process to integrate smart cards into their military in the *late 1980s*. It was a huge task, but they were able to figure out what makes for great eGovernment—interoperability. There aren't 12 different smart cards for 12 different elements of life here—there is one. At the time, those of us involved in the RFP process couldn't believe the pains they were taking to examine and choose their partners for creating the military version.

It took nearly five years. Today, that military smart card that once served as an ID now applies to the whole country. The UK, Germany, the United States, and France are all still struggling to get their smart card initiatives off the ground these 20+ years later.

There are two regulations worth pointing out in Singapore. Its Electronic Transactions Act of 1998, although broad in scope, puts legal liability only on the owners and originators of unacceptable or hostile code. It exempts all the systems that handle such code, which makes it harder to prosecute some international cases.[4] Also enacted in the 1990s, Singapore's Computer Misuse Act, fashioned after the UK's, can impose both fines and imprisonment for computer hacking, virus creation, and spamming.

Singapore has also built a superb, national technology infrastructure base. Its migration to the general populace created the world's most inclusive and profitable eGovernment. Again, one smart card is used as a national ID and one-stop debit card. You enter a cab, swipe the card, and you are billed for the ride. The cabby is taxed through his or her own smart card. You can file your taxes or buy a soda with your smart card. It sounds outrageous, but head over there, live a bit, and you will come home a believer.

The Problem of Smart Card Evil

Although the smart card technology may seem invasive, I do not believe it is an active reflection of the government and government control. Benevolent governments will use it for good, and malevolent governments will use it for ill.

Singapore is also very security aware. Its SingCERT, housed out of the National University in Singapore, is on top of constant vigilance. It touts itself as the one-stop-shop for the "prevention, detection, and resolution of security-related

---

4. *"Electronic Transactions Act 1998." Infocomm Development Authority of Singapore (IDA).*

incidents on the Internet."[5] Security talent is abundant, and the university also churns out bright practitioners year after year who can be your bridge to the rest of the continent.

Between Singapore's smart card technology, the openness of its government, the amenities of its lifestyle, and the awareness of security's importance, it is the easiest place to do business if you are interested in countries between Australia and Japan. There are hoards of multinationals there already. Finding a trusted partner should be easy. What's more, the United States has recently passed the Singapore Free Trade Agreement, which sets up the country as a jewel for Asian-headquartered operations.[6]

Australia (.AU)

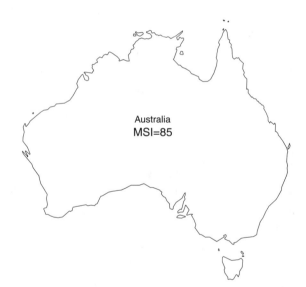

Australia
MSI=85

Figure 12-4 Australia

MSI = 85

Pros: World-class security and English in Asia

Cons: Time difference and distance

---

5. "About SingCERT." n.d. www.singcert.org.sg/ (10 August 2004).
6. "President Signed U.S.-Singapore Free Trade Agreement." Whitehouse.gov. 6 May 2003.

Tucked beneath continental Asia is the region's best-equipped cross-border partner. Australia drives Asian global corporate security awareness and provides more than 40 percent of the corporate security services from Malaysia to Hong Kong. Its friendly, open society is combined with a strong rule of law and a first-class infrastructure. The country carries a very strong commitment to global security standards, and an educated English-speaking workforce will make an Asian transition easier and more efficient. Regulations are light touch, and contracts need to be carefully written. They are generally enforceable. In Australia, as with other parts of Asia, it is important to enlist local partners when starting an operation.

Kevin Shaw, a Melbourne-based security expert, reports that Australia tends to watch the United States as a major adopter of new technologies to see what works. "We let them undertake the learning curve and then we will perfect," he jokes. Security drivers include public safety, financial institutions, and the airline industry.

Domestically, large telecom companies and smaller regional banks have taken the lead in setting the standard for security best practices. Look at some of the security initiatives of Telstra, the largest telco in the land, and National Australia Bank, the leading banker in a country dedicated to online banking, to find a good baseline for your own security operation in Australia.

Key Regulations

There are a host of public agencies designed to help multinationals navigate corporate security issues and deal with security events. Foremost is the country's E-security Coordination Group, which serves as the central government's core entity for corporate and infrastructure eSecurity policy development and coordination. It focuses on the public and private sector's development of "trusted and secure operating environments, awareness raising on eSecurity and reporting of incidents." Similarly the Australian CERT or AuCERT, offers incident response coordination and assistance. Housed at the University of Queensland in Brisbane, it has become the "most trusted contact in Australia for the Internet community."[7]

In 1997, Australia organized the *National Office for the Information Economy* (NOIE), which is known as the nation's agency for information economy issues. When founded, it was tasked with creating a globally competitive online economy and society. In terms of corporate security the NOIE seeks to do the following:

---

7. *Andreas Wenger, Jan Metzger, Myriam Dunn, ed., International CIIP Handbook: An Inventory of Protection Policies in Eight Countries (Zurich: Swiss Federal institute of Technology, 2002), 26.*

- Foster cooperation between the public and private sectors.

- Integrate electronic and physical security and response.

- Encourage ongoing development of a response capability.

- Accrue a database of threats and vulnerabilities.

- Outline review arrangements of security in the public and private sectors.[8]

The *Australian Security Intelligence Organization* (ASIO) is the national security agency and intelligence-gathering wing. It is important to underscore here that the Australian government has been reported to participate in ECHELON, the cooperative intelligence tool that's been widely reported by the media. This may mean your business could be vulnerable to tapping.

For all of its agencies, Australia's regulatory environment is not as far reaching as its American or European counterparts, and it remains opt-in. Its Privacy Act was passed in 1988 and consolidated in 1997. In 2000, it was amended to afford further guidance on the Internet and the use of personal data by corporations that house and use Australian citizens' information. More and more companies are factoring in both this act and international privacy compliance guidance as they build or refine their global corporate security posture. Kevin Shaw says that he is unaware of any noncompliant company that has faced prosecution so far.

Best Practices

With its skilled security personnel in global demand throughout Asia, Australian companies have or will voluntarily conform their security practices with the growing international standard ISO 17799. The communications giant Telstra is one company viewed internationally as innovative on security for itself and its clients. Companies around the world watch what Telstra does on the security scene.

Shaw, who in past years has been on the road (or on the sea or in the air) more than 80 percent of the time, reports that he is spending much more time in-country this year than last, because many of his domestic clients have come around to the understanding that security needs to be proactive with an enterprise-wide scope, not reactive firefighting, chasing down the next virus, denial-of-service attack, or break-in. Identity management in its fullest sense, which includes not only password provisioning but also access and smart card use, is on the rise in this country and is being driven by the government at a state level—Queensland and Victoria are the most aggressive.

---

8. *Ibid.* 27.

Australian Headlines

Incidents do happen. In 2003, the names and addresses of Australian Supreme Court justices were inadvertently published on a government Web site. In the 1990s, a justice was assassinated in a car bomb—this type of information leak was both an embarrassment and a safety hazard.

Because Australia supplies Asia much of its security talent, there is a shortage of homeland personnel. For example, one of the nation's largest multinational banks has 50 corporate security practitioners globally. This contributes to a newer business risk facing Australian companies—the outsourcing of business operations. Companies are still coming to grips with the fact that when something is outsourced, they still own the risks and responsibilities. On the other side of the outsourcing coin, as some of the developing nations stumble with their own growth, Australia's stable political environment, solid technology infrastructure, strong commitment to global security standards, and an educated English-speaking workforce will start to make it a preferred spot for co-location of globally outsourced operations.

Note that a lot of industries in Australia (and the whole of Asia Pac) are in a different position than Europe or North America. There is more of a process of understanding and taking a balanced and considered approach to security. They have watched and learned from the hysteria of the U.S. ".com" phenomenon, and they have seen the trend surrounding security moving forward and its critical components. I think you will see in comparison to Europe and the United States, a shorter period of time for the fragmented approach to security, and a rapid transition into "What am I doing as an enterprise?" "What's my enterprise approach?" "If something something's happening in my network, how's that affecting other areas of my business?" "If I think of one project, how is that affecting other particular projects?" Furthermore, marrying the security case with the business case has been rare. That said, Australian companies can move very quickly now because of the lessons from the other regions of the world. For example, United States and European companies there have already done the expensive testing, refining, business benchmarking, and implementing elsewhere, so when they bring it home, it is there and they can leverage it for a better ROSI than their global partners.

Final Australian Thoughts

Australia is an ideal starting point for companies that work between Singapore and Japan, and an excellent destination for security operations unto itself. It touts a regulatory environment that is business- and international-friendly. Use of international standards and an understanding of the enterprise-wide imperative—along with its strong inroads to China and other developing nations throughout the region—make it a potentially ideal partner for cross-border business and security-strategy development.

Japan (.JP)

Figure 12-5 Japan

MSI = 71

Pros: Strong business environment, good use of IPv6 and Wireless

Cons: Japan-only mentality, slowly recovering economy

Japan is one of the most technologically advanced countries on the planet. Its business prowess is equal to Europe, and the quality is better. It boasts the world's second largest trading economy, one of its finest infrastructures, and a better-than-average rule of law. Some of the brightest security personnel live there. However, there are two main vulnerabilities that plague this island nation:

- A general apathy to global corporate security risks
- One of the strongest ethnocentric business environments in the free world

No Code Talk
Public discussion of codes in Japan has been seen as inappropriately symbolic of past militarism.

Security indifference has stretched to critical infrastructure and national security. Japanese security expert Raisuke Miyawaki has pointed since the 1990s that his homeland "[has] not yet fully realized that Japan is vulnerable to a cyberterrorist attack, and the effects such an attack would have on Japan. In general, Japan's most powerful leaders have demonstrated a lack of technology understanding and a 'leadership void' that have stalled the development and implementation of a comprehensive, effective cyberterrorism strategy and policy."[9]

Although security might not be the biggest driver in Japan, they have embraced it as the great enabler. In 2001, they created an Imperial edict to get behind the IPv6 emerging standards. Not because they wanted the security, but because they wanted the profits that the security would unlock. In one test underway in 2004, they outfitted 1,000 taxicabs in Tokyo with IPv6-enabled windshield wipers. Why? Because they knew that when it was raining in one part of the city, they should send extra cabs immediately to capture the extra customers. To make this stuff work in real life, it will require extra granularity, and end-to-end security and privacy that IPv6 offers. Look for Japan to be the number one global supplier of next-generation networking, based on their early commitment to these new security technologies.

Sony Wins
Remember the standards battle between VHS and Beta for video? Although Sony's BetaMax had better pictures and longer recording time, it lost out to the VHS format and was forever confined to the garage next to OS/2, and the eight-track tape. But did you realize that one of the key reasons Beta lost that race

continues...

---

9. Raisuke Miyawaki. *"The Fight Against Cyberterrorism: A Japanese View." Center for Strategic and International Studies. 29 June 1999.*

Sony Wins   Continued

was that Sony refused to allow pornography to be sold on its tapes, whereas the VHS folks had no such rules. That decision has been credited with tipping the popularity scales against Beta, and leading the VHS format to dominance for decades. With IPv6, Sony is clearly backing a winner this time. Sony has stated that 100 percent of its communications products will be IPv6 enabled by 2005, and is well on its way back to market dominance for it.

The business environment is one of the most relationship-based on earth, and although there is a fun, interactive component to this—I once took an 18-hour flight to Tokyo, was off the plane in the evening for a night of karaoke and revelry that culminated in my having a wokfull of hot oil accidentally torch my trousers (a painful trip)—there is also a high degree of distrust and the need to find local partners. There are no corners that can be cut. Patience and strongly trusted local business partners will get you in the door, and even then, you haven't touched a global corporate security posture that could be exposed to less-than-strong awareness and intellectual property law. Proceed with caution.

Key Regulations

The country's Law for the Protection of Computer Processed Personal Data took effect in 1988 and covers and protects "all personal data held by the public sector. Private sector legislation has never been drafted because of an agreement in Japan on what constitutes the ideal balance between protection of personal privacy and the need for the efficient flow of information." Many private companies have voluntarily created guidelines to retain customers.[10]

Perhaps more important than regulations concerning corporate security and accountability are the various laws that deal with foreign companies landing on Japanese soil. To be fair, the government has tried to eliminate barriers to foreign investment, which has been accelerated since its economy's practical crash. Most goods and services can be imported freely and without a license. Its tariff has been reduced and is among the lowest in the world.

---

10. *PrivacyExchange.org. 25 September 1998.*

Best Practices

In 2003, the Japanese Ministry of Economy, Trade and Industry, described the defects in their information security measures as having "increasingly serious effects on the nation's economy and society, bringing about infringements of human rights, financial damage to corporations, and the failure of the entire information system." The Ministry went on to advise Japanese companies to not only step up their own internal security measures, but that it was also "vital to make good use of external specialists."[11]

To give you an idea for how far behind Japanese companies are in the global corporate security game, its first ever BS 7799-compliant company, NTT Data, was certified in 2001. Although this cues you to the particular standard that's in play domestically, you should expect to very carefully export your own corporate security strategy. Above and beyond imposing your own standard that is based on the BSI version of the convention, note, too, that nothing will serve you better in Japan than building close, trusting relationships that convey a strong image for the company, demonstrating visible patience, carrying out follow-up with your contacts, and fully adapting products and services to the Japanese culture. After you have done this, security awareness and training must accompany any work you do in the country. You will also need to have someone on the ground to manage, implement, and serve as a liaison for your security strategy.

Encryption and Japanese Financial Services

In contrast to the United States, the Japanese financial industry does not have any special Japanese encryption standards, and the market for business applications for crypto is well below that of its global peers. There tends to be a greater reliance on the use of leased lines, with the (false) hope that restricting access will limit risk. As Japanese banks start to rely more on the Internet as a communications medium, expect to see a quick upturn in their adoption of encryption, based on the international SWIFT standards. Although the Bank of Japan's BOJ-NET does employ the Data Encryption Standard and its cousin, Triple DES, this is reserved for wholesale settlements and not standard banking operations—which are much more susceptible to risk.

---

11. *"Information Security Auditing System." Japan Ministry of Economy Trade and Industry. 29 January 2003.*

Final Japanese Thoughts

Just two days after it launched in 2002, a personal data leak from Japan's national identification system triggered fear that it might be further prone to privacy issues. More than 2,500 individuals in Osaka received the information of other citizens in a letter designed to verify information on the system. The displaced data included the correct name, address, and phone, but it also included the national ID numbers, gender, and birth dates of other citizens. Perhaps this story highlights the fear expressed by Raisuke Miyawaki—Japan's security strategy does not reach the level of its technological proficiency. When combined with the closed nature of security business in Japan, you would do well to be patient domestically, and to look elsewhere for a regional security platform. The factor to watch, however, is whether their early adoption of the security in IPv6 will help them overcome cultural and operational issues and push them into a leadership position with the Next-Generation Internet.

Chapter 13

Outsourcing and Your Map

Outsourcing research and development, application development, business support functions (that is, customer service), business processes and next-generation product development to countries where quality talent can be married to reduced costs is pervasive. Europe and the United States have been the most enthusiastic outsourcers, dispatching work to established locales such as China, India, and the Philippines. The first two countries account for 38 percent of the world's population,[1] making jobs competitive and poverty levels typically higher among outsourcing havens.

With costs and risks both rising in the larger outsourcing havens, it is now a good time to inventory your needs and expand your search to include other potential candidates. If culture is important (as this book has been pointing out), you might want to look at South Africa and its highly skilled yet underutilized technical workforce. If price is still number one, look to whom India itself outsources to, any of the "young tigers" throughout Southeast Asia or North Africa. If specific skill sets are desired, such as IPv6 security features, perhaps China and Russia would be a better fit.

Outsourcing has always existed. The business shift facilitated by technology's rise that I outlined in Part 1, "Charting a Course," has invigorated the practice worldwide. At this book's writing, tension has surfaced about outsourcing's effect on the depletion of domestic workforces and the risks it poses to the security of intellectual property and consumer data. Early fervor has been tempered with uncertainty.

---

1. "U.N. Sees Slowdown in Population Growth; forecast is for 9 billion people by 2300." News on Rednova. 12 December 2003.

Outsourcing As Political Football

Pitched battles over the ills of outsourcing have become a source for political and corporate mudslinging. U.S. Representative Ed Markey of Massachusetts and the ranking Democrat on the House Energy and Commerce Subcommittee on Telecommunications and the Internet has said that outsourcing is costing U.S. citizens their privacy. Writing letters to major U.S. corporations who out-source, he stated, "I am concerned that in their rush to cut costs and increase their bottom line... companies may be sacrificing the privacy protections the law affords to American citizens. The off-shoring of jobs processing, analyzing, or accessing sensitive personal, financial, or health information could put Americans' privacy beyond the reach of U.S. law and outside the jurisdiction of U.S. regulators."[2] These politically charged arguments have contributed to some companies—notably New York-based Citibank—to recall some of its outsourced operations for fear they will be singled out as an insecure, un-American financial institution.

I believe outsourcing's incumbent challenges are not unlike those involved with the mass migration of business and consumer data to the Internet and its empowerment through other technologies just more than a decade ago. By focusing on outsourcing as a final chapter in Part 2's "Reality, Illusion, and the Souk," a natural convergence with Part 1 ensues. Using India as a geographic reference point, I illustrate how this country's nascent boom accurately poses the host of opportunities and challenges to global corporate security and cross-border business practices. This combination provides an example of how you can capitalize on mapping security.

India: Outsourcing's Poster Child

India's rise as an outsourcing haven has helped that country realize double-digit growth in revenues from IT services. As outlined in Chapter 7, "Constant Vigilance," the outlook is rosy. NASSCOM, in a joint study with McKinsey & Co., has projected ".com era" escalation in revenue, with numbers expected to reach

---

2. *"Markey Investigates Corporate Off-Shoring of Personal Privacy Rights: Americans Losing Jobs and Privacy in One Fell Swoop." News from Ed Markey. 23 February 2004.*

$57 billion in 2008.[3] The labor force is highly educated and skilled. The work ethic is unparalleled due to fierce competition for jobs.

Samir Kapuria, a Boston-based outsourcing security expert, reports that "the country's primary focuses are lower cost and higher quality—from shoeshiners to software developers. Because the market is so competitive, there is a heavy emphasis on reputation and integrity in the way people do business. The business culture in this country is a lot like that of Texas, where your word and handshake can be stronger than a contract. If it is not, people have many choices and can take their business elsewhere."

Catalyzing of an Outsource Haven

Understand that outsourcing countries pushed work to India. Now India's wising up and understanding the market opportunity for serving as an outsource haven. In doing so, it has created the Indian Action Plan that outlines 38 steps that will empower its IT firms' funding and tear down bureaucratic roadblocks while wiring the country and increasing its Internet user base, which currently numbers approximately 200,000.[4]

This observation is backed up by San Ramon, California-based NeoIT, whose Bangalore office helps facilitate outsourcing for its clients to India. It worked with 40 U.S. firms in 2002, including 25 of the Fortune 500, representing $250 million in offshore service contracts. Speaking on behalf of a client base "who wishes to remain anonymous," Avinash Vashistha, NeoIT's Bangalore-based project manager, told ComputerWorld, "None of these companies want us to mention their names, but we have a well-defined planning process that will show the [U.S.] client what can be achieved for cost and quality." [5]

Because it specializes in service-oriented outsourcing, there is a high level of customizable development work that can be done in India. Prototypes can be developed in advance of venture funding—proof of concept is instant and personal. Applications can be tweaked and reworked to fit the technology needs and

3. *"NASSCOM-McKinsey Report Predicts Robust Growth for Indian IT Services and IT Enabled Services Industry." NASSCOM. 10 June 2002.*

4. *Larry Press, William A. Foster, Seymour E. Goodman. "The Internet in India and China." Internet Society. n.d.*

5. *Mark Willoughby. "Offshore Security: Consider the Risks." ComputerWorld. 15 September 2003.*

framework of almost any corporation. With English as a primary language, customer support can be delivered cheaply. Yet India's greatest asset—its service orientation, price, and talent—carry a host of threats for companies moving across its borders.

Perils of Outsourcing: Indian Focus

From a global corporate security perspective, the unbridled shuttling of operations has been done with little to no eye for the dangers of taking business to India. Several threats will face new companies, and in India, such perils present a host of universals facing corporations seeking any outsourced relationship with any country:

- **There is little corporate security expertise or regulation.**

  It is here that the Israeli Mossad trains and Kashmir is a flashpoint for violence. Yet as the military practices strong operational security, little of it has trickled into the corporate setting. Furthermore, there is no indigenous driver of security. Do not expect as ready an understanding or urgency about your security strategy or methodology.

- **There is no application of physical security as it relates to global corporate security.**

  On a recent trip to India, Samir Kapiria, our Boston-based risk management expert, entered an office of a software company and told the front desk personnel that he was there to visit the CEO. Without pause, he was led to a conference room and poured coffee. Soon, he was joined by the company's host of C-level executives who have championed some of India's largest outsourcing contracts. Without an NDA, the executive team divulged the entirety of their business plan and SWOT. Samir had shown no ID and had left his business cards at his hotel. "I left the meeting feeling a little dirty," he said. "They were just oblivious, and the guy at the front desk was essentially manning a log book; there was no physical deterrence whatsoever."

- **Digital security knowledge is limited to firewalls, VPNs, and passwords.**

  This type of posture has been referred to as "circa 1993," and it generally prompts multinationals to ship in their own security teams, which I also recommend later in this chapter.

- **There is very little knowledge surrounding U.S. and EU compliance related to third-party audit requirements.**

Indian companies may be able to build you anything you want, but at the implementation level these same companies will likely not grasp the urgency or importance of how such regulations affect a company's liability. Many believe that until an Indian-based company is sued, its business community will continue to recognize this as a lower-order priority.

■ **Piracy.**

Because the average Indian makes $500 in six months, a copy of Windows XP is not a feasible purchase. Pirated versions run rampant. There are 15 "Nikes" in the country. Holders of intellectual property must beware when crossing into India.

■ **Staff retention and backgrounds.**

There is a persistent entrepreneurial bent in India that creates a strong work ethic and creativity. Yet it also poses a staff-retention issue. On the technology side, if a software engineer works a large R&D project that was designed for a general or mass audience, chances are the engineer will leave the company and redesign that product for a niche or vertical audience. They simply start their own business. Additionally, there is no such thing as a background check in India, and this makes the hiring process very difficult.

■ **Insecure development.**

Most application development is done with speed and quality in mind—not necessarily security. It is important for companies to understand that such silo methods lead to products that can carry abundant vulnerabilities depending upon their application and what operating system who will eventually run on.

The Promise of Outsourcing Through Mapping Security

Outsourcing hazards have prompted multinationals who were once freely moving to major havens to stand with a toe in the water because they have found that they cannot outsource securely. Often companies do not fully realize the main benefit of outsourcing, which is nearly pure business enablement. Outsourcing lowers the cost of goods sold, R&D, and production. For the host country, investment capital, increased market awareness, and training flow into its economy. Both entities have vested interest in creating a heightened global security posture.

To move across borders in an outsourcing environment requires that companies marshal all the resources contained within an existing security map built in Part 1 and all the knowledge gleaned from Part 2.

On top of this, you should consider five things when you outsource.

First, count the cost. Few people realize that although salaries are often half the price of their home country, the price of investigating, managing, and maximizing an outsourcing relationship can offset that savings post haste. One director of Web services at a major entertainment company in Hollywood says that in his industry, outsourcing wears out its potential benefits quickly when you figure in the hidden costs. "Offshoring to India is good and cheap," he says, "but we use up as much of the savings on management and quality control. Plus, there the type of security we have to implement creates a break-even proposition at best."

There are more than just management costs at stake when moving into outsourced relationships. Finding a partner, as I have recommended below, and then adapting your security strategy to their knowledge or lack thereof can prove expensive. Numbers range from the low to high hundreds of thousands of dollars. Both endeavors are riddled with potential delays that cost you more than you anticipated in both the setup and production/development phase.

The business side of the outsourcing proposition can predictably cost time and money, but the human resource side of the equation can trigger potentially overlooked costs. On the one hand, there is an issue of severance packages for laying off a domestic workforce. On the other hand, there is the necessary training that must take place among new employees who will not have—and I guarantee this—the same expertise and intuition, especially as it relates to your security strategy, of your old employees.

If your cost-benefit analysis clears you for takeoff, remember to re-establish your coordinates in the outsource partner's country. Doing due diligence and acclimating your security posture to a new, host country is an important step in creating a secure environment for outsourcing. Knowing that information security is more than likely going to be driven by you and your team, glean first-hand knowledge of the track record of your outsource vendor. Understand what they know of global corporate security in general and get a reference list. Note that in India and other similar outsourcing havens—China excepted—major players are usually on the ground (for example, IBM or the Big 4) and will be used by the companies you outsource to. Also, with the speed of growth and the quick transition to a secure environment, companies you deal with may be so overwhelmed with the choices and diversity of security offerings, you will more than likely need to adapt your existing strategy yourself.

Don't BITS the Dust

Washington, D.C.-based *Banking Industry Technology Secretariat* (BITS) has offered guideline questions for managing business relationships with outsourced IT service providers, many of whom reside in India and other outsourcing havens. They provide a firm first step in managing your new relationships:

- Do IT services firms have appropriate security policies and management procedures in place?
- Have they developed systems for maintaining an accurate inventory of IT assets?
- Are outsourcing workers and business partners qualified to fulfill their responsibilities?
- Are data centers physically protected against access by unauthorized individuals?
- Have comprehensive business continuity plans been developed and tested?

This reestablishment of coordinates must be followed with a reminder: do not forget the people. This means maintain a presence to check, train, and manage employees while implementing your security strategy on-site. Background checks in India and many outsourcing havens are unheard of. However, you will have to find a culturally sensitive way to execute one. Set aside both time and money. In the United States, a typical background check conducted by an online provider such as USSearch.com provides you a comprehensive report on an individual for about $50. It takes about a day. In a place such as India, where that same check is neither automated nor even available, budget $20,000 and two months.

Fully vetted workers will more than likely require thorough security training. In a 2003 study by Jobsahead and NASSCOM, it was determined that only 2,500 of India's workers—less than .5 percent of the total Indian workforce—had any corporate security skills as related to technology.[6] Training and ensuring that your outsource teams are as skilled in security as domestic workers will take time, but ultimately, it will be worth the toil.

---

6. *"IT Security Set to Boom: NASSCOM." Indian Express. 31 March 2004. egov.mit.gov.in/news.asp (22 March 2004).*

Training must be accompanied by management on the ground, and that means that companies that outsource must make a fundamental commitment to housing a manager on-site in the country of choice. Royal Hansen, a Boston-based security expert, has recently traveled to India and found many expatriates on the ground who were telling him sob stories about their Indian assignments. "Many have told me, 'I was asked to come to Bangalore until I can prove to my bosses and the C-level that what we have here is an ability to control and manage any risk as information moves in and out of this country,'" he said. "Of course there are benefits. These same security personnel are living in tropical environment with palatial estates, two butlers, and battle pay that's lucrative."

In most cases just having someone working alongside your outsourced partner is not enough. You must also develop strong legal partnerships in the outsourcing country. In India particularly, finding strong patent, IP, and trademark lawyers who have a firm grasp of Napoleonic law can creatively develop contractual elements that might not otherwise be enabled via the existing law. Craig Chrétien, Vice President of International Operations for the *International Protective Services of America* (IPSA International), Inc., spent 25 years with the Drug Enforcement Administration, spending his last few years as head of intelligence and prior to that as chief of their international operations responsible for DEA's 72 offices across 54 countries. He recommends that if you are unsure of where to begin, join the American Chamber of Commerce or talk with an American law firm that has established outposts overseas.

In addition to strong legal help, hedge your liability bets and take care with what types of data you send to outsourcing partners. Hansen said that he was amazed at the amount of real data that was being used in the development of database architecture in India. "The development companies I have connected with often have real data being used for application development. I was told that U.S. companies had simply turned over whole databases to the developer, and said, 'Here's what we want the application to search, now rock with it.' Indian providers were shocked. 'We're surprised we got the real stuff,' they said. I can only imagine how they figured out it was real data—'Oh, that credit card number actually *worked!*'" This oversight will continue to dog companies that do not take control of their data before it is shipped; although obvious, this appears frequently and unfortunately overlooked by corporations that are sending work abroad.

Outsourcing, although it is a hot-button issue in the near term, will continue to evolve as a chief reason for companies to take their business across borders. As discussed in Chapter 10, "The Middle East and Africa," this requires a fully baked security strategy that is grounded in Part 1 of this book. Outsourcing and India offer a strong case study for how you can use the information in Part 2 of this book to get a jump on establishing your coordinates and find that perfect partner in a cross-border setting. Upon counting the cost, you can transition your strong security framework with the help of local assistance, and depending on the country, deploy on-site management for an ideal and enabling experience. When looking at risks, watch out for "subsourcing," where you outsource in one country, and they further outsource it to an even cheaper place. You may never know, and your contract may not even preclude it unless you watch for this threat. Part 3, "Whose Law Do I Break?", examines in greater detail the implications of global corporate security across borders, providing further insight that will prove helpful as you begin to make your move abroad or revisit established multinational operations.

PART 3

WHO'S LAW DO I BREAK?

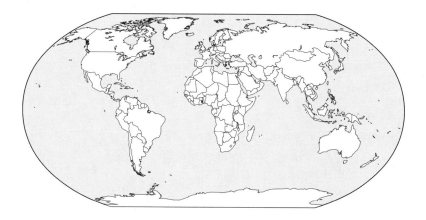

Chapter 14

Mapping Solutions

How far will [modern man] remain dark, obdurate, habitual, and traditional, resisting the convergent forces that offer them either unity or misery? Sooner or later that unity must come or else plainly men must perish by their own inventions.

—H. G. Wells, The Outline of History (1923)

Part 1, "Charting a Course," outlined six "tricks of the trade" best practices that should help you create an organization-wide security strategy that's ready for global business. In Part 2, "Reality, Illusion, and the Souk," you saw how your core geocentric security, when confronted by regional differences in local rules, regulations, customs, best practices, and conventions, magnify in relevance. Qualitative and quantitative differences in countries are accounted for in both the MSI and anecdotal accounts. Even so, there are still significant conundrums to untangle when working as a multinational, and you may be asking yourself, how do I do this? What are some ways I can begin to prepare my company if planning a first foray or shoring up an existing cross-border presence? Part 3, "Whose Law Do I Break?" begins to answer those questions and empowers you to secure your company today.

Part 3 is informed by some of the world's most experienced, thoughtful global security players. My practical, real-world advice is colored by these experts who have been working around the world longer than you. Many of the solutions proffered will not be absolutes; instead, they illustrate that good decisions can be made even amid the vagaries met in an evolutionary, and often outright conflicting maze of country-specific business around the world. Again, as in the first two parts of this book, these wizened international professionals are not the techie icons who lent their initials to an encryption standard, or the first ones to invent a firewall, or even bad-boy hackers "gone good." They are, however, some of the most influential people in the world who are routinely solving cross-border issues.

First, you have to understand the regulations and laws in each country, and then look to what is currently customary in terms of compliance. Second, you have to have a fine-tuned technology architecture that does not lump all customers into the same security group. Third, you have to be able to demonstrate to your auditors and regulators that you are complying with their laws. As a bank that works globally, we understand that the myriad regulations are critical to our success, and focus executive attention on them. Treating regulations like boxes to be checked on a compliance form is the quickest path to failure.

—Douglas Graham, CEO, Circle Trust Bank, Stamford

I have encountered these experts in my decades of global business. Although very knowledgeable about security technologies, they have made their names by finding ways to be successful, to negotiate solutions, and to make the world's systems work for—instead of against—them.

In Chapter 15, "Mapping Law," you learn how to negotiate cross-border contradictions. Your home law says one thing; your cross-border partner's law says something else. How do these internal and external disputes get solved? You will soon find out how.

Chapter 16, "Mapping Technology," looks at ways you can shore up your existing systems to be more secure and secure enough to transition across your borders. Although investments in new security technologies are inevitable, you have unexploited potential that can work for you today.

Solving and managing cultural differences requires a sensitive touch and positive, broad use of training. In Chapter 17, "Mapping Culture," you will discover how to ready for new business environments that require anthropological sensitivity to maximize and ensure the safety of your employees, systems, and key business assets.

Chapter 18, "Mapping Your Future," distills the whole of mapping security, ensuring that you understand the holistic nature of security and helping you set a course for your future in global corporate security.

Easy!

Chapter 15

Mapping Law

Is Greenland really bigger than South America? Look at a map. Then look at a globe. Then visit. It is all about perspective. The United States has a law that decrees banks must capture and report customer information. The UK has a law that says you must not capture or report customer information without specific customer authorization. So, whose law do you break? That, too, is all about perspective. Time to get a new map—one that impacts both your legal team and your technology group.

In an increasingly transnational business environment, you can't afford to ignore unique national requirements.

—*Alan E. Brill, CISSP, CFE, CIFI, Senior Managing Director, Kroll Ontrack, New York*

Standards and regulations are the biggest drivers for security around the world, and a wrong step here could have you facing business impairments, fines, or even prison.

Although it sounds easy to say that everyone just supports the "international standard," you have seen proof positive in Part 2, "Reality, Illusion, and the Souk," that almost every country you deal with has its own principles that they hold companies to. Perhaps you are hoping to find a chapter that allows you to simply examine a cross-section of laws that are neatly prioritized and denoted with a recommendation on whether or not to follow it. It is not that easy, but shy of it, I do recommend solutions you can put in place that will jumpstart your ability to steer the maze of regulatory environments on your map.

Solution 1: Find a Local Partner

The one thing global experts universally agree on is getting local help. Reasons for tapping local firms are myriad, but let's simply start with the law itself. Pick any one of the unique regulations from any one of the countries in Part 2 and compare it to your home country's. There is bound to be a difference at either the macro or micro level. "If you know that the Brits want you to use British-sanctioned encryption and the French want you to use 40-bit encryption, you must retain a local consultant to help you sort through the minefield of technical and legal issues," says Mr. Lynn McNulty, formerly in charge of the security group at NIST—the National Institute of Standards and Technology. He pioneered cross-border information security when he was the first CSO for the U.S. Department of State. He's helped secure U.S. outposts all around the world.

The classic story comes from South Korea where an executive is in his hotel room sending encrypted data back to the home office. There's a knock at the door and a policeman walks right past the guy, and in four whacks of his nightstick, the officer effectively powers down the computer. You can't afford to not have the guidance on the ground.

—Mr. Lynn McNulty, Former Associate Director of Computer Security, National Institute of Standards and Technology (NIST), Washington D.C.

Encryption and export controls on cryptography are two exemplary cases where local legal help is a prerequisite to doing business. As your data passes from country to country, and you want to maintain its confidentiality, you must know the laws governing encryption. To push it through, you might have to show some nations your key, and in others, they may just want you to use a weaker class of code. That is just the start. What if permits are required? What if you can send some data from the office or the factory but not from your corporate apartment? "This kind of stuff mandates local regulatory help," adds McNulty.

Internal security compliance issues are just one side of the in-country legal counsel mountain. There's the subject of local credibility, nuanced understanding of any local law, and the ability to maneuver and negotiate with some semblance of leverage, all of which require a local hero. Bruce McConnell, who has participated in IT and security policy debates for the past 20 years and directed the UN/World Bank's International Y2K Cooperation Center, believes that enlisting the help of local partners—including relationships with government officials—is absolutely necessary for navigating local terrain. "For example, laws may be vague or not enforced and you need to know if these need not be mentioned," he said. "Whenever you go abroad you also have to think about your reputation, and a gaffe with a dormant law could ruin it locally."

Establish that local help is a necessary component to your corporate security posture in other countries. Make finding a partner a first priority and budget for it as a component of your overall global corporate security posture that, in turn, should be figured into the full mix of your organizational risk.

"It's key to think about security risk as a part of your overall risk portfolio that accounts for the entirety of operational risks you will encounter going overseas. Try to put it in that context. It's one in a series of areas. You do not want to focus on it either more or less, but focus on it," says McConnell.

Do not head to the sale rack for legal help. Do not be lulled into thinking that by local partner, I mean simply flying law in and out of countries on the next Boeing. Remember if you are doing cross-border business—especially in a place such as China or Japan—it had better be for the long haul, and this demands that you have a trustworthy firm. Where do you find such counsel?

Craig Chrétien, vice president of international operations for the International Protective Services Association (IPSA International), Inc., spent 25 years working in the intelligence security wings of the U.S. Drug Enforcement Agency, in charge of its 72 offices across 54 countries. He recommends that "if you are unsure of where to begin, join the American Chamber of Commerce or talk with an American law firm that has established outposts overseas."

McConnell agrees to a certain extent. "Don't go blindly and find a law firm in a foreign country—quality can be iffy. I would also start with industry organizations. For instance, if I were a banker, I would go to the Bank of International Settlements and try to get connected and push from that side. Note that the American Chamber of Commerce and the local U.S. embassy can both be helpful, too, and you shouldn't neglect them."

He also believes that good people on the ground make a big difference: "You know, the biggest thing we learned through Y2K was that infrastructures are very resilient. We also found that at the operator level, there are very sharp, reliable people around the world who can come up with a workaround to keep things going. That's what you need in an on-site partner—those types of people who will enable you to forge ahead amid what are seemingly endless obstacles posed by standards and regulations."

Lynn McNulty thinks that looking to mainstream, Big 4 consultants and independent, CISSP security consultants that have a track record and no ties to the government can be strong resources abroad. He also thinks that former government and international business people resident in your country of origin can also prove helpful.

Legal Eagles

For those of you in Europe, Asia, and Africa, the United States is number one in a category all of us can agree on: the litigious nature of American society. There are so many laws and contracts that you will have to abide by: SOX, HIPAA, GLB and these are just for starters. What's more, contracts are enforced tooth and nail. You will need a local partner. This increased regulatory environment may seem constricting, but it can also prove very helpful—as judicial systems go, the United States is one of the least biased toward foreign companies.

As he did with encryption, McNulty once again raises the specter of national biases and threats based on a country's leadership wanting to give its hometown business a leg up. It is important to balance this issue. It is real. It exists. Just do not let it prevent you from moving into countries that are MSI-worthy.

"Did the Israeli's backdoor Checkpoint's firewall? Everyone asks that one, but my sense is that at only the highest level (meaning huge, national security interests such as defense or aerospace) is it a concern. There's not much connection between business and government in terms of information sharing in the industrialized countries. I cannot tell you how many business people from other countries have told me, 'There's no way we would do that, because in today's world that would be found out and our market would go to hell'."

As discussed in certain country profiles in this book and among many developing countries, government funds business and fuels intelligence as a way to catch up and, at times, even feed its people. Do not let it paralyze you; when choosing a partner, however, take an opportunity to be circumspect, careful.

Solution 2: Compromise Counts

In 2004, the European Parliament (EP) voted 439 to 39 in favor of a report that openly objected to the handover of airline passenger data for inbound flights to the United States as a terrorist countermeasure—something the United States had fought for since 2001. The Europeans believed that the data transfers would break existing European privacy law. The EP cited the fact that non-European countries require certification under some continental data-protection standards before receiving data, and the United States had no such certification.

For three years at an impasse, U.S. hopes for acquiring the data seemed doomed. Then in 2004—breakthrough. The Washington Post reported that "European airlines would soon share information about their passengers with U.S. officials so they can be screened for security reasons, under an agreement approved... by the European Commission."

So what was it that prompted the EC to override the EP's objections and fork over the data? Compromise. Both the EU and the United States will share the confidential passenger data. The United States also clarified to whom the information would go through by agreement—to U.S. Customs and Border Protection agents (who in turn would correlate the information against terror watch lists). Additionally, U.S. Homeland Security assured the EC that the information would not budge beyond Customs unless the agency could prove that it was pertinent to a criminal investigation or necessary intelligence. This created a win-win situation.

"This example is different because it includes the help of the government, and a lot of times you are going to be in a new country without government support," says McConnell. "Consider how big the market is. Consider how big the penalty is for breaking any relevant regulations. Consider if it is an easy place for the negotiation of a settlement.

"Also think about who you are going to offend. For example, are you going to offend the Europeans at a continental level? It may be that consequences are less harsh because of the local culture."

Enforcement Varies

The ability to negotiate and compromise becomes increasingly crucial as you anticipate contract law. In some nations, it is strong; in others, it is not. As was illuminated in the government intervention discussion in Solution 1, contracts hold up more readily in industrialized nations. Developing countries are less concerned about enforcement. Be aware of this and make sure your partners can negotiate effectively with powerbrokers of all stripes.

The fact is, business people everywhere are not exactly giddy over regulation. Many European countries and the EU have stringent privacy requirements, and for companies to do business across borders, these amount to a trade barrier. Believe me, they will want to do business, and they and you will compromise. This second solution obviously fortifies an argument for the first solution—find local help. Of course, sometimes compromise is shaded in a different hue. There are also technological compromises that can be made when examining regulations.

Your data may be sent through an array of countries when you house operations across borders. Where data is saved, where it is backed up, and where it is housed for the sake of business continuity may be different when you have gone global. Part 2's roster of laws could cripple you. Enter Akamai, the Boston-based company that successfully warded off MyDoom through its innovative hosting solutions. Akamai carries another product that could be tantamount to your survival. Called the Safe Harbor Package, it permits businesses to store and send data from any one of its 20,000 worldwide servers. Your company could circumvent certain privacy and data-protection laws in countries that prove unfavorable or even crippling. Technological compromise of this sort illustrates well why mapping law requires a team that is able to synthesize the legislation and technological innovation that can maximize ROSI.

Conclusions

The corporate Internet is just 10 years old and in its absolute infancy. As it has reached the decade mark, laws, regulations, and standards have increased in complexity. As you create a global corporate security strategy for cross-border business, make sure that you carefully establish your coordinates and build your base abroad by finding the right local people who are in a way country "streetwise" and who become your trusted partners in navigating what Lynn McNulty calls the "minefield."

As you find that partner, remember that compromise—as in any partnership—will become an important ally at the macro and micro levels. With the right mix of legal counsel and technical expertise working in concert, you can find a resilient, ingenious alchemy for negotiating potential survival-related hazards as you step into the new country of choice.

One last element I ask you to consider as you find that local partner and that perfect innovation to successfully map law is constant vigilance. Make sure that whoever you have in place to run your global operations is surrounded by people on the legal and technical fronts who can recognize important regulations and technologies, can translate them into business-relevant terms, and can enable them and you to make the necessary adjustments to your global corporate security policies. Laws change, regimes change, and new laws are emphasized. Do not get caught like a loud-mouthed American complaining about his double-decker bus tour in a Kensington café.

If you look at the history of information security, there has been more hype about the threat than actual incidents. But it is like the boy who cried wolf—his town was eventually confronted by the wolf. There is a threat there, but make sure your people understand that it has materialized to the degree that it could seriously impact your business.
—Bruce McConnell, Former Director, U.S. Government's International Y2K Cooperation Center, Washington D.C.

As we move on to Chapter 16, "Mapping Technology," a theme will begin to emerge: Localization is waiting in a new form, and the same elements of constant vigilance will apply. Remember that as you map law, you must really map technology at the same time. You cannot skimp, and you cannot be fooled into thinking that out of sight equals out of harm's way. Take the time and plan your legal strategy alongside your technological strategy. This is the new reality of the shift, and the further we move, the more attention must be paid in the new country to make your presence there pay off.

Chapter 16

Mapping Technology

At this juncture, many cross-border aspirants like you make glaring mistakes. After legal considerations have been dealt with, some companies go ahead and deploy technologies with a chosen naiveté. They close their eyes and cover their ears. They inaccurately gauge technology-based corporate security by their own country's standard. Worse, they have a false sense of security—their technology group is on it, or they have outsourced work and therefore believe they have also outsourced security. Consider these facts:

- In outsourcing alone, every keyboard you have abroad may have ten users... even though just three may be working on your project. All ten may have direct access to your intranet, your customer data, your financials, and some of your company's most valued assets.

- Your foreign IT managers may be deploying pirated software; it is the norm in many countries. Moreover, intracorporate privacy is rarely regulated.

- Certain countries mandate that you never move employee or customer data across any border.

- If you're like most banks and other businesses, you're giving those outsourcers real customer data—not test data—to build your database or CRM tool.

- Depending on your industry, you will have the same team working on your database *and* your competitor's database and yet *another* competitor's database.

- Those doing your work know they are getting paid dramatically less than their counterparts in your office. They do not like it. They just do not have a choice.

- In these environments, data is freely shared: your data, your competitor's data.

Such stark realities of outsourcing represent just a single facet of cross-border technology risk, but you immediately get a sense for its severity. Access to company information and your network architecture is high. Pirated software can lead to an exponential increase in vulnerabilities resulting from code that is using unpatched and incorrectly updated versions. Data is not secure. Data cannot be backed up normally without breaking laws. Surly outsourced employees may not have a personal investment in your well-being.

Ensuring that you develop a sound global corporate security strategy means you not only budget for the legal and regulatory issues you will face into overall risk. It also lies in the time and money you set aside for *mapping technology*. This chapter helps you figure out and begin to manage some of your own technology risk by offering two more solutions that will make a difference today.

Solution 1: Adapt and Localize Your Technology and Security Policies

Part 2, "Reality, Illusion, and the Souk," should have helped you establish your coordinates, paving the way for you to carefully find a cross-border partner. Once identified, you can begin to develop and implement a cross-border security strategy using the six imperatives from Part 1, "Charting a Course." Both steps in the process require that your technology be security-empowered so that you mitigate risk and maximize what you do abroad. Although these universal steps may lead to issues of adaptability and localization, they can also seem diametrically opposed to a secure global operation that requires a painstaking, tailored approach. They're not. You develop the global corporate security strategy and then engrain it into the fabric of your cross-border partner's operation. This investment in localization can make the difference between a secure or insecure company.

Chapter 11, "The Americas," discusses this in detail, but localization is no less relevant when it comes to technology—it is a mantra that requires an investment of time and resources to find that perfect, trusted partner abroad and adapt your operations to aforementioned, ensuing nuances. In this context, localization must be pursued in two ways: through technological appropriateness, and the implementation of a locally relevant global corporate security policy among a well-drilled cross-border team.

Be aware of greater use of local technology. Higher use of wireless in Japan, or more use of cable modems in Latin America needs to be screened for the increased risks you will face there.

—Dan B. Pietro, Professional Staff, Select Committee on Homeland Security, U.S. House of Representatives and International Affairs Fellow, Council on Foreign Relations, Washington D.C.[1]

Technologically, you must customize to your new region, or your new region's technology must be examined and customized for your culturally sensitive global corporate security strategy. IBM doesn't give any product "general availability" status until it has been localized for 100 different countries. Investing in IBM products may cost you more up front, but these costs may deliver the highest ROSI depending on your particular business needs.

Short of a new technology purchase, note that software manufacturers in your global outposts can also be tapped for gauging the appropriateness, legality, and security of your cross-border applications. For instance, Oracle will visit your Shanghai office or your Shanghai outsource partner's office and report back to you what they find—whether software is pirated or unpatched.

It is very common for corporations to assume that because English is the corporate language, then that will do, ignoring how graphics and even colors can be just as important. Understanding of English is good at the speaking level but often poor at the written level. A graphic style that works in Europe rarely translates as well to Asia Pacific and so on. In Asia face-to-face training is the norm largely because of cultural issues about communication and authority impede the acceptability of e-learning.

—Terry Hancock, CEO, Easy-i Group, Los Angeles

Wholesale deployment of legal, country-apropos software doesn't complete the localizing process. Make sure your global corporate security policy is culturally relevant and legal in the country you have chosen as a cross-border partner. Then find a professional who can superbly translate it into the native tongue. Do not muddle your way through a transliteration that renders your direction too literal and plain unintelligible. You will need the subtlety of idiomatic expression and common nomenclature.

---

1. *The views expressed by Mr. Prieto are solely his own and do not reflect the views or positions of the House Select Committee on Homeland Security or its members.*

Know that after it is translated well, training must ensue. Terry Hancock, CEO, Easy-i, a leading global provider of information security training and awareness solutions, asserts that "if English-speaking countries are divided by a common language, then the analogy is magnified by numerous cultural assumptions and references on an international scale." He contends that global training implementation must pay the closest possible attention to the cultural context across locations. "This doesn't just mean with effective language translation," he said, "but also with content, presentation, and delivery; there is simply no shortcut to this."

It also does not mean just a simple workshop on how to access the company database. Like the international community needs culturally customized depth, it also demands training that figures in both how to use secure technology and how to prepare people to behave securely on the job. Whiteboards with customer data scribbled in plain view and chocolate for passwords imply how widespread and serious it can be.

"Globally, employees are one of the weakest links in the security chain, and organizations need to ensure that all staff is aware of security threats and how to protect against them," says Hancock. "Social engineering has become a major security issue, and organizations need to work fast to educate their staff on how to identify and prevent social engineers from obtaining and exploiting sensitive information, often with disastrous consequences."

Locally readied technology matched with an on-the-ground team that is apprised of your security culture and lives by it in ways that respect their country's unique security challenges are necessary solutions that can prepare your company right now. There is another, often-ignored leverage point for ensuring a globally secure multinational that exploits existing software capabilities, and it is my second solution.

Solution 2: Granularity

Just as technology enables your business, granularity is the key that unlocks it on a global scale. Technology can be your greatest ally for a secure operation in another country, and not just new technology. Existing equipment and software can undergo retrofitting to make you safer and more productive. I briefly outline this global corporate security concept, granularity, which is solidly ensconced in technology that clearly assimilates the prescribed, all-encompassing global security posture while affording ultimate, localized deployment.

Granularity posits that the more customized your access to technology becomes, the more universal control you can exert over it, and it is readily accessible to you right now through your existing technology backbone! Each of your Oracle databases or Microsoft Office systems or SAP human resources systems allow for as much granularity as you desire.

Granularity is seldom touched when setting user access privileges. In a single-country operation, it has been easier or faster to allow your personnel either complete access or no access to your network or intranet. Usually, your technology group has collaborated with HR to provide this right or denial of entry. HR has thoroughly vetted new employees, and trust is implicit. This is changing rapidly, even in the single-country scenario, through a granularity functionality available on most applications known as *discretionary access control* (DAC).

If you have a new laptop, you can see DAC immediately at work. The laptop allows you to log on to your system using one name and user ID, and it allows friends or family to log on under their own names and user IDs. If it is your computer, you can set what those friends and family have access to. Take that to a corporate level, and DAC requires that companies create classes of employees who enjoy customized suites of access. Technicians do not have the same suite as the sales manager or the comptroller or you, the CSO or CEO.

Today most employees get into your network and see everything, but DAC enables you to very easily let your developers in China see all they need in terms of object libraries but nothing about the finances, intellectual property, or customer data resident on your servers. Remember, this concept is usually embodied in existing technology. As your operations move overseas, the level of granularity must refine beyond simple title-based access.

Therefore, if you are locating a manufacturing operation in China, you have developers in California and Germany, and now new developer team in Shanghai, you must "go granular." Maybe because background checks have been thorough and rule of law is more enforceable in your Redwood City operation, the "U.S. developer" access classification receives comprehensive entrée to your full developer resource suite. Because both factors of background and rule of law are less in your control in China, perhaps the "Shanghai developer" access suite allows that team to read and edit documents but not copy them. Again, localization moves to the fore, and with it arrives uncommon cultural sensitivity.

Mike Rossman, CSO of global manufacturer McCormack & Co, believes that granularity is key, but not without role-based standardization. "Allowing too much granularity does not provide for a return on your security investment. You need to standardize and simplify," he says. Neither are mutually exclusive, but they do take a better-than-average understanding of your enterprise resource planning (ERP) systems. Being able to achieve a single instance of SAP or Oracle in your home country is tough enough, but when you go abroad the hazards are greater. Make the best use of groups, roles, and classes—then customize as little as possible to keep it manageable but still reflect the realities of your localities.

Another way to make your systems more granular is to leverage the new IPv6 rollout that is coming. Latif Ladid, the trustee of the Internet Society and the president of the IPv6 Forum, calls IPv6 the ultimate granularity tool, and says that "IPv6 will provide the granularity that is necessary for global businesses to adapt to the cultural differences in security encountered around the world. Whereas now you have a 'one person, one IP address' mentality, the future will allow for dozens of addresses for each person, place, or thing. Do not think of the overused 'eRefrigerator,' but now add the eButter-dish and the eIceMaker, too. In business terms, that means that you will have different addresses for the different facets of you, your employees, their computers, your products, your suppliers and your customers. Everything will be able to be addressed directly and securely and privately, which will allow for a much greater degree of granularity for your global operations. Look for China, Japan, France, and the Nordic countries to be the earliest adopters, along with eGovernment initiatives around the world."

In Part 2, you learned how the Nordic states value trust and equality. When you develop a DAC policy that touches your presence in Stockholm, you will want to deploy it seamlessly and subtly. This is not press release fodder that announces "limited access for our Nordic team leads to a more secure global operation." Security in its most local form should remain quiet to remain adaptable and receive local buy-in.

This becomes even more important as you examine granularity from an enforcement perspective, insisting that you word your security policy with equal cultural sensitivity. Angering a cross-border employee who causes at the least internal political mayhem and at the most takes down your system isn't the goal.

After granularity takes hold through such means as DAC, other elements of your security strategy outlined in Chapter 4, Building the Base," must be thoroughly conceived or adjusted to accommodate it. If you have been able to implement an indentity management system, that would give you a single point of management for your global workforce, including partners and outsourcers. Those identities simply get mapped to the various DAC systems that run your operations. Your security technology and the security aspects of existing technology such as server security systems and network security systems must also undergo modification with any add-ons accounted for before going live in the cross-border country.

Strong user and device authentication coupled with security oversight and management that is local is a cross-border security ideal posture. There have to be means deployed to allow for continuous monitoring and surveillance—you need to know what your people are doing on your system, detecting anomalous behavior no matter who is at the keyboard, and access control can assist in kick-starting that process. So monitoring (see Chapter 6, "Developing Radar") increases in importance. You need to monitor all the levels and then analyze them in a way that makes sense to you, whether you are the finance officer, the legal officer, or the board member in charge of oversight.

Conclusions

When taking your technology security posture global, listen to the experts: In combination, adaptability and localization are the premises abroad. Achieve this using technological means such as DAC, building it in to your global corporate security strategy, and implementing it faithfully in a subtle manner. This type of methodology demands increased monitoring and management, but through technology that's becoming easier and easier. Elements from Part 1, such as building the base and developing radar, and embodied by tools such as identity management and intrusion detection, can aid in its swift deployment and potent use. Map your technology without paranoia and find your trusted partner to translate and train—if you have taken time and invested in developing your security posture accordingly, you will have little to fear. That is, except the culture itself! That's what Chapter 17, "Mapping Culture," covers.

Chapter 17

Mapping Culture

In the world of cross-border security, it is easy to overlook and marginalize its softer side. Most would rather focus on the differences in the allowable encryption key lengths or the specific laws governing storage and backup of customer data. In each of the 30 countries I highlighted in this book, however, consulting with local experts along the way, the most critical success factor that they insisted on was getting the new culture "right." Culture cannot be measured precisely, and it is not as quantifiable as core infrastructure or numbers of regulations. Data cannot be extrapolated from a computer, and it doesn't necessarily allow for rules that can be automatically popped into a policy. Often this is why it is crammed to the margins.

However, if each of our experts ranked it as their top issue, and it has been my number one priority since I began my security career outside the continental United States in the 1970s, know that it is vital for you to take the time and identify your culture risks. Find ways to map them into a successful security deployment.

In Chapter 8, "Wells and the Security Guy Travel the Globe," I described my 1989 arrival at Prague's Wenceslaus Square and my witnessing of the "Velvet Revolution." Reviewing how I got there delivers a potent lesson in cross-cultural awareness and perception. I reached the Czech border in my borrowed Mercedes sedan just as the Eastern Bloc was beginning to crumble, and I offered the border guards some fresh fruit that I had picked up in West Germany. This enabled me to strike up a friendly conversation with the soldiers, and I was quickly waved into the crossing. After the gifts of oranges and a plastic St. Nicholas, I was quickly waived through one of the most imposing borders in the world—the Iron Curtain—which had been shut off from the West when the Soviet Union laid claim to it following World War II.

I had been taught for years by my schools and my government about the dangers of this border crossing. I had been taught about the land mines, and snipers, and the well-armed armies lining the border. However, soon after I cleared the gates, soldiers began appearing with AK-47s strapped to their backs and with their thumbs raised—they were hitchhiking home for Christmas! Because I was alone in a giant four-door, I pulled over and three soldiers piled their guns into the trunk and hopped in.

We all spoke bad German, and with this we talked about our families on the way to Prague. They had as many questions for me as I had for them. At that time, no one really knew what was going on, what was about to happen, or whether it would last, but we became fast friends. I told them what respect the West held for their border guards, and they started laughing. Pulling out their weapons, they revealed that each one of them had only been issued three rounds of ammunition! It turns out that the USSR didn't have the money or the trust to outfit the Czechs properly. Meanwhile, NATO had spent years arming itself to the teeth, attempting to protect Europe from a series of three-shot armies. Our perceptions about that side were largely false—an illusion.

Those guards might not have been killers, but those same false perceptions of risk can just as quickly kill a global security rollout. Reality is elusive. Local staff may reject background checks and *discretionary access controls* (DACs) that preclude them from seeing the big picture. Even a simple security assessment, generally carried out annually, relies on successful strategy workshops, extensive staff interviews, and testing of both the people and the process. Trying to do this in your headquarters is hard enough, but trying to carry it out within the confines of foreign cultures requires extraordinary touch and extraordinary people. Failure to modify your security plans for cultural shifts will cause costs to soar and risks to be magnified due to local disbelief of you or overconfidence in themselves.

In reviewing each country, you received both quantitative and anecdotal evidence to support it. Now this chapter discusses how you can deal with it—overcome your own cultural biases, put on the hat of a participant-observer, and become a true world citizen and global corporate security ready. As with mapping law and mapping technology, mapping culture posits two solutions that will equip you to develop positive relationships with your cross-border partner(s).

Solution 1: Listen to Local Culture

The opening of Part 2, "Reality, Illusion, and the Souk," provided a series of steps for considering a cross-border move. After you have made that decision, it is time to begin equipping yourself for the new country, and this can happen in a variety of ways. Whereas leaning on your partner has been the touchstone of localization in the previous two chapters, mapping culture takes personal initiative on your part to read up on and study every facet of local customs that are brought to bear. Culture is paramount to the administration of security, including policy, procedures, classification, planning, configuration, and deployment. Further, it is of equal concern in the landscape of your security organizations, including personnel, their roles, training, and compliance.

Mark Goulston, senior vice president of executive coaching and emotional intelligence for U.S.-based Sherwood Partners and a professor at the *University of California at Los Angeles* (UCLA) is a psychiatrist. He is also a former trainer of FBI and police hostage negotiators and an expert at equipping executives for leadership by helping them "get out of their own way so they might get on their way." He says that doing the work up front to move into a new global corporate security setting will increase chances for your success.

"Anticipating the situations you will find yourself in and examining who the opinion and thought leaders are, trying to learn about them, is vital. Take time to find out about what's important to them and what the negotiable and non-negotiable issues will be," he said. In almost every case I have been involved with abroad, deep-seated issues have been lurking in at least one key component of a security policy that I was trying to implement. In some cases I was smart, and I drew them out before I delivered my plan. Other times I just ordered my team to comply with my plan. Both methods generated the exact same response in the boardroom, but listening first always made for greater acceptance and, thus, better security. Anticipating some of their cultural concerns and adapting your security to account for them will ultimately exceed their expectations.

The "precrossing" due diligence from Part 2 is more than reconnaissance. It can provide you intelligence that fosters the emotional intuition necessary to take Goulston's advice. The considerations merit reexamination and redefinition based on the decision to move:

- **"Why do you want to do security in this country?" becomes a beacon.**

  This question will remain your guiding force as you begin to transition and should work to keep you focused on decisions made in the new country.

- **"Where are the hardest workers?" becomes "What makes these workers tick?"**

  What will motivate and drive your newest security team members? How will you adjust rewards and recognition to match the culture? Will your security team hold meetings best at the local pub or at the local karaoke bar?

- **Travel to that country on vacation: Be anonymous, and now, in this phase, immerse yourself.**

  How and when do people eat? What is talked about at what times? How do people dress and carry themselves? In concert with an on-the-ground visit of your potential cross-border country—hopefully wrapped in the stealth of a second vacation—you must learn the language. Do not rely solely on your partners to do all the talking for you. The better you are at speaking the nation of choice's dialect, the more respect and appreciation you will command. Several language resources can help you. Previous to my appointments in Germany, I learned and then brushed up on the language by leveraging the Goethe Institute. In-person immersion is best, but you can also begin with books and tapes provided by individuals such as Michel Thomas, the self-styled "language teacher to corporate America and the stars."

- **Pay attention to the new culture by networking.**

  Do so both inside and outside the global corporate security scenes. Make sure that every facet of the cross-border partner's government, private, and corporate sectors that touch your company and that will potentially touch your business are accounted for as you become visible in the community. What are the local organizations that will further your cause? Your industry association's local club? ISF and ISSA local user groups? Tradeshows? The ex-patriot community will be a big help. If you like to drink beer or exercise, check out the local Hash club. The Hash House Harriers, whose motto is "drinkers with a running problem" are the hangout for ex-pats in every city on the globe.

- **What will make my security project successful or unsuccessful?**

  Now that you're on the ground, here's where Goulston's comments prove even more important: What are the deal makers and breakers for corporate security? What are the key points of difference between your corporate security styles? Where are the red flags? Differences in standard interpretation? Find them out and synthesize them into your global corporate security strategy. Make sure that your common risk language from home is truly a common risk language abroad.

- **Decide on a security partner and create a team of expatriate and local experts.**

  At this point you're thinking *ad nauseum*. You're right! The help of a trusted, local team is the only way to succeed. Again, learn the language: You *cannot* leave the whole of communication to them, especially when they're deriding your ISO interpretation over saki and you join them in laughter not knowing you're the joke.

Pick Personnel Carefully

When I worked in Germany, I carefully handpicked a secretary who was a German citizen and who had spent 15 years in America. Her U.S. experience was invaluable, providing a second layer of cultural translation that enabled me to more accurately perceive the actions of those around me—both nonverbal and verbal.

Launching security in a new country means self-equipping through due diligence. This can drive you toward a smooth transition and minimize a host of cultural issues that, without preparation, can be problematic. You are not done there, however. Below the surface are some universal matters as you hone your anthropological savvy. With a foundation of knowledge and budding network developed, understanding, intuiting, and remaining alert to the details of listening and communication when cultivating relationships in new countries is the next solution. How you are perceived and how you perceive must become an intentional part of your global corporate security theory and practice. It is here that Mark Goulston becomes important once more.

Solution 2: Listen Well, Communicate with Care

Americans have the toughest time perceiving foreign cultures and are often the most inaccurately perceived in foreign lands. In the interest of the best security possible, responsibility for overcoming these perceptions rests on Americans.

Goulston has made a mission of helping senior executives begin to map their and others' internal terrain by helping them focus on what he calls *emotional intelligence.* Coaxing individuals to understand how they come across in myriad situations—how they seem to those in cross-border settings—affords them the emotional intelligence to know how to act and react. Often what you think is the opposite of what is observed by those with whom you communicate. This is amplified in cross-border settings, and when applied to global corporate security, where the stakes are much higher, ignoring it may be tantamount to disaster. Imagine flying in to roll out a new security procedure amid a culture that you do not understand. If you are trying to get them to adopt your plan, and they are sitting there nodding politely, laughing at your jokes and taking you out in the evening, mark my words: You have failed. You need them to buy-in, not buy dinner.

"Often, Americans doing business abroad come off as disrespectful of culture and history because they have what I call an MBA mentality," said Goulston. "That is, find the deal, negotiate the deal, do the deal, deal done. This type of transactional myopia, to someone from a culture that is deep and touched at times by ancient history, may find Americans too impulsive and adolescent. Americans also take too many turns—taking the first and last word is greedy."

This tendency can poison a global corporate security environment. Like the souk transaction I described in Part 2, form must go before function when planning and implementing global corporate security. Know the countries that do not hold a straightforward style and know that your security training, earmarked as vital in Chapter 12, "Asia Pacific," must account for it. Make sure you are not delusional about countries that operate in a more straightforward manner: As an American, you are still under a perceptual microscope.

"One problem with ambitious, aggressive, and successful business people is that they are unaware of how what makes them successful in their own culture can be perceived as pushy, bullying, inconsiderate, and even inappropriate in other cultures," Goulston said. "The problem lies in a common, cross-cultural, universal human experience that takes place when you communicate—before people give you their minds, you have to pass the sniff test of their senses, meaning that as soon as you speak, the way you speak, the way you carry yourself, and the way you address them. People are comparing you with the hard disc of memories of people they like or dislike, people who have screwed them or people they've trusted."

So while you are attempting to develop a security posture in a new country, people there are listening to you. They will either be drawn toward you, wanting to hear more, repulsed by you and driven away, or, almost worse, fall somewhere in between, wherein they act polite but do not really seek to give your more than the time of day.

"The best first impression you can make with anyone in a cross-border setting is by getting where they are coming from without them having to put out a lot of effort in the process," Goulston continues. "You've studied the culture, and that's almost problematic if you do not intentionally account for the awkwardness of cross-cultural communication."

Brush Up Your Analogies Abroad

On my first trip back to South Africa after the death of apartheid, I tried to demonstrate my cultural sensitivity by including some thoughts about their fledgling black empowerment programs. I did so by relating some of my experiences with the U.S. government's 8A minority set-aside program. So right out of the box, I referred to black empowerment as a minority program, only to be immediately interrupted and shouted down. Yes, I know that blacks are the majority in South Africa... and in this instance I learned that cross-cultural hell is paved with good intentions.

When you sit down for your first global corporate security meeting, it will be critical to verbalize such awkwardness. When something comes off as awkward because of cultural differences, alarms can sound inside each party—something doesn't feel right. If it is coming from you, this awkwardness can be mistaken for evasiveness or your trying to pull the wool over their eyes. Security role and responsibility meetings are especially vulnerable to such cultural moments of inelegance. Usually detailed, they touch on sensitive issues such as access and who gets the blame when something goes wrong. Make yourself understood in sensitive, culturally apropos ways.

The ability to diffuse these triggers is key. "Being able to articulate potential and existing awkwardness while being polite and respectful plays well in any culture," says Goulston. "If you were to say something like, 'I have read up on your culture and the differences between both of our cultures, and yet I am certain I will say and do things that may not fit. I'm not planning to, but it may happen. However, before we get started, I'd like to find out what might be the best result of our talk together for you. If we can keep in mind the best end for doing business together and allow that to somehow make up for some of the gaffes or some of the things that I hope not to do but probably will based on my culture—what will be the best result of our dealings together?'"

Listening. It is a lost art that can be a tool for ROSI if you apply it to the ongoing transition of your global corporate security policy, embedding it in a new culture. When you show sensitivity and practice de facto "internal constant vigilance" your cross-cultural partnership can blossom. Goulston believes that even as arrogance triggers defensiveness and more arrogance, such humility is incredibly disarming. Vesting your cross-border team with importance by listening to them, their concerns, their wants, and the threats and vulnerabilities they face will begin to crack open a door of respect for you. It works both ways.

"If the other person's impression of you is severely biased, and yet they see that you are aware of some of their negativity and fears, you will find some footing. Then reframe it: 'You and I will probably do some things that wouldn't be in keeping with each others cultures, but if we can keep our eye on the prize of the best result, I am hoping that will offset any of the things that each of us might do that could rub both of us the wrong way. Are you okay with that?'"

This type of humility leads to respect, and respect, especially when it comes to enterprise-wide corporate security where even domestically the whole of a business's culture can be turned on its head, is imperative to ensuring its proper implementation and your overall security. This is especially vital when you are engendering support for security-enabled business processes and when you are multiplying the geographic cultural concerns, with the various business cultures from accounting, marketing, sales, development, and executive. A little humility goes a long way, and even further when it is not expected. Yes, you can be humble when rolling out strong security. Be clear about the threats and your reasons for your plan, and solicit local input on how to best carry it out in their country.

"When I train leaders," adds Goulston "I tell them if you command respect, especially in a foreign country, know that universally even though we're not consciously searching for a mentor or that terrific person, down deep, when we run into someone who is just really solid—solid in every way and admirable—we want their esteem and it makes us all behave better. So keep as a guiding principle that if you can command respect you won't have to command obedience."

Listening begins to catalyze respect, and fairness can solidify it. If in your cross-cultural communication you can clearly deliver fairness to each person you touch, explaining how you came to the conclusion as to why it is fair through the footwork you've already done, you have a principle to stand on. Again, in the cross-border security setting—from agreeing on standards implementation to making security policy real among personnel—fairness stated can ease tensions and enable your business more immediately abroad.

These foundational elements of cross-cultural listening and communicating must be tempered with an anticipation of situations where relationships do not automatically "click." Remember my fist pounding, symbolic cannon-aiming story? Case in point. Such situations can quickly devolve at a personal level. Inherent bias against your culture can make for nasty situations where individual prejudice emerges verbally and even viciously. Take a deep breath and maintain composure. Remind that person that he or she has not known you long enough to be so adversarial.

"This comes up often in other countries. You are an American, and they remember an American in the past who has either lied or flat out done them wrong in the corporate setting," said Goulston. "You can say something like, 'You haven't known me long enough to be this nasty with me. My wife has known me long enough, but you haven't. This leads me to believe that you've been in a conversation like this with another American and something was promised to you and you got screwed or burned or you were just deeply disappointed, and you're determined to not let that happen again. You do not know then if that's going to happen with me—isn't that true?' Again, articulating fear is disarming and respectful."

The final element of listening and communication are just both considerations in reverse—mistakes not to make. Perhaps the biggest miscues that follow Americans abroad is tied to not listening, to not reading verbal cues, and to not noting how their counterparts are reacting nonverbally. Lack of involvement from them, matched with a clear politeness, could mean you are boring them to tears.

Ignoring cues that communicate "no one cares any longer" will only heighten the sense of impatience and feelings of antagonism surrounding your cluelessness. In settings where you are trying to gain buy-in or adoption for what you're doing with your cross-border partner, and you have been tuned out, they will more than likely teeter on decisions and attitudes toward your proposals of how you will secure your business in their country.

Conclusions

You have made the decision to move cross border, and this means that all the cultural issues outlined in Part 2 must be thoroughly researched. Note that this chapter didn't talk much about the bits and bytes of security, and yet it is the single most important factor between success and failure in a global security deployment. It is the global corporate security best practice issue that must not be marginalized. Go forth prepared with the data, customs, network of trusted partners and friends, and fluency in the language. Upon arrival, remember that listening and communicating are the two biggest factors for security success. Remaining humble and fair will open the door to commanding respect and provide real ways to navigate difficult situations. Track your listeners and take care to practice emotional intelligence, combining it with "internal constant vigilance." This will lead to better security—trust me.

Chapter 18

Mapping Your Future

This book has examined how technology and the global marketplace have ushered in a shift in the way business gets done. The global economy has provided a deep pool of resources, but it has also unleashed security threats that are growing in quantity and veracity of scale and complexity. Crossing borders opened you up to more than your fair share of these threats. You are at risk every time you send an e-mail, patch a system, or train a person. However, significant market and profit expansion is afoot, and countless companies are trying to leverage both. This shift has also delivered what I call a moment of inflection, because most companies have sailed forth without giving much thought to global corporate security, and they are just now encountering how their environments are more vulnerable to risk, fraught with an array of vastly different threats, regulations, and demands. This renders security as an add-on reactive cost, and it will slowly bleed you into obsolescence. Global corporate security must now be global in its truest sense—touching each part of an enterprise in relevant, efficient ways.

The most common question that I have gotten over my career has been, "What are my peers doing elsewhere in the world?" One of the best places to find the answer to this is with groups of your peers who are all focused on security. Three great places to find such people are the auditor-focused *Information Systems Audit and Control Association* (ISACA) (compliance-centric), the non-U.S.-multinational-led Jericho Forum (within the Open Group) (focus on borderless security, and advancements in technology), and the Information Security Forum (ISF) (CSOs sharing stories), which is open to all (except vendors). Each of these three groups will help you work out many of the real-world problems that many companies share. I have tried to provide you with some of the common denominators from many industries, across the 30 countries that are of most interest from a global corporate security viewpoint.

In Part 1, "Charting a Course," I attempted to provide a fresh lens through which to view this idea of global corporate security. I also discussed how the combination of potent technology, mass globalization, and stricter accountability, when mixed with increased, more severe threats, forces security from corporate margins and into its core. By defining a new role for what is sometimes termed the *corporate information security officer* (CISO) but what I refer to as the CSO, I have elevated security to the boardroom, where it should become an integral part of the senior management team. I then imparted what I consider to be six keys to success that facilitate an holistic view of how to enable and secure business:

- **Key 1: Establishing your coordinates**

  Examining your own business issues, comparing them to applicable standards and investing in the security technology and procedures necessary to make it all work together

- **Key 2: Building the base**

  Constructing a global corporate security base that is operationally efficient, and allows for the differences that local geographic conditions of cross-border partners will impose

- **Key 3: Enabling businesses**
  and
  Key 4: Enhancing processes

  Optimizing operational units within an organization, including human resources, customer relationship management, supply-chain management, and financials reporting in ways that make you money

- **Key 5: Developing radar**

  Monitoring global corporate security internally and translating true threats in business-relevant terms

- **Key 6: Constant vigilance**

  Identifying new threats, changes in technology, countermeasures, and business risk (new rules, regulations, and locations governing business) that are necessary to stay on course

Armed with your global corporate security map, you moved into Part 2, "Reality, Illusion, and the Souk." You learned how the homogenous application of the six keys is beyond naïve—it is absurd. I showed you how disparate motivations and cultural customs driving security practice require a broad-based view of how security is practiced across borders.

I discussed how security starts and ends with people, so now is the time to become culturally aware of any differences. Failure to adapt to your new culture is simply failure for your security plan.

In addition, I sought to supply you with an arsenal of knowledge that could possibly make or break your global security's implementation. Quantitative data and cold facts were married to qualitative, firsthand stories that took you where real difference must be ironed out—inside the culture. I also used four quantified components to deliver an accurate gauge for measuring potential cross-border partners. I used metrics on communications throughput, risks, use of security, actual threats, and a cultural cross-border designator. The actual results of each component were then ranked, and combined they created the *Mapping Security Index* (MSI).

Mapping Security Index

Argentina 67	Israel 66
Australia 85	Italy 69
Belgium 82	Japan 74
Brazil 50	Mexico 72
Canada 93	Netherlands 90
Central America 38	Nordics 73
Chile 74	Russia 26
China 51	Saudi Arabia 32
Columbia 48	Singapore 80
Czech Republic 71	South Africa 87
France 71	Spain 66
Germany 73	Switzerland 77
India 65	United Kingdom 75
Ireland 68	United Arab Emirates 55

www.MappingSecurity.com

Figure 18-1 The MSI country by country.

After successfully equipping you with some basic knowledge about every continent, I then presented some tangible solutions for major themes that emerged in the first two parts of the book in Part 3, "Whose Law Do I Break?" Informed by some of the world's most experienced, thoughtful global security players, I sought to demystify and afford tactical components that can be acted upon today to effectively map law, map technology and map culture. I illustrated how good decisions could be made even amid the vagaries met in an evolutionary and often outright conflicting maze of country-specific business around the world and find success. I have shown how you cannot manage global security by edict—although it might work at home, it will fail abroad; the only question is whether you will see it fail.

Mapping Security

I sincerely hope that you will take seriously the arguments that I made for creating a global corporate security strategy in Part 1. With shrinking budgets and tougher regulations pushing you on one side, and threats that are increasing in intensity and ferocity on the other, you need to leverage your global infrastructure—not fight it. When combined with your global journey that's peppered with advice in Parts 2 and 3, you are ready to make global corporate security a priority within your company. This, in turn, will empower you to function well domestically and abroad while complying with regulations, remaining transparent and honest and furthering the objectives of your business.

The real changes in security are global. Corporate officers and board members are becoming personally accountable. Suddenly, they care. No longer can they hide behind an intentional lack of understanding—now they want to know what is wrong and what to do about it. When companies cross borders in search of profit from growth, supply chains, customer relationships, or outsourcing, they are significantly altering their risk profile.

Global companies must embrace security throughout. They must share common systems to find a return on security investment and must use security to enable new businesses and processes. They must start to use some of the more intricate features of their existing, larger systems. They must "go granular" where possible to be as globally inclusive as possible. They must understand the local rules, study them for intent and compliance, and then find the best way to be technically compliant, yet optimally business functional. Compromises are a must. They must monitor what is going on inside and out and must adopt a constant vigilance that keeps them competitive into the future. They must do this by understanding the world in which they work, the differences in laws and practices, and most of all, the differences between cultures.

So what do your next steps look like? Well, think about it this way: The shortest distance between two points is no longer a straight line. Don't believe me? Send an e-mail to your friend one door down.

In mere milliseconds, it left your computer, traveled over a network and through a few routers to a server, then to another server, through a network and another router, into another server, then down to your friend. It could have also hopped towns, across the country, and even around the world.

Still, e-mailing is faster than walking down the hall and delivering the same message.

This example is simple. Now think of the line between you and your customers, or between you and your manufacturers, or between you and your staff, business partners, and operations centers. Of course technology has changed the old line—it is transforming the whole of business, leaving it more powerful, but more vulnerable than ever. Accordingly, companies must quickly address their security, their customers' privacy and, ultimately, their survival based on new maps defined by how and where they use technology.

So you are faced with a lot of questions. How will you respond? Do you follow the cost-cutting herd of lemmings to India, or do you blaze a new trail to Jo'burg? Do you stick with reactive responses, or do you plan ahead and avoid them all together? Will you focus only on your home rules, or will you incorporate each of the geographies and industries that you now encompass?

Will you keep overpaying for stovepipe security measures, or will you build out a manageable base of security that is shareable throughout your world? Will security still hold your business back, or will its creative use start to enable cross-border business? Will you make decisions based on tech-speak you do not understand, or will you have a security dashboard that tells you what you need to know when you need to know it?

Is "set and forget" security your wish, or will you maintain constant vigilance? Are you stuck with security only as part of IT, or can you become the enabler and bring in the rest of the business owners? Can you stay ignorant of foreign laws, or will you strive to understand how they now impact you? Can you buy software the same old way, or will you ensure that it supports your global differences? Furthermore, is it possible to push your culture on the rest of the world, or will you embrace theirs and make your global security really work?

In the final analysis, only you can map your own security. Now that you have some key ingredients for a security posture, local breakdowns, an MSI, and some sage advice in hand, I hope this book (and mappingsecurity.com) will serve as a trusted, long-term guide along the way.

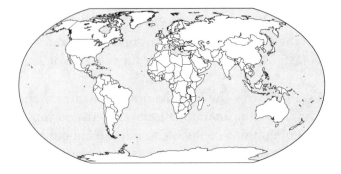

Appendix

Local Security Resources by Country

Many resources cross borders, but for the sake of brevity, I tried to include them under their most obvious country of origin. Some resources are listed in their native language, and rather than translate for you, I suggest you make use of one of the fine online web-translation tools (I use google.com/language_tools). In many smaller countries in which I have worked, there continues to be a lack of authoritative sources for information security, so I have gotten in the habit of looking at their central bank's Web site for clues. This is usually the most security-conscious site in the country and often has relevant links, policy, or guidelines. As such, where I could find no better source, I have listed central banks. I apologize in advance for dead links, a risk we all face when trying to confine the Internet to paper. Please send any updates or corrections to me at updates@MappingSecurity.com, and look for them to be posted at www.MappingSecurity.com after verification. Finally, I deliberately did not list specific vendor contact information in the appendix, except for some hard-to-find companies mentioned in the book—though you are all free to share vendor stories on the Mapping Security blog.

Albania

Albanian Securities Commission
www.asc.gov.al
The Albanian Securities Commission is the main and sole regulatory authority of securities market in Albania.

Africa

African Development Bank (AFDB)
http://www.afdb.org/
AFDB is a multinational development bank supported by 77 nations (member countries) from Africa, North and South America, Europe, and Asia.

African Union (AU)
http://www.africa-union.org/
The AU is Africa's premier institution and principal organization for the promotion of accelerated socioeconomic integration of the continent, which will lead to greater unity and solidarity between African countries and peoples.

Busy Internet
www.BusyInternet.com
This is a U.S.-based company that is building out Internet capabilities throughout Africa. Their center in Ghana is packed solid, 24/7, with locals surfing the Internet and establishing commerce at the local level. This is where you'll find the best talent in each town.

Empowerment for African Sustainable Development (EASD)
http://easd.org.za/
EASD seeks to promote the empowerment of Africans in the area of sustainable development.

Teaching Business
www.teachingbusiness.co.za/
Teaching Business is a firm of governance and strategy practitioners with a systems approach to building effectively governed organizations in a global economy.

Argentina

Argentine National Securities: Argentine Digital Signature Law
www.cnv.gov.ar/FirmasDig/ProyLeyCamaraDiputados.htm
A law that will enable the country to transition its federal government operations to digital format. Under the terms of this law, the federal government must use digital signature technology for all laws, decrees, administrative decisions, resolutions and sentences.

Ulpiano Informacion Juridica en Internet: Personal Data Protection Act
www.ulpiano.com/Dataprotection_argentina.htm
This act grants full protection of personal information recorded in data files, registers, banks, or other technical means of data treatment to guarantee the honor and intimacy of persons.

Australia

ACT Auditor-General's Office
www.audit.act.gov.au
The ACT auditor-general's office promotes a well-informed electorate in the Australian Capital Territory by ensuring legislative assembly members are provided with accurate, complete, and useful information about the management of public-sector resources.

Attorney-General's Department
http://www.ag.gov.au/
The Attorney-General's Department serves the people of Australia by providing essential expert support to the government in the maintenance and improvement of Australia's system of law and justice.

Audit Office of New South Wales
www.audit.nsw.gov.au
The New South Wales auditor-general is responsible for audits and related services.

Auditor-General Victoria
www.audit.vic.gov.au
The Victorian auditor-general's office is a public-sector audit organization providing auditing services to the parliament and Victorian public-sector agencies and authorities.

Australia Institute of Company Directors (AICD)
http://www.companydirectors.com.au/
AICD is a body for directors, offering board-level professional development, director-specific information services, and representation of directors' interests to government and the regulators.

Australia's National Computer Emergency Response Team (AusCERT)
http://www.auscert.org.au/
AusCERT is the national Computer Emergency Response Team for Australia and a leading CERT in the Asia-Pacific region. As a trusted Australian contact within a worldwide network of computer security experts, AusCERT provides computer incident prevention, response and mitigation strategies for members, a national alerting service, and an incident-reporting scheme.

Australian Government Attorney General's Office: Freedom Of Information Act 1982
http://scaleplus.law.gov.au/html/pasteact/0/58/top.htm
This act extends the Australian community's right of access to information in the possession of the commonwealth.

Australian Government Entry Point
www.fed.gov.au
The Australian Government Entry Point offers comprehensive and integrated access to Australian government information.

Australian Government Information Management Office (AGIMO)
www.agimo.gov.au
AGIMO fosters the efficient and effective use of ICT by Australian government departments and agencies. It provides strategic advice, activities, and representation relating to the application of ICT to government administration, information, and services.

Australian National Audit Office (ANAO)
www.anao.gov.au/
ANAO is a specialist public-sector practice providing a full range of audit services to the parliament and commonwealth public-sector agencies and statutory bodies.

Australian Securities and Investments Commission (ASIC)
www.asc.gov.au/asic/asic.nsf
The Australian Securities and Investments Commission enforces and regulates company and financial services laws to protect consumers, investors, and creditors.

Australian Security Intelligence Organization (ASIO)

www.asio.gov.au

ASIO's main role is to gather information and produce intelligence that will enable it to warn the government about activities or situations that might endanger Australia's national security.

Australian Stock Exchange (ASX)

www.asx.com.au

ASX operates Australia's primary national stock exchange for equities, derivatives, and fixed-interest securities. It also provides comprehensive market data and information to a range of users.

Australasian Council of Auditors-General (ACAG)

www.acag.org.au

The objectives of ACAG are to foster and promote the development of public-sector auditing in the Australasian region.

Australasian Legal Information Institute (AustLII)

www.austlii.edu.au

AustLII provides free Internet access to Australian legal materials.

Australasian Legal Information Institute: Telecommunications Act of 1997

www.austlii.edu.au/au/legis/cth/consol_act/ta1997214/

Provides the legal framework for the industry and its suppliers; this legislation establishes the rights and responsibilities of the supply-and-demand participants.

Australasian Legal Information Institute: Telecommunications (Interception) Act 1979

http://austlii.law.uts.edu.au/au/other/media.OLD/7005.html

Empowers the ombudsman to inspect the records of telephone interceptions by commonwealth law enforcement agencies (the AFP and the National Crime Authority).

Chartered Secretaries Australia

http://www.cicsa.com.au/

Chartered Secretaries Australia is an education and membership organization committed to advancing corporate governance.

Defense Science and Technology Organization (DSTO)
www.dsto.defence.gov.au
DSTO's role is to ensure the expert, impartial and innovative application of science and technology to the defense of Australia and its national interests.

The Institute of Chartered Accountants in Australia (ICAA)
http://icaa.org.au/
ICAA aims to enhance and promote the reputation and role of chartered accountants.

Investment & Financial Services Association (IFSA)
http://www.ifsa.com.au/
IFSA is a national not-for-profit organization that represents the retail and wholesale funds management and life insurance industry. IFSA has more than 100 members who are responsible for investing approximately $655 billion on behalf of more than 9 million Australians.

Minister for Citizenship and Multicultural Affairs and Minister Assisting the Prime Minister
http://www.minister.immi.gov.au/cam/index.htm
This Web site contains information pertaining to Gary Hardgrave MP, the minister for citizenship and multicultural affairs and minister assisting the prime minister.

Newcastle Business School
http://www.newcastle.edu.au/school/newc-business/
The Newcastle Business School is one of five academic units within the Faculty of Business and Law. It is responsible for teaching and research in the disciplines of Accounting and Finance, eBusiness, Employment Relations, and Marketing and International Business.

Northern Territory Auditor-General's Office (NTAGO)
www.nt.gov.au/ago/
NTAGO provides parliament knowledge of issues of substance arising from audits of financial information, internal controls, and performance management systems of the Northern Territory public sector.

Office of the Federal Privacy Commissioner: Federal Privacy Act 1988
http://www.privacy.gov.au/publications/privacy88_240103.doc
Protects personal information when handled by the private sector and governmental bodies.

Queensland Audit Office (QAO)
www.qao.qld.gov.au
QAO provides parliament information on audits of financial information from Queensland.

Reserve Bank of Australia (RBA)
http://www.rba.gov.au/
The RBA's main responsibility is monetary policy.

South Australian Auditor-General
www.audit.sa.gov.au
South Australian Auditor-General's Department provides the parliament and public-sector entities with independent professional opinions on matters related to financial management, compliance with legislative requirements, and, where appropriate, comments on the efficiency and economy with which public-sector resources are utilized.

Austria

Austrian Working Group for Corporate Governance
http://www.corporate-governance.at/
The Austrian Working Group for Corporate Governance created international standards with the Austrian Corporate Governance Kodex; a set of rules for the responsible guidance of enterprises in Austria.

Oesterreichische Nationalbank (OENB)
http://www2.oenb.at/english/index_e.htm
The Austrian National Bank sets monetary policy and promotes knowledge and understanding among the general public and decision makers owing to its comprehensive communication policy. "Security, stability, and trust" are their guiding principles.

Bangladesh

Bangladesh Bank
http://www.bangladesh-bank.org/
Bangladesh Bank, the central bank of the country, aims to regulate the issue of the currency and the keeping of reserves; manage the monetary and credit system of Bangladesh; preserve the par value of the Bangladesh taka; and promote and maintain a high level of production, employment, and real income in Bangladesh.

Belgium

Banking, Finance and Insurance Commission (BFIC)
www.cbfa.be
The commission is the single supervisory authority for the Belgian financial sector and is a great resource for privacy information.

Belgian Directors Institute (BDI)
http://www.ivb-ida.com/index.asp
Comprised of 50 Belgian companies, the BDI is the knowledge center for corporate governance in Belgium.

Centre for European Security and Disarmament (CESD)
www.cesd.org
The aim of the center is to provide information and advice on topical defense and foreign and security policy questions that affect Europe, especially within European security institutions.

The Conference Board of Europe
http://www.conference-board.org/
The Conference Board creates and disseminates knowledge about management and the marketplace to help businesses strengthen their performance and better serve society.

Corporate Governance Committee
http://www.corporategovernancecommittee.be/en/home/
The Corporate Governance Committee aims to update recommendations by drafting a single reference code for listed Belgian companies.

European Committee for Electrotechnical Standardization (CENELEC)
www.cenelec.org
CENELEC is a nonprofit technical organization set up under Belgian law and composed of the National Electrotechnical Committees of 28 European countries. CENELEC's mission is to prepare voluntary electrotechnical standards that help develop the Single European Market/European Economic Area for electrical and electronic goods and services removing barriers to trade, creating new markets, and cutting compliance costs.

European Committee for Standardization (CEN)
www.cenorm.be
CEN is contributing to the objectives of the European Union and European Economic Area with voluntary technical standards that promote free trade, the safety of workers and consumers, interoperability of networks, environmental protection, exploitation of research and development programs, and public procurement.

Federation of Enterprises in Belgium (FEB)
www.vbo-feb.be/vbosite/home.asp
The Federation of Enterprises in Belgium is the country's only multisector employers' organization representing small, medium-sized, and large companies.

Fondation des Administrateurs
http://www.administrateurs.be/
The Foundation of the Administrators is an initiative of several managers of undertakings aiming at offering the members' boards of directors a framework organized for the exercise of their mission.

North Atlantic Treaty Organization (NATO)
http://www.nato.int/
NATO is an alliance of 26 countries from North America and Europe committed to safeguard the freedom and security of member nations by political and military means.

Bhutan

Royal Monetary Authority of Bhutan (RMA)
www.rma.org.bt/
The RMA aims to regulate the availability of money and its international exchange, supervise and regulate banks and other financial institutions, and promote credit and exchange conditions.

Bosnia-Hertzegovina

Central Bank of Bosnia-Hertzegovina (CBBH)
www.cbbh.gov.ba/en/index.html
Central Bank of Bosnia and Herzegovina maintains monetary stability by issuing domestic currency.

Forum on Corporate Governance
www.korporativno-upravljanje.ba/eng/osnovna_eng.html
This site presents a public/private-sector dialogue and partnership to enhance the business environment in Bosnia and Herzegovina.

Botswana

Bank of Botswana
www.bankofbotswana.bw/
The national bank of Botswana.

Brazil

Foreign Trade Information: Industrial Property Code, Law No. 9279
www.sice.oas.org/int_prop/nat_leg/Brazil/ENG/L9279eI.asp
Regulates the rights and duties of intellectual property.

Fundacao Procon SP: Consumer Defense Code, Law No. 8078
www.procon.sp.gov.br/lb8078ingl.asp
Product liability law to protect consumers. Outlines consumer rights, including privacy and security. Brazil's national policy for consumer relations and liability of products and services.

Ministerio da Ciencia e Tecnologia: Policy for Information Security Management
Decree 3.505
www.mct.gov.br/legis/decretos/3505_2000.htm
Sets the policy for information security management.

Ministerio da Ciencia e Tecnologia: Information Treatment Decree 518
www.mct.gov.br/legis/decretos/518_92.htm
Provides guidelines for information treatment systems' interoperation
and communication.

Normas Juridicas: Brazilian Copyright Law, Law No. 9610
www1.senado.gov.br
Regulates copyright issues, the terms encompassing the rights of authors and
neighboring rights. This law also ensures reciprocity in the protection of copyright
or equivalent rights.

Normas Juridicas: Brazilian Software Law, Law No. 9609
www1.senado.gov.
This law regulates the sales and sets provisions on the intellectual property of a
computer program to protect the author's rights and registration.

Normas Juridicas: Directive 2.556
www1.senado.gov.br
Governs the registry as per article 3 of Law No. 9.609, which provides for the protection of intellectual property of computer programs.

Normas Juridicas: General Telecommunications Law, Law No. 9472
http://www1.senado.gov.br
Developed to regulate and supervise the performance, marketing, and use of the
services, and of implementation and operation of the telecommunications networks. This includes the utilization of orbit and radio-frequency spectrum
resources.

Normas Juridicas: Law No. 9296
www1.senado.gov.br
Provides the guidelines applied in the interception of communications flow (wiretapping) in informatics and telematic systems.

Bulgaria

Bulgarian National Bank

www.bnb.bg

The Bulgarian National Bank is the central bank of Bulgaria. Its main objective is to maintain the stability of the national currency, the lev, through the implementation of adequate policies and of an efficient payment system.

Center for the Study of Democracy (CSD): Corporate Governance Initiative in Bulgaria

http://www.csd.bg/

CSD is an interdisciplinary public-policy institute dedicated to the values of democracy and market economy. CSD is a nonpartisan, independent organization fostering the reform process in Bulgaria through impact on policy and civil society.

Canada

Canadian Department of Justice: Access to Information Act

http://laws.justice.gc.ca/en/

This act extends the present laws of Canada that provide access to information under the control of the government of Canada.

Canadian Department of Justice: The Freedom of Information and Protection of Privacy Act

www.gov.ns.ca/just/foi/foisvcs.htm

This act provides the public access to most records under the control of the provincial government while protecting the privacy of individuals who do not want their personal information made public.

Canadian Department of Justice: Personal Information Protection and Electronic Documents Act

http://laws.justice.gc.ca/en/P-8.6/92209.html

Supports and promotes electronic commerce by protecting the personal information that is collected, used or disclosed in certain circumstances, by providing for the use of electronic means to communicate or record information or transactions.

Canadian Department of Justice: Privacy Act
http://laws.justice.gc.ca/en/P-21/94401.html
Protects the privacy of individuals and provides individuals with a right-of-access
to personal information about themselves.

Canadian Department of Justice: Regulation Of Canadian Communications
Networks
www.justice.gc.ca/en/cons/jeh/friesen.html
This regulates electronic communications (that is, the transmission and reception
of intelligence by way of any wire, cable, radio, optical or other electromagnetic
system).

Canadian National Research Council (NRC)
www.nrc.ca
NRC is the government of Canada's premier organization for research and
development.

Canada's Computer Emergency Response Team (canCERT)
www.cancert.ca/
CanCERT is to be the trusted center for the collection and dissemination of information related to networked computer threats, vulnerabilities, incidents, and incident response for Canadian government, business, and academic organizations.

Communication Research Centre (CRC)
www.crc.ca
CRC is the federal government's center of excellence for communications R&D,
ensuring an independent source of advice for public-policy purposes.

D-Net
www.dnd.ca
D-Net defends Canada, its interests and its values, while contributing to international peace and security.

e-Commerce Canada: Electronic Commerce Act of 2000
http://192.75.156.68/DBLaws/Statutes/English/00e17_e.htm
This act promotes the use of information technology in commercial and other
transactions while removing statutory barriers and resolving legal uncertainties
that may affect electronic communication.

Federal Association of Security Officials (FASO-AFRS)
http://www.faso-afrs.ca
FASO-AFRS works closely with government security organizations and the security industry to organize training seminars, workshops, and conferences, and to obtain briefings in such areas as new developments and new technologies.

Government-on-Line (GoL)
www.gol-ged.gc.ca
GoL provides information on the government of Canada's progress to serve Canadians better and to become the government most connected to its citizens.

Institute for Information Technology (IIT)
http://iit-iti.nrc-cnrc.gc.ca/
IIT conducts scientific research, develops technology, creates knowledge, and supports innovation.

Legislative Assembly of British Columbia: Electronic Transactions Act
www.legis.gov.bc.ca/2000/1st_read/gov32-1.htm
This act encourages the acceptance in law of the use of electronic records in circumstances where nonelectronic records are used.

Networks of Centres of Excellence (NCE)
www.nce.gc.ca
NCE's unique partnerships among universities, industry, government, and not-for-profit organizations aim at turning Canadian research and entrepreneurial talent into economic and social benefits for all Canadians.

Office of Critical Infrastructure Protection and Emergency Preparedness (OCI-PEP)
www.ocipep-bpiepc.gc.ca
OCI-PEP enhances the safety and security of Canadians in their physical and cyber environments.

Uniform Law Conference of Canada: Uniform Electronic Commerce Act
www.ulcc.ca/en/us/index.cfm?sec=1&sub=1u1
Designed to implement the principles of the UN Model Law in Canada, this act applies to almost any legal relationship that may require documentation.

Channel Islands

Channel Islands Stock Exchange (CISX)
www.cisx.com
The CISX's mission is to be the premier offshore stock exchange in the European time zone and the center of choice for the listing of investment funds, debt instruments, and the shares of companies.

Guernsey Financial Services Commission
www.gfsc.guernseyci.com
The Guernsey Financial Services Commission is the regulatory body for the finance sector in the Bailiwick of Guernsey.

Chile

Privacy Exchange: Act on the Protection of Personal Data
www.privacyexchange.org/legal/nat/omni/chilesum.html
This is a third-party summary of the act that applies to legal and natural persons in the public and private sectors and covers electronic as well as manual processing of personal information. Personal information available from publicly accessible sources receives less protection than information held by the data subject or other private sources.

NIC Chile
http://www.nic.cl/
NIC Chile is run by the Universidad de Chile and manages the Internet names registry for the country. This Web site is a wealth of current local security information.

Subsecretaría de Telecomunicaciones del Ministerio de Transportes
y Telecomunicaciones
www.subtel.cl
This is the ministry of telecommunications for Chile and is an authoritative resource on regulations.

China

China Education and Research Network Computer Emergency Response Team (CCERT)
www.ccert.edu.cn

CCERT is a nonprofit organization that provides computer security-related incident-response service for people and organizations all over China.

China National Information Security Testing, Evaluation and Certification Center (CNISTECC)
www.usembassy-china.org.cn/sandt/infscju99.html
An independent, government-sponsored organization designated the national certifying authority for specific security-related items and interested in pending changes to U.S. policy on encryption technology exports.

China Securities Regulatory Commission (CSRC)
http://www.csrc.gov.cn/en/homepage/index_en.jsp
The CSRC is the State Council Securities Commission executive branch responsible for conducting supervision and regulation of the securities markets in accordance with the law.

Chinalaw: Computer Information Network And Internet Security, Protection, and Management Regulations
www.qis.net/chinalaw/prclaw10.htm
These regulations have been established to strengthen the security and the protection of computer information networks and of the Internet, and to preserve the social order and social stability.

Chinalaw: Regulations on the Protection of Computer Software
www.qis.net/chinalaw/prclaw10.htm
Created in accordance with the provisions of the Copyright Law of the People's Republic of China, these regulations protect the rights and interests of creators of computer software during the development, dissemination, and use of computer software, to encourage the development and circulation of computer software, and to promote the development of computer applications.

Chinalaw: Revised Provisional Regulations Governing the Management of Chinese Computer Information Networks Connected to International Networks
www.qis.net/chinalaw/prclaw10.htm
Created to strengthen the management of computer information networks connected to international networks, these regulations safeguard the healthy development of the international computer information exchange.

Corporate Governance of China

http://www.cg.org.cn/english/index.asp

The center consists of research offices specializing in different areas, such as corporate governance theory, corporate governance principles and comments, governance of transnational corporations and enterprise groups, network governance, innovation on corporate governance, and business management.

German Industry and Commerce in China: Regulation of Commercial Encryption Codes

www.ahk-china.org/china-economy/berichte-analysen-encryption-codes.htm

Regulations that protect information security, ensure the safety and interests of the nation, and safeguard the legal interests of citizens and organizations.

Government of Hong Kong Special Administrative Region: Electronic Transactions Ordinance

www.info.gov.hk/citb/ctb/english/new/a001.pdf

Facilitates the use of electronic transactions (including commercial and other purposes) to provide for matters arising from and related to such use.

Hong Kong Computer Emergency Response Team Coordination Center (HKCERT)

www.hkcert.org

The objective of HKCERT is to provide a centralized contact on computer and network security incident reporting and response for local enterprises and Internet users in case of security incidents.

Hong Kong Department of Justice: Personal Data (Privacy) Ordinance

www.justice.gov.hk/blis.nsf/CurEngOrd?OpenView&Start=486&Count=25&Expand=486.1#486.1

Protects the privacy of individuals in relation to personal data.

Hong Kong Department of Justice: Telecommunications Ordinance

www.justice.gov.hk

An ordinance that provides the provisions and punishments of crimes relating to unauthorized access to a computer by telecommunications.

The Hong Kong Institute of Company Secretaries

http://www.hkics.org.hk

HKICS has in recent years concentrated very much on the role of the company secretary in a listed company environment.

The Hong Kong Institute of Directors (HKIOD)
http://www.hkiod.com/
HKIOD works to promote good corporate governance and advance the status of Hong Kong.

Hong Kong Institute of Investors (HKII)
http://hkii.org
HKII aims at protecting the interests of the general Hong Kong investing public.

Hong Kong Monetary Authority (HKMA)
http://www.info.gov.hk/hkma/
The HKMA is the government authority in Hong Kong responsible for maintaining monetary and banking stability.

Hong Kong Society of Accountants (HKSA)
http://www.hksa.org.hk
HKSA is the only statutory licensing body of accountants in Hong Kong responsible for regulation of the accountancy profession.

Hong Kong Stock Exchange (HKEx)
www.hkex.com.hk/index.htm
HKEx is the holding company of The Stock Exchange of Hong Kong Limited, Hong Kong Futures Exchange Limited, and Hong Kong Securities Clearing Company Limited. It brings together the market organizations that have transformed Hong Kong's financial services industry from a domestically focused industry to the global player it is today.

Infosec
www.infosec.gov.hk
Infosec serves as a one-stop portal for the general public to effectively access information and resources on information security as well as measures and best practices for prevention of computer-related crimes.

The Law Society of Hong Kong
http://www.hklawsoc.org.hk
The Law Society is the professional association for solicitors in Hong Kong.

National Computer Network Emergency Response Team Coordinating Center of China (CNCERT)
www.cert.org.cn
CNCERT is responsible for the coordination of activities among all Computer Emergency Response Teams within China concerning incidents in national public networks.

Novexcn: Interim Provisions on the Regulation of Computer Networks and the Internet
www.novexcn.com/inerim_reg_comp_net_inte96.html
Created to strengthen the regulations on computer information networks that connect to the Internet and ensure the proper expansion of international computer information exchanges.

Novexcn: State Council Directive on Strengthening Regulations in the Management of the Telecommunications Sector
www.novexcn.com/state_counc_dr_telecom_99.htm
In an effort to maintain order in China's telecom industry, provide safeguards and quality, and to create a competitive environment, this directive outlines six specific ordinances to strengthen regulations.

Novexcn: State Secrecy Protection Regulations for Computer Information Systems on the Internet
www.novexcn.com/state_secrey_internet.html
Regulations issued in line with the "Law of the People's Republic of China on the Protection of State Secrets" to strengthen the management of secrets in the computer systems on the Internet and to ensure the safety of state secrets.

Croatia

Central Depository Agency (CDA)
www.sda.hr
CDA was established in 1997 as a joint stock company.

Croatian National Bank (CNB)

www.hnb.hr/eindex.htm

The Croatian National Bank is the central bank of the Republic of Croatia.

Cyprus

The Cyprus Stock Exchange

www.cse.com.cy/

The Cyprus Stock Exchange is a regulated exchange where all transactions concerning corporate and public securities are carried out.

Czech Republic

Czech Institute of Directors

http://www.centrumcg.cz/institut-eng.htm

The Czech Institute of Directors is an independent and nonprofit organization whose main mission is, in compliance with OECD Principles of Corporate Governance and the Code of Conduct prepared by the Security Exchange Commission, to contribute to the enforcement of best practice standards of corporate governance in the activities of the board of directors and supervisory board of Czech companies.

Czech National Bank (CNB)

www.cnb.cz/en/index.php

Achieving and maintaining monetary stability is the central bank's ongoing contribution to the creation of conditions for a sustainable economic growth.

Czech Securities Commission

http://www.sec.cz/script/web/?Lang=EN

The Czech Securities Commission regulates the Czech capital markets.

Prague Stock Exchange (PSE)

www.pse.cz

The principal objective of the PSE is to further improve quality and make cheaper the services provided to its shareholders and members.

CESNET-CERTS

http://www.cesnet.cz/

Czech CERT provides the main network services (in Prague node mainly). Responsible for the hosts within cesnet.cz, cesnet2.cz, ces.net, ten.cz and ipv6.cz domains. The team is hosted by CESNET z.s.p.o.

Denmark

The Copenhagen Stock Exchange Committee on Corporate Governance
http://www.corporategovernance.dk/
The Copenhagen Stock Exchange Committee on Corporate Governance was appointed to ensure the continued development of a management culture and management structures in listed companies.

Danish Computer Emergency Response Team (DKCERT)
https://www.cert.dk/
DKCERT monitors IT security in Denmark.

Danish Corporate Governance Network (DCGN)
www.dcgn.dk/
DCGN is a nonprofit network among academics, government officials, and business representatives with a common interest in corporate governance.

Danish Shareholders Association
http://www.shareholders.dk/
The Danish Shareholders Association provides guidelines on good management of listed companies.

Danmarks Nationalbank
www.nationalbanken.dk
The overall objective of Danmarks Nationalbank is to ensure a stable krone.

Danish Venture Capital Association (DVCA)
www.dvca.dk
The leading Danish Venture Capital group, the DVCA sponsors conferences and has good downloadable information on security, privacy, and commerce in the region.

Egypt

Central Bank of Egypt (CBE)

www.cbe.org.eg/

The CBE is an autonomous public legal entity assuming the authorities and powers vested in it, including organizing private-sector participation in the capital of public-sector banks.

Estonia

Bank of Estonia

www.bankofestonia.info/frontpage/en/

The mission of Eesti Pank as the central bank of Estonia is to strengthen both domestic and international confidence in the stability and integrity of the Estonian currency and the Estonian monetary system.

TeliaCERT CC

www.terena.nl/

Look for Swedish telecom giant TeliaSonera to operate the CERT for Estonia.

Tallin Stock Exchange (HEX)

www.hex.ee

The Tallin Stock Exchange is the only regulated secondary securities market in Estonia.

Ethiopia

National Bank of Ethiopia (NBE)

www.nbe.gov.et/

The National Bank of Ethiopia plays a key role in the Ethiopian economy by formulating and implementing the country's monetary policy.

Europe

Organisation for Economic Cooperation and Development (OECD)

http://www.oecd.org/home/

The OECD groups 30 member countries sharing a commitment to democratic government and the market economy. With active relationships with some 70 other countries, NGOs, and civil society, it has a global reach.

Centre for European Policy Studies (CEPS)
www.ceps.be
Centre for European Policy Studies is an independent policy research institute dedicated to producing sound policy research leading to constructive solutions to the challenges facing Europe today.

Committee of European Banking Supervisors (CEBS)
www.c-ebs.org/
CEBS is composed of high-level representatives from the banking supervisory authorities and central banks of the European Union.

Committee of European Securities Regulators (CESR)
www.cesr-eu.org/
CESR is an independent Committee of European Securities Regulators.

Corporate Social Responsibility (CSR)
www.csreurope.org
CSR Europe is a nonprofit organization that promotes corporate social responsibility.

Council of the European Union
http://ue.eu.int/en/summ.htm
The Council of the European Union is a Community institution exercising the powers conferred upon it by the treaties.

The Encyclopedia about Corporate Governance (Encycogov)
http://www.encycogov.com/
Encycogov is an academic encyclopedia about corporate governance intended for use by students, academics, business people, and government officials.

European Bank for Reconstruction and Development (EBRD)
www.ebrd.com/
The EBRD uses the tools of investment to help build market economies and democracies in 27 countries from central Europe to central Asia.

European Central Bank (ECB)
www.ecb.int/

ECB and the national central banks constitute the Eurosystem, the central banking system of the euro area. The main objective of the Eurosystem is to maintain price stability: safeguarding the value of the euro.

European Corporate Governance Institute (ECGI)
www.ecgi.de/codes/
The ECGI is an international scientific nonprofit association that provides a forum for debate and dialogue among academics, legislators, and practitioners, focusing on major corporate governance issues and thereby promoting best practices.

European Corporate Governance Service (ECGS)
www.ecgs.net/
The ECGS covers all constituents of the FTSE Eurotop 300 Index and the leading local indices in each market such as the FTSE 100, CAC 40, and the DAX 40.

European Investment Bank (EIB)
http://www.eib.org/
EIB implements the financial components of agreements concluded under European development aid and cooperation policies.

European Network and Information Security Agency (ENISA)
http://www.enisa.eu.int/
ENISA is a new agency of the European Union, with aims to achieve a high level of network and information security within the Community. It will also seek to develop a culture of network and information security for the benefit of citizens, consumers, business, and public-sector organizations in the European Union.

European Parliament
www.europarl.eu.int
The European Parliament represents the peoples of the European states. Some 375 million European citizens are now involved in the process of European integration through their 626 representatives in the European Parliament.

European Union (EU)
http://europa.eu.int/
The EU is a family of democratic European countries committed to working together for peace and prosperity—and does well sharing security and privacy information.

International Security Information Service, Europe (ISIS Europe)
http://www.isis-europe.org/
ISIS Europe is an independent research organization that works to increase transparency, stimulate parliamentary engagement, and broaden participation in EU and NATO policy making.

European Union: The European Union Data Protection Directive (95/46/EC)
http://europa.eu.int/smartapi/cgi/sga_doc?smartapi!celexapi!prod!CELEXnumdoc&lg=EN&numdoc=31995L0046&model=guichett
Prohibits the export of personal data to outside countries that do not meet the EU's minimum standards for consumer privacy protection.

European Warning and Information System Forum (EWIS)
http://ewis.jrc.it
A European Commission initiative promoting action on the development of improved EU capabilities to provide early warning of network and information security threats.

Federation of European Securities Exchanges (FESE)
www.fese.org/
FESE aims to represent and promote the common interests of securities exchanges in Europe.

Organization for Security and Cooperation in Europe (OSCE)
http://www.osce.org/
OSCE is the largest regional security organization in the world with 55 participating states from Europe, Central Asia, and North America.

Finland

Bank of Finland
www.bof.fi/eng/
The Bank of Finland is Finland's central bank and a member of the European System of Central Banks (ESCB).

Finnish University and Research Network—Computer Emergency Response Team: CSC—Center for Scientific Computing (FUNET)
www.csc.fi/suomi/funet/cert/
FUNET network service that the Center for Scientific Computing provides to the universities, polytechnic colleges, and the research community.

HEX Integrated Markets
www.hex.com/en/index.html
HEX Integrated Markets is the largest securities market in northern Europe.

France

Banque de France
http://www.banque-france.fr/gb/home.htm
The Banque de France is the central bank of France and an integral part of the European System of Central Banks.

French Business Confederation (MEDEF)
www.medef.fr/staging/site/page.php
This popular French language business site has insightful articles on security, privacy, and governance.

L'Association Française de la Gestion Financière (AFG)
www.afg-asffi.com/afg/uk/afg/whatisafg_nad.html
AFG is the French Asset Management Association, representing investment funds and individual portfolio management.

Germany

Arbeitskreis Schutz von Infrastrukturen (AKSIS)
www.aksis.de

Aspen Institute Berlin
http://www.aspenberlin.org/
A nonprofit organization with a mission to foster transatlantic dialogue.

Berlin Information—Center for Transatlantic Security (BITS)
http://www.bits.de/

BITS has established a reputation for providing independent expertise on military security issues, especially in the field of nuclear and conventional disarmament and arms control, nonproliferation, and NATO-Russian relations.

BKAonline—Bundeskriminalant Wiesbaden
www.bka.de
Information on the responsibilities, jurisdictions, and particularities of the Federal Criminal Police Office.

Bundesamt für Sicherheit in der Informationstechnik (BSI)
www.bsi.de
The BSI investigates security risks associated with the use of IT and develops preventive security measures.

Bundesanstalt für Finanzdienstleistungsaufsicht
www.bawe.de
This is a great site for finance-specific information in Germany.

Bundesministerium für Bildung und Forschung (BMBF)
www.bmbf.de
This Web site is the official site for the Federal Ministry of Education and Research, with a lot of good information on security best practices.

Bundesnachrichtendienst (BND)
www.Bundesnachrichtendienst.de
This is the official Web site for the German Federal Information Service, with descriptions of security functions and current security facts.

Bundesverband Informationswirtschaft, Telekommunikation und neue Medien e.V. (BITKOM)
www.bitkom.org
BITKOM aims to promote the companies in the information, communications, and media industry, to make their views heard in politics and the press, and to advance Germany's progress toward the information society.

CERT-Bund
www.bsi.bund.de/certbund/index.htm
This is the site for information on Germany's Federal Office for Information Security. *The* source.

DCERT

www.dcert.de

The aim of DCERT is to provide its customers with up-do-date, high-quality security information.

Deutsches Aktieninstitut

www.dai.de/internet/dai/dai-2-0.nsf/home_en.htm

The association of German exchange-listed stock corporations and other companies and institutions with an interest in the capital market.

Deutsche Börse Group

http://deutsche-boerse.com

Deutsche Börse Group is a marketplace organizer for trading in shares and other securities. It is a transaction service provider. With advanced technology it affords companies and investors access to global capital markets.

Deutsche Bundesbank

www.bundesbank.de/index.en.php

The Deutsche Bundesbank, the central bank of the Federal Republic of Germany, is an integral part of the European System of Central Banks (ESCB).

DFN-CERT

http://www.cert.dfn.de/english/

This is a Web site from a private company (GmbH) that does level-2 response. It contains good information and it is a good site to have in your rolodex.

Europäisches Institut für IT-Sicherheit

www.eurubits.de

Eurobits' goal is to build a network involving cutting-edge research, companies, and the public sector.

German Accounting Standards Committee

www.standardsetter.de

The German Accounting Standards Committee is recognized by the Federal Ministry of Justice as the competent standardization organization for Germany.

German Corporate Governance Code
www.corporate-governance-code.de/index-e.html
The aim of the German Corporate Governance Code is to make Germany's corporate governance rules transparent for both national and international investors, thus strengthening confidence in the management of German corporations.

German Law Archive
www.iuscomp.org
The German Law Archive publishes cases, statutes, literature, and bibliographies on German law in the English language.

Informatikstrategieorgan Bund ISB (In German)
http://www.isb.admin.ch/internet/
The Computer Science Strategy Organ Federation (ISB) compiles the strategy, programs, architectures, and standards for computer science in the federal administration and guarantees their conversion by a suitable controlling authority.

Inforamtions-und Kommunikationsdienste-Gesetz
www.iid.de/iukdg/
Guideline to the information and communication services acts.

Ministry of Finance
www.bundesfinanzministerium.de
Germany's Federal Ministry of Finance, with good security and privacy information.

Secunet Security Networks AG
www.secunet.de
A leading German IT service provider in the field of highly complex IT security systems.

Sicherheit im Internet
www.sicherheit-im-internet.de
A state-run fundamental security reference site geared toward mid-market German companies.

Vereinigung Institutionelle Privatanleger (VIP)
www.vip-cg.com
VIP is an association of people in a European network who see corporate governance as a necessary prerequisite for a lively and fruitful financial market with credible ethical priorities and principles of steadfastness.

Ghana

African Security Dialogue and Research (ASDR)
http://www.africansecurity.org/
ASDR is an independent, nongovernmental institute based in Accra, Ghana, specializing in issues of security and their relationship with democratic consolidation.

Greece

Association of Greek Institutional Investors
www.agii.gr
This is a nonprofit organization that promotes and assists in the development of its members' activities, studies issues of common interest to its members, safeguards its members' professional interests, and promotes the institution of professional investment management.

Bank of Greece
www.bankofgreece.gr/en/
The Bank of Greece is the central bank of the country.

Federation of Greek Industries (SEV)
www.fgi.org
SEV is an independent, nonprofit association for employer and enterprise organizations in Greece.

Iceland

Confederation of Icelandic Employers
www.sa.is/page.asp?id=813
Confederation of Icelandic Employers is a service organization for
Icelandic businesses.

Iceland Chamber of Commerce
www.chamber.is/default.asp?webID=5
The Iceland Chamber of Commerce is an association of enterprises, companies, and individuals from all sectors of the Icelandic business community.

Iceland Stock Exchange (ICEX)
http://www.icex.is/is?languageID=1
The Iceland Stock Exchange is a regulated securities market, where securities are officially listed and traded.

India

Academy of Corporate Governance
www.academyofcg.org
Creating a corporate governance movement in India.

Asian Organisation of Supreme Audit Institutions (ASOSAI)
www.asosai.org
ASOSAI is one of the seven Regional Working Groups of the International Organisation of Supreme Audit Institutions (INTOSAI).

Comptroller and Auditor General of India
www.cagindia.org
The comptroller and auditor general of India functions on behalf of the legislature to ensure that the executive complies with the various laws passed by the legislature in letter and spirit, and ensures compliance by subordinate authorities with the rules and orders issued by it.

Confederation of Indian Industry (CII)
http://www.ciionline.org/
The Confederation of Indian Industry works to create and sustain an environment conducive to the growth of industry in India, partnering industry and government alike through advisory and consultative processes.

Department of Company Affairs
http://dca.nic.in
The Department of Company Affairs mainly administers the Companies Act.

Ministry of Finance
www.finmin.nic.in
Governmental body overseeing finance in India.

National Stock Exchange of India (NSE)
www.nseindia.com
The NSE was promoted by leading financial institutions at the behest of the government of India, unlike other stock exchanges in the country.

Indonesia

Forum for Corporate Governance in Indonesia (FCGI)
www.fcgi.or.id/English/
FCGI is responsible for disseminating the concept, practice, and benefit of corporate governance in Indonesia to the business community and society as a whole.

Indonesian Computer Security Incident Response Team (ID-CERT)
www.cert.or.id
ID-CERT responds to security issues in Indonesia.

International
Asia-Pacific Economic Cooperation (APEC)
http://www.apec.org
APEC provides a forum for facilitating economic growth, cooperation, trade, and investment in the Asia-Pacific region.

Asian Corporate Governance Association (ACGA)
http://www.acga-asia.org/index.cfm
The Asian Corporate Governance Association is an independent, nonprofit membership organization working on behalf of all investors and other interested parties for the improvement of corporate governance in Asia.

Asian Development Bank (ADB)
http://www.adb.org/
ADB is a multilateral development finance institution dedicated to reducing poverty in Asia and the Pacific.

Association for Investment Management and Research (AIMR)
http://www.aimr.org/
AMIR is an international, nonprofit organization of more than 60,000 investment practitioners and educators in more than 100 countries.

Bank for International Settlements (BIS)
http://www.bis.org/index.htm
The Bank for International Settlements is an international organization that fosters international monetary and financial cooperation and serves as a bank for central banks.

International

Global Corporate Governance Forum (GCGF)
http://www.gcgf.org/
GCGF helps countries improve the standards of governance for their corporations.

Information Security Forum (ISF)
www.securityforum.org
The Information Security Forum (ISF) is an international association of more than 250 organizations that fund and cooperate in the development of practical research about information security.

Easy-I
www.easyi.com
A global training company that is mentioned favorably in the book.

International Chamber of Commerce (ICC)
http://www.iccwbo.org
ICC supports world business and the global economy as a force for economic growth, job creation, and prosperity.

International Finance Corporation (IFC)
www.ifc.org/
IFC promotes sustainable private-sector investment in developing countries as a way to reduce poverty and improve people's lives.

Information Technology Governance Institute
www.ITGI.org
Home of COBIT (Control Objectives for Information and Related Technologies), an open standard published by the IT Governance Institute and the Information Systems Audit and Control Association. It's an IT control framework built, in part, upon the COSO framework.

Sustainable and Responsible Investment in Asia (SRI)
www.asria.org
SRI investments allow investors to take into account wider concerns such as social justice, economic development, peace, or a healthy environment, as well as conventional financial considerations.

World Bank
www.worldbank.org
The World Bank Group's mission is to fight poverty and improve the living standards of people in the developing world. It is a development bank that provides loans, policy advice, technical assistance, and knowledge-sharing services to low- and middle-income countries to reduce poverty.

World Trade Organization (WTO)
www.wto.org
WTO is the only global international organization dealing with the rules of trade between nations.

Ireland

Dublin Funds Industry Association (DFIA)
www.dfia.ie
DFIA is the representative body for the International Investment Fund community in Ireland.

Institute of Directors in Ireland (IOD)
www.commerce.ie/iod/index.html
IOD is an independent body affiliated to the Institute of Directors worldwide. Its membership manages a significant portion of the productive capacity of Ireland.

Irish Association of Investment Managers
www.iaim.ie/
The Irish Association of Investment Managers is the representative body for institutional investment managers in Ireland and represents virtually the entire industry.

Israel

Bank of Israel
www.bankisrael.gov.il/firsteng.htm
Bank of Israel is the central bank of Israel overseeing the regulation and direction of monetary policy.

Avnet
www.avnet.co.il
A leading consulting and integration company in security of information systems, communications, and telecommunications.

Italy

Banca d'Italia
http://www.bancaditalia.it
Banca d'Italia is the central bank of Italy.

Computer Emergency Response Team Italy (CERT-IT)
http://idea.sec.dsi.unimi.it/home.en.html
http://security.dsi.unimi.it
The main goal of CERT-IT is to contribute to the development of security culture in the computer world—in particular, the Italian computer world.

La INFN Certification Authority emette certificati a chiave pubblica (X.509) dei seguenti tipi
security.fi.infn.it/CA/
This is the certificate authority for the national physics program and is a trusted site for all Government business.

Japan

Bank of Japan
www.boj.or.jp/en/index.htm
The Bank of Japan's missions are to maintain price stability and to ensure the stability of the financial system, thereby laying the foundations for sound economic development.

Corporate Governance Japan
www.rieti.go.jp
Corporate Governance Japan aims to report fresh observations and promote lively debate about ongoing change within Japanese corporations.

Government Public Key Infrastructure (GPKI)
http://www.gpki.go.jp/
A good Japanese electronic government site, with emphasis on the use of public key encryption.

Japan Association of Corporate Executives
www.doyukai.or.jp
Japan Association of Corporate Executives is a private, nonprofit, nonpartisan organization that was formed in 1946 by 83 forward-looking business leaders united by a common desire to contribute to the reconstruction of the Japanese economy.

Japan Computer Emergency Response Team Coordination Center (JPCERT)
www.jpcert.or.jp
JPCERT gathers computer incident and vulnerability information, issues security alerts and advisories, and provides incident responses as well as education and training to raise awareness of security issues.

Japan Corporate Governance Forum (JCGF)
www.jcgf.org/en/index.html
JCGF attempts to put forward effective policies relevant to corporate governance and set a model for exploring new kinds of academic associations.

Japan Securities Investment Advisers Association (JSIAA)
http://jsiaa.mediagalaxy.ne.jp
JSIAA carries out a wide range of activities, including formulation of self-regulatory rules, studies on prospective expansion of the industry's services, and representation and advocacy of the industry before the relevant authorities.

Ministry of Economy, Trade and Industry
http://www.meti.go.jp/english/index.html
Japanese governmental organization overseeing the economy, trade, and industry.

Ministry of Economy, Trade and Industry CyberSecurity
http://www.meti.go.jp/english/special/CyberSecurity/index.html
This site provides a listing of Japanese regulations dealing with cybersecurity.

Ministry of Finance Japan
www.mof.go.jp
Japanese government agency overseeing finance.

Ministry of Public Management, Home Affairs, Posts and Telecommunications (MPHPT)
http://www.soumu.go.jp/english/index.html
MPHPT is responsible for creating the fundamental national systems of Japan. These systems include the national administrative organizations, the public service personnel system, local tax/finance, the election system, fire/disaster prevention, information and communications, postal services, and statistical systems.

Nippon Keidanren
www.keidanren.or.jp/
Japan Business Federation is a comprehensive economic organization that aims to achieve a private-sector-led, vital, and affluent economy and society in Japan.

Osaka Securities Exchange (OSE)
www.ose.or.jp
OSE provides a marketplace for securities transactions, to enhance liquidity of securities by concentrating a large volume of supplies and demands to the market, to form fair prices that appropriately reflect such supply-demand relationship, and to distribute such prices to the public.

Prime Minister of Japan and his Cabinet
http://www.kantei.go.jp/foreign/it_e.html
This site provides a listing of Japanese laws and policies pertaining to eCommerce, telecommunications, IT, and IT security.

Privacy Exchange Web Site: Law for the Protection of Computer Processed Personal Data
http://www.privacyexchange.org/legal/nat/omni/japansum.html
This law provides for the protection of data that is processed using computers owned by the government.

Telecom Information Sharing and Analysis Center Japan (TELE-ISAC Japan)
https://www.telecom-isac.jp/
An industry-wide database and forum that provides information about network vulnerabilities and provides effective solutions.

Tokyo Stock Exchange (TSE)
www.tse.or.jp
TSE promotes the fair and smooth transaction of securities, aimed to protect investors and the public good, and operates a securities market for the use of investors, brokers, issuers, and companies alike.

Jordan

Central Bank of Jordan
http://www.cbj.gov.jo/
The Central Bank of Jordan aims to maintain monetary stability in the kingdom, to ensure the convertibility of the Jordanian dinar, and to promote the sustained growth of the kingdom's economy in accordance with the general economic policy of the government.

Kenya

Central Bank of Kenya
http://www.centralbank.go.ke/
The bank maintains price stability and fostering liquidity, solvency, and proper functioning of a stable market-based financial system.

Korea

Asset Management Association of Korea (AMAK)

www.kitca.or.kr

AMAK strives to promote cooperation and exchange of information among the members, achieve consensus in the industry on important issues, provide support for the industry, and improve the common welfare of the members.

Bank of Korea

www.bok.or.kr

The primary purpose of the bank is the pursuit of price stability.

Center for Good Corporate Governance (CGCG)

http://cgcg.or.kr

The Center for Good Corporate Governance is Korea's first research institute specialized exclusively in the area of corporate governance. The center takes an interdisciplinary approach and analyzes governance issues from the perspective of law, economics, and management.

Korea Securities Dealers Association

www.ksda.or.kr

The KSDA was established under the Securities and Exchange Act and its principal function is to promote self-regulation in Korea's securities industry.

Korea Securities Depository

www.ksd.or.kr

The Korea Securities Depository is in charge of a wide range of securities-related businesses as the central securities depository in Korea.

Korea's Security Map

www.securitymap.net

A good local security business site with current threats, resources, and its own honeynet project.

Korean Corporate Governance Service (KCGS)

www.cgs.or.kr

KCGS is an independent, nonprofit institution that directs its activities mainly to enhance market discipline.

Korea Financial Supervisory Commission (FSC)
www.fsc.go.kr
FSC is created to achieve efficient and appropriate financial supervision in a rapidly changing financial environment.

Korean Financial Supervisory Service (FSS)
http://english.fss.or.kr
FSS maintains the integrity of Korea's financial market, ensures fairness of financial transactions, and protects the rights and interests of the general public.

Korean Stock Exchange (KSE)
www.kse.or.kr
The KSE is a securities exchange based in Korea.

Ministry of Finance and Economy (MOFE)
http://english.mofe.go.kr
The purpose of this Web site is to provide accurate, useful, and timely information about the Korean economy, government policies, and major organizational functions and activities.

Program in Law, Business, and Finance in Korea (LBFK)
http://lbfk.netian.com/
The objective of the program is to promote the understanding of law, business, and finance in the rapidly growing and globalizing Korean capital markets among international investment community, foreign governments, institutions, scholars, and practitioners, as well as other interested parties.

Kyrgyzstan

National Bank of the Kyrgyz Republic
www.nbkr.kg
The National Bank of the Kyrgyz Republic aims to achieve and support price stability by means of relevant monetary policy.

Luxembourg

Association of the Luxembourg Fund Industry (ALFI)
www.alfi.lu
ALFI is the official representative body for the Luxembourg investment fund industry.

Macedonia

Macedonia Corporate Governance and Company Law Project (CG&CL)
www.maccorpgov.com.mk/index.asp
The Corporate Governance and Company Law Project aims to help Macedonia's private sector develop and grow.

National Bank of the Republic of Macedonia
www.nbrm.gov.mk
The National Bank of the Republic of Macedonia establishes and conducts monetary policy.

Malaysia

Bank Negara Malaysia
http://www.bnm.gov.my/
Bank Negara Malaysia is the central bank for Malaysia.

NISER
www.niser.org.my
Malaysian National ICT Security and Emergency Response Centre.

Securities Commission Malaysia (SC)
www.sc.com.my/welcome.html
The SC aims to promote and maintain securities and futures markets and facilitate development of a capital market in Malaysia.

Malta

Malta Stock Exchange
http://www.borzamalta.com.mt/
The Malta Stock Exchange carries out all transactions concerning corporate and public securities in Malta.

Mauritius

The Bank of Mauritius
http://bom.intnet.mu/
The bank aims to safeguard the internal and external value of the currency of Mauritius and its internal convertibility and direct its policy toward achieving monetary conditions conducive to strengthening the economic activity and prosperity of Mauritius.

Mexico

CiberHabitat Navegos seguro en Internet
http://www.ciberhabitat.gob.mx/biblioteca/seguridad/
This Web site details Internet security systems.

CiberHabitat Bienvenido al Café
http://www.ciberhabitat.gob.mx/cafe/
This Web site details the importance of Internet security in regard to the new form of communication.

Mexican Stock Exchange
http://www.bmv.com.mx/index.jsp
The Web site for the centralized stock exchange of Mexico.

Nepal

Nepal Rastra Bank (NRB)
http://www.nrb.org.np/
NRB, the central bank of the Kingdom of Nepal, was established in 1956 to discharge the central banking responsibilities including guiding the development of the embryonic domestic financial sector.

Netherlands

Binnenlandse Veiligheidsdienst (BVD) (National Intelligence Security Agency)
www.fas.org/irp/world/netherlands/bvd.htm
The BVD is tasked to direct its attention to the gathering of information on the areas of intelligence and security, specifically on organizations or persons that/who may pose a threat to the national security or other important interests of the state.

Commissie Corporate Governance
www.commissiecorporategovernance.nl/
The official Corporate Governance Committee site for the Netherlands, with great links to other helpful information in this space.

Computer Emergency Response Team for the Dutch Government (GOVCERT.NL)
http://wwwe.govcert.nl/
This organization offers support to the government in the field of preventing and dealing with information- and communication technology-related security incidents, such as computer viruses, hacker activities, and bugs in applications and hardware.

De Nederlandsche Bank (DNB)
http://www.dnb.nl/dnb/homepage.jsp?lang=en
DNB is the central bank of the Netherlands and an active participant in the European central bank and many European-wide security and privacy initiatives.

Directoraat-Generaal Telecommunicatie en Post
www.ez.nl
The directorate for post and telecommunications (the post office) is part of the Dutch Ministry of Economic Affairs and has a great deal of relevant security and privacy information in all languages.

The General Intelligence and Security Service (Algemene Inlichtingen- en Veiligheidsdienst, AIVD)
www.aivd.nl
The Dutch General Intelligence and Security Service (think CIA) site covers relevant risks to national and international security, vetting of personnel, the new system for protection and security.

INFODROME
www.infodrome.nl
Infodrome is a think tank, sponsored by the Dutch government, tasked with a strategic exploration of the role the government will play in the information society of the future.

Ministerie van Verkeer en Waterstaat
www.minvenw.nl
The ministry responsible for mobility policy in the Netherlands and for protection against floods or falling water tables.

Netherlands Ministry of Finance
http://wwwminfinnl.econom-i.com/default.asp?
Ministry of Finance, together with the other ministries, shapes financial and economic policies.

NLIP—Branchevereniging van Nederlandse Internet Providers
www.nlip.nl
The Dutch Internet Service Providers Web site, loaded with good security information and statistics.

The Platform for Electronic Business in the Netherlands (ECP.nl)
www.ecp.nl/index.php?lang=en&PHPSESSID=320896bccb69a400fe06255e5db
62693
ECP.nl helps to accelerate the creation of conditions on behalf of a trend-setting role of the Dutch industry in electronic commerce.

Stichting Corporate Governance (SCGOP)
www.scgop.nl/
The Foundation for Corporate Governance Research for Pension Funds is a Dutch organization established in the light of "the Peters Committee," the corporate governance committee that has played an important role in intensifying and widening the corporate governance debate in the Netherlands.

SURFnet Computer Security Incident Response Team
http://cert-nl.surfnet.nl/home-eng.html
SURFnet-CERT is the Computer Emergency Response Team of SURFnet, the Internet provider of higher education institutes and many research organizations in the Netherlands.

KWINT (Vulnerability on the Internet)
www.KWINT.org
A great multi-lingual site loaded with content focused on security and privacy on
the Internet (look for their paper, "A Safer Internet for All," written in 2004—it's a
great overview).

New Zealand

Audit New Zealand
www.auditnz.govt.nz
Audit New Zealand is the leading provider of audit and assurance services to the
New Zealand public sector.

Institute of Chartered Accountants of New Zealand
www.icanz.co.nz
The Institute of Chartered Accountants of New Zealand is the country's only professional accounting body and represents nearly 27,000 members in New Zealand
and overseas.

Institute of Directors in New Zealand
www.iod.org.nz/
The Institute of Directors in New Zealand (Inc.) is the professional body for New
Zealand company directors. The Institute is a professional organization demonstrating leadership in corporate governance.

Knowledge Basket Research: Privacy Act 1993
www.knowledge-basket.co.nz/privacy/legislation/1993028/toc.html
This act governs the collection, use and disclosure of personal information and
access to such information in both the private and public sectors.

Local Government of New Zealand
www.lgnz.co.nz
The organization that represents the national interests of all 86 councils of
New Zealand.

The New Zealand Ministry of Economic Development: Electronic Transactions Bill
www.med.govt.nz/irdev/elcom/transactions/bill/bill.pdf
This bill is designed to facilitate the use of electronic technology and to contribute to the government's goal of growing an inclusive innovative economy.

Reserve Bank of New Zealand
www.rbnz.govt.nz/
The Reserve Bank of New Zealand is New Zealand's central bank and has three main functions: operate monetary policy to maintain price stability, promote the maintenance of a sound and efficient financial system, and meet the currency needs of the public.

South Pacific Association of Supreme Audit Institutions
www.oag.govt.nz
The auditor-general is the auditor appointed by parliament to audit all types of public entity.

The Treasury
www.treasury.govt.nz
The Treasury is the Government's lead adviser on economic and financial policy.

Norway

Direktoratet for Sivilt Beredskap (DSB)
www.dsb.no
DSB works to prevent loss of life and to protect health, the environment, and essential public functions and material assets in connection with accidents, disasters, and other undesired occurrences in times of peace, crisis, and war.

The Norwegian Network for Research & Education—Computer Emergency Response Team
http://cert.uninett.no
This organization provides assistance on handling and investigating incidents that involve one or more members of their constituency.

Norwegian Network for Research & Education
Computer Emergency Response Team (UNINETT CERT)
http://cert.uninett.no/
The Computer Emergency Response Team for Norway—a key site.

Oman

Central Bank of Oman
www.cbo-oman.org/
The Central Bank is committed to promoting monetary and financial stability and fostering a sound and progressive financial sector, to achieve sustained economic growth for the benefit of the nation.

Pakistan

Securities and Exchange Commission of Pakistan (SEC)
http://www.secp.gov.pk
The SEC aims to develop a fair, efficient, and transparent regulatory framework, based on international legal standards and best practices, for the protection of investors and mitigation of systemic risk aimed at fostering growth of a robust corporate sector and broad-based capital market in Pakistan.

Papua New Guinea

Bank of Papua New Guinea
www.bankpng.gov.pg/
The objectives of the central bank are to formulate and implement monetary policy, to regulate and supervise the financial institution, to promote an efficient and national and international payments system, and to promote macroeconomic stability and economic growth.

Poland

CERT Polska
http://www.cert.pl/english.html
CERT Polska responds to security incidents in networks connected to NASK (the Research and Academic Network in Poland) and networks connected to other Polish providers' reporting of security incidents.

Polskie Forum Corporate Governance (PFCG)
www.pfcg.org.pl/en/index.htm
The PFCG is a platform of professional discussion and a source of recommendations on corporate governance issues.

Portugal

Banco de Portugal
www.bportugal.pt/default_e.htm
The Banco de Portugal, an integral part of the European System of Central Banks
(ESCB), operates in an international and, mostly, European environment marked
by the Economic and Monetary Union (EMU).

Comissão do Mercado de Valores Mobiliários (CMVM)
www.cmvm.pt/english_pages/
The CMVM is the authority in charge of supervising and regulating securities and
other financial instruments markets, as well as the activity of all those who operate within said markets.

Romania

National Bank of Romania (NBR)
www.bnro.ro/def_en.htm
NBR, the country's central bank, is the sole issuer of notes and coins to be used as
legal tender within the territory of Romania.

Russia

Corporate Governance in Russia
http://www.corp-gov.org/
This site provides information and strategies on corporate governance in Russia.

Institute of Corporate Law and Corporate Governance (ICLG)
www.iclg.ru/english
The ICLG facilitates private initiatives to improve corporate governance practices
and protect investor rights.

Russian Institute of Directors (RID)

http://www.rid.ru/?l=en

The Russian Institute of Directors was created to improve corporate governance in the public and private sectors.

Russian Computer Emergency Response Team (RU-CERT)

www.cert.ru/Eng/

RU-CERT is an official name of the first Russian Computer Security Incident Response Team (CSIRT), which was founded 1998 on Russian Institute of Public Networks (RIPN). RU-CERT was established to serve RBNET (Russian Backbone Network) users' needs, but most of its services could be used by all Russian Internet users.

RB Net

www.RIPN.net

Russian Backbone Network (RBNet) has been established to provide Internet service for science and high school community in Russia.

Saudi Arabia

Islamic Development Bank (IsDB)

http://www.isdb.org/

The IsDB is a multilateral development financing institution that was established to foster social and economic development of its member countries and Muslim communities worldwide.

Saudi Arabian Monetary Agency (SAMA)

www.sama.gov.sa/indexe.htm

SAMA is the central bank of the Kingdom of Saudi Arabia.

Serbia

National Bank of Serbia

www.nbs.yu/english/index.htm

Core functions of the National Bank of Serbia include determining and implementation of the monetary policy, as well as that of the dinar exchange rate policy, management of the foreign currency reserves, issue of banknotes and coins, and maintenance of efficient payment and financial systems.

Web Site of Serbian Government
www.serbia.sr.gov.yu/
This site supplies information and news about current governmental developments in Serbia.

Seychelles

Central Bank of Seychelles (CBS)
www.cbs.sc/
CBS is the central banking institution for Seychelles.

Singapore

Council on Corporate Disclosure and Governance (CCDG)
www.ccdg.gov.sg/index.html
The CCDG aims to position Singapore as a key business and financial center.

Infocomm Development Authority: Code of Practice for Competition in the Provision of Telecommunication Services
www.ida.gov.sg/idaweb/pnr/infopage.jsp?infopagecategory=&infopageid=I488&versionid=6
Outlines the regulations placed on the telecommunications industry.

Infocomm Development Authority: Code of Practice for Infocomm Facilities in Building (COPIF)
www.ida.gov.sg/idaweb/pnr/infopage.jsp?infopagecategory=&infopageid=I1309&versionid=2
Regulations to ensure adequate provisions for in-building equipment, including cellular telephones and wireless LANs.

Infocomm Development Authority: Electronic Transactions Act
www.ida.gov.sg/idaweb/pnr/infopage.jsp?infopagecategory=regulation:pnr&infopageid=I1934&versionid=1
Establishes the legal validity, admissibility, and enforceability of electronic and digital signatures, as well as electronic records, while addressing the liability of network service providers and the formation and validity of electronic contracts.

Investment Management Association of Singapore (IMAS)
www.imas.org.sg
IMAS is a representative body of investment managers spearheading the development and growth of the industry in Singapore.

Ministry of Finance Singapore
http://app.mof.gov.sg/index.asp
The Mission of the Ministry of Finance is to advance the well-being and development of Singapore through finance.

Monetary Authority of Singapore (MAS)
www.mas.gov.sg/masmcm/bin/pt1Home.htm
The MAS aims to promote sustained and noninflationary growth of the economy as well as foster a sound and progressive financial-services sector.

National University of Singapore (NUS)
www.cgfrc.nus.edu.sg
The Corporate Governance and Financial Reporting Centre was officially established in January 2003 by the NUS Business School and is hosted by the Department of Finance and Accounting.

Pacific Economic Cooperation Council
http://www.pecc.org/
The PECC is a unique tripartite partnership of senior individuals from business and industry, government, academic, and other intellectual circles.

Securities Investors Association (Singapore) (SIAS)
www.sias.org.sg
The SIAS is the largest organized investor lobby group in Asia, with almost 61,000 retail investors as members.

Singapore Computer Emergency Response Team (SingCERT)
http://www.singcert.org.sg/
SingCERT is a one-stop center for security incident response in Singapore. It was set up to facilitate the detection, resolution, and prevention of security-related incidents on the Internet.

Singapore Exchange (SGX)

www.sgx.com

SGX is Asia-Pacific's first demutualized and integrated securities and derivatives exchange.

Singapore Institute of Directors (SID)

www.sid.org.sg

The SID promotes high standards of corporate governance through education and training and upholding of the highest standard of professional and ethical conduct of directors.

Slovakia

Bratislava Stock Exchange

www.bsse.sk

Ministry of Finance of the Slovak Republic (MFSR)

www.finance.gov.sk

The official Web site of the Ministry of Finance.

National Bank of Slovakia (NBS)

www.nbs.sk/INDEXA.HTM

NBS is the central bank of Slovakia.

The Slovak Republic Government Office

www.government.gov.sk/english/

This is the official site of the government of Slovakia.

Slovenia

Academic and Research Network of Slovenia (ARNES)

www.arnes.si

The main task of ARNES is development, operation, and management of the communication and information network for education and research.

BANK OF SLOVENIA

www.bsi.si/html/eng/index.html

The Bank of Slovenia is the bank of issue and the central bank of the Republic of Slovenia.

Slovenian Internet Service Providers Association (SISPA)
http://www.sispa.org/

Solomon Islands

Central Bank of Solomon Islands (CBSI)
www.cbsi.com.sb
The CBSI's primary functions are to formulate and implement monetary policies and to exercise discretionary control over the monetary system.

South Africa

Institute of Directors in Southern Africa (IOD)
www.iodsa.co.za
The IOD promotes the highest ethical and professional standards in business through education, sharing of knowledge, leadership, and information communication.

Johannesburg Stock Exchange (JSE)
www.jse.co.za
The JSE is a regulated exchange on which all transactions concerning corporate and public securities are carried out.

South African Reserve Bank (SARB)
www.reservebank.co.za
The SARB is the central bank of the Republic of South Africa and its primary goal in the South African economic system is to achieve and maintain financial stability.

South African Revenue Service (SARS)
http://www.securityforum.org/html/frameset.htm
SARS is a revenue and customs agency that enhances economic growth and social development, and supports South African integration into the global economy.

The South African Futures Exchange (SAFEX)
www.safex.co.za
SAFEX works with the JSE to regulate the exchange.

State Information Technology Agency (SITA)
http://www.sita.co.za/
SITA provides technology support for civilian, defense, and eService customers.

Arivia.kom
http://www.arivia.co.za/main/
Leading South African IT company operating throughout Africa, with the proven ability to implement customized, integrated IT solutions and provide services.

South Korea

Ministry of Commerce Industry and Energy Web Site: The Basic Law on Electronic Commerce
www.mocie.go.kr/
Clarifies the legal effect of transactions by means of electronic messages to ensure security and reliability and secure fair trade.

Spain

Banco de España
www.bde.es
Banco de España is the central bank of Spain and performs basic functions attributed to the ESCB including defining and implementing the Eurosystem's monetary policy, conducting currency exchange operations, promoting the sound working of payment systems, and issuing legal-tender banknotes.

International Organization of Securities Commissions (IOSCO)
www.iosco.org/
IOSCO cooperates to promote high standards of regulation, exchange information on their respective experiences, and unite their efforts to establish standards.

Sri Lanka

Central Bank of Sri Lanka (CBSL)
www.lanka.net
CBSL is a semiautonomous body that acts as the central bank of Sri Lanka.

Sudan

Bank of Sudan
www.bankofsudan.org
Bank of Sudan is the central banking body in Sudan.

Sweden

Aktiespararna (Swedish Shareholders' Association)
www.aktiespararna.se
The Swedish Shareholders' Association is an independent organization working in the interests of private individuals who invest in stocks, mutual funds, and other stocks-related securities.

Fondbolagens Forening (Swedish Investment Fund Association)
www.fondbolagen.se
The association is a trade organization whose purpose is to look after the collective interests of management companies and fund savers alike in all dealings with the public authorities and the legislature.

Försvars Departementet
http://forsvar.regeringen.se
The Ministry of Defence prepares government business connected with the total defense (that is, the military and civil defense, protection and preparedness against accidents, and preparedness for severe peacetime emergencies).

KTH Royal Institute of Technology
www.kth.se/eng/
The KTH provides one third of Sweden's technical research and tertiary-level education.

Swedish Alliance for Electronic Commerce (GEA)
www.gea.nu
The Swedish Alliance for Electronic Business is an association of most local IT and Banking companies and is a wealth of current information on domestic security issues that might affect business.

Swedish Defense Research Agency

www.foi.se/english/

The FOI is an assignment-based authority under the Ministry of Defence and is one of the leading institutes in Europe for applied research.

Switzerland

Center for Security Studies

www.fsk.ethz.ch

The Center for Security Studies specializes in international relations and security policy. The Center's activities include research, teaching, and the provision of information services.

CERT SWITCH

www.switch.ch/cert/

SWITCH represents the interests of Switzerland as a research center in numerous bodies and makes an important contribution to the development and operation of the Internet in Switzerland.

Comprehensive Risk Analysis and Management Network (CRN)

www.isn.ethz.ch/crn/

CRN is a Swiss-Swedish Internet and workshop initiative for international dialogue and cooperation between governments, academics, and the private sector.

Division for Information Security and Facility Protection (DISFP)

www.vbs.admin.ch/internet/GST/AIOS/e/index.htm

The main activities of DISFP consist primarily in the elaboration of basic principles and directives relating to information security (secrecy, classification, industrial security), IT security and facility protection (safety, security, access, environment, environmental impacts). To fulfill these tasks, DISFP collaborates closely with both civilian and military authorities.

Federal Office for Communication (OFCOM)

www.bakom.ch/en/index/html

OFCOM oversees radio and television, radio communications, and telecommunications services and installations. It enables efficient competition to take place and guarantees that market forces will have full play.

Federal Office of Information Technology, Systems and Telecommunication (FOITT)
www.informatik.admin.ch
This is a good information portal focused on up-to-the-minute data on Swiss companies.

Federal Strategy Unit for Information Technology (FSUIT)
www.isb.admin.ch
This is the computer and science strategy group within the Swiss government and has a lot of detailed technical information related to security.

Foundation InfoSurance
www.infosurance.org
The foundation aims at creating in close partnership with the public and the private sector the organizational and structural conditions to recognize and analyze the risks for Switzerland of its growing dependency on information technologies.

International Relations and Security Network (ISN)
www.isn.ethz.ch
The ISN is an instrument that links and supports research institutes, international organizations, and professionals working in the security community. It offers an electronic platform for the generation and dissemination of knowledge, as well as facilitates information exchange, dialogue, and cooperative interaction that reaches around the globe.

Security and Cryptography Laboratory (LASEC)
http://lasecwww.epfl.ch
LASEC aims to promote research and education on communication and information system security.

Symposium on Privacy and Security
www.privacy-security.ch
An annual event in Switzerland, one of Europe's foremost events concerning privacy and information security—well worth the trip to get an overview of what countries are doing about security.

Swiss Business Federation
www.economiesuisse.ch
Economiesuisse is the largest umbrella organization covering the Swiss economy. Economiesuisse, the Swiss Business Federation, has the support of more than 30,000 businesses of all sizes, employing a total of 1.5 million people in Switzerland.

Swiss Exchange (SWX)
www.swx.com
The SWX Swiss Exchange provides first-class exchange services in the interests of all involved.

Taiwan

Privacy Exchange Web Site: Computer-Processed Personal Data Protection Law
www.privacyexchange.org/legal/nat/omni/taiwansum.html
Regulates the computerized processing of personal data to avoid any infringement of the rights that pertain to an individual's personality and facilitate reasonable use of that personal data.

Taiwan Computer Emergency Response Team Coordinating Center (TWC/CC)
www.cert.org.tw
TWCERT/CC is a coordination center for the computer- or Internet-related incident response teams in Taiwan.

Thailand

National Electronics and Computer Technology Center: ThaiCERT
http://thaicert.nectec.or.th
Thai Computer Emergency Response Team.

Trinidad

Central Bank of Trinidad and Tobago
www.central-bank.org.tt
The bank aims to promote monetary, credit, and exchange conditions favorable to economic growth and development, monetary and financial stability, and public confidence.

Turkey

Central Bank of the Republic of Turkey (CBRT)
www.tcmb.gov.tr
CBRT is the central banking institution in Turkey.

Uganda

Bank of Uganda
www.bou.or.ug
Bank of Uganda is a monetary institution fostering price stability and a sound financial system that enables macroeconomic stability, economic growth, and poverty eradication.

United Kingdom

Association of British Insurers (ABI)
www.abi.org.uk
The Association of British Insurers is the trade association for the UK's insurance industry representing around 400 companies.

Association of Investment Trust Companies
www.aitc.co.uk
The AITC is the non–profit-making trade body of the investment trust industry.

Audit Scotland
www.audit-scotland.gov.uk
Audit Scotland provides the auditor general and the Accounts Commission with the services they need to carry out their duties.

Auditor General for Wales
www.agw.wales.gov.uk
The primary role of the auditor general for Wales is to provide independent information, assurance and advice to the National Assembly on the way in which it and other public bodies in Wales account for and use taxpayers' money.

Bank of England
www.bankofengland.co.uk
The Bank of England is the central bank of the United Kingdom. The bank is committed to promoting and maintaining a stable and efficient monetary and financial framework as its contribution to a healthy economy.

The British Accounting Association Corporate Governance Special Interest Group
http://www.baacgsig.qub.ac.uk/
Within the BAA, there is a stream of research on the relationship between corporate governance and capital markets and the effects of corporate governance on the choice of strategy, management control, and performance-evaluation systems both in the private and public sector.

British American Security Information Council (BASIC)
www.basicint.org/
BASIC is a progressive and independent analysis and advocacy organization that researches and provides a critical examination of global security issues, including nuclear policies, military strategies, armaments, and disarmament.

BSI
http://www.bsi.org.uk/index.xalter
The BSI Group is a global provider of professional services to organizations worldwide.

Centre for Corporate Accountability (CCA)
www.corporateaccountability.org/
CCA is a not-for-profit organization set up to promote worker and public safety by providing advice and undertaking research on matters relating to law enforcement and corporate criminal accountability.

Centre for Corporate Governance Research
http://business.bham.ac.uk
The Centre for Corporate Governance Research conducts and encourages high-quality research in corporate governance; engages in interdisciplinary and cross-border research through collaboration with contacts in the UK and overseas; consults with professional bodies, corporations, and other groups on corporate governance issues; and disseminates the research of the center as widely as possible through published research, presentations at conferences, and seminars.

Chartered Institute of Management Accountants (CIMA)
www.cimaglobal.com
CIMA represents financial managers and accountants who work in industry, commerce, and not-for-profit and public-sector organizations.

Confederation of British Industry (CBI)
www.cbi.org.uk
The CBI is UK business' most powerful lobbying organization.

Corporation of London
www.cityoflondon.gov.uk
The Corporation of London provides local government services for the financial and commercial heart of Britain, the City of London.

Department of Trade and Industry (DTI)
www.dti.gov.uk
The DTI works to create the best environment for business success in the UK.

Financial Reporting Council (FRC)
www.frc.org.uk
The Financial Reporting Council is a unified, independent regulator that sets, monitors, and enforces accounting and auditing standards, oversees the regulatory activities of the professional accountancy bodies, and regulates audit and promotes high standards of corporate governance.

Financial Services Authority (FSA)
www.fsa.gov.uk/
The FSA is an independent body that regulates the financial services industry in the UK.

Foreign & Commonwealth Office (FCO)
www.fco.gov.uk
The purpose of the FCO is to work for UK interests in a safe, just, and prosperous world.

Global Facilitation Network for Security Sector Reform (GFN-SSR)
www.gfn-ssr.org
The GFN-SSR is a project funded by the UK government's Global Conflict
Prevention Pool (GCPP). The team serves as a resource for the UK government as
well as other global institutional, organizational, and government partners to provide research that facilitates policy development and capacity building for global
security-sector reform initiatives.

Governance Magazine
http://www.governance.co.uk/index.htm
Governance is an international monthly newsletter on issues of corporate governance, boardroom performance, and shareholder activism.

Her Majesty's Stationary Office: Terrorism Act of 2000
www.hmso.gov.uk/acts/acts2000/20000011.htm
Includes measures that define terrorism and discusses measures to prevent acts of
terrorism.

HM Customs and Excise
http://www.hmce.gov.uk/
UK Customs and Excise is a government department with responsibility for
collecting billions of pounds in revenue each year in VAT, other taxes, and
customs duties.

Independent Directors Register
www.icaew.co.uk
The Independent Directors Register is a comprehensive database of chartered
accountants who are available to undertake independent director and other nonex-
ecutive roles in companies, voluntary organizations, and the not-for-profit sector.

Intellectual Property Institute
www.ip-institute.org.uk
The Intellectual Property Institute promotes awareness and understanding of intellectual property law and its contribution to economic and social welfare, through
high-quality, independent research.

International Compliance Association (ICA)

www.int-comp.org

The ICA is a non–profit-making professional organization dedicated to the further-ance of best compliance and anti–money-laundering practice in the financial-serv-ices sector.

International Corporate Governance Network (ICGN)

http://www.icgn.org/

The purpose of the ICGN is to provide a network for the exchange of views and information about corporate governance issues internationally and for the devel-opment of corporate governance guidelines.

International Security Information Service UK (ISIS UK)

www.isisuk.demon.co.uk

The International Security Information Service provides parliamentarians of all parties with independent information, analysis, and research reports on defense, foreign, and other issues related to international security.

Institute of Chartered Accountants of Scotland (ICAS)

www.icas.org.uk

The Institute of Chartered Accountants of Scotland received its Royal Charter in 1854 and is the oldest professional body of accountants in the world.

The Institute of Chartered Secretaries and Administrators

http://www.icsa.org.uk/

ICSA is the professional body for chartered secretaries. A chartered secretary is qualified in company law, accounting, corporate governance, administration, com-pany secretarial practice, and management.

Institute of Directors

www.iod.com

As a worldwide association of members, the Institute of Directors provides a net-work that reaches into every corner of the business community.

Investment Management Association (IMA)

www.investmentfunds.org.uk

The Investment Management Association is the UK trade body for the professional investment management industry.

Law Society
www.lawsoc.org.uk
The Law Society is the professional body for solicitors in England and Wales.

Law Society of Scotland
www.lawscot.org.uk
The Law Society of Scotland is the governing body for Scottish solicitors.

Manifest Proxy Voting and Corporate Governance Analysis
www.manifest.co.uk/
This Web site promotes discussion and sharing of information pertaining to corporate governance.

Ministry of Defence (MOD)
http://www.mod.uk/
MOD is responsible for defending the United Kingdom and promoting international peace and security.

National Hi-Tech Crime Unit (NHTCU)
http://www.nhtcu.org/
The NHTCU works to combat national and transnational serious and organized hi-tech crime within, or which impacts, the United Kingdom.

Northern Ireland Audit Office (NIAO)
www.niauditoffice.gov.uk
The NIAO provides guidance for improved financial reporting, including support for efforts to combat public sector fraud. This is a good resource for local audit and internal audit security regulation.

Police Information Technology Organisation (PITO)
http://www.pito.org.uk/index.htm
PITO aims to support the UK police and other criminal justice organizations in reducing crime and in administering justice more effectively by providing information and communication technology solutions, either directly or through contracts with suppliers.

Public Audit Forum

www.public-audit-forum.gov.uk

The Public Audit Forum provides a focus for developmental thinking in relation to public audit. The main role of the forum is consultative and advisory.

Securities Institute

www.securities-institute.org.uk

The Securities Institute is the largest professional body for those who work in the securities and investment industry in the UK with more than 15,000 members.

Scottish Corporate Governance Unit

www.scottishdirector.com

The Scottish Corporate Governance Unit encourages more effective practice in Scotland by providing information, research, opportunities for personal and professional development, and a program of events that will help all those who discharge their directorial and governance roles and responsibilities in the public, private, and voluntary sectors to do so to the highest possible standards.

Scottish Council for Development and Industry

www.scdi.org.uk

The Scottish Council for Development and Industry is an independent membership network that strengthens Scotland's competitiveness by influencing government policies to encourage sustainable economic prosperity.

Scottish Executive

www.scotland.gov.uk

The Scottish Executive is the devolved government for Scotland. It is responsible for most of the issues of day-to-day concern to the people of Scotland.

Scottish Law Online

www.scottishlaw.org.uk

Scottish Law Online aims to be the very first place that anyone with an interest in Scots law would visit whenever he or she goes on the Internet.

Scottish Parliament
www.scottish.parliament.uk
This Web site explains the parliamentary body of Scotland.

United States of America

AICPA
www.AICPA.org
The American Institute of Certified Public Accountants and its predecessors have been serving the accounting profession since 1887 and is a great resource for COBIT information.

American Civil Liberties Union (ACLU)
www.aclu.org/
An organization whose goal is to preserve America's Constitution and the Bill of Rights.

Banking Industry Technology Secretariat (BITS)
www.bitsinfo.org/
A nonprofit consortium that focuses on issues related to eCommerce, payments, and emerging technologies.

Carnegie Mellon Software Engineering Institute: North American Computer Emergency Response Team (CERT/CC)
http://www.cert.org/
CERT/CC is a center of Internet security expertise, located at the Software Engineering Institute, a federally funded research and development center operated by Carnegie Mellon University.

Center for Education and Research in Information Assurance and Security (CERIAS)
www.cerias.purdue.edu/
CERIAS is one of the world's centers for research and education in areas of information security that are crucial to the protection of critical computing and communication infrastructure. CERIAS is based at Purdue University.

Center for National Software Studies

www.cnsoftware.org/

A not-for-profit organization that provides objective expertise, elevates software to the national agenda, and provides studies and recommendations on national software issues.

Computer Professionals for Social Responsibility (CPSR)

www.cpsr.org/

An organization that provides the public and policymakers with realistic assessments of the power, promise, and problems of information technology.

Consumer Project on Technology

http://www.cptech.org/cpt.html

An organization that was started by Ralph Nader in 1995 that focuses on intellectual property rights, health care, electronic commerce, and competition policy.

Committee of Sponsoring Organizations of the Treadway Commission (COSO)

www.COSO.org

COSO was originally formed in 1985 to sponsor the National Commission on Fraudulent Financial Reporting and is now a great resource for implementing a risk management framework.

Critical Infrastructure Assurance Office (CIAO)

www.cia.gov

The White House's office, within the Department of Homeland Defense, focused on protection of America's critical infrastructure.

Department of Computer Science and Engineering University of California at San Diego: Theory of Cryptography Web Site

http://philby.ucsd.edu/cryptolib/

This site provides access to recent work on the theory of cryptography.

Department of Homeland Security

www.whitehouse.gov/deptofhomeland

The Department of Homeland Security covers areas including PATRIOT Act and Critical Infrastructure Protection. The Department of Homeland Security was created to make America more secure.

Electronic Frontier Foundation (EFF)
www.eff.org
An organization created to share our ideas, thoughts, and needs using new technologies, such as the Internet and the World Wide Web. Provides archives on privacy, free speech, and underground newsletters.

Electronic Privacy Information Center (EPIC)
www.epic.org/
A national organization dedicated to improving the quality of electronic media on behalf of children and families.

Electronic Privacy Information Center: Consumer Internet Privacy Protection Act of 1997
www.epic.org/privacy/internet/hr_98.html
Regulates the use by interactive computer services of personally identifiable information provided by subscribers to such services.

Electronic Privacy Information Center: E-Privacy Act
www.epic.org/crypto/legislation/eprivacy.html
Ensures that Americans have the maximum possible choice in encryption methods to protect the security, confidentiality, and privacy of their lawful wire and electronic communications and stored electronic information.

Electronic Privacy Information Center: Fair Credit Reporting Act
www.epic.org/privacy/fcra/#fcra
Promotes the accuracy, fairness, and the privacy of personal information assembled by credit reporting agencies.

Electronic Privacy Information Center: The Gramm-Leach-Bliley Act
www.epic.org/privacy/glba/
Provides limited privacy protection against the sale of an individual's private financial information.

Electronic Privacy Information Center: PATRIOT Act
www.epic.org/privacy/terrorism/hr3162.html
This act was created to deter and punish terrorist acts in the United States and around the world and to enhance law enforcement investigation tools. This is not that official site for the PATRIOT act (see whitehouse.gov), but rather opinion about it.

Electronic Privacy Information Center: The Right to Financial Privacy Act
www.epic.org/privacy/rfpa/
This act protects the confidentiality of personal financial records by creating a statutory Fourth Amendment protection on bank records.

Energy Information Sharing and Analysis Center (ENERGY-ISAC)
www.energyisac.com/index.cfm
An industry-wide database and forum that provides information about network vulnerabilities and provides effective solutions.

Federal Bureau of Investigation (FBI)
www.fbi.gov
FBI priorities include protecting the United States from terrorist attacks, from foreign intelligence operations, and from cyber-based attacks and high-technology crimes; combating public corruption at all levels; protecting civil rights; combating international and national organized crime, major white-collar crime, and significant violent crime; supporting law enforcement and intelligence partners; and upgrading FBI technology.

Federal Computer Incident Response Center (FedCIRC)
www.fedcirc.gov
FedCIRC is the Federal Civilian Agency's trusted focal point for computer security-incident reporting, prevention, and response.

Federal Trade Commission: Children's Online Privacy Protection Act of 1998
www.ftc.gov/ogc/coppa1.htm
This act applies to online personal information from children under 13. The new rules explain what a Web site operator must include in a privacy policy, when and how to seek verifiable consent from a parent, and what responsibilities an operator has to protect children's privacy and safety online.

Federal Trade Commission: Electronic Signatures in Global and National Commerce Act
www.ftc.gov/os/2001/06/esign7.htm
This act facilitates the use of electronic records and signatures in foreign and interstate commerce by ensuring the validity and legal effect of contracts entered into electronically.

Federal Trade Commission: Identity Theft and Assumption Deterrence Act of 1998
www.ftc.gov/os/statutes/itada/itadact.htm
This act states that identity theft is a federal crime with penalties up to 15 years imprisonment and a maximum fine of $250,000.

Financial Services Information Sharing and Analysis Center (FS-ISAC)
www.fsisac.com/
An industry-wide database and forum that provides information about network vulnerabilities and effective solutions.

Global Internet Liberty Campaign (GILC)
www.gilc.org/
An international coalition of privacy, human rights, and free-speech groups dedicated to fighting international threats to privacy and free speech on the Internet.

Information Technology Information Sharing and Analysis Center (IT-ISAC)
https://www.it-isac.org/
An industry-wide database and forum that provides information about network vulnerabilities and effective solutions.

Library of Congress: Consumer Identity and Information Security Act of 2003
http://thomas.loc.gov
Easy access to quick information on existing laws, like this one: Protects against the illegal use and display of an individual's social security number. Prohibits denial or discrimination in the provision of products or services because an individual declines to display his or her social security number. This act also prohibits the printing on any receipt at the point of the business transaction the following:

- More than the last five digits of the account number of a credit card, debit card, or consumer account
- The expiration date of such credit card, debit card, or other consumer account

Library of Congress: Government Network Security Act of 2003
http://thomas.loc.gov
Easy access to quick information on existing laws, like this one: Requires federal agencies to develop and implement plans protecting the security and privacy of government computer systems from the risks posed by peer-to-peer file sharing.

National Infrastructure Protection Center (NIPC)
www.nipc.gov
CYBER NOTES, their popular newsletters, are now distributed by the National
Cyber Security Division's (NCSD) United States Computer Emergency Readiness
Team (US-CERT), a division of DHS Information Analysis and Infrastructure
Protection (IAIP) Directorate.

National Institute of Standards and Technology
www.nist.gov
Great site with all of the federal security and privacy regulations, and guidance on
how best to implement. (Don't forget all the state rules too!)

National Security Institute (NSI)
http://nsi.org/
The NSI features industry and product news, computer alerts, travel advisories, a
calendar of events, a directory of products and services, and access to an extensive
virtual security library.

National Security Institute's Security Resource Net: Cyber Security Information
Act of 2000
http://nsi.org/
Promotes the security of information about cybersecurity problems, solutions, test
practices and test results, and related matters in connection with critical infrastructure protection.

National Security Institute's Security Resource Net: Encrypted Communications
Privacy Act of 1996
http://nsi.org/
Ensures that Americans are able to have the maximum possible choice in encryption methods to protect the security, confidentiality, and privacy of their lawful
wire or electronic communications and establishes privacy standards.

National Security Institute's Security Resource Net: Government Information
Security Act of 1999
http://nsi.org/
Reforms government information security by strengthening its own information
security practices throughout the federal government.

National Security Institute's Security Resource Net: National Information Infrastructure Protection Act of 1995
http://nsi.org/
This act revises current federal criminal code provisions regarding fraud and related activities in connection with computers. It also sets penalties with respect to anyone who knowingly accesses a computer without authorization, exceeds authorized access, or obtains specified restricted information or data—with reason to believe that such information could be used to the injury of the United States or to the advantage of any foreign nation.

National Security Institute's Security Resource Net: Promotion of Commerce On-Line in the Digital Era Act of 1996
http://nsi.org/
Allows businesses and individuals to choose the security features that they need to protect information being communicated in electronic commerce.

National Security Institute's Security Resource Net: Security and Freedom Through Encryption (SAFE) Act of 1999
http://nsi.org/
Enables U.S. citizens to use any kind of encryption. It also enables any person in the United States to sell any encryption product. Moreover, this act states that the government cannot mandate any kind of key escrow.

Partnership for Critical Infrastructure Security (PCIS)
www.pcis.org
PCIS coordinates cross-sector initiatives and complements public-private efforts to promote the assurance of reliable provisions of critical infrastructure services in the face of emerging risks to economic and national security.

Privacy Rights Clearinghouse
http://www.privacyrights.org/
Provides information to consumers about their rights.

Stanford University: Information Technology Security and Services
www.stanford.edu/~security/

Information Security Services helps Stanford protect its computing assets, while supporting the institution's broad, relatively open access requirements. (Stanford's SRI hosted node number two on the internet in 1969—they know their stuff!)

State PIRGS
www.pirg.org/
State Public Interest Research Groups are an alliance of state-based, citizen-funded organizations that advocate for the public interest.

Surface Transportation Information Sharing and Analysis Center (ST-ISAC)
www.surfacetransportationisac.org
ISAC provides a secure cyber and physical security capability for owners, operators, and users of critical infrastructure, and ST-ISAC provides this for the Department of Transportation.

United States Department of Health and Human Services: Health Insurance Portability and Accountability Act (HIPAA) Privacy Rule
www.hhs.gov/ocr/privacysummary.pdf
This act contains a set of national standards that protects the use and disclosure of a patient's health information.

United States Department of Justice: Freedom of Information Act
www.usdoj.gov/oip/foia_updates/Vol_XVII_4/page2.htm
Provides the ability for any person to make a request for government information.

United States Department of Justice: Unlawful Access to Stored Communications
www.usdoj.gov/criminal/cybercrime/usc2701.htm
A federal statute that protects the privacy of stored Internet communications passed as part of the Electronic Communications Privacy Act of 1986.

United States House of Representatives: Computer Security Enhancement Act of 1997
www.house.gov/science/hr1903.html
Reduces the cost and improves the availability of computer security technologies for federal agencies by requiring National Institute of Standards and Technology (NIST) to promote the federal use of off-the-shelf products for meeting civilian

agency computer security needs and enhances the role of the independent Computer System Security and Privacy Advisory Board in NIST's decision-making process.

US Copyright Office: Copyright Law
http://www.copyright.gov/title17/
A form of protection provided to the authors of original works. This includes literary, dramatic, musical, artistic, and certain other intellectual works, regardless of whether they are published or unpublished.

US Department of Energy and the National Nuclear Security Administration: Computer Incident Advisory Capability (CIAC)
http://ciac.llnl.gov/ciac/index.html
This is the site for the office of cyber security at the Department of Energy. It is loaded with great info and stats for everyone.

US Department of Energy Chief Information Officer: Computer Fraud and Abuse Act
http://cio.doe.gov/Documents/CFA.HTM
Describes the provisions and punishments of fraud and related activity in connection with computers.

US Information Technology Office: Measures for Managing Internet Information Services
www.usito.org
Regulates Internet information services (IIS) while promoting the systematic development of such services.

W3C Technology and Society Domain Micropayments Interest Group
www.w3.org/ECommerce/Overview.html
W3C focuses on core infrastructure technologies for electronic commerce and identifies common infrastructure needed in this area.

W3C Technology and Society Domain Security Resources Web Site
www.w3.org/Security/Overview.html

Worldwide Information Sharing and Analysis Center (WW-ISAC)
www.wwisac.com
An industry-wide database and forum that provides information about network vulnerabilities and effective solutions.

Vietnam

Hanoi University of Technology
www.hut.edu.vn
My Vietnamese friends tell me that this is the best source of domestic security information, but it's all Vietnamese to me and my translator can't read it.

Zambia

Bank of Zambia
www.boz.zm
Bank of Zambia formulates and implements monetary and supervisory policies that ensure price and financial systems stability, to promote balanced macroeconomic development.

Zimbabwe

Reserve Bank of Zimbabwe
www.rbz.co.zw
The Reserve Bank of Zimbabwe is the cornerstone upon which Zimbabwe's economic fortunes and developmental aspirations are anchored (their language, not mine). A focus on financial crime, and pointers to local resources is included.

Index

D

informIT

www.informit.com

YOUR GUIDE TO IT REFERENCE

Articles

Keep your edge with thousands of free articles, in-depth features, interviews, and IT reference recommendations – all written by experts you know and trust.

Online Books

Answers in an instant from **InformIT Online Book's** 600+ fully searchable on line books. For a limited time, you can get your first 14 days **free**.

Catalog

Review online sample chapters, author biographies and customer rankings and choose exactly the right book from a selection of over 5,000 titles.